The Pastor and His Anatomy

The Pastor and His Anatomy

A Biblical Examination — Volumes I & II

Derrick I. Temple, Sr. (PhD/MBA)

XULON PRESS

Xulon Press
2301 Lucien Way #415
Maitland, FL 32751
407.339.4217

www.xulonpress.com

© 2020 by Derrick I. Temple, Sr.

All rights reserved solely by the author. The author guarantees all contents are original and do not infringe upon the legal rights of any other person or work. No part of this book may be reproduced in any form without the permission of the author. The views expressed in this book are not necessarily those of the publisher.

Unless otherwise indicated, Scripture quotations taken from the King James Version (KJV) – *public domain.*

Printed in the United States of America

Paperback ISBN-13: 978-1-6322-1355-6
Ebook ISBN-13: 978-1-6322-1356-3

ACKNOWLEDGMENTS

I acknowledge the pastors within the ranks of my preaching family: To James Commodore Wade, Sr., *who laid his hands on me*. To James Commodore Wade, Jr., *who warned me*. To Melvin Von Wade, Sr., *who trained me*. To James A. Temple, *who nurtured me*. To Donald Ray Temple, *who spent time with me*. To Armond W. Brown, *who stretched me*. To Clyde Nichols, *who was hospitable to me*. To T. Ellsworth Gantt II, *who was candid with me*. To Mark Williams, *who is an encouragement to me*. To James Commodore Wade III, *who graced me*. To David L. Wade, *who invited me*. To W. Terrell Snead II, *who partnered with me*. To Charles L. Thompson, Jr. and Thomas Charles McKinley, *who are dear to me*. I discovered through M. V. Wade, Sr. and Ruth Wade-Murray that we have more pastors in the family, i.e., Darryl and Terry Webster, *who are a treasurable discovery to me*.

I acknowledge various professors who left an indelible mark upon my life and ministry: Dr. Troy Welch (former President and Founder of Channel Islands Bible College and Seminary), Dr. Danny Akin (President of Southeastern Baptist Theological Seminary), Dr. Paige Patterson (former President of Criswell College and Southwestern Baptist Theological Seminary), and Dr. Gary Galeotti (former Old Testament Professor of Criswell College and Southeastern Theological Seminary).

To the preaching fraternity of all who attended Bishop College of Dallas, Texas. Bishop College who had the best reputation for producing many of the greatest preachers the African American preaching culture has ever known. While attending Bishop College, I learned that none of us are originals and the value of a preaching fraternity. There was something special about *The Good Ol' Bishop Blue*.

Special honor must be given to Bishop James Edward Henry, the deceased father of my wife, Mellanie Henry-Temple. I remember a book written by Bishop Henry titled, *Biblical Fasting in the Local Church*. Somehow, it made its way to the campus of Criswell College. At the time, I knew nothing of his daughter (Mellanie). As a matter of fact, she would have only been around twelve years old. Although it was a little book filled with simplicity, knowing it was written by a Black man spoke volumes to me.

I am blessed to be part of a preaching dynasty on my father's side of the family, rooted in the Boyd-Frazier, Wade-Temple families. Although our preaching family is renown within the African American preaching context (largely due to the Wade legacy), none of us would be the preachers who we are without a praying family. It is my firm conviction that a family is no family if there is no loyalty. Most of the members within our family epitomize the scripture that commands to not touch God's anointed and do His prophets no harm (I Chronicles 16:22). If they cannot help, they will not harm.

However, the first sounds of my call to preach were heard in Van Alstyne, Texas where my mother was raised. Mostly every member of the family would gather at that church on any given Sunday. In my later years, I revisited that little church that sits on a hill. Once renowned, it dwindled to a few faithful members. A few were at rehearsal with a choir that totaled about four people and no musician. There, I recognized that the church had nothing

Acknowledgments

to do with numbers. I can at least remember Aunt Patricia Orr, Aunt Shirley Boddie, and Bob McKinney standing in the choir stand. Aunt Pat and Aunt Shirley were singing in alto and soprano while Bob McKinney was singing with a melodious bass-baritone voice. All they had were hymnals. It was one of those moments that you could have sworn you were under beams of Heaven. As a matter of fact, that is a vision of what I saw when they were singing. I saw a heavenly light shining down on them. I began to see Samaria Baptist Church for what it always was. I not only heard songs from hymnals, but I also heard the tones of ancestors who gave their lives for our freedom ringing through their voices. In that choir stand stood the remnant of a rich African American heritage. Years later, my Aunt Patricia Orr gave me the history of Samaria Baptist Church in a way that made my experiences with Samaria more understandable. I always hated Sunday School as a child except when I was under the teaching of Aunt Eloise Temple. Resisting Sunday School, my grandmother and aunts in Van Alstyne almost had to drag me to Sunday School. Aunt Melissa Orr was my Sunday School teacher. Although resistant, it was under Aunt Mellissa's teaching that I felt my first pulls to preach. As a matter of fact, she told my parents that I would be a preacher someday. The anointing of my ancestors was being poured over me. Then, I was only around nine or ten years old.

Twenty years after Abraham Lincoln's Emancipation Proclamation, Samaria Baptist Church was organized on August 5, 1883, by a council under the leadership of Reverend R. Curry. During unimaginable racism, Reverend Curry saw the need for a Negro Baptist church. If Blacks were allowed in the White church, they had to sit in segregated sections of the sanctuary. To curtail segregation, Samaria Baptist Church was organized under a Brush Arbor tree in the backyard of Pete Bowens, who is my ancestor. Later, a lot was obtained by Pete Bowens in Van Alstyne, and Samaria Baptist Church was moved there. That little country church became the training grounds for many young African American pastors who became well-known nationally. Among a few of them were S. C. Nash, Sr., C. L. Adams, Terry White, C. C. McNealy, J. C. Wade, Jr., Carson Adams, Lee Arthur Kessee, Abraham Campbell, and many others. This book is a family book. It is a *Bowens-Orr, Boyd-Frazier, Wade-Temple* book that I pray will be preserved for generations to come.

I thank the most influential person in my walk with God for sharing with me the Gospel of Jesus Christ around the age of ten years old. I credit preachers in my family for my preaching, and I credit Aunt Eloise for my walk with God in ways words can never express. Because of her royal disposition as a woman of God, I came to personally know the true definition of a virtuous woman who cherished and challenged my manhood, even to this very day.

I must acknowledge my hero and father (Alonzo Temple) for exposing me to the power of research and study as he taught me how to use encyclopedias when I was around nine years old. I remember him proudly glancing at me when I would refer to those books. Yet, he would never smile. Instead, he would look at me with piercing eyes and a seriousness that instilled within me the sobriety that attends an education. Although educated men suffer much criticism and envy, being a learned man is a sobering sanction. When I touch a book, I often think of my father. My prized possession was when he gave me the set of encyclopedias that I first knew. Knowing they were once my father's encyclopedias encouraged me even more. At a young age, I learned to continue asking questions and search for my own answers. I cannot forget those red, white, and blue Encyclopedia Britannica references with colors that were like silver and gold to me. Whenever I was writing a research paper or doctoral dissertation in seminary, my father's image would cross my mind. When I saw his face in my mind's eye, I would get to work.

Lastly, to my deceased mother, Peggy R. Temple. I like to describe her as a Diva. I guess I would describe a Diva as a woman who takes pride in being all she should be without feeling a compulsion to envy, compete with or demean men. She was proud to be a woman. If that is not the definition of a Diva, that sure is a fit description of my mother. Anyone who knew her would agree that inwardly and outwardly, she was a beautiful woman. She was just as passionate about accentuating a young woman's beauty as much as her own. Yet, my mother knew the difference between woman power and being a powerful woman. She did not believe in women's movements, but she did believe in moving women. However, I was her pride and joy. During my adolescent years, I did not realize what she meant when she advised me to take care of myself. She always said that I was too hard on myself and that I had too much on my mind. If I would have taken her advice much earlier, I could have avoided pitfalls at an early age and during my early ministry years. Although I occasionally struggle with perfectionism, I wish she could see me now.

DEDICATION

∞

I dedicate this book to my two sons, Derrick Irving Temple, Jr. and Alonzo Barrington Temple, my granddaughter, Aniyah Droughn-Temple, and my grandson,

Princeton Love-Patrick Temple.

My sons, God has an awesome call upon your lives. I pray that you will one day answer that call and experience the security of being in the center of God's will. I am proud to have you as my sons, and there is nothing that you can ever do or say that would cause me to be ashamed of you. You are my alpha males, and your strength is your glory (Proverbs 20:29). You both have been the most rewarding ministry that I ever had. I am depending on you to never forget what I taught and the God of whom I represent. Aniyah, you will always be my precious gift from God. I will always be your "Poppy". I take you to church as often as possible to leave a godly stamp on your heart as you grow older. You take notes of my sermons. Princeton, welcome to the family! You are my little prince, and never forget that you come from a royal family. I pray that God will give me length of days to see each of you grow to become who God ordained for you to be. If God sees fit to call me Home before then, I look forward to meeting you in Heaven.

If you never read this book, never forget this dedication, and let it be tattooed on your hearts and pierced in your souls for the rest of your lives. If you do read this book, you will grow to understand why I wrote it. I began writing this book in 2005. Sons, you heard me tell you how important it is that God is priority above everything and everyone else. I told you to never quit. God will be with you when you are right, and He can even be with you when you are wrong. God is faithful, even when we are faithless (II Timothy 2:13). No matter how rough your road, my prayers will guide you to Heaven's door, but it will be up to you to humble yourselves, knock, and ask God for what you need (Matthew 7:7). In no way would I lose you in a quest to save the world. I would never trade my sons for success. I dedicated my whole life to you. I would rather be at home with you than to be a successful stranger in the world. At home, day after day, I can easily see that God has His hand on your life. You are God's property, and He has the final word in your life. Money matters, but the greatest inheritance that I can leave you is Jesus. I owe you that. I would rather have Jesus than silver and gold (Acts 3:6). I leave you with one sentence that summarizes what I discovered about that I want to pass to you for the rest of your lives. Always remember:

God is not just your source…He is your *only* source

TABLE OF CONTENTS

∾

Preface . . . . *xv*
Introduction: The Pastor and His *Character* . . . . *xxvii*
Chapter 1: The Pastor and His *Head*. *1*
Chapter 2: The Pastor and His *Mind* *33*
Chapter 3: The Pastor and His *Ears* *47*
Chapter 4: The Pastor and His *Eyes* *69*
Chapter 5: The Pastor and His *Voice* *105*
Chapter 6: The Pastor and His *Shoulders* *129*
Chapter 7: The Pastor and His *Heart* *155*
Chapter 8: The Pastor and His *Rib* *209*
Chapter 9: The Pastor and His *Arms*. *275*
Chapter 10: The Pastor and His *Loins* *305*
Chapter 11: The Pastor and His *Thigh* *341*
Chapter 12: The Pastor and His *Knees* *379*
Chapter 13: The Pastor and His *Feet*. *403*
Conclusion: The Pastor and His *Conscience*. *443*

PREFACE

Preachers are not angels, gods, or demons. Usually, those who demonize us previously idolized us. It is as much of a sin to idolize a pastor as it is to demonize one. We are mortal men. Yet, we are uniquely mortal. I will seek to address areas of mortal combat preachers often experience within and without from a biblical perspective. Various attitudes carelessly condemn preachers on many fronts. God wills to bring self-righteous judgments under scriptural scope. *The Pastor and His Anatomy* is also written to overcome poisonous perceptions that dilute our definition within two realms of manhood, marriage, and ministry. We will examine malignant manholes we can fall into from a biblical bias and how God often deals with us in our ditches.

I understand many reasons why the publishing of this book had been delayed by God for the past eighteen years. Anyone who was in a close relationship with me over fifteen years ago heard me continually talk about publishing this book. I also thank wise pastors and friends for their timely advice. There is a truth I have been forced to discover and defend doctrinally and practically. I refuse to condone one's interpretation of preachers based on their own truth. Instead, my focus is on the only type of truth that will make people free, i.e., God's Truth. The truth is in the fact that God's men are God's property, and if they become a problem, they are God's problem. God takes good care of His property, and He solves His problems.

God often condemns what people usually condone, and He often covers what people usually condemn regarding the men He chooses to preach the Gospel. The things many people can condemn a preacher for doing, God can justify, and the things others justify a preacher for doing, God can condemn. God can severely chastise a preacher for some of the most seemingly innocent initiatives, even to the point of death. Usually, people and some of us as preachers overlook the activity that can sign a death contract on our calling. On the contrary, our Heavenly Father can pardon a preacher amid some of the most obvious offenses and spare his life and ministry.

Beyond what we do, *The Pastor and His Anatomy* has much to do with who God says a pastor is. This book is not a defense for preachers. Instead, it gives a better definition of who a preacher is. As a result, this book is a deliberate discourse on divine definitions and biblical beliefs for preachers and pastors. I in no way speak for all. Every preacher can speak for himself. I am primarily communicating with my fellow-preachers and those who have been wounded by distorted perceptions of preachers. *The Pastor and His Anatomy* is preacher-talk. Anyone other than a preacher who wants to dine on this discourse is welcomed to the table, but if they do, I advise them to take off their shoes, for the ground we stand on is Holy Ground. I am addressing ideologies that falsely discredit a preacher's worth as well as opinions that falsely credit a preacher's worth. Thus, I will be as biblical and candid as God has given me permission to be. I am only giving an expose' of truths discovered through failures, fortitude, fortune, and faith. Yet, I do share in preachers' self-same siftings and sufferings. Through much testing and temptation, God allowed me to learn some of the tragedies and triumphs that accompany sifted servants:

Preface

> "*And the Lord said* (to Peter), *Simon, Simon, behold, Satan hath desired to have you, that he may sift you as wheat: But I have prayed for thee, that thy faith fail not:* **and when thou art converted, strengthen thy brethren**."
>
> (Luke 22:31-32; KJV)

After Peter learned through much failure and satanic sifting. He could then write:

> "*Be sober, be vigilant; because your adversary the devil, as a roaring lion, walketh about, seeking whom he may devour: Whom resist stedfast* (steadfast) *in the faith,* **knowing that the same afflictions are accomplished in your brethren that are in the world**".
>
> (I Peter 5:8-9; KJV)

There are many self-imposed demands we can place upon ourselves that falsely calculate our pastoral net worth. Our net worth is the amount by which our assets exceed our liabilities. If prone to use false metrics to measure our value, we can miscalculate times when we are assets or liabilities. If so, we or others may believe we are more of a liability to the Lord than an asset. Because of the inhumane challenges of pastoral ministry, a human metric must never be used to measure our net worth, but there is a divine one. If we measure our worth on human scales, our critical appraisals, or the opinions of people, we may learn survival skills to keep our heads above the water, but deep down on the inside, we can drown from lack of definition. Unless we stand on scriptural scales, we may fall prey to vices and voices that attend overestimating or underestimating our self-worth. If we fail to biblically measure our true worth, we can become driven to compensate or medicate for what we believe are liabilities. We can be driven to become overachievers or underachievers. If we overachieve, we are prone to self-compensate. If we underachieve, we are prone to self-medicate. If we fall prey to harmful success habits, we may do so because of an unrealized drive to self-compensate. If we fall prey to harmful sinful habits, we may do so because of an unrealized drive to self-medicate. When we fall on the borders of either of these extremities, we are truly pastors in crisis.

There are misnomers of ministry that falsely suggest a pastor is succeeding or failing for many reasons. The days when pastors were fairly evaluated by the worth of their ministries instead of the width of their ministries are gone forever. Pastors with larger congregations have enough jealousy and envy from others to combat as well as internal bouts they must battle as mere mortals. The demons are unique when a man pastors on that level. The last thing they need is someone to put them on a pedestal and make them easier targets. Furthermore, at what number are lines drawn between micro, medium, and mega? As a native of the South and resident of the West. I can easily say, a mega-church in Los Angeles could be defined as a medium-sized church in Dallas or Houston. Who is authorized to determine the numbers? Church cannot be quantified. It can only be qualified. We either have a qualified or quantified church. Jesus' Church has no walls, especially during the Coronavirus crisis of 2020. That is the true definition of mega, i.e., wall-less and beyond human numbers. We only reach mega proportions when we reach a number no man can number (Revelation 7:9).

An incident that happened in 2019 regarding a mega-church Associate Pastor who took his own life. As unfortunate as that may be, we live in days that remind us of our need to not weep for dead preachers as much as we must weep for those of us who are still living. It is not just the pastors who surrender their lives to suicidal demons that is the issue. Many of us remain who have fallen prey to becoming walking-dead men who can do more for others than we can do for ourselves. The need for us to dedicate ourselves to spiritual self-help tactics is crucial. The line between self-sacrifice and servanthood can often be as thin as the line can be between love and hate. Thin line or not, there is a bottom line. The bottom line is that pastoring is a deadly calling, and it is life-essential that we dig deep and embrace God's grace that will sustain and protect us from assassinating assumptions that come from the judgmental guns of others, the guns of our guilt, or the revolvers of our repercussions.

In a sobering and simpler sense. We (pastors) must take care of ourselves and allow God to take good care of us. In the pastoral ministry, we minister within a vacuum. Within the pastoral office, we can always believe there is more for us to do and be. As Pastor Donald Parsons would say, "The angelic are pulling us up, and the beastly are pulling us down." We are in a constant state of awareness that we all have sinned and come short of the glory of God (Romans 3:23). For these reasons and many more, biblical measurements of our effectiveness must be the instruments that help us draw the lines and learn to live within our limitations.

The Pastor and His Anatomy is purposefully masculine. My goal in this book is to achieve more definitive definitions of what it truly means to be a man of God. I could write an entirely different book on women in the ministry. However, getting into unresolvable debates of whether women are sanctioned to pastor and preach or not is not my concern. I have written from the platform of who I am and to whom I am communicating. I am a man, and I am communicating with men. Much written in this book will require a little manpower and a lot of soul-searching. Yet, this is also a book of soul that extends from my soul to the souls of pastors, who are my soul-brothers and women of virtue, who are my soul-sisters.

Because I am somewhat apologetic that I do not address the reality of women preachers and pastors in this book, I must magnify my convictions that state why the discussion of women in the pastoral office is not my focus. While I do understand that countless women are dedicating their souls to pastoral vocations on sincere levels, my conviction causes me to state more imminent concerns. I have finally learned to discern a dysfunction far greater than who is right or wrong in the area of the confirmation of practices in the local church that will never be corrected until Jesus comes, regardless of how wrong they are.

The core concern of women in the preaching and pastoral ministry has much to do with our theology regarding sexuality, personal experiences, and most of all, our methods of biblical interpretation. In the local church and American culture, sexuality is becoming severely distorted. The distortions affect our marriages and ministries. Marriages and ministries must be biblically defined within the gender realm because our vocabulary of what it means to be a man or woman highly sentences our marriages and ministries. Furthering the discussion of sexuality from a theological thrust, since Adam and Eve, there has been a battle of the sexes that takes place in a marriage that has spilled over into how we do ministry. A power struggle between men and women will surface, even in the best of marriages and ministries (Genesis 3:16).

Instead of debating, more biblical discussion must be given to sexuality because the acceptance of gender roles has erroneously replaced the understanding of the roles of each gender. In our century, the general convictions of the nation, home, and local church rarely involve men and women who celebrate sexual distinctions.

Instead, our culture is attempting to recreate men and women to be the same. I agree with the equality of the sexes, but I disagree with the sameness of the sexes. Men are not the same as women, and women are not the same as men. Males and females are only similar in a few areas but highly distinct in over 6,500 biological ways.

What makes matters worse is the fact that beyond our greatest imaginations or intentions, our culture is heading toward a *nongender* direction that plants seeds for the evolution of another species altogether. A new breed is erupting that neither proponents for nor against sexual equality or sexual sameness will be able to claim genderism to because they will have no sexual distinctions whatsoever. Instead of the traditional norm of sexual distinctions, we are experiencing a new norm of sexual distortions. We are approaching an era of *locusts* whose hair will be like women, but their faces will be as men (Revelations 9:7-8). A demonized humanity and satanic sense of sexuality is swiftly encroaching. Satan desires for every organ and personality development God ordained in the anatomy of Man and Woman to be demonized. Beyond heterosexuality, unisexuality, same-sexuality, bisexuality, homosexuality, and transsexuality is the swarming of locust demons who are invading the local church and our culture with an Antichrist and anti-sexual spirit that is *against* the sexes whether they are Male or Female. Our society, local church, and marriage institutions must be on guard against how gender and gender roles are reversed, redefined, or removed.

While many are having needed discussions about our culture's rapid response to sexual segregation, there awaits a culture in the making that lays no claim to gender at all. Already in 2016, an Oregon judge made an unprecedented ruling that transgender individuals can legally change their sex to *Non-binary* rather than Male or Female. My address is not to transsexuals or those who check the non-binary box. Instead, it is to our non-gender mobilizing culture that has become the new doctrine of sexuality in our children's and grandchildren's elementary schools. Although *Non-binary* is a new category, it shows how just three years later in 2019, we are seeing a surfacing depreciation of gender within our culture. There is one thing everybody ought to know, Christians especially: God did not create any of that. America did. God created both Male and Female (Genesis 5:2).

Because of the sensitivity of the subject of the sexes, I am in no way condemning or condoning any who sync with a sexual or anti-sexual category. I am simply saying that the appreciation of gender is no longer an embraced or desired result within our culture and too many of our local churches and pulpits. Needed emphasis involves not causing future generations to stumble by not enlightening them of the dangers of defective biblical interpretations that refuse to accentuate our anatomical advantages. Because of poor biblical interpretation, there are multiple mistaken identities of ministry and marriage in the local church along with the gender issue. Eve misinterpreted God's word, and Adam deliberately disobeyed it. A weakness in biblical interpretation by men or women is as much of a sin as any other (II Timothy 2:15).

Male or Female, Binary or Non-binary, all human beings have souls that will be required of God at the point of death (Luke 12:20). On a more soulish level, I hope to serve generations in the local church by giving an anatomical x-ray of cultural and social precedents to guard against that will protect them from inheriting problems that neither male nor female pastors and ministries intended. My greatest concern is the extinction of biblical absolutes dismissed in exchange for cultural, ecclesiastical, personal, sexual, ministerial, and marital discontentment.

While we are in an era of diversity that defuses, dilutes, and destroys sound doctrine, I do know this: Men who have power

Preface

struggles and deep-seated issues with women struggle with biblical manhood, and women who have deep-seated issues and power struggles with men struggle with biblical womanhood. Those issues in and of themselves are enough to falsely slant one's approach to how the Bible is to be interpreted, justify one's personal experience, and redefine how ministry and marriage are to be governed. Men who are battling or belittling women are in a battle with themselves, and women who are battling or belittling men are at a battle with themselves. At the core of such concerns is a malpractice in biblical interpretation and implementation of biblical manhood and womanhood.

The Church who Jesus promised to build will march on whether we agree or disagree with women pastoring local churches or not (Matthew 16:18). Yet, if we embrace shallow interpretations of the Holy Bible, we all might as well retreat. If I were cornered into a debate regarding female pastors, preachers and prophetesses, I only defend how the Bible is to be interpreted instead of judging from an opinionated, traditional, trendy, cultural, or subjective point of view who is qualified or not qualified to do ministry.

I believe *the greatest weakness in the local church of our era is the poor quality of biblical interpretation within our leadership tiers*. Thus, too many Christians believe they are their own leaders, and they are subject to the heresy of privately interpreting the Bible. Thus, they are doing ministry without a fear of accountability (II Peter 1:20). As an old professor of mine would often say, "Like prophet, like people." Yet, I will say that the tsunami of poor biblical interpretation causes many of us to experience the drowning of our true calling. If we are truly one body in Christ, many of the ministries some of us aspire to embark upon can be more effectively done without the church titles a few of us assume or grant to another.

It is difficult to discuss biblical interpretation without discussing expositional preaching. Unfortunately, expositional preaching has developed into a trend more than a trusted tradition in the 21st century. Preaching should never become stylistic, success-driven, sex-driven, or status-oriented. Beyond expositional preaching, all our local churches are accountable to expository studying (Acts 17:11). If our approaches to how the Bible is to be interpreted are diluted, one word from witch and warlock ministries could bewitch our local churches in a malignant moment (Galatians 3:1). Too many witches and warlocks are ministers who practice magic. They come under the disguise of worshipers and witnesses who invite themselves or are invited into church pulpits without being severely screened. Many local church worship experiences evolve into witchcraft, and most people within those services have no clue that they are held in a spell by witches' brew they mistake for blessings.

Many dysfunctions accompany ministers, but there is nothing dysfunctional about their mantle. Many things are dysfunctional about chosen men, but there is nothing dysfunctional about the God who chooses them. When God chooses a man to preach the Gospel, He does not make a mistake regarding who He chooses. Anyone who intimately knows a *real preacher* will discover something grotesquely ugly about him. It is called, "sin". God cannot use a man or woman who thinks he or she has a monopoly or market on ministry and ministers. This is not to tear down those who think they fit that criteria. It is only to build up those who do not. God uses those who admit they are undone but are willing to say, "Lord, send me" and leave the glory to God (Isaiah 6:5).

Preachers are troubled on every side and acquainted with paradoxical extremes. When we are weak, we are strong. Although we may dread our infirmities, we are mandated by God to glory in them so the power of Christ may rest upon us (II Corinthians 12:9). In our greatest paradoxes, we as preachers are most powerful.

Preface

Our infirmities cannot kill us, but our pride can. The greatest weakness a preacher can have is pride. Interestingly, a preacher is rarely exposed for the sin of pride. When a preacher's pride is publicized, that does not make good marketing material or juicy gossip for the spiritual paparazzi who have a surfaced view of sin, salvation, and Scripture, and they also have an agenda. They think surface sins destroy a preacher's credibility. On the contrary, it is pride that will destroy a preacher. If they had any wisdom at all, if they were concerned about destroying a preacher's credibility, they would leave him alone because if guilty of pride, he would self-destruct. Yet, real preachers know a preacher's kryptonite is self-sufficiency.

God's men were more sinful than successful, but their victory was within heavenly feats amid a faded glory. God-chosen preachers are men in deep purposeful pain who seek no pity. Real preachers get no glory in playing the role of a victim or pointing the finger at someone else. Real preachers are too victorious to be victims, and they are in too much pain to be proud. In a strong sense, there is a threatening thorn in every pastor's side God will not remove. All who I pay tribute to have been *thorned* by God, including myself. Because I pay tribute to them, that in no way implies they endorse all my views. I am simply paying homage to a few men and women of God whose shoulders I stand upon. They would not trade their thorn for mine, and believe it or not, I would not trade mine for theirs. Instead, we embrace them. Like all men and women of God, they were not flawless, but they were faithful (II Timothy 4:7-8). As far as I am concerned, please be patient with me, God is not finished with me yet:

"But he knoweth the way that I take: when he hath tried me, I shall come forth as gold."

(Job 23:10; KJV)

Introduction

THE PASTOR AND HIS CHARACTER

∞

(An Exerpt from the Life of Paul:
A preacher whose character was under attack)

Tribute: To my cousin, Armond W. Brown (Pastor of the Fellowship Baptist Church of Oak Cliff, TX from 1997–Present: 2020)

*A*round 1989, my first conversations about authorship began with A. W. Brown. Pastor Brown is a pioneer in countless endeavors whose approach to ministry challenges me beyond my comfort zone. He has rarely been known to operate under conventional norms. Honor must be given to whom it is due. A. W. Brown picks his battles and compromises for the greater good. His meekness has often been misunderstood for weakness. He moves upon conviction and not personal aggrandizement. Armond Brown is the unseen glue that holds so many things and people together. He is ahead of his time, and he has one of the most ingenious minds of our age. Armond Brown can never be accused of being too high-minded to be of any earthly good. He wisely defined preaching as the ability to communicate the Truth of God. In countless ways, he has proven to be an Earth Angel. He founded two of *the best charter schools of our time. His passion for the education of our youth is evident, especially for young children of color. He understands the local church's limitations. Therefore, he is dedicated to the broader spectrum of endless alternatives for those who are bold enough to break into Kingdom possibilities in many of its overlooked social components. He is comfortable in his skin and that encourages me to be comfortable in mine. Armond W. Brown is a man of great character.*

One loss a leader never wants to experience is the loss of good moral character. Every God-chosen preacher will suffer scandal in some sort. It comes along with the preaching package. When we research the malignant motives of a minister's menaces, their vindictiveness is no longer valid. When it comes to the harassment of the hypocritical, a preacher will always be as guilty as sin, but he will never be guilty as charged. When the Corinthian church doubted Paul's character as a genuine apostle, he came to his defense by making sobering statements regarding those chosen to preach the Gospel. He did not defend himself by stating arguments to prove he was not guilty of being a sinful man. Instead, he defended himself by acknowledging he was a sinful man. In a paradoxical sense, his guilt coupled with God's grace made him innocent of their charges.

In the first four chapters of I Corinthians, Paul goes to great lengths to defend himself, but he never defended his sins. Instead, Paul defined his sins. In the very first verse, he was "called" to be an apostle by the will of God (I Corinthians 1:1). Paul initiates his address to Corinth because he received a report that there were divisions among them. One cause of division was because some were discounting his apostleship while giving preference to either Apollos, Cephas (Peter), or Christ (I Corinthians 1:12). Paul affirmed his apostleship by stating that it was Christ who sent him to preach the Gospel, not with wisdom of words (I Corinthians 1:17-18). The entire "wisdom" motif was central to Paul's defense because the Gospel was a stumbling block to Jews and foolishness to the wisdom of the Greeks in Corinth (I Corinthians 1:20-25).

Paul examined the anatomy of preachers of the Gospel in I Corinthians 1:27-28. While the Corinthian church lifted certain preachers but put Paul down, the apostle stated that all preachers have common despised denominators:

> *"For ye see your calling, brethren, how that not many wise men after the flesh, not many mighty, not many noble are called: But God hath chosen the **foolish things** (preachers of the Gospel) of the world to confound the wise; and God hath chosen the **weak things** (preachers of the Gospel) of the world to confound the things which are mighty; And **base things** (preachers of the Gospel) of the world, and **things which are despised** (preachers of the Gospel) hath God chosen, yea, and **things which are not** (preachers of the Gospel) to bring to nought things that are: That no flesh should glory in his presence. But of him are ye in Christ Jesus, who of God is made unto us (preachers of the Gospel) wisdom, and righteousness, and sanctification, and redemption: That, according as it is written, He that glorieth, let him glory in the Lord."*

(I Corinthians 1:26-31; KJV)

In the above-mentioned text, God chooses *foolish* men to preach the Gospel. In Paul's defense, he let them know how he fit that qualification. The word for *foolish* is μωρός [moros /mo·ros/]. The word refers to the *impious, godless, sinful,* and *immoral*. Paul even cataloged himself as the chief of sinners (I Timothy 1:15).

Our English word (*moron*) is derived from the Greek word (*moros*). In a blessed sense, God's preachers are preaching fools. However, chosen preachers do not use the pulpit as a platform to address foolishness, but they are examples of the foolishness of preaching (I Corinthians 1:21). If they are fools, they are only fools for Christ's sake (I Corinthians 4:10).

The text further describes how God chooses sinful men to preach the Gospel to shame the wise. The word for *wise* is σοφός [sophos/sof·os/]. It refers to those who are *skilled*, *experts*, *cultivated*, and *learned*. It also references *Christian teachers who form the best laid evil plans to plot the execution of the credibility of God-chosen preachers* (Strong, J. [1995]. Enhanced Strong's Lexicon. Woodside Bible Fellowship).

Paul further states that God chooses the **weak** to preach the Gospel. Paul also fit that qualification. The word for *weak* is ἀσθενής [asthenes/as·then·ace/]. It refers to those who are *sick*, *feeble*, *without strength*, *infirmed*, or *diseased*. God even selects the sick and infirmed to preach the Gospel to shame those who are physically healthy and strong. The word for *strong* is ἰσχυρός [ischuros/is·khoo·ros/]. It is about those who are *mighty*, *boisterous*, *powerful*, *violent*, *controlling*, and *forceful*. Paul also denotes the *strong* as those who pride in their strength or might, even in a physical manner.

While Paul's enemies and friends saw an ugly and shameful physical impalement that placed a stigma upon Paul's life, God removed Paul's stigma but ordained him to keep his sickness. Paul came to learn why his physical malady was the secret to the strength of his ministry. Therefore, it was something God wanted him to embrace. Paul described his demonic disease and satanic sickness as a thorn in his flesh, a demon messenger of Satan to afflict him with a harassing and humbling illness. Paul initially prayed for his disease to be removed because he believed it to be his hindrance. Paul later came to realize that which did not kill him only came to make him strong. Paul's illness was a gift from God that became his inspiration although his sin brought about his sickness.

The Apostle suffered from the peril of pride, but he came to appreciate the fact that he had a divinely designed disease that kept him humble. In his incurable illness, God's strength was evident in Paul's body, mind, and soul. It was to the testimony of God's grace to shame Paul's accusers that God could sustain and sanction such a sinful and sick man as he:

> *"For this thing I besought the Lord thrice, that it might depart from me. And he* (God) *said unto me, My grace is sufficient for thee: for my strength is made perfect in weakness. Most gladly therefore will I* (Paul) *rather glory in my infirmities, that the power of Christ may rest upon me."*
>
> (II Corinthians 12:8-9; KJV)

God also chooses **base** (ἀγενής [agenes/ag·en·ace/]) men to preach the Gospel. The word refers to those who lack nobility and have been mean, cowardly, of no family or from dysfunctional families. Base preachers are also referred to as, *the low-born*. Paul also fit at least one of those qualifications. Although Paul was from a devout Jewish family, he was previously a mean-spirited man who viciously murdered Christians:

> *"For ye have heard of my conversation in time past in the Jews' religion, how that beyond measure* (intensely) *I persecuted the church of God, and **wasted** it."*

(Galatians 1:13; KJV)

The Greek word for "waste" is πορθέω (portheō). It means to ravage, wreck, or destroy. It is used only here and in Acts 9:21. In the criminal world, to waste a man means to kill him. In a meaner sense, Paul wasted Christians. Luke recorded the same word in the book of Acts that Paul used when he (Paul) wrote to the Galatians:

> *"But all that heard him* (Paul) *were amazed, and said; Is not this he that **destroyed** (*πορθέω -portheō) *them which called on this name in Jerusalem, and came hither for that intent, that he might bring them bound unto the chief priests?"*

(Acts 9:21; KJV)

Lastly, God chooses **despised** men to preach the Gospel. The word for *despised* is ἐξουθενόω [exoutheneo/ex·oo·then·eh·o/]. It refers to least esteemed men, held in contempt, and those who no one counts. We also see how Paul was held in contempt in the very context of the doubting of his character by the Corinthian Believers along with most of the churches who eventually deserted him (Philippians 4:15). In conjunction with the *despised*, God chooses **those who are not**. In the Corinthian mind, "those who are not" was the most detestable description of a human being. Yet, Paul uses that same term to refer to those who are considered worthless. Thus, God uses men who most would consider useless and worthless to preach the Gospel.

When God chooses a man to preach the Gospel, He often picks the hard cases and men who many would consider to be the worst witnesses. Paul gives reasons why God chooses such men to preach the Gospel. God does so that no human can boast.

Therefore, the Corinthians were not to boast in Apollos or Cephas and demean Paul. Not even preachers can boast in themselves. God selects these types of men so that people who judge their character do not credit or discredit preachers for the good or bad they do. Instead, God gets the glory through a preacher's life in profound and confounding way:

> *"For ye see **your calling**, brethren, how that not many wise men after the flesh, not many mighty, not many noble, are **called**: But God hath **chosen** the foolish things of the world to confound the wise; and God hath **chosen** the weak things of the world to confound the things which are mighty."*
>
> (I Corinthians 1:26-27; KJV)

In the text above, Paul describes the Christian's salvation as a *calling*, but he refers to a preacher as one who is not only called (I Corinthians 1:1), but he is also *chosen*. Notice how the text makes better sense with the context suggesting that preachers of the Gospel, including Paul, Apollos, and Cephas are defended by God because of those in the Corinthian congregation who considered themselves to be superior enough to have preacher preferences. The preacher who they threw away was the one who God kept. The preacher who they disqualified was the one who God qualified. To exalt one preacher meant the downgrading of the other(s):

> ***"But God hath chosen the foolish things of the world*** (preachers of the Gospel, including Paul, Cephas and Apollos) ***to confound the wise*** (those who considered themselves more wise according to

> the wisdom of the Greek culture); ***and God hath chosen** the weak things of the world* (preachers of the Gospel, including Paul, Cephas and Apollos) ***to confound the things which are mighty*** (those who considered themselves superior and stronger who discredited Paul because of his iniquities and infirmity)."

(I Corinthians 1:27; KJV)

While many commentators interpret the above text regarding those who are *chosen* to simply refer to the calling of a Christian to salvation, most interpretations are either an oversight or assumption. Either way, the principle remains true of preachers. Preachers are called and chosen. They are saved by Jesus Christ and sanctioned by God. If we are to consider a more probable interpretation, the context preceding and succeeding I Corinthians 1:27 dealt with how God sanctioned sinful men to be His servants. The depth of Paul's defense was in the fact that the Corinthians were saved (*called*) through the preaching of sinful men (*the chosen ones*). The salvation of the Corinthians was secondary to his defense because the argument was not over their salvation. The argument was over their spirituality. Due to their carnality, the Corinthian church had an immature way of perceiving who should be warranted or unwarranted to be preachers of the Gospel.

The fact that God uses sinful men to preach the Gospel for God's glory was primary. Paul even challenged their salvation by categorizing many of them as carnal or natural people who could not understand spiritual things (I Corinthians 2:6-16). As they were challenging his sinfulness, he was also challenging their salvation and spirituality. If they were to consider themselves to be

Christians who were saved by God's grace, Paul was reminding them of the preaching means by which they were saved:

> "***What Paul is dwelling on** (compare 1 Co 1:27, 28) **is the weakness of the instrumentality (preachers of the Gospel) which the Lord employed to convert the world*** " [HINDS and WHATELY; so, ANSELM]. However, English Version accords well with 1 Co 1:24. "***The whole history of the expansion of the Church is a progressive victory of the ignorant over the learned, the lowly over the lofty, until the emperor himself laid down his crown before the cross of Christ***" [OLSHAUSEN]. (Jamieson, R., Fausset, A. R., & Brown, D. (1997). Commentary Critical and Explanatory on the Whole Bible (Vol. 2, p. 265). Oak Harbor, WA: Logos Research Systems, Inc.)

Paul does not give a general description of Christians by describing them as the *foolish, weak, despised,* or *worthless*. The context before and after I Corinthians 1:26-28 and to the end of the fourth chapter aligns more in defense of ministers of the Gospel. The first four chapters align systematically to support such a view. In the second through fourth chapters, Paul continues to defend his apostleship, the Christological basis for preaching and reasons why the Corinthians were not to show partiality, prejudice, or preference towards preachers.

Consequently, we see in the very next chapter how Paul states how he came to the Corinthians in much *weakness* (I Corinthians 2:3). This is the same word he used to describe "the weak" in I Corinthians 1:27. Thus, when Paul was referring to the *weak* in I Corinthians 1:27, he was referring to himself. When Paul came to the Corinthians, he came in bodily weakness (sickness). Nevertheless, God's grace granted him supernatural strength to be a preacher of the Gospel and to preach the Gospel supernaturally:

> *"And I was with you **in weakness**, and in fear, and in much trembling. And my speech and my preaching was not with enticing words of man's wisdom, but in demonstration of the Spirit and of power: That your faith should not stand in the wisdom of men* (as was the case with the Greek philosophers and eloquent orators), *but in the power of God."*

(I Corinthians 2:3-5; KJV)

Paul defends how he preached. The amazing truth about the above-mentioned passage is the fact that Paul came preaching to them in a sickly but supernatural style. Picture a preacher who is stumbling with sin or sickness to the pulpit to preach. However, as soon as he opens his mouth, he receives supernatural strength and preaches with power from above. God-chosen preachers do it all the time. They come to the pulpit as staggering men with weaknesses in one form or another. They stagger up to the pulpit, but they stand down to preach.

Paul further defends what he preached. He described the Gospel as the hidden wisdom of God (I Corinthians 2:7). He continues to defend *how* he, Apollos, and Cephas preached (I Corinthians 2:13).

Paul then defers to how he could not preach. He could not preach to them as ones who were spiritual, but he had to preach to them as carnal babes (immature Christians) in Christ (I Corinthians 3:1). They were babes in Christ because they had preacher preferences (I Corinthians 3:4). Paul defended his credentials by stating the fact that he, Apollos, and Cephas were all laborers together with God (I Corinthians 3:5-9).

Notice how Paul concludes his argument for preachers. He exhorts the Corinthians to not glory in preachers (I Corinthians 3:21-23). Instead, the Corinthians, along with all Christians, should view preachers as stewards of the mysteries of God who must be found faithful to preach the Gospel with power and are not to be judged by people. Preachers are to be judged by God (I Corinthians 4:1-4). He reiterates that the Corinthians were not to think of preachers above or even below what is already written (I Corinthians 4:6-15). There is no judgment a Christian should have regarding preachers. Thus, opinions and prejudices about preachers from any human antagonist has no biblical value or godly merit.

Paul in no way condones moral failures of preachers, worships preachers' agonies, or breeds acceptance of unjustifiable actions of preachers, but it is a reminder that God's men are humanly sinful but divinely chosen. It is our sin that justifies us and our self-imposed righteousness that condemns us. God's grace is greater than our sins, but God's grace has no space for self-righteousness. That does not imply in any way that we continue in sin (Romans 6:1-2). We (preachers) do feel God's painful purging in a more severe sort that is separate from the injuries of common folk, and we do experience almost unbearable chastisement more harshly from a God who has a loving and giving heart but a heavy and restricting hand (James 3:1).

No pastor escapes fragility and failure. Paul reminds all that preachers are prone to perversion. To discredit a preacher because of his infirmity, iniquity, or past identity only offends Christ's methods by which He chose to spread the Gospel through the means of corrupt men. Paul teaches how God puts His treasure of the Gospel in preachers, who are comparable to corrupt clay (II Corinthians 3:7). Preachers are described as earthen vessels, who are fragile and failing. Although we as preachers may look invincible to some, we are extremely vulnerable.

Many vices make us vulnerable. Unlike any other leadership position, pastors are rarely authorized by God to make executive or vetoing decisions. Instead, we are to be servant-leaders (II Corinthians 4:5). Pastoring is the only official leadership position in the world I can think of that has authority but no control. Dr. John Taylor (New Testament Professor of Gateway Seminary) made a profound statement:

> *"Paul was not in the apostolic business of building something larger than what the next guy had. Paul did not exercise apostolic authority in a way that demanded his way. He realized that Jesus Christ had full control over the churches he founded."*

Paul wanted his accusers to understand that he was sinful, but what separated him from their satanic sneering was the fact that God could trust Paul to be a servant. Servants do not have control issues, but their accusers do. Only God-chosen preachers have been entrusted to preach. One who becomes a preacher by his own volition cannot be trusted to preach Jesus only. They preach something else. Because God-chosen preachers know they were born with a criminal character, they obey pulpit laws that protect them from being arrested by God. The first pulpit law states that a preacher must always be cognizant of the fact that he is too sinful, infirmed, and unworthy to count himself worthy to preach the Gospel. Thus, it is the grace of God that gives him sufficiency to preach. Because of a God-chosen preacher's continual awareness of his afflictions and affinities, he takes preaching seriously and soberly.

God did not ordain the essence of the Gospel to be found in a preacher's lifestyle. God ordained the essence of the Gospel to be found in Jesus' lifestyle. Regardless of how morally upright many may think preachers are, none of them are sinless. The Gospel can only embody a sinless lifestyle. Neither Paul, Apollos, or Cephas fit the description of being morally upright, and neither do we (preachers) or our accusers. Because no preacher meets that qualification, God-called preachers preach Christ and not themselves:

> *"For we* (preachers of the Gospel) *preach not ourselves, but Christ Jesus the Lord; and ourselves your servants for Jesus' sake."*

(II Corinthians 4:5; KJV)

Are pastors' sins condoned by God? Of course not. Paul became an example for us to hold ourselves accountable to brutal beatings of self-examination (I Corinthians 9:27). Therefore, we (pastors) must have a solid system of accountability. Unfortunately, not many members of the local church are qualified or spiritual enough to hold pastors to an adequate accountability system, even if they have the best intentions. God forbid if they have the worst intentions. There is a plateau of leadership that exists where many will not dare challenge their leader to be on his best behavior. Pastors' systems of accountability are often defective because of executioners, exposers, or enablers. While exposers and executioners are tagged as the most dangerous threats to a preacher's character, enablers are just as dangerous. Very few are encouragers. Our enablers also display a deadness to our true definition by placing us on undeserved pedestals we must never stand upon. Our Lord also warned us to not to be placed, stand or be thrown off pedestals nor jump off pinnacles. If we make prideful assumptions about God and ourselves from high religious platforms, neither God nor angels will catch us if we fall (Matthew 4:6).

VOLUME I
Chapter 1

THE PASTOR AND HIS HEAD

∞

Power from on High
(An Excerpt from the Life of Elijah:
A preacher who ran from a woman)

<u>Tribute</u>: To my spiritual father in the ministry, Derek L. Winkley, Sr. (Founder-Pastor, Holy Tabernacle Church International of Dallas, TX)

God used Derek L. Winkley to birth me into ministry in a way that kept me faithful to my frame. Around the age of fourteen, I would sit on the front row with the deacons as I was drawn to the dynamic he demonstrated. I was more impressed by his disposition than his delivery. When I could not see myself, Winkley saw me. He would smile, knowing God was calling me to preach, and he would keep walking. When we are called into the ministry, we are reminded that we are to operate within the context of how God uniquely molded us for ministry. Pastor Winkley allowed me to be "Me." I always think that he is pulling my leg, but he says that I am one of the best preachers he has ever heard. That more than humbles me. Because of "Wink", I can say that preaching is a supernatural thing. Yet, a preacher must pay a great price for the anointing.

On April 19, 2016, the temple of Baal was scheduled to go up in New York's Times Square and London's Trafalgar Square. What has been hidden from secular history is the fact that adults would offer their children as sacrifices to Baal. Amidst horrific screams of children burned alive, worshipers would surround the altar and engage in illicit sexual orgies, including bisexuals and homosexuals to invoke Baal to bring rain for the fertility of who Baal worshipers called, "Mother Earth".

God's people always had a dramatic attraction to the gods of this world. Local churches are churches in Satan's cities who can never afford to compete with our culture by sacrificing that which is holy on anxiety-stricken altars. When the local church starts doing what our culture does, our culture can always do it better. We are to have holy altars instead of relative ones. Among the idols, there is a screenplay form of worship in the 21st-century church, full of actors and actresses who are stricken with the need for notoriety. Because there is a thin line in our newer and unimproved brands of Christianity that barely distinguishes church arenas from secular ones, our objects of worship and objectives must be severely screened. Holy Fire purges our passions, refines our purpose, and directs our ultimatums toward God's holiness in a way that leads to wholeness.

Our cultural context can be perceived as a creative context of ministry for God to sharpen our focus on church health above church growth. One quick and most dangerous way to grow a church is for it to become idolatrous. Our churches must be protected from being their own self-preserving societies and cities. When a church becomes too autonomous, it loses accountability and becomes a secret society and underground city (Matthew 5:14). The lack of accountability becomes the main ingredient for toxic faith ministries when idolatrous altars have never been consumed by *Holy Fire*. When we exchange church growth for church health, our philosophies of ministry shift for the better in purging proportions. We are called to focus on the nature of our membership instead of the number of our members. Elijah was outnumbered, but he did not need an army to take down Queen Jezebel. Pastors of churches with few and many members understand pastoring as a people ministry and not a numbers game.

The new Baalism we are to steer clear of are the compromising alliances that abandon the God of the Bible for priorities that may be good, but they are not of God. In no other time in history are we faced with tempting options to develop creative ways of impacting our society. The mantles of pastors that are trampled belong to men who are trying to remove the demands of those who assemble in anxious arenas. Anxiety has stricken people in such a way that they have screaming demands for God to comfort them on their conditions. Prophets are called to never fear threats by pacifying the gods, goddesses, prophets, and prophetesses of our world instead of prophesying against them. Thus, **a true anointing is accountable.** It is not isolated or insulated from the attack on real Christianity only to be confined to scared sanctuaries with paranoid prophets. Out of fear, Elijah resorted to self-preservation.

One day, I was playing with my granddaughter (Aniyah), who was five years old at that time. Evidently, I was intruding her little space as we were playing with her toys. As I reached for one of her toys, she said, "Poppy, respect the bubble!" It tickled her pink when she said that. She jovially justified her joy and wanted me to let her have her little world of make-believe and not burst her imaginary bubble. She taught me a lesson about ministry. Because ministry is not child's play, I must not demand respect for my bubble when Jesus invades my play space (Matthew 11:17).

A counterfeit Christianity that ignites strange fires attempts to personalize Christ's agenda and Christianize personal agendas. When ministry is about people's pain instead of Christ alone, an idolatrous bubble develops that will eventually be deflated. Counterfeit worship in Elijah's day was deflated because of selfish agendas the self-entitled felt Baal should satisfy. Thus, they would not stop cutting themselves in a religious fit when Baal did not answer (I Kings 18:28).

The new Baalism is a counterfeit Christianity that grants people permission to throw religious fits when God does not go their way (I Kings 18:27). They persecute preachers, refute sound doctrine, and reduce worship to victimization. Instead of attention focused on God, attention is focused on them. God is more concerned with worship than our wounds or worries. Instead of seeking healing, they demand that their gods hear them. The sin of self-entitlement causes them to focus on being heard rather than holiness. Thus, they are loud and lethal. God will never bend an ear to selfish screaming. God does not compromise His essence to console anyone. If comforts were to come, they had to listen to God first. Deaf and dedicated to their own desires, they had to learn the hard way by doing things their way.

The first tactic Elijah used was to allow wounded worshipers to build their own altar and get their own wood. God did with them what He would do with everyone who takes matters into their own hands. Before God could help them, He had to give them enough rope to hang themselves. So, God allowed them to develop their own terms for worship. Knowing worship as a lifestyle, we are referring in our day to how God allows people to live on their terms by temporarily removing accountability from them to prove their *goddish* and goddess allegiances will only disappoint. In this battle of the gods, God allowed His people to run wild in worship with a display of drama to a distant and detached deity. Whenever people do things their own way, they enlist in a sympathetic screenplay that only causes them to play the role of drama kings and queens. As in Elijah's day, we are in an even more vicious era in which people demand tremendous amounts of victimized and vindictive attention. People who refuse to submit to God on His terms have destructive ways of drawing attention to themselves. They do not mind shedding their blood for all to see.

To get Baal's attention, worshipers of Baal sought the religious rite of cutting themselves. In the world of psychology, cutting is a sign of an attention disorder. Many who suffer from cutting are not trying to kill themselves although they appear to be doing so. In fact, they have a high tolerance for pain and a self-medicating way of punishing themselves. They are craving for attention and screaming for relevance. They are crying through the act of cutting, "Can anyone see me? I am bleeding!" Christian cutters have the same psychological patterns. Yet, they cut themselves spiritually instead of physically. They believe themselves to be very unloved people. So, they define the love of God in the context of a deity who condones victimization. They leave the altar a bloody mess in the local church by their worship, witness, and words. Christian cutters are also careless in how they tend their wounds. They crave confirmation of their cutting condition.

Therefore, publicity can become their priority. They are addicted to attention. Although hurting, they do not want their wounds closed. They want to keep them open for the world to see. Although wounded, they wound others, sometimes unknowingly. If you insist on healing, they curse the cure. They have only one way in their minds to be made well, i.e., to let them have their way. They claim to be mature, but they seek pampering instead of taking responsibility to have right priorities. If people tamper with cutting forms of Christianity, there are sins they get hold of they cannot cut loose. Among those sins is the sin of satanic sympathy. An *Elijah-anointing* ensures sanctuaries are not be filled with people who inhale the smoke of selfishness while sharpening their vengeful knives on devotions to gods of gore. A preacher who carries a miraculous mantle cannot afford to blow smoke in their faces regardless of his fears or failures.

People who possess a victimized mentality have a way of slicing prophets with the sword of sympathy. It is nearly impossible to beat sympathy. I later learned how God beats sympathy. He has no pardon for pity parties. God only has pardon for confessed sins. All some people see is their pain, but God and the godly know how they are harboring some form of anxiety due to a sense of abandonment. The self-entitled have a wicked and worshipful way of broadcasting their bleeding to induce blame with a hidden blade. Christian cutters can be religiously devoted to that which is destroying them. They do not know how to stop bleeding and blaming. Because they are never satisfied, they increase destructive dosages of drama and have a manipulative method of attack upon whoever challenges their choices.

Within the culture of parenting in which I was raised, if any of us as children would have decided to cut ourselves, our parents would have cut that out of us in one line: *"If you don't stop all that cryin' and cuttin', I'm gon' give you somethin' to cut and cry about!"* That would have been the end of the pity party. Our parents would have known why we did not need comfort. They would have known our need of correction. However, our local church era is even more filled with spoiled adult-children who defy God's discipline toward their brat-like behavior as they throw tantrums when God and people with good religion do not dance to their music (Luke 7:32). They cannot comprehend God as their Father because they have no idea of what is required to be a son or daughter. They do not know how to honor Father God because they are too disenchanted with His authority to focus on why He distances Himself from their devilish demands. Ironically, they claim God as their Father, but they act as though they are God's only children. They have an unrealistic view of family, corporate responsibility, and they can be poor partners because all they truly know who to draw attention to is themselves. Because of victimization, we minister among a culture of constituents who avoid submission to God because they are addicted to passive aggression. Their scabs never heal as they age and become more dysfunctional as victims or proponents of codependence, toxic faith, and religious addiction.

Preaching that *cuts it straight* entails battling the psychological illusion of believing the lie that real preaching is irrelevant to our times. Preachers who *tell it like it is* are not irrelevant. It is virtually impossible to reach a culture of people who are more deeply devoting themselves to idols of insecurity who crave condoning their cutting conditions. As a result, the local church is satanically seduced by mutilating ministries led by hurt people who hurt people. They insist that God only prescribes scriptural pills they can swallow. They are selective servants and part-time patients who have serious problems with the medicine cabinet of the whole counsel of God. While they select some scriptures to swallow, they vomit others that command them to sit down and be humble. They manipulate Truth to defy truths that convict them of their craving for comfort. People addicted to pain fall for these types of medicating ministries, testimonies of torment, heroes of hypocrisy, and *sheroes* of selfishness. They are too victimized for true victory. They fail to understand that peppering their lives with a few scriptures and twisting the truth will never be enough to break free from the choking chain of codependence.

The cataloging of this type of conduct is not some soapbox for me to stand upon. These realizations are necessary for the prophet to deliver people or defend himself against people who have a perverse and persecuting form of pain. Elijah had to mock them before he could minister to them (I Kings 18:27). Ministering through mocking is a psychological response to people who have hidden demands masked by their miseries. The ministry of mocking cannot be underestimated. Mocking people who have a victimized mentality is a spiritual effort to warn them to not take themselves so seriously. They must understand the fact that their terms will always torment them. They must learn to worship God His way. Neither God's world nor the gods of this world revolve around them. They will learn one way or another. They will learn God's way, or the lethal way.

As horrific as that may be, these hidden hurts must be surfaced because God has compassion for Christians who cut, and prophets must never become bitter with bleeders and blamers. However, Christian cutters must be willing to stick their swords in the sands of their own surplus of sins instead of pointing a crooked finger at the prophet (I Kings 18:17-18).

Those who flow in a genuine anointing know how to distance themselves from believers of blame and ministries and members of madness. In referring to distance, I am referring to Elijah's ability to draw attention from their anxious attitudes, antics, and agendas unto God. After they had their turn putting themselves on display, it was God's turn to put His holiness on display. God allowed Elijah to set the record straight. Whenever things get twisted, men with meaningful mantles let mutilators make their moves and stay sacredly silent unless God summons them to supernaturally surface. God sometimes allows prophets opportunities to straighten people's twisted accusations against them.

Elijah shifted to compassionately gather vindictive victims to observe how God operates. Elijah was responsible to repair the very altar they destroyed (I Kings 18:30). Real preachers do not retaliate. They seek to repair. The altar of God is where we come to know the truth about God and ourselves. If the altar of God has been profaned, God ensures that it is prepared properly. Elijah quadrupled water in the trenches in triple cycles (I Kings 18:34). He continued to create distance by praying aloud to God with the content of his prayer revealing where real Fire resides, i.e., in the word of the Lord (I Kings 18:36). As God's people were picking their wounds, Elijah prayed according to God's word. It all came down to fire, and only the true God could rain down fire. After Elijah's prayer in I Kings 18:36-37, the Bible depicts that it was *then* when fire fell:

> "***Then*** *the fire of the Lord fell, and consumed the burnt sacrifice, and the wood, and the stones, and the dust, and licked up the water that was in the trench.*"
>
> (I Kings 18:38; KJV)

Think about the first few minutes after Holy Fire had fallen. I can imagine screams of shock and awe that shrieked from the mountain as they fell flat out of fear of being in reach of divine consumption. A God-awful silence or scared scream had to have stricken all who were spared. Their ears had to have been deafened by the volume of divine destruction that fell from Heaven like lightning. Their eyes had to have been blinded by the illumination of the Fire of God. The most condensed description I can imagine is in two words: "Holy terror!" Holy terror is the theme of real worship. When we encounter God's holiness, it causes us to bow our heads instead of lift them. Real worship causes our hearts to tremble. Far too many of our contemporary worship services are too assuming. We assume too much in many of our anxious arenas. We assume we can come to worship dead and come out alive instead of reverence the fact that we can go to worship alive and be carried out dead if God is not pleased with us.

Once real worship was established, God had unfinished business with those on a higher leadership tier who refused to acknowledge Him. The parties must be distinguished. There was wicked Queen Jezebel and her weak husband, King Ahab. Then, there were the prophets of Baal, and finally, there were their followers. Love was the benefit the followers of Baal received once they acknowledged God on His terms. Lethality was the curse the prophets of Baal and Jezebel received as they refused to acknowledge God. Jezebel's husband (Ahab) was a coward who later died of cowardice (I Kings 22). Make no mistake about God and His prophets, God does have killing instincts, and his ministers do have murdering mantles. One never wants an angry God and a God-angry preacher as an opponent (I Kings 18:40).

Notice how Elijah killed false prophets singlehandedly. Scripture teaches us about at least eight hundred and fifty false prophets who were present (I Kings 18:19). Those who were once Baal worshipers turned against Baal when they turned unto God. It was they who captured the same false prophets who they were once devoted to. It is important to not mislead people because they can turn on the one who misled them, and rightfully so. Yet, mindless followers of mad ministries must understand that a leader who makes mistakes is not always as toxic as one who misleads. Elijah made mistakes, but he never misled God's people. The victimized congregation was misled by jealous Jezebel. While they had a problem with God's leader, they should have had a problem with their own.

When a person has problems with a real preacher, they must be careful if they join forces with pioneers of bitterness. Queen Jezebel was a female force to be reckoned with. She was beautiful, but she was bitter. You could not see it on her painted face as much as you could see it in her eyes. Once her subjects came to their senses, they no longer fed off her bitterness, but they learned to taste and see that the Lord is good (Psalm 34:8). As they learned to develop their own minds, Jezebel could no longer brainwash them.

Yet, the war against vengeful spirits has many battles. The war of the goddesses of this world lasts a long time, and the enemy stronghold does not give in easily. Jezebel's servants fell in love with God, but she and her prophets continued to have vengeful issues with God's men. Her subjects were common folk, but she and her mad ministry team were bent toward twisted truth. Therefore, Jezebel refused to straighten up.

It is important that a preacher becomes bold when he deals with antagonists of this nature. Elijah was anointed to become murder-minded against Jezebel's ministers, but he trembled when it came to his ability to pull the spiritual trigger on Jezebel. Although Elijah was using tools that stuck the core of Hell's workings, he stopped digging when he hit bedrock with Jezebel, who was the embodiment of a core that appeared impenetrable to Elijah. His jabs did not even jolt her. The hellish core of her fury consumed his courage. That is the only mistake that we see of Elijah, and it was a grave mistake to make.

Cowardice has been the sole stigma placed upon Elijah's flight from Jezebel. There is biblical evidence to expose additional components of Elijah's paranoia. Many psychological manifestations surface when a preacher's courage is consumed. The absence of courage is not only cowardice. The absence of courage is also a form of **dis-couragement**. Discouragement is one of Satan's greatest weapons used against a preacher. With a little play on words, when it comes to *discouragement*, it is vital for the pastor to not allow evil to *"dis"* (disrespect) his courage. Discouragement can cause a pastor to feel all alone, especially when he comes down from triumph to only become a target. It has been said that if a man is the last man on Earth, his deepest human need will be for companionship. It is lonely at the top, but it is even lonelier at the bottom. God assigned

Elijah to the mountain and the valley. A Gospel preacher must never allow his mind to think linearly. He must think perpendicularly. Ministry is full of ups and downs, highs and lows, victories, and valleys. Mt. Carmel was one thing, but the Valley of Jezreel was quite another.

When discouragement sets in, a preacher may no longer want to show up in certain rings of ministry. When a pastor stops showing up, that is a strong sign of discouragement. Discouragement can kill a pastor quicker than any Jezebel spirit can. Discouragement will also cause a pastor to retreat to secular securities and cave-like comforts. If we do not do so geographically, we may do so psychologically and develop manageable ministries void of anything confrontational and supernatural. The answers to why prophets died too soon is within their caves and fossils that reveal fear factors that made them discouraged and dead targets.

Discouragement can stem from ***disillusionment***. A pastor must always know the game is not over until it is won regardless of the score. If the score is nine-to-one, and the game is won by the one who scores ten points first, if a pastor only has one point, he must not think the game to be over. Instead, he must see himself as one who is nine points from winning. Progress is one of the greatest weapons God uses against an enemy. A pastor's enemies detest his success, and they do not want others to win if they are members of his mantle. In Jezebel's mind, she was down by nine points after Elijah won the battle on Mt. Carmel. Like any bitter rival, Jezebel was fast, fueled, and furious because of Elijah's progress. With such great *Fire*, I can imagine how Elijah believed that would be the end of his troubles, thinking victory on Mt. Carmel would send a quenching message to Jezebel. Instead, it only fueled her flame and made her meaner.

In Bible history, the suicidal state of mind many prophets found themselves in was due to their disillusionment that came from unexpected enemies and demons of delusion. Whenever we are in pastoral ministry, we must lower our expectations and never be surprised. There are some people who a prophet would expect to turn against him, but there are others who can catch him by surprise if he has no supernatural suspicions. We as pastors must have a grounded perspective of what real ministry is about. Ministry is not a corporate ladder we climb to get to higher ministry. Ministry does not get higher. It gets lower. Ministry is spiritual warfare that involves demons of deeper depths. Therefore, it demands tremendous amounts of humility. Ministry is a supernatural thing. Thus, little that occurs in our tenure is simply human. We are in the context of gods and goddesses, and we are mortals in the middle of immortals, i.e., angels and demons. As a result, the repercussions we experience from human foes can be quite fiendish and frustrating if we fail to focus because we do not war against flesh and blood (Ephesians 6:12).

A pastor's greatest defeats of his enemies can become some of his greatest disillusionments. We can reach peaks of purging progress only to discover that our troubles have only just begun. It is hard for the human mind to put in perspective the resilience of evil and the end of all hope. There is a built-in capacity for humans to cry for mercy when pushed to the limit. Yet, God had no mercy on Elijah when he felt like quitting. Instead, God kept mercilessly mashing him into more malicious ministry. Elijah could have died with the mental frame of mind he adopted. He was so discouraged and disillusioned that he wanted to curl up and die. A large percentage of prophets in the Bible wished they could just disappear instead of continuing in a ministry surrounded by people who refused to fear God. We hear a lot about preachers' failures, but in the same context, we do not hear much about people who do not fear God. There is a grave difference between the two. People who do not fear God run the risk of being on the borders of insanity.

They are capable of the most reckless routines and demonic decisions. Therefore, Elijah could not mentally process her personality. Because Jezebel did not fear God, she was demonically devoted to destroying Elijah.

Elijah's discouragement developed into being **drained**. I have never seen a discouraged preacher with a high energy level, including myself. Elijah led the execution of over eight hundred of Jezebel's prophetic constituents. He also exerted a great amount of energy running from the Lord. When a preacher runs from his calling, he will run out of breath in a season of seconds. Elijah exhausted everything he had in fighting and fleeing. However, he could not do both at the same time. One overtook the other. Whenever we run from the Lord, we will always tire ourselves out because there is nowhere to run. Speed can never outrun omnipresence.

There are three runs of Elijah that contributed to his collapse. He ran *for* the Lord, he ran *because* of Jezebel, and he ran *from* the Lord. He did not do all three runs simultaneously. However, he made all three runs in the same track meet of ministry. Jezebel's husband (Ahab) was no match for Elijah, and she knew it. Elijah miraculously outran Ahab on foot while he was in his chariot. After the battle on Mt. Carmel, he ran in the rain to the entrance of Jezreel (I Kings 18:44-46). Running in the rain, Elijah is speedy and supernatural instead of soaked. He was more miraculous than muddy. The rain was not a drizzle. Make no mistake about it, Elijah was running through a storm. He was at peak performance, a victorious velocity, and a supernatural speed, running for the Lord, outrunning Ahab's chariot horses. After Elijah's discouraging report that Jezebel was after his head, the text never tells us that he ran *to* the Lord.

If we (preachers) are to have supernatural speed, we better make sure that we run faster toward our enemies than we run from them. God gave Elijah supernatural speed to run toward Jezebel in Jezreel. When he ran from her, he was so cowardly slow that Jezebel could not only catch up with him, but his fears, failure, and fatigue also caught up with him. If he would have continued in that type of fear, God would have taken him out long before Jezebel could have. When we run from our calling, God will cause us to realize how much we were part of something much larger than ourselves. By then, it is too late unless we rely on God to turn back the hand of time by supernaturally fortifying us for a fortunate future. Elijah was sinfully slow to get over his post-deliverance trauma he experienced on Mt. Carmel, remaining in a stale, psychological and ministerial state. He was on a dangerous path to becoming like Jonah, ending his ministry with a question mark (Jonah 4:11).

It is easy to outrun Satan's horses when we have come down from the momentum of a miraculous mountain. When we run for the Lord, we can outrun tormenting Trojans, but when we run from threats, stress can quickly stampede our stamina. When we come down from the mountain into the valley, our speed must never slow down to muddy momentums. A tired preacher must always be careful how he treads on lower ground. We must be careful how we ground ourselves after a major victory and guard ourselves against post-adrenaline syndromes. At the bottom of the mountain always lies some evil that threatens us to never reach high prophetic peaks ever again.

As Elijah descends from greatness, he ran from God's call to descend into greatness. Ahab informs Jezebel of their defeat on Mt. Carmel. *The assassination of a preacher frequently starts with a cowardly confidant and instigating informant.* Ahab informed Jezebel of Elijah's progress. Jezebel's response was a death contract issued against Elijah (I Kings 19:1-2). God never commissioned any individual to assassinate a true prophet or turn him in, especially when under the context of satanic snitching. The assassination of a prophet was a job God only left for beasts, angels, or God would do it Himself. Any man who thought Jezebel loved and was loyal to him was highly disillusioned. Jezebel had issues with rejection, and she had a mean view of men. She would terminate anyone who frustrated her future or one who did not align with her agenda, including her husband (Ahab). When it came to her threats against Elijah, she crossed a line with God by threatening to cut off Elijah's head. It teaches a powerful warning: ***Never go for a preacher's neck.***

"Touch not mine anointed and do my prophets no harm."

(Psalm 105:15; KJV)

As word gets back to Elijah, he changes the definition and destination of his run. He runs away because of Jezebel and exhausts himself under a juniper tree, requesting to die. Elijah was in a suicidal state with a fleeing focus. Then, Elijah ran from the Lord to a cave where the Lord showed up in a still small voice (I Kings 19:9). The angel of the Lord refreshes Elijah and tells him that the journey is too great to make while fatigued.

It wasn't until the 1980's that professional boxing numbered between thirteen to fifteen rounds. Prior to that time, Joe Louis and Abe Simon went twenty rounds on March 21, 1941. The last title match scheduled for fifteen rounds was in 1982 with the death of lightweight, Duk Koo Kim after his fourteen-round fight with Ray Mancini. Duk Koo Kim died from the fight. Two loyal fans were so devastated by his death that they committed suicide. Nearly instantly, the World Boxing Council (WBC) declared WBC title bouts would be shortened to twelve rounds.

If a prophet is in the ring of battling relentless evils for a certain amount of time, he could get killed due to poor conditioning. There is danger in quitting too soon in the twelve rounds of Truth. If we quit too soon, it will be hard to resume our rightful place as conditioned contenders. When a prophet dies in the ministry from a collapse of courage, it also disheartens his loyal fans. God does not shorten a prophet's rounds of ministry. Ministry is a long sport, even if we have a short life span. Only God determines when we have been in the ring for too long. The process of battling vindictive spirits is long and brutal. Whenever Jezebel's nest is stirred, Pandora's box opens. We are in for a long battle. We save our breath, condition our souls, and get ready for the next battle (Ecclesiastes 3:8).

At this juncture, Elijah focused more on his inertia than God's intelligence. God is a supernatural and smart warrior with eternal stamina. He outwits and outlasts His enemies every time. Granting the stamina to go the distance is God's responsibility, but the duty to show up in the ring is the preacher's responsibility. A tired prophet can quickly drop his mantle. A preacher must always have a good grip on God regardless of who is after him and never grow weary in well-doing (Galatians 6:9). A skilled and structured fighter can sometimes lose against an unorthodox fighter because unorthodox fighters can be unpredictable and swing by surprise.

Elijah did not know how long he had to continue before unpredictable and unorthodox Jezebel was knocked out. Her tank of torment never tumbled. It just appeared to get even fuller. He was not conditioned to go the distance, but Jezebel was. Resilience was her middle name. She was not devoted to some idol god in her mind whose name was Baal. She was devoted to Satan because she was rebellious. Her rebellion was as the sin of witchcraft (I Samuel 15:23). She was devoted to her god more than Elijah was devoted to his. Thus, she was bitter and would not break. A prophet must never fear people who have blood running warm in their veins. Every human being has at least one weakness, and so did Jezebel. As a matter of fact, she had at least five.

Firstly, *she did not understand the partnership God has with His preachers*. She did not realize how hard God hits those who seek to harm His prophets. Secondly, *she had no self-control when her world fell apart*. When Jezebel could not get her way, she became destructive. Thirdly, *she had no diplomacy when people defected from her demands*. Anyone who opposed her was not released to live their lives. Instead, she detained and maintained lethal leverage over them. Fourthly, *she refused to humble herself*. Jezebel could never say, "I'm sorry. I was wrong". Instead, she changed the rules to justify her ambition. Fifthly, *she had tunnel vision*. She was so consumed with knocking Elijah out that she failed to realize her arms were too short to box with God.

As far as Elijah's greatest weakness was concerned, he was afraid of losing his head. Little did Elijah realize the more important truth that **a preacher's head should only be vulnerable to the guillotine of godliness**. In other words, only God determines when a preacher is to die. If a preacher does not understand that, he may find himself reduced to an embarrassing sense of simplicity, resigning to a life of seclusion, eating nothing but bread and water (I Kings 18:4). At that interval, all he wants is just enough to get through the day. Although Elijah was content with bare necessities, Jezebel wanted to take that from him also.

Pastoring is a dangerous job. Seclusion makes us easier targets if we play it safe by resigning to more cave dimensions of pastoral ministry. If we play it too safe, every way we minister hinges upon job security. We will begin to preach safe sermons, conscious of how we sound and who we offend instead of being sound (II Timothy 4:3). It is critical to know an important truth when God pushes a preacher back into the pulpit, even if he knows he doesn't deserve or desire to be there: God called us to preach boldly and not develop a cowardly calling (Acts 4:29).

There are times when staying off the radar is wise, but most of the time, it is not, even if a prophet faces fear and failure. Running from a person is one thing but running from God is quite another. A prophet could be minding his own ministry or even cuddle in his own cave, and some bitter rival can surface years down the line. Seclusion did not deter Jezebel from hunting for Elijah's head. It just made her come looking for him more because she knew he was hiding. Since Jezebel refused to put up her sword, Elijah needed to know God's will in allowing her to die by it (Matthew 26:52).

Real ministry takes a lot out of a Gospel preacher (Romans 8:36). Any other style of ministry we commit to that is void of peril and persecution is one that seeks to protect our prosperity. If we allow our ministries to become constructed to a cave-like comfort zone, we become predictable and complacent. God does not anoint complacency. Self-serving safeties never give a real preacher stamina. If we become dedicated to docility, we will reconstruct our reputation to avoid confrontation and create compromising alliances. If we coward down, we may save our reputation, but we will lose respect and our reward. We may save our lives, but we will never know what it truly means to live. It is being used by God on our contemporary *Mt. Carmels* that keeps prophets covered, not our caves. Obedience to God strengthens our ministries while compromise only weakens them.

If we fear the valley of the shadow of death, the remainder of our ministries will be nothing but a process of God transitioning us from service to be replaced by a successor who has twice as much of an anointing as ourselves (II Kings 2:9). There are not many things more unattractive to God than a comfortable and cowardly prophet who misrepresents his mantle. God has a quick temper when it comes to His prophets quitting out of fear. A prophet may anger the spirit of Jezebel when he stays in the ministry, but he will anger God infinitely more if he strays from his ministry. God has little to no sympathy for preachers who commit prophetic suicide. In the Bible, whenever a prophet flirted with quitting, God was far from sympathetic. Instead, God was serious, and He warned prophets of the danger of refusing to preach (I Corinthians 9:16).

The character of Jezebel is quite interesting. Like her husband (Ahab), men who she used were too compromising to confront her. They became her assassins who executed her agendas. They put their necks on the line while she protected her own. That is a skill she hid from her resume', but God revealed it in Scripture. Most men who did not challenge her were charmed by her at some point in time. Her charm is how she weakened men to get her way. Once she was done hypnotizing them, they could never admit how they fell for her or became soft through her seductions because that would make them look like fools. So, they tucked their tails and never told the truth about how much she was a trick more than their treat. As a matter of fact, that was one of the ways she muzzled men. They could not attack her because they were at one time attracted to her. Jezebel had no tolerance for disloyal or disinterested men. She only recruited dumb men. She was a woman easily scorned. Thus, Jezebel had control over her submissive, shady, and silent husband. She needed a man she could manage. If seduction did not work, this type of wickedness got straight to the point and made it known that madness was the motive because regardless of all she acquired, she had nothing to lose. Jezebel lived every day of her life in hell because her life was a living hell. She demanded faithfulness while she remained an adulteress. Yes, she was a queen with a kingdom, but a castle means nothing if God is not on the throne of one's heart. Yes, she had a house, but it was never a home. She had riches but no real relationships. Because of her lust for power and commitment to control, everyone in her life was a pawn on her chessboard, and most of them were too weak-minded to know they were being played.

The story of Jezebel is not just a history lesson. It forms the theological foundation of what pastors and faithful members of the local church are to guard themselves against today. The Bible does not only speak of Jezebel as a woman. The Bible also speaks of her as an evil spirit. Like Jezebel who is now dead, her spirit appears to live on. In the local church, the Jezebel spirit has a way of spiritually soliciting passive people by marketing a ministry of manipulation. It is not just prophets who God calls to defeat the spirit of Jezebel. It is also the local church's responsibility to hold Jezebel demons accountable. This Jezebel spirit loves to target local churches under the disguise of Truth. Although this spirit has a ministry within some local churches, her spirit has a deep-seated resentment against the Church. Jezebel's evil spirit talks down to the Church rather than learns from the Church. Her spirit does not openly acknowledge the fact that the Church is the Bride of Christ because her spirit is that of an adulteress.

Jesus has a strong word against this demonic spirit that He wants His Church to realize. Although Elijah and many prophets feared her spirit, Jesus does not. Not only does Jesus have a problem with the spirit of Jezebel, but He also has judgment against Christians who coward down and pastors who become passive when her spirit visits churches with a manipulative ministry:

> *"I (Jesus) have a few things against thee (the pastor and the church), because thou (the pastor and the church) sufferest that woman Jezebel, which calleth herself a prophetess, to **teach** and to seduce my servants to commit fornication, and to eat things sacrificed unto idols."*

(Revelation 2:20; KJV)

Notice the text closely. Jesus teaches us how this Jezebel spirit has a *teaching ministry, and she even calls herself a preacher (prophetess).* Yes, there were true prophetesses in the New Testament Church, but Jezebel was not one of them. Jesus was angered because the angel (pastor) of the church along with the church allowed her to slither her deceptive doctrine within the local church setting. In this text, God's prophets were not the only ones who were guilty of fornication. Jezebel had something to do with it as well. While she gloated in being a prophetess, Jesus called her an adulteress (Revelation 2:22). She was not faithful by a long shot. The physical Jezebel had man problems with more than one man, and the spiritual one has a misguided ministry and preacher problems with more than one preacher. Jesus told the church of Thyatira that He was going to clean house if they didn't repent and remove her evil spirit from their midst as they overlooked the root of fornication that originated from the seed of Jezebel's spiritual adultery.

It is not the spirit of Jezebel who a prophet must fear. It is God who a prophet must always fear (Matthew 10:28). A preacher must never forget that. We must fear God more than our foes, failures, or our future. The battle on Mt. Carmel was *not* about Elijah versus Jezebel. It was about God versus Baal. No preacher should allow some *Jezebel* to make it about the two of them. It is spiritual warfare. Surely, Jezebel would have loved for Elijah to have stooped to her level by giving her all that negative attention. As a matter of fact, when Elijah let it become personal, he played right into her hands. A bigger picture was at stake Elijah needed to be reminded of. If God wanted to take a prophet down, He did not need Jezebel's help. God would do it Himself. God calls us into the ministry, and God calls us out of the ministry. **God never uses a bitter spirit to assassinate a preacher.** Satan and his constituents do that. If God has not taken a prophet out, he is still in.

Instead of running, Elijah needed to get to the point in which Jezebel was afraid to face *him*. From then on, Elijah would have stood at an anointed angle of attack. "If you come for me, I will surely come for you" was a better ministry motto God wanted Elijah to have. As long as he ran, his back was always in her view. That made him easy prey. What even made Elijah more of an easy kill was the fact that he turned his back on God. Whenever a prophet turns his back on God, he can never face his foes. Whatever our fears, discouragements, failures, or disappointments are, we as preachers must settle them with God. If not, God will settle them with us, and it is not always a nice settlement if God rearranges the contract of our calling. When Elijah could not get the courage to continue in his calling, God fired him in a friendly way. A friendly firing from God is one that keeps a preacher in the ministry, but it also triumphantly transitions him out of the ministry at the same time. God works in mysterious ways when it comes to how he deals with us as preachers when we are paralyzed by paranoia.

Another reason for Elijah's flight from Jezebel was *failure*. Discouragement can come when we feel as though we have not only missed the mark, but also when we feel as though there is no mark to strive for anymore. When we miss our season of service, all other ministry efforts are just chasing the wind. This happens when we fail in what we consider to be our most defining moments. Elijah cried to the Lord that he was no better than his fathers (I Kings 19:4). Elijah knew he failed because Jezebel was still standing strong while his knees were knocking. It is baffling to the prophetic mind that God still has a mantle for a minister who is weak at the knees.

To get Elijah to a level of fortitude, God was not pleased with His depression. Depression is a silent killer of our calling, and it tries God's patience. Our seasons of depression are running ways that we make statements to God that we no longer appreciate our anointing. Instead, we have allowed some change in circumstance to precede our purpose and paralyze our preaching. When a prophet is suffering from depression, it is important that he eats. An angel fed him with food, but there was no food God or an angel could give to replenish his confidence. Instead, *"he ate, drank, and lied down again"* (I Kings 19:5-6). Elijah had no desire to move forward. He just wanted to spend the rest of his life in one spot. Elijah chose to eat the bread of sorrows. He ate the bread of the Earth, but he had difficulty eating Bread from Heaven. Elijah was losing an appetite for his anointing and passion for preaching.

Ministering to a depressed person is a delicate duty. It is even more fragile when a preacher is that person who is depressed. When a person is suffering from depression, you cannot always break into their space without being invited. If so, you can easily tilt them over into the death zone. The Earth, Wind and Fire did not shake Elijah out of his depression, but God's still small voice did (I Kings 19:11-12). Everything God commissioned Elijah to do from that point on was in a still small voice. God let Elijah know why Elisha was soon to be anointed in his stead (I Kings 19:16). In a graceful, yet still-small manner, God was transitioning Elijah from Earth to Glory.

Loneliness was also an issue. Sometimes, our journey is from the mountain to the valley. All preachers are not called to the top. Some are called to descend into greatness. God keeps a record in low places as well as high places. It is more dangerous to land a plane than take off in mid-air. Elijah's ascension on Mt. Carmel was successful, but his dissension into Jezreel was a total plane wreck. It takes staying power, descending power, and landing power. Every preacher must always know he is not the only preaching pilot on the planet. In God's master plan, He always has an Elisha and *a pack of sevens* who know how to fly:

> *"Yet I (the Lord) have left me seven thousand (prophets) in Israel, all the knees which have not bowed unto Baal, and every mouth which hath not kissed him."*

(I Kings 19:18; KJV)

Here is where numbers matter. Seven is the number of perfection. In God's perfect plan, He has preachers on front lines operating in perfect partnership with Him. Our ministries are not the only ones on the map. There is an invisible norm of prophets with *Fire* who are flamethrowers against the new *Baals* of our day. At Bishop College, we always knew there was some unnamed preacher who was back in the woods faithfully tilling the soil, and opportunity was going to come knocking on his door one day, in God's own time.

Elijah did not understand God's strategy of defeating Jezebel's method of attack. Although Jezebel tried to bury Elijah, she was digging her own grave. When people set traps for prophets, they will get caught in it themselves. If they roll a boulder down on the ones who they are seeking to crush, it will crush them instead (Proverbs 26:27).

Some of us can know we are the chosen ones, but everything within and without can convince us otherwise, including our own failures, fears, and fatigues. When we have experienced severe trauma to the brain, it is difficult to regain consciousness of the context of our calling. Elijah allowed Jezebel to get in his head. Whenever threatening spirits get in a preacher's head, it hurts. It is a form of mental pain that is unbearable. ***Not many evils are as painful to a pastor as a satanic migraine.*** Since Jezebel could not physically touch Elijah, he allowed her to psychologically torment his mind.

I watched a television special about Michael Jordan. I am always touched by the man behind the basketball more than the basketball in front of the man. The death of Michael Jordan's father caused trauma to his thought-life. I can only imagine. During times of retirement and returning, there was always some demon telling him to quit too soon while another was telling him to stay in the game too long. Pastors may know what Michael Jordan went through. There is always at least one demon telling us to quit too soon and another telling us to stay longer than we should. We are tormented by stopping, starting, and stopping all over again. When we want to quit, God reminds us that we only just begun. When we feel as though we have more miles to run, God buries us on some unknown mountain. One of the most profound sights I have seen under the sun is seasoned pastoral and preaching veterans suffer and sacrifice for much of their ministries, reach a peak of a major victory, and then, God calls them *Home* before they have time to enjoy the fruit of their labors. Just when they learn to live, it is time to die. God's definition of finishing strong is not the same as ours. The most important point when crossing the finish line of faithfulness is simply in celebrating the fact that we finished (II Timothy 4:7-9).

When we have divested our heart and soul into the ministry prior to and after great failure, God can spare us of an embarrassing finish. God prepared chariots for Elijah to carry him *Home* and new challenges for his new successor, Elisha. Elijah would soon come to know a bold prophet coming even better behind him to seize his torch who did not mind doubling his efforts (II Kings 2:9). God's naming of Elisha as a successor came in the context of Elijah fleeing the call. For Elijah, this was a double-edged sword. God was letting Elijah know that his ministry would soon come to an end, but He was also letting Elijah know that he still had work to do. This is what I call a friendly firing of Elijah.

Yet, it was not time for him to resign. A raw resignation is not the same as a running resignation. A raw resignation is one in which we know our time is up simply because God said so. A running resignation is one in which we fear greater failure if we do not diplomatically fade off a scene we believe we no longer play a role in because we are defeated, drained, discouraged, or disillusioned.

Elijah had to learn how to regain his relevance with the Redeemer. Thus, God moved him up the mountain of mentoring. It is just my opinion that every credible retired pastor ought to be given an honorary seat in a school of the prophets. I have been to seminary on a respectful scale, and I have no doubt that professors and students would benefit from these seasoned shepherds. Every young Elisha who succeeds his Elijah should champion Elijah's training him for triumph. ***Whenever a prophet succeeds an older prophet who has overcome, he can never be successful using a different mantle.*** There will always be something wrong with the man, but there will never be anything wrong with his mantle. A successor must not attempt an Elisha ministry without an Elijah mantle.

Because there is scarce mentioning of Elijah after his great depression, one can presume Elijah was not as strong as before. That is a great fallacy. Although we do not hear much of Elijah from that point on, it is only because the remaining chapters of the life of Elijah prove his ministry was reduced to precision. If we study the biblical data, everything Elijah was commanded to do from that point on, he did it. Ministry became simple for Elijah. When God told him not to fear, he did not fear (II Kings 1:15). As a matter of fact, he called down *Fire* at least two more times to consume enemy commanders before Heaven's chariots came to carry him *Home* (II Kings 2:10-12). Elijah had a strong finish. He was a man of fortitude who never flinched at the face of evil from that point on. Elisha was not being trained by a coward. Elisha was being trained by a man whose relevance was recovered. Elisha's grief over Elijah's transition into Heaven is further evidence that Elisha was clinging to a mentor of great value (II Kings 2:1-18). Thus, Elijah went out strong and in style (II Kings 2:3-9).

Elijah was not hiding from Jezebel anymore. He repositioned himself while God did a tragic number on her. God pushed Elijah back into the ring, and he even boldly participated in the prophecy of Jezebel's demise. God rarely spares those who relentlessly seek to destroy God's work and workers. God eventually caught up with Jezebel, and Elijah's anointing caught up with him. Jezebel was on God's *Most Wanted* list. God did not want her alive. God wanted her dead, and God always gets what He wants. God was just planning the perfect timing for her tragedy. When God moved, everything else had to move:

"In II Kings 9:30-37, Jezebel meets her demise at the hands of Jehu, her own eunuchs, a team of horses, and a pack of dogs. It takes a lot to kill a queen. When she hears of Jehu's arrival in Jezreel, she arranges her hair and paints her eyes; actions that are often seen as sexually suggestive. However, these acts are those of a proud and powerful queen. She arrays herself in full royal splendor and stands at the window to await the usurper…She throws out a taunt: "Is it peace, Zimri, murderer of your master?" Her reference is to the earlier coup of Zimri, who killed King Elah and all of the other claimants to the throne (1Kgs 16:8-14). Her statement may also be a curse meant to thwart the success of Jehu's insurrection, since Zimri ruled for only one week before he too became the victim of political violence (1Kgs 16:15-20). Jezebel's last words are clearly meant not to entice but to deride Jehu; her last beautifying acts can be understood in the same way. Jehu responds, "Who is on my side?" Responding to his call, Jezebel's own eunuchs throw her out the window, her blood splattering as she hits the ground. Jehu's now bespattered horses then trample her. The image of an adorned woman at a window suggests not only royal power but

also goddesses (especially Hathor, Asherah, and Astarte), who are also depicted looking out windows. In this way, the death of Jezebel is not just the death of a Phoenician princess who became queen of Israel but also the symbolic death of the goddesses she worships and represents. It is not enough simply to kill her; she must be violently expelled from the political and religious community. Jezebel's body mangled and lifeless, Jehu goes inside for dinner. Almost as an afterthought, he commands her burial. While he has been inside eating, the dogs outside are feasting as well—on Jezebel's body. Dogs are powerful symbols in Canaanite religion, especially associated with the goddesses Anat and Astarte and the god Baal. There is a deep irony here. She who was devoted to these deities is devoured by them, all to the triumph of Israel. Only her palms, feet, and skull remain. A further reference to Anat may explain why only these fragments of her body are unconsumed. According to Canaanite mythology, Anat wore a necklace and belt of human skulls and hands. The religious rituals and images of ancient Near Eastern religions are inverted, perverted, and overturned in the death of Jezebel. Consumed by animals, Jezebel becomes an animal; her dehumanization is complete. She is a foreign woman, a powerful queen, and a worshiper of deities other than Yahweh. She is ethnically and religiously different, transgresses proper gender roles, and she is a danger. The death and destruction of Jezebel eradicates the other to protect and preserve the proper Israelite community"

(Jennifer L. Koosed, "Death of Jezebel").

I preached for my father in the ministry (Derek L. Winkley) for his 40th-year celebration of preaching in 2018. In his closing remarks, he mentioned a series of rounds he fought in the ring of pastoring. I noticed strength drain from his body. I saw tears springing from his soul before they touched his eyes. Then, he broke out in tears. He did not cry like an infant. He cried like a weeping prophet. Although he has a mantle, it would be wise for most to remember he is also a man. Anyone who knows "Wink" knows he does not back down if he is cornered or challenged. However, what many do not know is the fact that his life has been one fight after another, from childhood to manhood.

In the fight, we must take as much punishment possible. During other times, it comes from other prophets. A preacher's worst enemy is usually another preacher. In time, a man gets tired of fighting, and he gets tired of getting shot down by other preachers. When some preachers aim for another preacher, they aim high. There will always be some obstructing opponent whose words are subtle suggestions that real preachers are not worth knowing or hearing. Then, there are times when our wounds are self-inflicted.

In the realm of boxing, a fighter cannot take off his own gloves. They are tied so tightly that his trainer must take them off. While boxing, his gloves were designed to be put on and not taken off. In the realm of pastoring, we cannot take off our gloves. The wrists of our ministries are tied so tightly to glorious gloves that God must take them off. We may step out of the ring and quit, but we cannot take off our gloves. If we step out of the ring, we will be left with gloves and nothing to faithfully fight for. If we quit too soon, we will lose our standing behind the pulpit with a burning desire to preach. The bell that rings has a heavenly timer, and God will not pull off our gloves until our fight is over.

Our God is more acute to the level of punishment a pastor can take more than the WBC is to the boxing profession. God does not need to experience a loss of His most prized fighters to make new rules that state when enough is enough. There are no new rules to determine how much we can take, just old ones to remind us that God will not put on us more than we can bear (I Corinthians 10:13). God knows the pain we feel, even when we are numb. He knows how to catch up with us, even when we run.

Pastoring is a deadly sport. It can kill a man. We do not wish this sport on anyone. A man must be called and conditioned to be a contender. It is a sport that demands stamina. Pastoring is a serious sport. The local church can be strange, fickle, and unpredictable, and so are many of the people we gave our lives to. Yet, so can we. Many have deadly cases of amnesia. They quickly forget the good we have done and hop on some runaway train, lethal lane, or hypocritical highway that will get them nowhere. Even our accusers were sometimes the ones we helped most, but they rarely admit that. I heard Pastor Donald Parsons say, "People do not always change. They just get tired of pretending."

God has invested too much in us as His prized fighters to quit on Him. We must take as many blows to the head and knives to the throat possible until God says we had enough. Not only must we take punishment, but we must also dish it out. Each time we do good, we punish evil (Romans 2:21). Just because we are commanded to love our enemies, God sometimes grants us *Fire* to level them. Pastoring is a sport with evils in every round. After we contend in the long bout of life, God will wipe every tear from our beaten eyes. When we reach our Eternal Corner, God will heal every blow we took if we stood strong in the arena of adversity. Most of all, our Trainer will wrap His everlasting towel around our swollen brows and say, "Well done, thy good and faithful servant. Thou hast been faithful over a few things, I will make thee ruler over many. Enter into the joy of thy Lord" (Matthew 24:23). Until then, to every preacher...box on!

Chapter 2

THE PASTOR AND HIS MIND

∞

A Beautiful Mind
(An Excerpt from the Life of Paul:
A preacher whose theology was threatening)

Tribute: To the late, Dr. Manuel Scott, Sr. (former Pastor of Calvary Baptist Church of Los Angeles, CA and St. John Missionary Baptist Church of Dallas, TX)
Sunrise: November 11, 1926; Sunset: December 18, 2001

In the dorms of Bishop College of Dallas, Texas, audiotapes of seasoned preachers echoed through halls as we studied the style, substance, and stamina of preaching giants. Sometimes, we would even try to mimic them. At Bishop College, I first heard of Manuel Scott, Sr. I was intrigued by the intellect of a man who was small in stature but large in substance. Apart from his preaching prowess, two high points leave an indelible stain on my mind. Firstly, Dr. Scott was a gentleman. While attending Criswell College, I worked at Highland Park Cafeteria as a busboy and server to help pay for my tuition. I noticed Dr. Scott walking through the door for dinner. A lady walked through the door, and Dr. Scott gave her the greeting of a gentleman and not a secret admirer. He smiled, tipped his hat to the woman, and clicked his heels. I never saw a man greet a woman like that except in movies. I walked over to him and introduced myself. Although he was a man of national renown, he took the time to speak with me as if I were the only man in the room. The first impression that came to my mind was, "This man is for real. He is not just a preacher on a platform for the public. He's a personal preacher." I realized a scholar must also be a gentleman. Lastly, Dr. Scott was a scholar indeed. In his own words, "Reading makes a ready man."

A passion for true theology mandates the pastor to be flexible enough to allow his thoughts about God to be deprogrammed or deleted. Paul's conversion on Damascus Road is a prime example. Paul' conversion sheds light upon those of us who had zealous concepts of God who needed our theological hard drives wiped and our ministries reprogrammed. To be transformed theologically may require the trashing of years of work and the sacrificing of previous modes of the way we do ministry. Most of all, as was the case with Paul, it may require swallowing large amounts of pride.

Theological leans can be lethal. Paul was emphatically knocked off his beast by Jesus Christ and blinded on his way to further perpetuate his zeal through escalated policies that would execute followers of *the Way* (Acts 9:2). Theological errors thrown have a boomerang effect. The further thrown, the more deadly they return to strike the one who threw them. If so, many discover their doctrine had no distance. Before conversion, Paul's doctrine did not get him far. Theological error never travels far. He thought he was on his way to accomplish his agenda, but God blocked him. Then, God buffeted him.

When challenged to confrontations with Christ, what happens afterward is a domino effect of death or deliverance, depending upon how we respond to the blinding Light (Jesus Christ). If Paul would not have obeyed Christ's instructions on Damascus Road, in no way would our Lord have allowed him to go any further. Paul would have died on the spot as a murderer. Christ confronts our convictions, and we can no longer ride our beasts into murderous ministries. The average theologian has enough savvy that dares not resist the encounter because his feet cannot withstand the pricks if he kicks against them with theological temper tantrums when things are not going his ministerial way (Acts 26:14).

It is a gracious act of Christ when He knocks us down. Sometimes, that is the only opportunity to get back up and do ministry the right way. I remember my cousin, David Wade (Pastor of Mt. Calvary Missionary Baptist Church of Mesa, Arizona) refer to a sermon by Dr. Gardner Taylor. He shared with me that Dr. Gardner Taylor once stated a tragedy he had seen in his lifetime, especially among young preachers. Dr. Taylor stated that a young preacher can get so caught up in a destructive pathway that they can never make a comeback.

Before conversion, Paul's theology was highly experiential and subjective. He formed a false understanding of God based on his personal prejudices rooted in Pharisaical tradition. A personal experience does not automatically imply one is theologically justified to harm an individual. If a man does not look both ways before crossing the street and gets hit by a truck, he personally experienced getting hit by a truck, but that does not mean he knows much about trucks. What it may reveal is his deficiency in safely crossing the street. In this sense, one's experience can also show how much one *does not* know. There are things experienced I just could not understand. Yet, I was hit and humbled. I did not understand a lot about what hit me, but I learned to look both ways before I ever crossed that street again.

Paul was going to come to terms with who hit him as well as not going down that road of threatening theology and mean ministry ever again. When Jesus struck him on Damascus Road, Paul discovered the fact that when he thought he knew everything he needed to know, he did not know anything at all. A beautiful mind is in the making when we are hit so hard by Heaven that we are humbled to learn all over again. As our knowledge is diminished, our spiritual wisdom broadens (I Corinthians 13:12). When we mount our beasts, we do it cautiously, recognizing the fact that it is a longer way down than up.

Paul was previously in a hurry, going nowhere fast. One major character trait of men of God with beautiful minds is the fact that the longer they travel the road of ministry, the slower they become. The strongest preacher fellowships are the ones who have the slowest men. They move with precaution, humility, wisdom, and an acute Christological and cautious conscience. They are not in a hurry to preach, pioneer, or practice principles that terminate generations of preachers and churches to come. They are more concerned about precedents than popularity, ecclesiastical, or cultural relevance and acceptance. Their theology hinges on the axis of being true to Christian theology as a support system for those who build on that foundation in the future. They are more concerned with leaving a legacy behind than being legends in their own eyes.

Manuel Scott, Sr. was a prime example. Dr. Scott was deliberate and intentional. He gathered his thoughts before he spoke, and he collected his emotions before he acted. Such men consider what the outcome of their principles and procedures produce long after they are dead and gone. When he stood behind convention platforms, he did not stand as if he reached his peak with a look of satisfaction that he made it to the top. He stood behind the pulpit like a man on a mission. He was not preaching to impress preachers. He was preaching to leave an impression upon preachers. What he said was notarized. None of his convictions had the potential to evolve into something he never intended or to be something new. What he said then applies now. His truths were timeless. Dr. Manuel Scott preached his way into major theological institutions because he was a mental minister, thoughtful theologian, and gentle giant. He was also welcomed because his poise and preaching reminded many of our Afro-theocentric heritage. Dr. Scott also provided many White scholars the groundbreaking opportunity to express their sincerest apologies for the sins of their fathers. Because he preached in the Southern Baptist Convention, colleges, and churches, I could walk through the doors of southern seminaries with my head held high. I cherish many of my White brothers because if just one had the integrity to say, "I am sorry", I could at least avoid the sin of feeling entitled to four acres and a mule.

Doors must be opened for the next generation and not closed in their faces. Turf-guarding among the Titans of Truth must be tamed. Slow men are not as quick to draw conclusions about God and what is good. Slow spiritual men are flexible and bend towards godliness over and against greediness. The greed I am referring to is not just about money. There is also ministry greed. The longer godly men endure real ministry, the less greedy they are for anything that would give them an arrogant advantage over another preacher or denomination. Such men spread the jam for preaching generations to come as well as those who are struggling in this present age. They extend Jesus to those who think they already know him because they never will forget the transforming day when God blinded them by *The Light*. They are not in a hurry to get to a place God already ordained, and they do not attempt to persecute the Church with new ideologies that are methods of modern-day Pharisees. Such men also extend Christ because the Lord is the only hope for a pastor to change his mind when he is sinning theologically. These seasoned veterans of the Gospel preached slowly, realizing how much young ministers were watching their every move. They made a *B-line* to the Cross in every sermon. Slow sages gave us time to process what it took to be great. They had a low tolerance for proud or prosperity preachers. Such thoughtful theologians preached in a way that laid an example for those in a hurry to become great to do real ministry one day at a time, one church at a time, and one member at a time. They warned young ministers that it takes time. It takes time to truly know what it means to be great or partner with God in building a great church.

When Jesus knocks us down, it hurts, but it also helps. It will kill you if you do not get up slowly and humbly. If God gives a man a chance to stand after he has been stunned by the Savior, he must get up and get to the business of exercising himself unto godliness and leave all the prideful elements of ministry to those who refuse to respect the fact that the mind is a terrible thing to waste. If a man has been called by God, he will eventually come to his theological senses, cut out nonsense, and keep ministry simple. He will also minister to people who he would have previously theologically murdered through misinterpretations of Scripture and malfunctioning methods of ministry. When a minister has been transformed, he will return to the simplicity of the Gospel and the simplicity of worship. Changed men keep it simple, and they keep it slow.

The wrong theological swords are more lethal than any military weapon, and many have been slashed by their power. God opens our eyes to see how zealous convictions can bring injury to those within reach of our theological strikes. None of us will reach theological perfection in this lifetime (I Corinthians 13:9-12). No one has the right to destroy the ministry of a man. Although many of us may be in the right theological lanes, hermeneutical and homiletical laws demand that we stay within the scriptural speed limit. The most defining numerator is Truth, but the most common denominator is love (I Corinthians 13:13; Ephesians 4:15). When Truth is spoken in love, our theological threats can be transformed into more loving brushes of the Master's hand in ways others are delivered and not damaged by our doctrine and disciplines.

Dr. Scott had more brain power than most of his contemporaries, but he did not cause them to feel as though they had anything less. He did not parade his genius in a way that persecuted those whose thoughts were not as thorough as his. He was not a threat to any preacher who had struggles with his theology or who was cut from a different cloth.

God graciously allows us to struggle in certain areas, but when *pride* becomes the suffix of our successes, we have taken on the disposition of another beast. There is expository pride, ministry pride, mega-church pride, micro-church pride, mission-church pride, family pride, man-pride ministries, and woman-pride ministries. To maintain humility, God had to enlist Paul in a life of transparency. The Apostle Paul clearly stated he was chief of sinners (I Timothy 1:15). If Paul was living today, many might be tempted to label him the chief of Christians.

To slow Paul down, God had to inflict him with pain. God trusts his greatest men with the greatest of pains. He had to stop Paul by giving him a sickness. God had to keep Paul dependent upon Him by giving him a demon as an unwanted deterrent. He had to stop him to save him. When God stops a preacher, He often uses pain to do so. The more giftedness a preacher has, the more God afflicts him with pain. God must hurt us before we can help others. We must learn to live with pain, pray in pain, preach in pain and pastor in pain. Jesus has ruthless ways He hurts a man to humble him for ministry. The text emphatically states the thorn in Paul's flesh was a demon (messenger of Satan) sent by God to beat Paul (II Corinthians 12:7). Think of that awesome truth for a moment. What if people in today's church discovered their pastor had a demon *in* him? The demon was not only with Paul, but it was also in his flesh. A spirit afflicted a body. **Paul had a demonic**

physical health condition designed by God. It was not a malignant spirit that periodically attacked Paul from the underworld. The demon was ever-present within Paul to keep him humble.

I always admired the poise and preaching of Pastor Terry K. Anderson. Like so many great preachers, that type of preaching comes with a great price. I was watching his ministry on television and thought these exact thoughts: "Man, that must be nice!" Then, I heard Pastor Terry K. Anderson (Pastor of the Lily Grove Missionary Baptist Church of Houston, Texas) testify in a sermon. He asked God to give him strength and wisdom to lead his people into their new building venture due to their explosive growth. Pastor Anderson then addressed his congregation and let them know God answered his prayers, but He did so by giving him a brain tumor. According to Pastor Anderson, the brain tumor was his thorn in the flesh to keep him depending on God.

There is a certain level of God-ordained satanic pain that attends a minister when he has received certain revelations. There are challenges that come with being chosen. With revelation comes responsibility. Pride is almost an automatic sin that will come before our fall if God does not put us on the pavement first. Like the Apostle Paul, those who do not have obvious flesh wounds are more susceptible to internal injuries. For that reason, I cannot condemn myself if I have flesh wounds or compliment myself if I do not. In no way was Paul guilty of the flesh wounds of sexual sin, drugs, drinking, stealing, or anything of that nature. As bad as those sins are, his sin-level of pride was far deeper. Paul suffered from sins of supremacy.

The best preachers are their own worst critics. They are hard on themselves because they know what they are capable of if they fail to hold themselves accountable to brutal beatings of self-examination (I Corinthians 9:27). Unless we have a paradoxical sense of failure in what we do, we will not know what it truly means to succeed. Every great preacher has a sense of failure attached to his greatest fortunes. He knows there is always room for improvement. We truly succeed when we realize how much we will never be masters of the ministry or professionals in the pulpit. Just when we think we figured it out, we discover that we know nothing at all.

The saga of the Damascus Road reveals Paul riding on more than one beast. There were two beasts Saul (Paul) was riding that he needed to be knocked off. The first was the literal beast he was riding in the wrong direction to persecute Christians. The second was the beast of pride he developed about his ministry when he should have been ashamed of it. His ministry was huge, but it was hurtful. His ministry was successful, but it was sinful. It was theological, but it was threatening. His ministry was large, but it was lethal. His ministry was a beast of its own. Paul was accomplished, but he was arrogant. Pride is a beast too powerful for a truth-teller to tame.

Previously, Saul was not struggling with murdering tendencies. He was proudly killing Christians with ease. He had no convicting Christian clue to what he was doing. When pride consumes us, we start sinning with ease, and we have no idea of how we are in danger of being leveled by the Lord. We start sinning in a religious way that eradicates the humility that comes with riding on a donkey (Matthew 21:2). Ministry should always be done with struggling steps. When ministry gets easy, that is a serious indicator that something has gone pridefully wrong. Pride keeps a preacher popular only among his peers. If Saul would have remained a Pharisee, he would have meant something only to other Pharisees. Now that Saul became an apostle, his ministry base continues to widen to this day. When we are transformed, we touch the lives of those who matter most. Sinners and common folk are never impressed by our sermons or the size and structure of our sanctuaries. They do not care if we have an attention-getting introduction, three points, parse our verbs or have a motivating conclusion. All that matters to them is that we have spent time with Jesus (Acts 4:13).

We do not have to learn the hard way. Humility insulates us from painful knockdowns and allows us to land more gracefully on our feet (I Peter 5:6). Such was the case with Paul *after* his Damascus Road experience. God's wisdom in converting this Pharisee into a true theologian was not in giving Paul an interpretation of a scripture he could understand but in giving him a fall he could feel. On Damascus Road, it was the burning of God's blinding Light within Saul's eyes, the impact of his fall from his beast, the open wounds on his pre-mature Gospel feet from kicking against the pricks, and the headaches from Heaven that humbled him. Out of all the things he knew, he could not comprehend the deity of Christ. On Damascus Road, Paul crashed. He ran straight into Christ in a head-on collision. There is a point in a pastor's life before, during or after his calling when Jesus says, "Enough is enough!" When we persecute Christ's purposes, He strikes back. If Christ hits us with a blow that socks us to our senses, we consider ourselves blessed. Thank God, He did not kill us (Numbers 22:21-41). To transform us from stubborn to servant-mindedness, Jesus deals us blessed blows to remind us of who He is and who we are not.

When humility is practiced, we become pro-active in the gelling of our theology. Although Dr. Manuel Scott was a great preacher and teacher, he was an even greater student. He put himself in a pupil's posture. He was not learning just to get another degree. He was learning to improve his pedigree. He was an avid reader, and he listened enthusiastically, respectfully, and attentively when another preached regardless of his race, status, or age. Humility tenderizes the pastor's mind to be more of an absorbing agent of God's Truth that only beautifies with time.

When we have a humble approach to learn who God is, less radical transformations are necessary, and God allows us to mount our beasts with grace to platforms that promote Christian virtue rather than be radically removed from them. Humility is fundamental to a meaningful mental ministry. When God clothes a transformed pastor, He clothes him with the garments of His grace. Yet, he wears his religious garments loosely. Religious grandeur is something he is willing to take off at any given moment and lay at the Master's feet instead of spending his entire life guarding the garments of his own glory.

Those of us who had some hard falls from beastly ministries can testify that we know what we know because we have been struck by Divine Lightning. Pastors who had encounters with a God who afflicted their anatomies should be appreciated. Just as Paul was mindful of his past prejudices, sacred secrets have been revealed to preachers who previously kicked against the pricks. Although God had to hurt us, He only hurt us to heal us from the sins of misguided enthusiasm. Because we are familiar with the humbling process of hitting the pavement and starting all over again, we are confident that it is by God's grace that we are who we are (I Corinthians 15:10).

Pastors who challenge pride are the modern-day *Paul's* who simply warn those with misguided zeal that it is a long way down when you get too high on your horse. Now, we spend our years doing our best to keep others from doing ministry in a way that will get them maimed by the Master. Not only have we learned the hard way, but we also learned the long way. Descending from pride is a long way down. We are simply saying, "You don't need a high horse to get to the place God wants you to go." You can do ministry from a mule if Jesus says so (Matthew 21:2-3). The Master is still in need of mule ministries.

Many discouraged pastors think their ministries are insignificant because they do not have Trojan ministries. Look at Saul before his conversion riding pompously on his beast, wearing garments layered with religious regalia. One can say he had a new clerical robe for every occasion. Yet, his Christology was confusing, and his attitude was arrogant. He had earned theological degrees, but he had not experienced God. He had a stallion ministry, but he was stampeding the Church with it. His ministry was messy and murderous. He was a prejudiced theologian. I am a living witness that a prejudiced theologian is a scary sight. He was riding his beast on the borders of blasphemy. Everything Jesus was for, Paul was against, and he did not even know it.

One of the greatest virtues of a beautiful mind is peace with God. It is possible to have all the amenities in ministry and have no peace. When a pastor has made peace with God and has the peace of God, he can stand amid any congregation and declare God's Truth in a way that confirms his calling. When he is in the center of God's will, the humblest settings have a way of expanding in his soul. If his ministry grows to magnitudes, he appreciates the little things because the greatest achievement is what happened to him attitudinally.

When God strikes any who insist on persecuting followers of *The Way*, He often strikes them with delusional diseases. Many reach the brink of insanity, paranoia, amnesia, schizophrenia, or they become bipolar. Preachers who have been humbled by God can never have that said of them. Instead, they have peace of mind. Pride has no room in ministry, and Jesus will ensure that He shines brightly and exposes every arrogance. Proud Saul came to recognize strength in weakness. If we boast, we boast not in our accomplishments but in our infirmities that the power of Christ may rest upon us. We do not brag about our sicknesses or sins, but we boast in a way that gives glory to a God whose grace sustains us in the center of our struggles. To those of us who are infirmed, our weaknesses are what cause us to know we are unworthy of the call, powerless in preaching, and too wicked to worship unless God's grace gives us sufficiency. Then, we begin to act like, preach like, and lead like men who recognize that without Christ, we are nothing. Yet, God decided to save and use us anyhow. If God's saving grace does not change minds for the better, nothing else will.

Chapter 3
THE PASTOR AND HIS EARS

Listening to the Call
(An Excerpt from the Life of Jeremiah:
A preacher who resented his ministry)

Tribute: To Dr. Gary Galeotti (former Old Testament Professor of the Criswell College of Dallas, TX and Southeastern Baptist Theological Seminary of Wake Forest, NC)

Dr. Gary Galeotti was known for bringing to life the most intricate details of the Old Testament and simplifying them in the most profound ways. I never heard a man teach from the Old Testament the way that Dr. Galeotti taught. He taught from a prophetic realm. As we listened to his lectures, it was difficult to tell if he was bringing us into the history of the prophets or if he was bringing the history of the prophets to us. Either way was fine because he connected us to the God of the Old Testament. In that sense, the old became new. Those who knew Dr. Galeotti were familiar with his emphasis on maintaining "the prophetic voice". Other than "God takes sin seriously", Dr. Galeotti's signature sentence was in three profound words that thundered through his lectures when it comes to the call of God as he spoke these words with authority: "God comes down!"

The Pastor and His Anatomy

The rich history of preachers from which I originate within the culture of the African American preaching context made it crystal clear regarding the need to be *called* into the ministry. It was a given that he must first come to a saving knowledge of our Lord and Savior, Jesus Christ. The pastor, church, family, and friends constituted a village that groomed young Black preachers to learn how to preach. The calling was not imposed upon any young man. Our village just watched, prayed, and waited when they saw signs of a boy who God was calling into preaching manhood. One day, young men would avoid the call until they could hold out no longer and finally say, "God has called me to preach."

Three boys confessed that they could not hold out any longer. My cousins, James C. Wade III, David L. Wade, and I announced our calling to preach in consecutive weeks at Bethlehem Baptist Church of Dallas, Texas on 4401 Baldwin Street. Instead of giving theme speeches at my church that were sermons in disguise at the age of ten years old, I officially announced my calling to preach at the age of seventeen. The village just nodded because they knew it had been seven years in the making. Others shouted for joy as another of the tribe of preachers in the African American context had been born. Yet, seasoned Saints whose still waters ran deep stilled their souls before God in sober reverence because they knew the call of God meant we were God's property from that time forth. They committed us to prayer by asking God to keep us through dangers seen and unseen. We were to be groomed by our father in the ministry, Derek L. Winkley.

During an E. K. Bailey Expository Preaching Conference, S. J. Gilbert heralded the Gospel from the genius of the Afro-centric context by stating why the God-called preacher can never quit, even if he wanted to. In the lament of Jeremiah's concluding tenure, he experienced what would have been most pastors' nightmare, i.e., the dissolving of their congregation. Jeremiah was the last man standing in the womb of a burned city, chastised assembly, destroyed temple, and shattered pulpit as he declared God's new mercies and great faithfulness (Lamentations 3:22-23).

God's command to Jeremiah was going to last for what appeared to be a lifetime. The six-word exhortation to *"Be not afraid of their faces"* possesses an expose' of the nature of the call to preach (Jeremiah 1:8). When *faced* with a strange apathy towards the inevitable, it can be deafening to a preacher's sense of hearing what God called him to do. God's people were to experience the irrevocable consequences of disobedience through the invasion of the Chaldeans (Jeremiah 37:8). Truth confronts us with the inevitable. Paradoxically, as Jeremiah packaged Truth in a flawless fashion, it only hardened God's people toward what was to come. Jeremiah was called to collapse his congregation. He was called to root out, pull down, and destroy before there was to be planting and building (Jeremiah 1:10). This was the process necessary for God to cultivate His own garden.

The digression of a congregation can be progressive. Digression involves a temporary departure from the subject at hand. Judah was to experience the weeding process of temporary departure from the subject. God was the subject. Exile was their temporary departure because of disobedience. Yet, a remnant would eventually get back to the subject, i.e., God. Progress is not always forward movement, especially if we are pastoring through a period of purging. At the core of progress is a hearing that can only be developed through the discipline of disaster. God will go through weaning means to bring a pastor and people to the point of return, even if it means the massacre of our ministries and memberships. Finances and attendance have been said to be the distinguishing marks of a flourishing church. However, just because a congregation does not increase in membership or money, that is not always the sign of a stagnant congregation or failing pastor. When God's hand is on a chastised minister and ministry, there is no such thing as failure. Instead, the minister and ministry are under the forging faithfulness of God that molds them for God's new mercies. If we allow the culture of western civilization to frame our approach to pastoral leadership, we will pastor our churches with deafening definitions. Yet, when we pastor according to a true biblical paradigm, we may discover we are doing poorly when we think we are doing well, and when we think that we are doing poorly, we are doing quite well.

The diseases of *less* and *more* are cancers to our calling. Although some churches are blessed to thrive, God called us to build inevitable ministries. If ministry progress were measured by the responses of people, very few pastors would be considered successful shepherds. If we allow management to replace ministry, what do we do when we are assigned to ministries God called us to uproot? We are not called into the pastoral vocation to demand growth. We are called to have the expectancy that God will be faithful when all else fails. If God furnishes our churches with His great faithfulness, the results will be godly, even if we stand amid an ashy assignment.

We as pastors are faced with a dangerous brand of ministry in our times that refuses to accept the inevitable. Sin creates inevitable consequences beyond human control. Careful attention must be given to what is purchased when it comes to ministry. If we develop a marketing mentality that only has a vision for increase and are deaf to what God has told us to lose, we may buy into a style of ministry we can't return, and we may build a ministry that can easily become spiritually bankrupt. When it comes to ministry, some things we acquire do not come with a receipt. We are in it for the long haul, even if it means dedication amid disintegration.

Jeremiah could have easily thought he failed as a leader when his congregation dissolved into Babylonian captivity. Later, Jeremiah discovered God was mercifully reducing the congregation to ashes to bring about a revived remnant. Because of sin, there is no way to avoid structuring a ministry that makes us chastisement-proof (Hebrews 12:5). We must choose between our congregations and consequences. We preach faithfully until God's people either run in or out of our churches. Either direction they run is fine if we are disciplined under divine directives and an inevitable inspiration. Good preaching will either draw people or drive them.

With today's social media and web-based resources, we can be encouraged to know that we don't have to put make-up on our churches to impress anyone or choke when chastised as we bear the yoke of God's restricting reigns. We do not have to use a spiritual form of *Photoshop* to portray accentuated angles of our arenas. It is okay to post a picture of God's chastising hand because His great faithfulness will eventually lift that same hand off our lives. The best camera angle of a church is one that can capture our calling from convicting and corrective lenses. Then, we all stand a chance of touching somebody's life through a purging portrait of God's plan, even if it is a snapshot of a ministry going up in smoke. We do not have to apologize for what we do not have, especially if God faithfully removed some things and people from us. If we lose our sense of hearing, we can be embarrassed by what we do not have and too proud of what we do have.

Regardless of the size, structure, success, or strength of our churches, all churches are missing members, especially during the Coronavirus crisis of 2020. It is only a sign of our times. Scripture consistently foretells a decline of the desire for Christ from generation to generation. When there is revival, we are reminded that it is a revival of a remnant at stake. We are called to be compositions of a Christian congregation and not a comfortable crowd.

A farmer who plants seeds is no better than one who uproots weeds. A farmer who reaps from the field he has sown is no better than one who must wait a while longer until harvest time. A farmer is a farmer. Likewise, a pastor is a pastor. According to the Bible, pastors do not come in ranks. We are no better, worse, more, and we are no less than the next pastor regardless of what we gained or lost. Pastors are no more failures in ministries to which they are faithful than God is to the world. This world is whirling away from God, but that is not a reflection of failure in God. It is not a sign of failure on the pastor's end if he remains under God's devastating directives. Jeremiah had thousands of members, but each had to suffer God's chastising hand, including himself. Jeremiah's chastised congregation was Judah. We know Judah to be the line from which Jesus would descend. Thus, a chastised ministry does not diminish its value. It only heightens it.

The pastor who hears from God avoids pseudo tones of success that ring loudly in the ears of many in this success-driven culture. Success is a loud sound, but faithfulness is confirmed through the sound of smoking debris. Jeremiah had to be still enough to see the morning dew of God's mercies that extinguished the remaining flickering flames of Babylonian torches. God called us to be faithful, even if our ministries do not appear to be fruitful (Matthew 25:21; I Corinthians 4:2; Ephesians 6:21; II Timothy 2:2).

As Dr. Gary Galeotti would lecture, he would accuse Jeremiah of "whining". Although that may appear to be a harsh and arrogant criticism, the call of God is so faithful that if we don't hear echoes of mercy amid our despair, everything we are aching about is nothing but the whims of an infant preacher. Preaching is a high privilege and high calling, and that settles it. When we comb the tangibles within the hairs of God's servants in the Bible, we will discover they had little of what we consider to be "much". Our road is from Earth to Glory and not from Glory to Earth. The road to Glory cannot be turned upside down. Today's deaf brand of discipleship has greatly erred by materializing the Kingdom of

God and spiritualizing material things. The Kingdom of God is not food and drink but righteousness, peace, and joy in the Holy Ghost (Romans 14:17).

The standards of western civilization's success limit pastoral ministry while the biblical mandate to appreciate God's faithfulness only broadens it. The farmer knows how possible it is to faithfully till soil, plant seeds, and yield no harvest. Yet, the same humble farmer can possess a strange satisfaction in sowing. The only solution to dedicated planting and an unyielding harvest is realizing when the harvest is at the mercy of nature's fury. The pastor is mandated by God to resist the temptation to grow resemblances of a fruitful harvest that bears fruit that is not organic. Whatever seeds we plant, that very well may be the type of church we grow. It is important to not plant churches in a way they come back to haunt us or the next pastor. If we depend upon numbers, we are nothing more than a *big church*. If we depend upon branding, we are nothing more than a *relevant church*. If we depend upon marketing, we are nothing more than a *business church*. If we depend upon money, we are nothing more than a *wealthy church*. If we think small, we are nothing more than a *small church*. If we look to politics, we are nothing more than a *Right- or Left-Wing church*. If we depend upon a building, we are nothing more than a *church building*. If we depend upon Christ, we are no less than a *Christian church*.

I interviewed pastors with inevitable ministries of all shapes and sizes, and each had one common denominator when I asked about the key to their merciful ministries. I am inspired by their rural responses. Each of them stated they could not explain it. According to their testimonies, *it was just something the Lord made*. Make no mistake about the price successful shepherds pay. I am referring to success on spiritual terms. Many of these great men of God were taken down before God lifted them up. They had to sink before they could swim. As they would shout faithfully in their sermons, "The Lord has delivered me from the muck and miry clay", they meant it:

> *"Then took they Jeremiah and cast him into the dungeon of Malchiah the son of Hammelech, that was in the court of the prison: and they let down Jeremiah with cords. And in the dungeon, there was no water, but mire: so, Jeremiah sunk in the mire (*mud*)."*

(Jeremiah 38:6; KJV)

Some men pastor from a pit, and they are ministers in the mire. Thank God for men who have miraculous ministries, but we also praise God for most men who have muddy ministries. Whenever a preacher ministers in a way that satisfies the selfish demands of people, he will always land on dry ground. However, when a pastor stands faithfully, void of the fear of losing popularity, he will find himself in sinking sands.

Jeremiah had no problem standing tall against the stubborn stoutness of his congregation. Jeremiah's problem was with God. The backlash experienced was irrelevant if God would have confirmed Jeremiah's ministry on terms he could understand. However, God did not compromise to temper Jeremiah's tantrum. Jeremiah was thrown into a pit for preaching on God's terms and not his whims or the whims of those he served.

If a God-called preacher hears what God calls him to preach, he can never select his sermons. If he preaches from a listening unction, he will eventually be dumped into defining dungeons with vicious but victorious vocabularies. He must be careful how he serves God when he plummets into a pit. If we curse our prisons, we must be careful of the disciplines we develop when we become free. If we curse calamities that accompany our calling, we may be tempted to preach in a way that protects us from the liberty of being on lockdown. Pulpit prisons must rehabilitate us regardless of whether we are guilty or not. If not, we will spend our freedom planting and harvesting ministries that sanction a selfish form of freedom defined by material success instead of servanthood.

Like Jeremiah, many pastors learn to stay faithful when they answer a summons of subtraction. Make no mistake about it, countless ministries have flourished spiritually and numerically due to the faithful sowing and suffering of their pastor or pastors who preceded them. Yet, we have the critical call to neither acquire nor build ministries that restrict us from accepting the call to be downsized by God. When we build and acquire more, we are called to ensure we are not doing so in a way that leaves an inheritance the next generation can no longer occupy or overcome.

There is no need for a pastor to apologize for a devastating work God has done in his ministry. When sin is in the picture, God gives devastating directives, and He takes us through purging and painful procedures. When we understand the fortune in fire, there is no need to sweep our ashes under the rug. Instead, we can put those same ashes in a bottle and set them on a shelf of merciful memories. Jeremiah's confusion, complaining, crisis, and calamity did not alter God's mercy and faithfulness to use him to maximum capacity. Jeremiah was like many of us pastors at one time or another. He resented his assignment. Breakthrough hearing came when Jeremiah discovered he was powerless to alter the callous decisions of God's people or turn down the volume of his call to calamity. As a matter of fact, Jeremiah's preaching only amplified the song of the purging of a people whose chastisement was unstoppable. The purging of God's people reminded Jeremiah of His own sins also (Lamentations 3:27).

Healed hearing came when Jeremiah matured from a young deaf prophet to a seasoned and sensitive sage. His confusion was distilled through objective observation as well as deductive reasoning (Lamentations 3:23). When he stopped complaining about his calling and finally listened to the rebuking ramifications of God's great faithfulness and new mercies, he began to observe opportunities arising from ashes of a scorched sanctuary. Jeremiah concluded the ashes were on assignment. They were to remind him of God's hatred toward sin and His love for the sinner. As he saw ashes of a decayed temple, he realized that although the temple was consumed as they were carried into Babylon, they could still sing in a strange land.

It does a world of good for a pastor to discover beauty for ashes and strength for tears. We have many pastors who are products of the mercies of God that transcend the stench of burned ministries, deferred hopes, and the foul flames of foes who God uses to chastise us and our churches. It was not until Jeremiah smelled smoke that he discovered how his ministry was flawless although he was faithless. Although Jeremiah was faithless, he was faithful. God wants the pastor to have faith *and* be faithful. A poor sense of hearing can cause some of us to lean more towards one of the two. Sometimes, we can be faithful but never believe anything good will come out of our gloom. Others of us can even have faith that keeps us optimistic, but it is also a type of faith that moves us away from the redemptive reality of the reprimanding and restoring reasons for our repercussions.

Previously, Jeremiah was committed, but he was not convinced. Ministry is hard to measure. Thus, the pastor must never become result oriented. Tangible results rarely determine an accurate assessment of our accomplishments. ***Faithfulness is flawless regardless of the felt or perceived outcome.*** When a faithful pastor who once had it all is reduced to nothing, that does not mean a thing in the eyes of God. That is not the end of his world, and it is not the consuming of his calling, regardless of what happens to his congregation. Regarding Jeremiah, if there was a flaw, the flaw was not within his work but within his wisdom to worship God during it all. Finally, the rubble and ravished people became pressurizing agents to squeeze Jeremiah into a stillness to hear the call of God in the past and His promises in the future (Jeremiah 29:11). As Jeremiah stood amid ruins, he no longer had amplifiers of his own ambitions to deafen him to the meaningful message of a massacred ministry.

The loud sounds of our amenities can deafen us to the tune of God's new mercies and great faithfulness. When we hear the sizzling sound of burned walls and howling wolves of the inevitable demanding our surrender, we can often hear the faithfulness of God louder than ever. As Jeremiah heard the crackling debris from a burned temple, shrieking echoes of the captive cries of God's people as they were carried into Babylonian captivity, and the silence of the lambs (Judah) who had been ravaged by the wolves of the Chaldean army, "Great is Thy Faithfulness" became the title of Jeremiah's new sermon and song. With the consumption of our creature comforts, we are more prone to hear the voice of God because we have no one to comfort us but God. When everything was silent, all that remained was the call of God in its merciful melodies. The music of God's mercies was playing the whole time, but Jeremiah could not hear them because what he heard from his inner ear of complaint caused him to march to the beat of a deafening drum.

Among our calamities, our calling cannot be consumed, but our preaching must be purged if it is to be precise. Jeremiah must listen because he is in a season of silence, point of frustration, confusion, and desperation. He has no choice but to sit still and bear the yoke of God's chastising hand upon his juvenile understanding of the call of God (Lamentations 3:27-28). His prophetic ears were eventually unstopped because his success-driven sense of sound had been deafened by the volume of divine destruction. Then, Jeremiah could hear more clearly from Heaven as his unrealistic expectations of ministry had been unplugged by the providential hand of God.

God's faithfulness to Jeremiah teaches us to remember it is not *what* we have, but it is *who* we have that defines our destiny and confirms our calling. No matter what we have or do not have, the pastor can never afford to be *Godless*. If his ministry is all God, it is all good. God assures the preacher that his assignment is deeper than resigning under the yoke of his own resentments or the rebellion of those he leads. A pastor does not have to quit for fear of not going out on top. There are no corporate ladders to climb in ministry. There are only ladders that call us to descend into deepening and defining dungeons.

Now that he has no rebellious nation to preach to, Jeremiah is left alone with God and the ashes. Jeremiah's work is done. He preached his whole congregation out. Whenever we are left with God and ashes, our capacity to appreciate not being consumed reaches a crescendo. We are called to refuse to only count how much fruit has grown in God's garden. When we hear the call of God in its subtracting sounds, we learn to also count how many weeds God's faithfulness has uprooted. Thus, we can count the people God extracted instead of the number of people we attracted. It is wise to count how many have gone instead of how many have come. If only the people who left us were returning members to our churches, every pastor in this world would have a mega-church. In no way is this a demonization of the mega-church. It is a sarcastic soberness of the numbers of fickle people who promised to be faithful but fainted. They fled due to fear of God's forging fire rather than remain faithful to God's faithfulness.

That also shows us how important it is to not want to win members who God no longer wants. Everyone we lose is not a loss. When we count how many have gone, we are also counting the number of headaches God spared us from and how many disappointments we spared God from. People who fail to cherish chastisement have weak staying power. Their strength is small because they faint in the days of adversity (Proverbs 24:10). As we deepen in our definitions of our duty, we learn to live on both ends of the spectrum. We learn to see them come, and we learn to see them go.

In the end, Jeremiah listens the way a preacher should. Interestingly, Jeremiah does not say that it is of the Lord's mercies that *he* was not consumed Instead, he stated that it was of the Lord's mercies that *we* are not consumed (Lamentations 3:22). A pastor who detaches himself from the sins of the congregation is no longer useful to God or the people. He was able to see the connection between the condition of his congregation, himself, and the compassions of our Creator. A pastor who understands his call does not disengage himself from his congregation and lose sight of his own sins. In addition, he does not fall into the sin of self-preservation. Although Jeremiah was faithful to the call, he could have easily been consumed for the sin of craving a convenient calling. ***A bitter pastor who stays is no better than a rebellious member who leaves*** (Philippians 2:14). If we do not acutely hear what God called us to be and do, our pastoral presence is no better than their aggressive absence. Bitterness is one of our most subtle and silent killers. God usually killed His people and prophets if they complained. God always kept his prophets on a short leash when it came to murmur or complaint. Thank God, Jeremiah didn't have the sinful luxury to submit his resume' to another church when the chips were down. Although Jeremiah cursed his calling, he was not a hireling who would flee when the Chaldean wolves were coming. Yet, they persecuted Jeremiah for having the gall to call himself a *real preacher* when he at least had the fortitude to stick it out with them, even when they failed to be faithful.

Even if Jeremiah went through a purging pastoral process, he was still made of the kind of material God could mold. Before Jeremiah could hear God's call clearly, his ministry was defined, but his manhood was defective. While Jeremiah was conscious of the consumption of his comforts, God was making him into a man of non-combustible material (Jeremiah 20:9). For these reasons and more, the man of God must align with what God left him in ministry and not the members who left. His anatomy must align with his assignment and not with those who attend. His congregation did not call him, but God did.

Pastors under divine obligation are more concerned with ratios and proportions than stats. Any sportsman knows a player's success stats mean nothing if his team is losing. During the NBA playoff season, Charles Barkley gave words of rebuke regarding an NBA player who was looking at his stat sheets while his team was losing. No matter how skilled, we can never afford to look at our stat sheets if those who we minister to are losing in life. At the end of the day, all our churches are losing a winning battle. Our awards, compensations, numbers, reputations, engagements, degrees, and full calendars can all be burned and come out as wood, hay, or stubble if we are irrelevant to the ministry of rebuke that precedes restoration (I Corinthians 3:11-14). When we are confined to the dusty plains of the Earth, we cannot celebrate yet because we have not won the championship. Our most important trophies will not be issued until Jesus comes (I Peter 5:2-4). The pastor's crown will be the Crown of Glory received if he faithfully feeds the people of God the word of God and faithfully leads them.

Yet, we must be concerned with ratios. The need for correction from the Lord is due to the corruption that most of our churches contain at the core. Pastors with churches large and small must deal with the 20/80 spiritual corruption-ratio. Most pastors can only depend upon twenty percent of their members to be committed to the true ministry of the Church and Jesus Christ while eighty percent are casual attenders and nominal by nature. Pastors with larger churches have the same ratio of corruption as those of smaller ones, but they are in larger portions.

My father was faithful when it came to how he disciplined me. Back in the day, he would often spank me. When he did, I would squirm, and I even tried to run, but I only pulled that stunt one time. When I tried to run, he said, "Don't you ever run from me!" Then, he spanked me even harder. Running seemed to anger him more than what I did that brought about the spanking. When God gives us blessed beatings, we cannot afford to run from those types of callings or churches. Members sometimes flee when they see the church or pastor taking a beating from God. There are always blessings in God's buffetings. God never allows us to run from Him. No matter what we do to escape to greener pastures, God will meet us at the end of our running road, and we must learn to lead on God's level all over again. The first time was free, but the second will cost us.

The life of Jeremiah teaches us that preaching may come with purging paradoxes the preacher can never flee from. Calamity comes with our calling. Lies come with our loyalty. Prisons accompany powerful preaching. Conspiracies come with commitment. Obstacles accompany obedience. Scandals accompany successes and sins. Adversity attends our assignment. The list of paradoxes continues, and we can never run from them. However, there is not much more powerful to a pastor than learning the art of paradoxical praise amid purging. When we are deafly despising our divine duties, we resign to attitudes God never sanctioned. Then, we truly come to know the definition of defeat. Paradoxically, Jeremiah complained when in Jerusalem, but praised God in Babylon. It was not until all was lost that he began to appreciate God's mercies that were there all the time.

Dr. Gary Galeotti was a praising paradox. I never heard him complain. He was not only a wonder to listen to, but he was also a wonder to watch. There was no doubt his calling consumed him. As a matter of fact, Dr. Galeotti stayed faithful amid sickness. He accepted the call on whatever level God called him. He could not help himself. God's word was like fire shut up in his bones. The blessed blaze within often burns hottest when the pastor is at his most scorching seasons. Quitting will only imprison us in a dungeon more deafening than the calling that corrects us. If we quit too soon, we will be behind bars of uselessness with a Holy Fire that yearns to preach (Jeremiah 23:29; I Corinthians 9:16). Believe me, I wanted to quit. I had every selfish, suffering, sinful, and satanic reason to quit. I just did not have a spiritual one.

Without a crystallized consciousness of our calling and a worshipful welcoming of God's weaning works, our sensitivities can evolve into stress. A ministry surrounded by conditions that are not in alignment with God's ultimate good uniquely irritates a preacher who has a good set of ears and a pastor's heart (Jeremiah 3:15). We undergo an almost untreatable type of cardiac arrest when our pastoral anatomies are out of alignment with our assignment. Our heart problems are God's problems. We can confuse godly burdens with codependent compulsions to claim them as our own when they are inherently God's. Jeremiah had to learn how to be more impacted by God's will than his whims.

As Jeremiah noticed the divine details of deliverance and the fine print of God's faithfulness during God's contract with a collapsing congregation, he began to learn that *a captive calling is better than no calling at all*. God calls us to appreciate what we have and not just what we hope for. I learned after thirty-four years of ministry to lower my expectations and raise my reality. God wants us to be grateful for our calling on an *as-is* basis. A ministry in Babylonian chains is a sign of a greater hope. If God's mercies leave us standing when the smoke clears, a divine rebuilding process begins in our character and congregations immersed in the mercies of God in a fashion that makes us fire-proof. No pastor should be discouraged when God's hand is upon His life and ministry, even if it is a chastising hand. The chastising hand of God is better than no hand at all.

Prayer for mercy is extended to many who have everything except God's chastising hand. A pastor never wants to sell his soul to Satan for a successful sanctuary and smooth style of servanthood. No matter where we go, there will be trouble. Everything that glitters is not gold. The grass always *looks* greener on the other side, but that is about it. Every God-called preacher who has a good sense of hearing can be thankful and never fall into the sin of complaining or comparisons when God removed the consumables from his life.

Jeremiah's complaint about his conditions climaxed to the ultimate crossroad of pastoral ministry by regretting his life. We can never minimize the number of occurrences in the Bible when God's men began to lose hope in living. We may have subtle ways of looking over the panorama of our preaching and wonder if it was even worth it all. A man must have a sense of accomplishment in life. If we feel as though we have not accomplished much, to some of us, we believe life is no longer worth living. If we fail to see the benefit of preaching for our lives, our confusion has reached fullest maturity. It is at this point when we are in our deepest distresses. If any of us adopt suicidal stances or invisible initiatives, we may not always want to end our lives, but we may have hidden desires to disappear from our present scene and start a whole new life.

Like Jeremiah, a pastor can feel as though he has been cursed with calamity (Jeremiah 20:14). Please note, Jeremiah's cursing the day he was born was *after* he acknowledged the fire of God's word that burned within (Jeremiah 20:9). One would think the order would have been reversed. Preaching fire plus cursing life equals a personal desire to quit while maintaining an indistinguishable fire to preach. Preaching has little to do with feelings, but it has everything to do with God's faithful fire. God's word is like fire shut up in a preacher's bones. Our most powerful sermons are often the ones we preached when we did not feel like preaching, but we still had the fire to preach anyhow. Yet, when we deliver God's message through seasons of struggle, it often proves our dedication, even during our despair. Since creation, God spends most of human history grieving over the stubbornness of His people, but He did not grieve over the stubbornness of His prophets. He simply removed and replaced them. Yet, we can never escape the pulsating pleasure of God's heart in redeeming sinful mankind. Redemption is hard work. As a matter of fact, it is God's work. Dr. Galeotti had a phrase I never heard before. Although it was simple, it was quite profound. He would often say to us young ministers in the making, "We can't appreciate God's holiness until we recognize our sinfulness."

Thus, ministry is deeper than a shallow quest for the pursuit of happiness. Ministry is a pursuit of holiness. Jeremiah was not confused about his calling until he was personally purged and persecuted. God's mercies override sin, but they never ignore our sin. His mercies are the calm assurance that anguish derived from the carelessness of His creation will not cancel His compassions. God's faithfulness can be easily traced when we take our eyes off ashes of crushed buildings, Believers, and beliefs, and focus on the hands that crushed them. Sometimes, God must crush us to cure us. It was Jeremiah's recollection of the darkest days of his destiny that inspired nocturnal praise. When we recollect our dark days, we also see that God's grace helped us make it through the night. How we may wish we could put everything we experience in a bottle. If so, we would be able to appreciate the ashes that we experience today and realize how the ashes are not always remains of what was, but they can also indicate the future and hope of what is to come.

Recollecting God's faithfulness involves a process of enduring the sting of God's sanctifying stroke upon our lives. Because God loves us, He chastises all of us; the best of us and the worst of us, the least of us and the greatest. Thank God for the men whose victories are not beyond the reach of those who struggle for better days. They are within the sinner's reach because they are pastors who do not portray a lifestyle or ministry absent of the afflicting hand of God upon their lives. Whenever God afflicts us, it is good because it helps us to not go astray. Any person who is committed to taking responsibility for his or her own sins will love leaders like these and not leave them. There is also a faithful fragrance that accompanies a pastor whose ministry smells like smoke. He passed through God's refining fire. He may smell like smoke, but he looks like pure gold. His ministry transparently exudes the carats of God's compassion. Then, sinners can appreciate the fact that they have a pastor who can teach them to live their lives like it is golden. Those who lost hope and feel their lives are up in smoke have these types of pastors to faithfully remind them that God's faithfulness will also pass them through the fire. When people see pastors who have been purged, they should not see men who secured success without being scorched. They must see men who bear blessed burns that made them better men and ministers.

The drama of Jeremiah's ministry has little to do with a captive congregation and destroyed city. Everything had to do with the new mercies and great faithfulness of God although it has been said by some scholars that only 128 out of 4,060 Jews (not including women and children) returned from Babylonian captivity (Jeremiah 52:28-30). God can do more with a small core of submissive members than He can with a crowd of members dedicated to denial. Many Jews did not want to leave Babylon because they became accustomed to the good life of living in a strange land. This is the condition of many today. They love this land more than they love the Holy Land. Only a few good Christians desire their home in Heaven.

Despite his struggles, Jeremiah stood among Judah and proclaimed a message of chastisement none wanted to hear. As he was preaching, not even he could hear God's mercies amid maladies. He paid an awful price for preaching as even family members and preaching contemporaries were part of the conspiracy to destroy his ministry. These are a few of the *unexpected enemies* mentioned in the second chapter that can suck the desire to live out of a God-called preacher.

One dark night, every sermon he preached surfaced. The hellish hoofbeats of Chaldean horses were heard as they approached the city like threatening thoroughbreds. Lives were slain as they resisted the inevitable. The Jews were a remarkably interesting people. They were an enormously proud people. Regardless of their sins, they detested the thought of surrender to slavery. They were not people who could be taken captive willingly. They often put up a fight, even as we see this in the Jewish Revolt between AD 66-73. Yet, when God comes for us as His people, He breaks our backs, and we have no option but to bow. As the temple went up in smoke, Jeremiah thought his ministry also went up in smoke. His belief was temporarily bound to a building. Jeremiah lost his tangibles, but God was tailoring him to temper his trust in God. Pastor Jeremiah lost the temple, but he gained God's blessings through buffetings. Smoke that came through Babylonian torches of God's chastising love was a burnt offering unto the Lord that would become a sweet aroma of His mercies and great faithfulness. Why should that matter when Judah desecrated the temple? The temple deserved to be burned down, but so does ours (I Corinthians 6:19). All our church buildings deserve to be burned down because none of us deserve to be there. Our best righteousness is as filthy rags to the Lord. Unless God is honored, He can burn down everything sacrilegiously built in His name.

Among the rubbish stood a man who came to hear the meaning of it all. *Jeremiah came to terms with the amazing graces of God that saves wretches like us.* The salvation of souls involves us never forgetting a forging fact: We are in the *soul business* and not the success business. We are never to sell our souls in the process. We are called to minister to souls. We are *soul men* (Hebrews 13:17). Every detail of Jeremiah's ministry was a salvific act although God allowed His prophet and His people to be sacked by Satan. Jeremiah did not realize God's redemptive reasons until all was lost. A strange peace comes to a preacher when God's mercies and great faithfulness has made him right when he felt so wrong.

No matter how dark the night, we serve a God who shines the light of His mercies all around us by day and by night. God is a keeper, even if He must use the Devil to detain us. God accomplishes His purposes by wrenching our ministries out of our hands and placing His mercy on our minds. God keeps us when we cannot keep ourselves. He keeps us when others throw us away. He may confine us to keep us but thank God that He did not consume us. He knows our frames are dust. There is no need for God to reduce us to rubbish if we settle our sins of indifference by staying on speaking terms with God.

Chapter 4
THE PASTOR AND HIS EYES

The Vision and the Valley
(An Excerpt from the Life of Ezekiel:
A preacher who had a dead congregation)

Tribute: To Dr. Gardner C. Taylor (Pastor of the Concord Baptist Church of Christ in Brooklyn, NY from 1948-1990)
Sunrise: June 18, 1918; Sunset: April 5, 2015

A perk of being the Assistant to Melvin Von Wade, Sr. was meeting some of the greatest Black preachers of our era. While I served under Pastor Wade, Gardner C. Taylor was the guest preacher. I inherited the privilege of observing a dynamic that contributed to Dr. Taylor's prophetic voice. The key to true biblical prophets was not just about what they said, but it was also concerning what they saw. Dr. Taylor could "say it well" because he could "see it well". He was a discerner of the times. He had an uncanny and keen insight into the political and spiritual climate of our world. He saw the plight of African Americans, government, and civil rights. His vision allowed him to sit with presidents and kings. While sitting next to Dr. Taylor, he initiated an interest in me as a young preacher and began a small conversation. Only because he communicated with me first did I risk breaking protocol and ask him a question. I gambled on his greatness by believing he had the humility to make time for this little preacher. I leaned and asked Dr. Taylor a question with trembling trust: "Dr. Taylor, what would you say a young preacher's greatest asset is in his ministry?" Gardner C. Taylor leaned over and kindly responded with piercing eyes and a thundering smile: "To be available to the Lord." Being available often entails God assigning preachers to dead places and dead people with the call of God to preach the Gospel of good news in the graveyard.

Our times demand vision in the truest sense, realizing the bones of our 21st-century cemeteries are not just the house of Israel, but they are also dead remains of people destroyed by technology, social media, modern-day new age cultures, racism, capitalism, oppression, universalism, humanism, ecclesiastical idolatry, and contemporary ministry movements of an Antichrist spirit that holds deceptive claims to Christianity. We preach amid a system of commerce that reminds us that we are pilgrims, and this world is not our home (I Chronicles 29:15; I Peter 2:11). Today's world systems do not allow the pastoral visionary to do his work freely and unhindered. While we do have freedom of religion, we do not have freedom to fully express the ethics of Christianity. We are shackled by indifference towards God's intended purposes for us in the Earth, and we preach with chained freedom as we are amongst a contemporary graveyard of the walking dead.

Ezekiel practiced his ministry in literal shackles. He was a contemporary of Jeremiah. Ezekiel continued the prophetic theme of an inevitable chastisement upon God's people that would come through Babylonian chains. Ezekiel was taken captive from Judah along with Jehoiachin. Within the first three chapters of the book of Ezekiel, a depiction of the prophet's residence is given along the Chebar River in Babylon.

Vision is often birthed in the context of cataract conditions. God's men need to have the transparency to see a way out of no way. The crux of Ezekiel's vision exemplified such a trait. However, he was misunderstood by his constituents because the details of his vision involved revelations of the extent of Judah's idolatry.

A true biblical sense of vision can be blurred if it has taken on a corporate, sinless, and trendy quality unlike that of God's major *seers* in Scripture. Biblically, vision has nothing to do with church prosperity or hallmarks of short or long-term corporate goals. A biblical visionary is distinguished from those of our day who only see prosperity while the sin element is placed within the periphery. Like Ezekiel, true pastoral visionaries can become outcasts because they do not envision carnal success for the Body of Christ. Instead, they see idolatry in the very context of the local church and world. When prophets of profit clamor for a vision void of the consequences of sin, they are preaching from petrified pulpits. There is no life in ignoring sin. The wage of sin is the same death revealed in Ezekiel's vision of skeletal remains. Pastoral visionaries see the deadly consequences of sin and reviving measures God takes if we would only preach and hear the word of the Lord. Biblical visionaries see the elements that accompany a graveyard. They see dead remains, epitaphs on tombstones of people who lived pointless lives, the spirits of the dead who forfeited entrance into the Heavenly City, and the forces that killed them.

Not only was it a valley full of dry bones, but it was also an evil hovering over the valley Ezekiel saw. This valley encompassed a graveyard that was not a heroic memorial of soldiers slain in the line of duty. On the contrary, Ezekiel saw the battlefield of a dead army slain by the gods of this world and a decaying nation embalmed in demon love. This rotting nation was God's own people who refused to be one nation under God.

Ezekiel's ministry teaches the difference between vision and fantasy. Fantasy is a world of make-believe with no relevance to what we are experiencing. Fantasy involves living in a disconnected world due to a twisted sense of boredom with reality. Vision has to do with coming to terms with the real world in all its impossibilities and possibilities of death and life. Vision enables a pastor to raise his congregation to the level of fighting fantasies and coming to terms with death-boned discoveries. The discoveries are in the fact that most premature deaths are self-inflicted. Because God's people were engulfed in the pursuit of happiness, even the sweet voice of Ezekiel was not enough to communicate the correlations between their present captivity and their previous corrupt conduct (Ezekiel 33:32).

Vision is a lifestyle. Much is said about *casting* a vision. Ezekiel cast his vision by the way he lived. Ezekiel was instructed to outline Jerusalem on a tablet (לְבֵנָה–leḇēnâh). It could have been a large and soft clay tablet the Babylonians used for writing material or a hard-baked brick that was used for building material. Then, God instructed Ezekiel to lay siege to the brick as a sign that God would disrupt their flow of resources. The brick was symbolic of Jerusalem. They were to be sieged by the Babylonians. It is possible that Ezekiel also used clay models to depict the Babylonians encircling Jerusalem under King Nebuchadnezzar's leadership. Ezekiel was commanded to build a ramp, illustrating the incline used for battering rams to be pushed above the foundation stones of the city. The constant hammering of Babylonian battering rams would eventually break down the city walls. He was instructed to place an iron pan between himself and the clay city-model he made. The iron pan (maḥăḇaṯ) was most likely a griddle made of iron the Israelites used for baking. He was instructed to face the iron pan while on his side. This type of imagery depicted the sin and judgment barrier that separated them from the face of God as they would cry out for deliverance, but God would not hear them. Ezekiel's posture on his side has been difficult to interpret, but the imagery is strangely powerful. God instructed Ezekiel to lie prostrate upon his left side and place Israel's sin upon himself. When he would lie toward Jerusalem on his left side, he would face the northern direction. This would be for 390 days with each day signifying a year. After he prostrated on his left side for 390 days, he was to turn on his right side and face southward bearing the sin of the house of Judah. This was to be for 40 days with each day signifying a year. Ezekiel was tied with ropes to symbolize the confinement of the siege. It may symbolize his powerlessness to help during this time because it would be too late. They should have taken advantage of prophecy before judgment fell (Ezekiel 4:1-8). Ezekiel had to be willing to inconvenience himself and lie on the ground for over a year. Many thought he lost his mind. Yet, Ezekiel had to become a human vision board for a year and two months. This shows how much vision will cost and the life we must cast when we bear the burden of vision. Pastoral visionaries are human vision boards.

Vision is not voluntary. A God-called pastor cannot pick his pulpit, and he cannot project his own perspective of what he is to accomplish in ministry. In Ezekiel's vocation in the valley, the text says the hand of the Lord *carried* and *caused* him to pass by the bones and inspect them (Ezekiel 37:1-2). True vision is a work of the apprehending hand of the Lord that carries us to places He wants us to preach that override our consent. True visionaries can often portray a human reluctance to see what God is revealing because being transported from an earthly perspective to Heaven's point of view is a retinal ride. Seeing ministry in the natural can be disillusioning and daunting. In the natural, excuses are made for the human condition by blaming it on government, racism, crime, pestilence, oppression, pandemics, epidemics, or economics. The root problem in the urban and rural cities is neither. The problem is the same throughout the open valley of our nation, i.e., sin. In the natural, Judah could have looked like an oppressed people victimized by Babylonian yoke, but supernaturally, Ezekiel could see they were dead in their sins.

God's hand must carry us into the valley. God-called men travel in the hands of God and not with the times. God did not call us to be relevant. He called us to be revivalists. If we become relevant, we are only allying with the forces that kill. There is no need to relevant to be a blessing to those who live in boneyards. Bones must be revived. When we see the human condition, we discover many of the tangibles we are tempted to acquire for ministry are a waste of God's time and our energy. We are to be available to be divinely transported from one dimension to another more than we are from one geographical location to another. The valley God carried Ezekiel to was more dimensional than geographical. We will always be available for revival when we have a vision of a living dimension to avoid saying all we have done is preach around the world. When God carries us, we go to worlds unknown. God took Ezekiel to a place unknown while he was in the location he was called to. He took him to a land of vision that saw the upside of despair. God gave Ezekiel a vision of hope for people who were dying before they ever truly lived. In Babylonian chains, God took Ezekiel to a valley that was not on the map.

Some preachers have not travelled far geographically, but they have gone to places unknown supernaturally. They have gone to places in God. When they stand to preach, there is a *Wind* that accompanies the Word they preach that sobers people to the reality of the forces that kill and a God who can revive the living dead.

Dr. Taylor preached around the world because he had been to worlds unknown in God. To Gardner Calvin Taylor, the world was an open valley. The world was part of his vocation and not a vacation. When he landed in a city, he reminded Saints and sinners of that city of another City. In a celestial capacity, you could hear through his sermons that he had a glimpse of the City of God. His conclusions in his sermons were celestial. His mannerisms were majestic. His sermonic stamina was seraphic. He was the Black Church's *Earth Angel*. Gardner Taylor was like a 20th- century John in the Book of Revelation. He saw revelations of what he described in his own words as "something he couldn't quite communicate but could never stop trying."

When God carries us into the dimension of decay, we are not allowed by God to powerfully preach if we are more impressed with that city than God is. We must see more tombstones than tall towers and more mortuaries than monuments. God did not call us to dead cities to be impressed by them, but He called us to make an impression upon them. We can see the cities. The tall buildings and skyscrapers are tombstones. The hustle and bustle of those in the streets who we view from our hotel rooms are a valley full of victims. Of course, not all of them, but the city is an urban underworld. Some of them are in the right army, but most are not. Yet, they are fighting for their lives to fill that empty void only God can fill.

Look at our churches…lifeless, especially during the Coronavirus crisis of 2020. Mortuaries are beautifully structured, and so are many of our churches. Many of our churches are morgues of the blessed dead. Yes, the dead move, but they only move if something moves them. Many are hyper-sensitive. They move like puppets at the silliest strings, pulled by the chords of drama and not sound doctrine or the deity of Christ. They have nothing in them that is an already existing internal inspiration. Like wooden dolls, they are petrified souls that must be inspired. If we do not come up with something to keep them motivated, they will no longer be members. If they are not animated, they will not attend. As with God's own people returning from Babylon, only the faithful few in our churches are alive enough to operate on their own.

Pastors who have a burden of vision for the spiritual state of people maneuver in ministry from the context of a completely different dimension. They rarely do what most are doing. When you rub shoulders with them, you get a close-up view of what makes them into momentous men. When I sat next to Dr. Taylor, I could feel the *Wind* blow. He would often say, "A ship must be careful not to miss the tide. So, I think I better sail on." One thing is true: Men of vision are not of this world although they are in this world. There is a Wind that carries them, and a Word that comes out of them. They are just as human as Ezekiel, but their anatomy is built for altitude. They are the eagle-eyed seers who can stand the sobering sight of the valley. They preach from above but quicken the dead below. God has taken them to places that were Meccas of their ministries. Their anatomy is accented with an eagle's anointing. They preached in the valley and have seen what God can do. They have seen the lightening flashing and have heard the thunder roll.

Boneyard preachers are not trying to gain the world because it is too small compared to the worlds their eyes have not seen and their minds have not been able to imagine (I Corinthians 2:9). They have such a concern for the condition of mankind that they give our skeletal societies nothing short of preaching in its truest form. They do not waste words. They choose their words carefully. They preach. Because the world is an open valley, our Lord transports most pastors into graveyard gatherings. When they look at the congregational condition from lifeless lenses, they only see decay. When they see the human condition from the Lord's lenses, they see the causes of decay. True vision addresses the lethal loves of our lives. The gods of the love of the world that include the lust of the flesh, lust of the eyes, and pride of life are killing too many of us softly (I John 2:16).

Like Ezekiel, true visionary pastors cannot help but inspect the real causes of the slaying of our societies, Saints, and sanctuaries. Pastoral visionaries see beyond the heights of the city's skyscrapers and the church's steeples. Instead, they see acres upon acres of people with dead demeanors. They gaze beyond the size and style of congregations and see a vast memorial sight of dead soldiers slain in the sanctuary.

Most of our churches do not need to grow as much as they need to be revived. Growth and revitalization endeavors are not in the hands of men or church growth strategies. Revival has nothing to do with our intelligence initiatives. Everything starts and ends with what God wants and with what God wills. More attention must be given to the power of God when revival and growth are concerns. The best strategy for church growth and health are supernatural in scope. They also reside in God's sovereignty. God knows exactly how many people will be engrafted into His Kingdom, and He knows exactly how many people who do not want entrance into His Kingdom. Understanding Ezekiel's vision allows us to be available to God and learn to acknowledge how much we do not know, especially when it comes to strategies for survival and revival. It should be encouraging for any pastor to know the wisdom of the providence of God. Only God knows if, how, and when bones can live. God's men have little to say when they see the condition of congregational corpses from Heaven's windows. For them, the word of God must do the talking. Preachers who make the pulpit priority are wise wonders to watch. When we see the condition of our culture from God's eyes, we are speechless, (Ezekiel 37:3). Yet, we preach.

Vision embodies cultural relativity. Dr. Gardner Taylor did not preach propaganda or a weak-branded gospel. His Gospel had social, spiritual, and racial implications. He was keenly aware of the plight of the world, and he refused to allow the United States to leave African Americans out of the salvific equation. He could have been likened unto *a preaching Frederick Douglas* if one ever existed. Very few of his sermons failed to address the oppressors of Black America. I would not be surprised if most Black preachers who are faithful to our preaching legacy would agree that Dr. Gardner Taylor had the keenest set of eyes among Black preaching pioneers.

Gardner Taylor had supernatural substance. Sadly, substantive preaching is being replaced by stylistic preaching. Without a vision to realize the valleys of dead disciples and petrified pulpits, we will never have much to say anyway. Only preachers who discern the gods of our times are men who never run out of material to preach. They mount the pulpit like men on a mission with a massive message. Discerners of our times have a sober view of the critical condition of our churches and pulpits. Many of our churches and pulpits are in intensive care, surviving by artificial life support systems of trends, technology, and technique. Men who see these deadly forces are panoramic preachers. They see that it will take more than a plexiglass podium, big bands, big budgets, big boards, big wheels, big screens, inviting big boys to preach, big buildings, big productions, and big ideas. Men with vision are aware of the truth that the preaching graveyard is much less animated than that. They see an open valley of cartoon souls who are impressed with idealized images instead of cold realities and hard facts. People live in a real world and not a fake one. It is a cold world full of cold wars, and our congregations are compositions of people who are bleeding from the battle. We are in a big battle for the souls of mankind.

Dr. Taylor was falsely accused by many in other theological circles of preaching a social gospel. Little did they accept the fact that Gardner Taylor realized how social gospels become the new idols for the oppressed. We all can stand behind a pulpit and preach against injustice until Jesus comes. That is easy. Injustice is not what kills us. The iniquities of social injustice are what kills. Dr. Taylor taught us that just because we were slaves, we did not have to settle for being sinners. Our slavery did not entitle us to be slaves to sin.

Dr. Taylor's Gospel understood the ramifications of slavery and injustice, but he also understood the implications of making a *B-line* to the Cross in his sermons. Although he identified racism, he took on the daunting, deadly, and divinely appointed task of teaching our tormentors and preaching to our persecutors. He realized they also needed to be resurrected from racism because they made racism a dead theological issue. They had a decaying way of representing Christianity in a style that condoned slavery and White Privilege. Thus, Dr. Taylor was not preaching to start a revolution. He was preaching to start a revival. Because our oppressors feared a revolution, they could not attack Dr. Taylor on justifiable grounds. Because he preached the Gospel, they could not resist his greatness.

Falling prey to Revolutionary Theology does nothing but produce mad ministers and members. Thus, our oppressors are given grounds to stand on an *eye for an eye* theology. Gardner Taylor did not have an angry anointing. He had an activist anointing. Instead of arousing madness due to injustice, he mobilized us to channel our anger into Christlike action. He was quickening a dead Black community who had been slain by the same gods Dr. Martin Luther King, Jr. sacrificed his life to save us from. While Dr. King died for our freedom, he also realized he would not be alive to challenge us to never be content with our freedom. Gardner C. Taylor summoned us to be resurrected by the power of God and war as soldiers in the army of the Lord by living above and beyond the perils of politics that sanctioned slavery in its newest forms. He also reminded us of our own sins that could slay us. Thus, his preaching revived a race of people who had a spirit that taught us to refuse to be victims of anyone's valley. Thus, when he preached, we said "Amen" and endured the chains of racism until our change comes.

Getting angry about injustice for too long dilates our pupils. If we preach against injustice more than we preach the Gospel of the Kingdom of God present but not yet, we lose sight of true vision for our valley. Thus, we fall prey to a victimized theology that subconsciously acknowledges our weaknesses instead of our worship. In other words, Dr. Taylor knew a lot about oppression, but he also understood there was not a lot his people could do about it other than wait on God and watch God. When he taught the Black church how to wait and watch, they began to develop pupils of perseverance and praise because they saw the hand of the Lord operating sovereignly on their oppressors amid their mental chains. Thus, Black churches learned to continue the rich heritage of codifying their intelligence because they knew how much their oppressors were threatened by a theology Black Christianity practiced that was more reviving than the one their oppressors preached. Thus, Black churches were full of the *Wind* and *Word*. Black churches had inspiration and intelligence, the burning, and the learning.

Although there was great focus on our oppressors, Gardner Taylor's greatest focus was on the Kingdom of God. Black, White, Red, or Brown, if we catalog too many of the sins of our oppressors, we will leave no room to catalog our own. Thus, we will begin to make more demands on our oppressors than we place upon ourselves. Then, we play right into the hands of our tormentors. The only level of intelligence that victims can rise to is one that pardons them from their prisons. Dr. Taylor taught us to be more than victims. He taught to be victorious. Thus, our central level of intelligence was in living Cross-shaped lives that taught us to suffer for Jesus' sake. So, when we knew that our oppressors thought they had us bound, we continued to sing in their strange land. They could take everything from us but our freedom in Christ. Although we raised their children and built much of this country, they could have this whole world, but we continued to sing, "Just give me Jesus".

When we lower ourselves to the level of victims of our valleys, we feel as though we cannot be free unless we begin to make material, social, and political demands. If so, history repeats itself all over again, and we become like certain of Jesus' day who wanted a tangible kingdom that would overthrow the Roman government while refusing the Kingdom of God that was designed to rule in their hearts (Acts 1:6). As Christians, there are certain things in life that we cannot overthrow. As in Ezekiel's day under Babylonian yoke, we must bow to God and trust that oppression of any sort will be dealt with in God's own time, especially if we handed our oppressors the key. Jesus' mission was not about recruiting revolutionaries. Jesus' mission was to renew the rationale of renegades. Therefore, our Lord succeeded John's message of repentance. A rebellious people can never become true revolutionaries anyhow. If we want a revolution, we will have to wait until Jesus places the government on His shoulders instead of demanding for it to be upon ours (Isaiah 9:6).

The vision in the valley was for the reviving of God's people because they offended Him more than anything or anyone else. Dr. Taylor taught Black Christians that we cannot fall prey to revolutionary idolatry and lose patience with the Kingdom of God. He educated us about the dignity we must demonstrate when we have been detained. No one in his or our time could preach about Heaven like Gardner Taylor. He preached about Heaven in such a majestic manner that he left us wondering if he had not been there, even in some small capacity. Because He taught us about Heaven, he taught us how to hold out. Overcoming injustice takes time, a whole lot of time. Impatient initiatives embrace practices that are abominable to God. When that happens, the gateway is open for local churches and us as pastors to eventually erase our own sins from our vocabulary. No matter how we are enslaved by tormentors of any sort, we are not victims. If so, the guards drop against practices the government accepts while the Bible rejects them.

Gardner Taylor taught us that we will never be able to address our sin issues if we substitute them for social ones. A social gospel removes accountability for our own actions. Then, it becomes by any means necessary. We do not have to put political, revolutionary, or social bricks on our churches to evangelize the world. Preachers do not have to become presidents or politicians. All we need is the Cornerstone (Ephesians 2:20). Dr. Taylor preached Christ and taught us to have the mind of Christ. Christ is not the cornerstone of the world, but He is the Savior of the world. Christ, who holds us together is the Cornerstone of the Church. Regardless of the battering rams of injustice that strike the Church, we will not crumble because we are compacted in Christ. A preacher who is devoted to revival with the Gospel at the core is not ashamed of the Gospel (Romans 1:16). The world can only be saved by a bold Gospel and not a timid one (Acts 4:29).

When other prophets commit to a social gospel in America, allegiances shift to the United States instead of God. It is not only many Liberals and their social gospel who need revival. We must also have vision to revive many Conservatives who worship a political gospel. Evangelicalism has gotten more enmeshed in racial supremacy on levels only visionaries can see while Liberalism extinguishes biblical absolutes that condemn a new morality of human rights over what is right. Biblical lines are erased at the expense of partisan ones on both the Left and Right. Truthfully, we are one nation under many gods. If we were one nation under

God, we would have only one Law and Lord (Deuteronomy 6:4). To make America great again would entail a return to idolatries that originate from the shaping of our nation by secret societies, slavery, capitalism, and classism.

Although Dr. Taylor did not preach a social gospel, his Gospel had something social to say. The sin of some of our most reputable expositors who criticize any preacher devoted to Dr. Taylor's sermonic style, social substance, and supernatural sight is the sin of silence when the eyes of those discriminated against are gauged by those who are devoted to racial gods. Yet, many of us saw and heard them, even in this decade. We heard them silently speak of the god they serve who considers oppression a social issue instead of a spiritual one. Racism and religion cannot be separated. To say their god is the God of the Bible would be taking the name of the Lord in vain because God never sanctions oppression. As a matter of fact, the silence of many is a social gospel in and of itself. Their silence represents the screams of the silent majority.

The eruption of White Supremacy supporters in the last few years quickened minorities and uncovered the graves of many in our local churches. Out of the woodworks came a culture who many minorities thought to be extinct. Although there was turmoil during many marches, not only was half of the world silent, but half of those within popular and powerful pulpits who remained in blind denial were silent also. If they could see, they closed their eyes and pretended they could not. If that is not the case, they surely squinted. It is amazing how their expositional prowess or preaching popularity could not expose the culture of oppression that minorities are enslaved by. They knew that if they preached against injustice on that level, they would be issued death threats aimed at their ministries and even their lives by their own peers and persuasion. They did not need Hebrew or Greek Bible study tools to give a word study for racism. All they needed to do was open their eyes, open their mouths, and preach against the forces that kill the oppressed.

We saw how polarized our nation has been for a long time as racial corpses erupted from graves that were buried since the 1600's. Those who were oppressed were not heard. Even more so, far too many who have mega-ministries and relationships with the rich as well as those who champion expository preaching never preached one sermon against it.

In the month of June of 2020, our nation is in an uproar. The Coronavirus crisis coupled with daunting racism against Back folk, young black males especially, has created a two-headed monster in our century. Apart from the Coronavirus pandemic of 2020, a silent lamb has been forgotten that must be saved who says much about the theology of too many of my Conservative Christian brothers and Right-Wing Republicans. That little lamb who has been forgotten is Hether Heyer.

In 2017, the Sunday following the day that dear little White girl (Hether) was killed in Charlottesville by a White Supremist, many preached about something totally irrelevant to the wake-up call for America the following Sunday. If we were at war with some other country, nearly every Evangelical pulpit would have been preaching about it, including mine. However, they refused to acknowledge the resilient war of racism was still raging since the 1600's. Silent preachers of the silent majority and many confused preachers of the screaming minority missed the opportunity to sound the Gospel trumpet to bring revival to our nation. Instead, that dear little White girl became the scapegoat because to have vindicated her would have meant the vindication of Black America and White supporters of people of color.

Since Jesus' day, the sacrificial lamb has always been one who was of the same ethnic persuasion. Jesus dying as a Jew meant little to many Jews who were responsible for His crucifixion, as even a Roman prefect governor by the name of Pilate found no fault in Jesus. Black folk have been sacrificed on the altar of racism for over 400 years, but when a White girl is sacrificed on the altar of racism, the conscience of the crucifiers of people of color is obviously seared. Therefore, blind expositors let her murder run away into a tragedy that has not been remembered for what it truly was. America can remember 9/11 annually, but America cannot memorialize the day when our nation was a threat unto itself.

In God's eyes, that dear little White girl became the sacrificial lamb, but very few racists and religionists repented. Her death was a contemporary crucifixion as she sacrificed her life. The voice of that little White girl's blood was crying out to God from the ground, but many of God's own prophets failed to remind her killers that they *are* their brothers' keepers (Genesis 4:9). Many Saints in sanctuaries remained sleep because countless expository preachers hit the snooze button from both White and Black pulpits. Very few had a word from the Lord in the open valley although they had sixty-six books in their Bibles to validate them if they only would have said something. In too many Black churches, the Uncle Tom theology prevailed by supporting those who had the gall to say two wrongs do not make a right. They failed to see that a person who is protesting oppression never places that person on a level playing field but a person who stays accountable for their demons of discrimination does.

Sadly, these are a few of our new idolatries that true visionaries see. Sometimes, it is what a person is not saying that speaks loudest. Dr. Taylor's style of preaching and seeds of inspiration to younger preachers such as myself has opened our eyes. We see how Dr. Taylor's topical style of preaching and social emphasis has been demonized by some expository preachers who fail to understand the true spirit of expositional preaching. Not only does expositional preaching expose the scriptures, but true expositional preaching exposes the Truth whether one wants to call it topical preaching or not. The Gospel that Gardner C. Taylor preached was far more Christological than religiously not saying anything against discrimination, sexual harassment, racism, and capitalism. To not see and confess such sins of silence is a salvific concern.

All these idolatrous ideologies are spawned by many rich churches who need to be revived due to their dedication to dead presidents in the literal and financial sense. Presidents in the past would have also condoned such unrighteous acts. To only attack one president would mean the figurehead has been identified, but the sin of racism has not. Financially, to identify the sin of racism at the core would have taken billions and even trillions of dollars out of many Evangelical and political pockets. These are also the dead bones of our days. Unfortunately, with far too many, it is personal.

Ezekiel's ministry helps us guard against personalized vision. If one is a visionary, he should be able to see horizontally, far, wide, globally, and vertically with a biblical worldview. Ezekiel's vision was for the nation of Israel. Abraham's vision was for the innumerable beneficiaries of the Abrahamic covenant. Joel's young men were to see visions in the context of a progressive outpouring of an evangelistic Spirit until the final countdown of Jesus' ultimate victory over the powers of darkness occurs. Peter's vision was for a perpetuation of the Gospel to Gentiles. Paul's vision was so powerful that it could not be marketed, or he would have been *thorned* to death (II Corinthians 12:7). John's vision was for the substantiation of true worship of the exalted Son of God and the sentencing of Satan and demons due to God's majestic vengeance upon the gods of this world, culminating in the establishment of His Kingdom overthrow.

Packaging vision into *vision statements* has the ideology that must be expressed within the context of a corporate mentality (as if the Church is an organization or business). Vision has nothing to do with what happens in the four walls of a local church because the Church should have no walls. More than the Church being an organization or business, the Church is an organism comprised of people who are wanted by God, dead or alive (Ezekiel 37:3; Ephesians 5:14). Vision is deeper than a statement to get our parishioners to buy into or have ownership of the corporation. No one has stock in the Church but the Holy Trinity. We have membership and stewardship, but we have no ownership. The concept of getting people to buy into the vision is a *dead-boned* solicitation. In the corporate world, getting stakeholders to buy into the vision is a necessity, but in the local church, it is a travesty.

If a man is a *seeing* preacher, people will never see what he sees, but they can hear if he preaches what God told him to preach. Biblical vision involves being transported by God into a heavenly consciousness of sin and decay and faithfully preaching from a graveyard context, letting the *Wind* and *Word* do the work. When a pastor has true vision, he is not marketing consumers. He is summoning the Spirit to bring souls back into corpses. Anything we solicit from members to buy into our vision is dead profit. Visionaries never get people to buy into their vision because their sins cannot afford it, and the preacher cannot sell it (Acts 8:18-20; I Corinthians 9:18).

If we are preaching amid corporation graveyards, we do not need the majority vote of bones, even if they consider themselves major stakeholders in our churches. Contrarily, we must have the hand of the Lord upon us approving our efforts and the power of the Holy Spirit enabling us as we prophecy (preach) in God's name. We cannot put this type of vision on a PowerPoint presentation or new member's orientation church manual. It is too supernaturally implemented to do so. It must be preached. The question is not, "Can these bones buy into this vision?" The question is not,

"Can you get these bones to agree with the vision?" The question is, "Can these bones *live*?" If we see vision in marketing and corporate terms, we have no choice but to view our congregations as consumers. If so, we need *them* to stay in business. When we need people to keep us in business, they become our new idols, and our pastoral paradigm will shift from preaching the whole counsel of God to pacifying, programming, or persuading people because we need them to make a profit and preserve our position. Then, we almost have no choice but to use business practices to establish sustainable customer relationships. Rather, God commands preachers to *eat* the whole counsel of God and preach:

> *"And he said unto me, Son of man, cause thy belly to eat, and fill thy bowels with this roll* (scroll of the Law) *that I give thee. Then did I eat it; and it was in my mouth as honey for sweetness."*
>
> (Ezekiel 3:3; KJV)

When asked about our vision statement, we are often interrogated about our niche. Niche and vision are as exclusive for valley ministries as night is from day. Niche is what we have the human capacity to be most comfortable doing, but vision is the God-given capacity to do what we are most uncomfortable doing. Ezekiel had an extremely uncomfortable assignment. I am not sure if there is such a thing as a comfortable calling. Ministry discomforts everything our fleshly frame desires, knows, or has the human capacity to do. After sin entered our bloodstream through Adam, there is nothing supernaturally divine that compliments the human condition. Since then, it has always been flesh against Glory.

Rather than a niche, **vision is a burden placed upon us that makes our inadequacies obvious**. God does not use adequate men.

He only uses inadequate men. I am forever humbled and awed at pastors who led mega and meaningful armies of Christians into new life. They abandoned all new-age forms of resuscitation and learned to go with the Wind. Vision makes no assumptions. It leaves the results to prophecy (Ezekiel 37:4). As we come together in fellowship, we may also hear the question, "What's your vision for your church?" It is almost as if this type of vision must be a certification of whether we are purpose-driven or not. The proponent of the purpose-driven philosophy has not claimed to be an authority on that subject as much as many have. So, this is in no way an attack on the founder of that philosophy who I admire. However, if the purpose-driven paradigm was such a viable strategy as others have proposed, God would have made such implementations available when He first birthed the Church. The same power that birthed the Church is the same power that will revive and keep it alive. Only the Wind (Holy Spirit) revives people (Ezekiel 37:9; John 3:8; Acts 2:2). A vision statement may certify flows in modern church trends, but it can never be the birth certificate of a church. The supernatural component must be seen for our ministries to be validated in our valleys.

Furthermore, the supernatural can never be reduced to a shallow humanistic display of signs, wonders, and miracles. The realm of supernatural supply is eternally greater than that. The supernatural component that must exist in the 21st-century church is the silent force of the power of the word of God and the wind of the Holy Spirit quickening dead people who have material things, but they have no meaning. They are prosperous, but they have no purpose. They have valuables, but they are still victims of their own valleys.

I understand ideologies that believe local churches must never compromise the message but change methods if we are to reach this generation. Although I once made those statements, I learned to not do so anymore because the message *is* the method. When I cut out all the nonsense and began to preach and minister with simplicity, I was then able to reach all nations and ages by having a multicultural church. Only because of the Wind and Word, I can see that my little church is a small congregation of leaders and not a large congregation of followers. I am not suggesting that a multicultural church is superior to a church that maintains its ethnic identity. I am simply saying that preaching with simplicity crosses all racial, cultural, and social barriers. When we understand the power of preaching the Word, we understand how it is pregnant with supernatural methodology. In other words, the Word *works*. It is living and active (Hebrews 4:12). One who sits under the context of the preaching of the word of God will radically be shaken regardless of the various graveyard eras in which one lives.

It takes the Wind and the Word to do the work of ministry. Supernatural preaching must be the core of true expository preaching or any other style of preaching. Man-made expository styles of preaching quench the power of the Spirit of God. If a preacher has no spiritual power and claims to be an expository preacher, he is only preaching in an essay format if he only utilizes a thesis statement, attention-getting introduction, supporting points, and a motivating conclusion. I do not mention such a statement as a criticism. I only made that observation as an encouragement for any preacher who believes he must be confined to a cultural way of communicating. Instead, he can be released by a more supernatural way to preach. Whatever style we choose to preach, we are mandated to know that it is powerless unless God breathes upon it. Preaching is a supernatural event and not a homiletical discourse. We experienced that through Gardner Taylor's preaching. He did not preach the Bible verse-by-verse or use three points, but he did preach Truth, and he preached with power. Instead men with vision preach with an unction for the underworld (Luke 4:18; I Peter 3:19). They preach in a way that is a revivalist attempt to raise people from the comforts of contemporary caskets.

Vision involves strategic supernatural implementations of life in the context of killing fields. God asked Ezekiel a question that weighed heavily upon his shoulders in Ezekiel 37:3: "Son of man, can these bones live?" Sense Ezekiel's weight as he sighs, "Oh, Lord God, only thou knowest!" That is how a visionary sometimes feels. If a pastor is questioning if he has a true sense of vision, I will not doubt that he is also questioning the weight of the work before him. The most admirable pastors who I know have heavy eyelids and beaten brows. They are not satisfied due to what they see. They do not see their sanctuaries as a success. Instead, they see a sobering summons. Pastors with the burden of vision understand the weight of their work. They are the true heavyweights of the Gospel. There is a heaviness about the way they do ministry. Gardner Taylor was a heavyweight.

I have lived to witness pastors literally and subliminally resign from God's Gospel for graveyards because they feel as though they lost their voice. They feel as though they are mute regarding the needs of the Millennials. A pastor does not always have to appoint a Millennial to be his successor. All he needs is a God-called messenger who will deliver God's message. Seasoned pastors have not lost their voice. Millennials can hear quite well, especially if God speaks to them. God does not speak in Twitter, Instagram Facebook, or Snapchat language. He speaks through His word.

Social media has become the new Bible of the Millennials. Much of that has to do with the erosion of family and Christian values along with the deadness of the local church. Through social media, our children prophecy to one another. They are a social media society. As the generations pass from age to age, our children and grandchildren become less inclined to live because the abuse of social media has left them with a deep sense of insecurity, disillusionment with reality and demons of depression. Many who are in social media graveyards post their liveliest faces on social media although they are barely breathing. If they do not get enough "likes" and "followers", they cannot live. So, our depressed children, grandchildren, and even our own peers who are addicted to social media between the ages of 50-65 view these pages as though they are being left behind. To them, it appears that everyone is living well but them. Many manufacturers of apps designed them to keep people devoted to their devices. If one believes social media is the *sole venue* to reach Millennials, they are falling prey to a media massacre. Pastors who mastered the media can testify that it can be an invaluable resource, but it can also be a crutch to cripple congregations with a false sense of connectivity. If lifeless members connect to our church and ministries through social media, they deadly believe they are connected. Yet, they are dead in attendance, giving, and lifeless in loyalty to local church gatherings because they perceive that they made the connection through social networks. These are new bones that are disconnected from their parts. When components that comprise relationships are revived, we see how worship of social media disconnects relationships.

Connecting does not constitute life. Ezekiel preached and the bones connected, but there was no breath in them. Bones were connected and well-organized, but they were still dead (Ezekiel 37:8). Imagine the scene. Scattered and decayed bones came together. Flesh came upon the skeletal structure of each soldier. Like many, they had flesh and bones, but they had no life. There they lay in an open graveyard by the thousands. They were all lined up, just lying there; just...*there.* For Ezekiel, it was the spiritual measures of the *Wind* and *Word* that were the vital signs of a conscious congregation.

God commanded Ezekiel to preach to the mountains of Israel (Ezekiel 36:1). He then told Ezekiel to preach to the hills, rivers, and valleys (Ezekiel 36:6). During Ezekiel's revival series of sermons, God commanded him to preach to the bones (Ezekiel 37:4). However, when he did so, there was still no life. It was not until God told Ezekiel to preach an additional sermon to the *Wind* when they came alive (Ezekiel 37:8-10).

We are freed from using organizational tactics to structure and mobilize the local church, only to ask God to blow on them *after* we organized them. If we do so, people may attend church, but they will be just…*there*. God's method is the opposite. He blows on people, and they all come together in His order. God does not blow on buildings or budgets, but God blows on Believers. God blows on what constitutes or complements human anatomy (Genesis 2:7).

As massive and structured as many of our churches are, you would think that would cause severe climate changes in our cities. However, our cities and citizens are deathly cold. That is not always a reflection of our churches. Sometimes, it is. More importantly, it is a lesson to teach us how powerless we are. Only the breath of God can warm the souls of people who are chilled by sin. God was not concerned about congregating corpses or structuring sanctuaries that were synonyms for cemeteries, but He was concerned about reviving the slain. God has not called us to add more corpses to our congregations. If we only organize bones, we cannot expect life once they gather. If so, all we have is a graveyard group. So, pastors are frustrated because their people are spectating but not participating. The pastor has finally attracted them into the arena, but those who are attracted are not activated. Then, we are nothing more than bone collectors. It is impossible to get the unregenerate or carnal into the arena and initiate real worship once they arrive.

Vision is not only something you see, but it is also something you feel on a much deeper dimension than sheer emotionalism or a treatise of religious affections. When a pastor has true vision, he experiences a chilling effect. Death is cold-blooded. Morgues are cold and so is ministry. The cold cell floors of our pastoral prisons call for a coat from at least one trusted companion (II Timothy 4:13). A pastor cannot help but shiver and cover his nose at the stench of the autopsy of a dead church. Ezekiel's vision was a chilling challenge. His vision was not warm and welcoming. What he saw was wicked. The people of God were impaled by idolatry. If we placed that type of vision in our church manual or on our website, too many people would deathly defy it.

We need more fellowships that unite for pastors who have cold-blooded callings. Within our preaching conventions and fellowships, a valley preacher cannot afford to prejudicially pick other preachers to preach based on their peer, peak, or popularity levels. Instead, they must pick other preachers to preach based on their prophetic levels. We avoid being inundated with conferences and workshops that suggest we have some part to play in building a 5-Star church. We are not mandated by God to showcase our sanctuaries or shrink them to fit a success paradigm. Instead we must enlarge them to fit a supernatural one.

Consequently, the pastoral vocation is a vacuum. It is too large and above our heads to be placed on a system of measurement or a matrix. Because none of us have arrived, we never have to addict ourselves to a relentless pursuit of prestige. Every sincere preacher will always know there is more work to do and more room for steering clear of portraying ourselves as preaching experts. The graveyards of lifeless souls never afford us the privilege of preaching on plateaus. Instead, they validate us for the valley.

Two professions that will always have a high demand are those of the mortician and minister. People die before their time, and people live until it is time to die. Our preaching unction has been so far removed from Ezekiel's preaching mode that the mortician is the one who usually gives people hope while blind preachers bury them by speaking well of the dead more than against the forces that killed them. When we fail to identify and preach against the forces that slay us before our season, we are burying people instead of giving them new life.

There is a move that suggests a pastor has failed if he has not reached certain plateaus of preaching. Ezekiel's valley and the valley we walk through in this life is a shadow of death (Psalm 23:4). I can see the breath taken away from many pastors because they will never reach the plateaus of their peers. They must be revived to know that real ministry is more about valleys than skies. I do not take that fallacy personally. By the chastising hand of God, I know better. I take it corporately. I desire to encourage pastors who are of the valley norm. There are more pastors in the valley than on mountaintops. False prophets on some mountaintops have peaked out in their ministries and have picked the pockets of cold-blooded saints who cannot defend themselves because they are too dead to realize they have been robbed. Many Christian's consciousness of their own sin is dead while they are deadly conscious of the sins of others. They rob themselves and mob others by thinking self-worth and self-preservation can substitute for God's forgiveness. They think swine can substitute for the Lamb (Mathew 7:6; Mark 5:16-17).

On the other hand, we as pastors in the valley must not become victims of our own valley. If so, we will become vicious and vindictive. The pastors of old had vocations in the same valley. They did not congregate as preachers to complement one another in ways that only bury the dead and compliment a dead delivery style of preaching. They gathered to compete with one another in an iron-sharpening way that would chisel people from the four walls of their contemporary caskets.

The valley preachers of old served their churches instead of their churches serving them. They had a status that was not predicated upon the churches they pastored. Instead, their status was predicated upon their preaching. They reached a level of greatness because they were great preachers. Now, status is predicated upon the size, style, and structure of our churches whether we are great preachers or not. Back in the day, you had to be a good preacher to be a pastor. It did not matter how large, small, prominent, or poor the church was. Members of valley churches did not tolerate a preacher who could not or would not preach. Now, one can pastor without being a good preacher. As a matter of fact, one can pastor without knowing how to preach. A person can pastor a church without being called to preach. Even worse, one can pastor many of today's churches without preaching at all. If one is a good administrator who can give culturally acceptable messages that keep people dead in their sins and alive to their selfish successes, such a one will likely get the job.

Dr. Taylor was a preacher whose eyes were like an eagle soaring over the valley. What made preachers of Gardner Taylor's era great preachers was the fact that they were faithful in preaching to their own context. Now, greatness is defined by being invited to comfortable and convenient contexts. While I am always more than humbled to preach behind pulpits of some of the greatest preachers of our age, I realize such pulpits are not suffering from a lack of preaching. While I tend to feel accomplished when I preach behind the pulpits of some of the greatest pulpit-masters I know those are not the pulpits where I am needed most.

If God willed to raise dead bones of Israel to be an exceeding great army, Ezekiel had to learn how to be a preaching general. Gardner Taylor was one of our greatest generals. True preaching

The Pastor And His Eyes

generals are concerned with being more supernatural and significant than successful. If a preacher has a blind vision for success and wings for the world, he will not see nor soar far. The ministry is the last place he would want to be if success is his objective. He could have done better at being successful in the corporate world, entertainment industry, or some secular career.

Because blinding success eclipses the light that resuscitates souls, pastors who are the valley norm have rare resources and relationships that encourage perseverance in preaching in their valleys. Not too long ago, we went to conventions to hear great preachers. There was a day when you left conventions, the guest preachers preached so hard that you could not wait to get back to your valley to preach because when they preached, even preachers' bones came together. Even in my era, I remember those days. Valley preachers gave the total of servanthood in a sermon. Those days are gone forever. In many of our gravesite gatherings, the average preacher sits below prosperous platforms viewing a man he can never be while valley preachers view prosperous platform preachers as those who they would never want to be.

Gardner Calvin Taylor was a valley preacher who gave boney Believers something to believe in, poor preachers something to feel rich about, ashamed preachers something to be proud of, young preachers something to mature into, theologians something to think about, and exegetes something to interpret. He was sober and quickened by the Spirit, carried, and called to a vocation that infused hope that we could come out of our caskets.

No true visionary sees only possibilities. Visionaries see problems that impede possibilities, obstacles that must be turned into opportunities, and the scarcity of human resources for revival. Thank God for the valley of pastors who see the fallen conditions that brought about such a slaughter of the Saints. Ezekiel embodied a series of visions. His need to see beyond the chains of

Babylon necessitated vision regularly. Vision was such a natural occurrence that his visions became his reality. Vision is a reality that we must live within and not some dream to reach for without. Vision has nothing to do with making dreams come true or living our best days now. Vision is operating within the realm of God's revelation now and later by adapting our frame of reference to what God enabled us to see and governing our lives, churches, and ministries by His word for a world full of conscious corpses. Ezekiel needed to realize that he could not leave the valley until he fully processed the purpose of preaching. Thus, God caused Ezekiel to sit where they sat (Ezekiel 3:15).

We sit or stand in the valley long enough to be victorious and not abandon the callous contexts of our calling. There are no such things as greener pastures for the pastor other than those that come from God (Psalm 23:2). As far as the local church is concerned, the grass is never greener on the other side. If anything, moving to another church has higher grass and more weeds that require more cutting. Pastors who have acres of members need larger lawnmowers. They are not to be envied, but they are to be encouraged. They have more soil to till, and only they and God know the toil that accompanies their soil. Wherever we go, we will constantly be confronted with the call to rely on the *Wind* and *Word*. The best legacy we can leave behind is one that has marks of where the *Wind* blew.

When Ezekiel completed the process of preaching that involved both the Wind and the Word, the Bible describes the bones coming together as an *exceeding great army*. The fact that they were an army implies they were resurrected to continue in the battle against the forces that killed them (Ezekiel 37:10). True revival of the soul often births a militant mindset. When God has truly delivered us from fatal forces and foes, we are relentless to war against anything that threatens our potential to live again. When

God brings us back to life, we never want to return to the tombs we were delivered from unless we are there to rescue those from the graves we once knew.

Ezekiel had to inspect the bones. As God endows pastors with vision to survey their corpse contexts, they conduct an autopsy that reveals the misery that attends real ministry. They begin to see how *very many* are in a dead existence. Pastors with the burden of vision begin to see that there are more than realized in a decayed disposition. They collect bones of all sorts, disconnected from their parts with one thing in common: They are disconnected in the same condition and context, i.e., in an open valley. Just when the pastor sees things coming together, God sharpens his sight to see people who have fallen apart due to multiple maladies, failing to dodge the arsenal of the Adversary.

God's grace has a sustaining buffer that allows such men to survive unexplainable odds and not be contaminated by the toxic stench of dead men's bones. When we understand that our anatomy is unique in every sense of the word, we fulfill our calling with an unusual sense of the supernatural regardless of how horrifying the site of the valley may be. When we walk through the valley of the shadow of death, we should not fear. We move beyond the insecurity and discomfort that comes with preaching in a graveyard and are thankful that we are not buried in the cemeteries of the same bones we inspect. Whatever many say about supernatural spokesmen, they cannot say that we are lifeless and *Lord-less*. By the Gospel, the grave is defeated, and that is what we preach.

Life can be lonely for the pastor in the center of an open valley. Even if you stand in a cemetery with thousands of buried bodies, you may feel eerily alone. In graveyard ministries, there is a creepy loneliness God sanctions. In the prophetic realm, valleys are good news graveyards from which life is spoken into departed souls. Our vocation in the valley is not about establishing social networks with dead people. Contrarily, our vocation is about connecting to a supernatural network for the salvation of souls. Most of our ministries will be spent with skeletal remains in need of a visionary who sees beyond their graves to the potential they have in becoming an exceeding great army of militant members of Christ's Church who can stand triumphant against the grave (Matthew 16:18).

When vision is restored, loneliness will not provoke us to envy a codependent relationship with bones that will enable them to remain in a lifeless state. Pastors must seek to be their own individuals because individuality is loneliness in maturation. A pastor will never be at peace until he has come to terms with his own individuality. When a pastor embraces this divine loneliness and individuality, he will cease from being contemporary. Being contemporary may lead him to contentment with the graves of our times. Furthermore, he will not seek to be too traditional because that may cause him to eulogize those in the grave instead of preach against the forces that killed them.

Now is not the time to bury God's people in the dust of opinions, great ideas, and secular sameness. Now is the time to revive slaughtered Saints by preaching the timeless truth that God takes sin seriously. Sometimes, our objective is to silence the crowd. Graveyard preachers do not need an "*Amen*" to get their point across. They are not slain by silence. They realize dead people cannot talk or agree. Pastors who bear the burden of vision do not need confirmation from corpses or comfort from the callous. They accept the fact that their assignment is to bring dead people to life rather than compliment or condone cold-blooded conditions.

Vision is a spiritual solution to a lethal problem. Lack of vision keeps fog in the graveyard and clouds the sight and source of decay. Vision is a supernatural insight into iniquity. As we embrace that truth, the audience to whom we preach is seen for who they truly are, i.e., a sleeping giant. Consequently, real preaching becomes a battle cry. Through the dynamism of preaching, dead disciples are supplied with endowments to increase mobility as a resurrected army along the unfolding timeline of a Kingdom agenda. The Kingdom of God is violently advancing, and vision enables sleeping entities to awaken to an aggressive advance and seize the possibilities by force. To advance, God does not reveal irrelevant vision statements that confuse pastoral generals of dead armies. After God explained to Ezekiel that new life would be infused to transform them into a marching army, He caused Ezekiel to understand the meaning of the vision:

> *"Then he said unto me, Son of man, these bones are the whole house of Israel: behold, they say, our bones are dried, and our hope is lost: we are cut off for our parts."*

(Ezekiel 37:11; KJV)

Notice how God's people stated that their hope was lost. When we have been slain by sin, hope is a precious commodity. If sinners have no hope, they can never be saved. Someone must see a light at the end of their tunnel. Preaching the *Word of Life* to people who pay the wages of sin lets them see how God will foot the bill.

Vision is not to be cheered as if the Church is attending a spiritual pep rally or heralded as if it was a first-place medal of an Olympic game. If vision is likened to a medal of honor, it is to be worn reverently because Jesus won the cold war against sin. Vision exemplifies the fact that we can be revived from sin over and against vision becoming a trophy of saintly superiority or lofty leadership. Vision is not something we persuade people to see because dead people cannot see. God causes the preacher to see heavenly horizons for hopeless humans.

Before Ezekiel saw the vision of dry bones in the spiritual realm, he ministered among people who lost all hope that they would ever return to the Sender (God). Marketing, branding, and casting a corporate projection of short and long-term goals would have been totally irrelevant to Ezekiel's assignment. As a matter of fact, those are some of the ecclesiastical idols that snuff the life out of our churches and transform them into secular arenas instead of sacred assemblies. God desires to resuscitate His children who died before their time and reclaim people who are digging their own graves.

Thus, vision involves seeing the dysfunction of people despite layers of prosperity they portray. Such are those who ignore consequences of their own sins and those who reached a level of selfish success. Their dead money cannot deliver them. Their success haunts them in their sleep, keeps them awake at night, knowing what they gained, they gained from devilish devotions. Visionaries see the comforts many acquire that are nothing but open caskets waiting to be occupied. The dysfunction our congregations or communities possess need not be embarrassing. If we are on this Earth, we are all subject to the deadly elements of a plethora of killing fields. I am well acquainted with what it is like to have been slain by sin and the gods of this world. The gods are seeking to devour anyone who possesses purposeful potential (Ephesians 6:12).

Much honor should go to pastors who remained faithful in the valley who are now seeing seasons of life within their congregations because they faithfully summoned their people to hear the Word of the Lord. As they soar with wings as eagles over their valleys, may we celebrate their soaring, fly with them, and protect them from scissoring spirits of the self-righteous and judgmental who try to clip their wings. If we are still in the valley while they minister on mountaintops, may we praise God for their ascension and encourage them to fly as far and faithfully as they can, even if

God leaves some of us on lower ground. These pastors are flourishing and flying high because they are preaching the same way that they preached long before their congregations revived. Their gift of preaching has made room for them. They preached the same way in their graves that they do in their glory.

On the mountaintops or in the valley, the Word works if one is dead or alive. The possession of vision should not be perceived as an elitist badge to soothe the insecurities of an arrogant organization or leadership. On the contrary, vision validates the supernatural supplies God grants graveyard ministries soon to be revived rather than religiously eulogizing those who deathly claim to have already lived.

Chapter 5

THE PASTOR AND HIS VOICE

A Voice Crying in the Wilderness
(An Excerpt from the Life of John the Baptist:
A preacher who felt abandoned)

<u>Tribute</u>: To Dr. Sandy Frederick Ray (Pastor of the Cornerstone Baptist Church of Brooklyn, NY from 1954-1979); Sunrise: 1898; Sunset: 1979

Although I was too young to have rubbed shoulders with Dr. Sandy Ray, I was privileged to have learned from those who had. Sandy Ray was a mentor to my mentors. His sermons and writings had a word for preachers. Dr. Ray was an advocate for young preachers understanding what he coined, "The Wilderness Theology". He was concerned about young preachers leaving the pulpit to serve the secular job market because they had become disenfranchised with the wilderness of preaching. Soberly, pastors are obligated to stay faithful to be a "voice", even if they must cry out from the wilderness. One of Sandy Ray's most notable accomplishments was the publishing of a book that I am grateful to Pastor L. A. Kessee for sharing with me that is entitled, **Journeying Through the Jungle**.

John the Baptist was born in the year 5 B.C. and was noted as *"A Voice Crying in the Wilderness"* (Matthew 3:3). The Baptist emerged as a preacher in A.D. 26 in the wilderness region near the Jordan River. His preaching is noted throughout Christian history to be decisive with Christological content. To be the forerunner of Jesus Christ, proclaiming for the world to prepare the way of the Lord demands a Christology that cannot be countered. John's distinguishing characteristic was his hard message of repentance.

While positions are taken regarding the cessation or non-cessation of the prophetic office, accepting the responsibilities of such claims to be a prophet is an even more difficult position for many to embrace within the local church. Biblical prophets experienced persecution because they preached convicting messages. Their voices were heard although they were rarely heeded. Prophets and persecution go *hand-in-hand* while prosperity gospels and fortune-telling come from a different set of hands. Prophets in the Bible were also poor. Yet, they were sustained by God and free-will offerings of people. None were ordained by God to have money flowing through several streams. They were forbidden to do so (Mark 6:4-11). They were commanded to drink from one brook at a time. When they received sustenance, it was only to strengthen them on their journey to more preaching and persecution.

For the sake of establishing the *Prophetic Voice* within the pastoral ministry, such claims can be biblically founded for every preacher while avoiding debate about the validity or invalidity of the prophetic *office* in the 21st century. The prophetic office and maintaining a *prophetic voice* can be distinguished. The pastor's voice should be prophetic in the sense that it is loaded with a vocabulary of terms related to repentance. At the heart of repentance is the pulsating need to be challenged in the ways we think about God and ourselves.

The *Prophetic Voice* is distinct from fundamental preaching. Sermons can be hermeneutically sound but homiletically deficient. Hermeneutical soundness has biblical *interpretation* at the core, but homiletical efficiency involves *communication* in a way that calls hearers to rethink the spiritual matters at hand. The *Prophetic Voice* maintains the authority of communication that powerfully flows from a consecrated man into the inner sanctums of the minds of the recipients. The *Prophetic Voice* cannot be ignored because of its force and power. The *Prophetic Voice* has nothing to do with exegetical exactness, style, volume, or preacher tones, but it has everything to do with the inspirational impact that exudes from a vessel sanctified for the Master's use.

I recall taking my uncle, J. C. Wade, Sr. (a well-known contemporary of Sandy Ray) to hear a minister preach. After the sermon, I asked "Daddy Wade" what he thought of the sermon. He simply said, "He didn't shake me!" Preaching should challenge the listener to rethink his spiritual direction. Preachers are to also experience an internal shaking as they preach (I Corinthians 2:3). Preachers during Sandy Ray's era had sermons that shook. There was a fraternity among those pulpit masters, but when they mounted to preach, their preaching peers expected them to hold nothing back. Most preachers of that era understood pulpit ethics. A component of pulpit ethics was a prophetic ethic. The ethic involved *telling it like it is* regardless of whether people or peers liked it or not. Those seasoned preachers lived for that moment to mount the pulpit and prophetically proclaim what God laid heavily on their hearts, even if they were personally shaken by their own sermons. Their sermons were not just eloquent and accurate interpretations of Scripture, lofty theological insights, or innovative ideas to impress their peers. They were not just rightly dividing the Word for the sake of cutting it straight by trying to impress preaching peers with the accuracy of their hermeneutical knives. There was something about their message because there was something about the man that produced a harmony between the message and messenger. Their pulpit ethic was dignified. They were distinguished gentlemen. There was something about them that made them worth listening to. That *something* was consecrated preaching that feared God as well as a calling that took preaching seriously and soberly.

Many were not as educated as we are, but they were more consecrated than most of us are today. While these men had faults (as is the case with every God-called preacher), they were never at fault for not being able to preach. They established an ethic for generations to come that reminded us: **Out of all the things that people say about a preacher, a preacher must never let it be said that he cannot preach.** Their lifestyle revolved around their craft instead of their craft revolving around their lifestyle. If their lifestyle infected their preaching, they quarantined themselves from anything that would cause them to be guilty of sick preaching. Anything that caused them to have prophetic strep throat was done away with. Preachers of that era were not loose with words behind the sacred desk. Their preaching was not verbose, but it was vicious. It was what Dr. Sandy Ray called, "fierce preaching".

John's mode of consecration inevitably contributed to the fierceness by which he spoke. His days of solitude and seclusion, periods of fasting and consecration as well as total devotion to a ministry that was immaterial, garbed in rugged wear and nurtured by locusts in the wild were preludes to prophetic power. To maintain a prophetic voice, the preacher must have a consecration that transcends human weakness. When a preacher has consecrated encounters with God, most people believe he should come out of that encounter less sinful. Little do they know that the very opposite is true. When we have consecrated encounters with God, we recognize how sinful we are, and that's exactly where God wants us (Isaiah 6:5).

John was a preacher who maintained consecration to God in ways that heightened his sensitivity to any patterns of intimacy with Jesus that had been broken. When there was a break in John's intimacy, he sought for the break to be mended immediately. If John was not successful in His connection to Christ, he was even bold enough to question if he should look for another Jesus (Matthew 11:3). When John requested another Jesus, it was not that he questioned the *real* Jesus. John's doubt stemmed from being acquainted with sweet communion with Christ. Because he was in prison, he lost that sweetness with his Savior, and it was unlike the Christ he knew to not confirm their communion. John did not want vindication. He just wanted Christ to pay him a visit. Thus, Christ immediately responded when John was interrogating from prison (Matthew 11:4). The Christ who John knew would not ignore the distance prison bars established within their devotion. He was not questioning Jesus as much as he was questioning what was happening in the free world. All he heard were rumors of Christ healing the sick, giving sight to the blind, and blessing others while he was buffeted. To him, that was foreign to the Christ he knew. The Jesus who John knew would not ignore his work or worship.

Consequently, Jesus confirms John's persecution and preaching and leaves him to die in his cell. From that point on, John never raised another question about Jesus or jail. While in prison, all John wanted was communion with the Lord and confirmation from the Lord. Once he received both, it did not matter to him if he was dead or alive. As long as he was a prisoner of Christ, he knew he could die a free man in a celebrated cell.

Similarly, what a pastor really needs is communion and confirmation that the Lord is sanctioning his sermons and service, even if he is in a context of solitary confinement. Our freedom is in Christ and not in the breaking of our chains. Therefore, chained men are champions. As I listened to Sandy Ray's sermons, I gleaned it far better to be in a consecrated confinement than an unsanctioned freedom. Adverse circumstances we face can become an illusion of abandonment by Christ and tempt us to look for another Christ-like option. Of course, looking for another Jesus is too obvious to admit. Instead, our consciences are at ease if we simply refer to it as establishing a new brand of ministry, developing new methods for ministry, adjusting our ministry style, reinventing ourselves, recovering our relevance, or looking for greener pastures. If we adopt a brand of preaching that becomes disenfranchised with the jungle or jail, we may attract to urban life and lose our rural edge.

When we preach the Historical Jesus, Christ's methods of staying connected to us are not always predictable and identifiable. Often, we may feel deserted when we see little results of Jesus' approval in our preaching and pastoring. It is during those times that we must resist perusing the environment of our peers. If we look too long with a sense of abandonment, we may see the success of our contemporaries and hear reports of Jesus' power in miraculous dimensions in their ministries but fail to see the impact of our own. Then, we must avoid being critics of our contemporaries when we feel threatened by the paradox of preaching. The paradox of preaching is perceived when we give our best, and it appears our best was not good enough, especially when we see Kingdom breakthrough in the lives of those who exert minimal or no effort.

If a preacher fails to be the guardian of his own prison cell, he will pick the lock and free himself from the blessings of ministerial misery. One of the greatest disillusionments a pastor can face is what he believes when he is behind bars. Our paradigm and perspective of ministry can shift when we are constricted to a confined calling and muzzled ministry. With a prophetic voice, there will be restrictions placed upon us, but such restrictions are redemptive (Romans 8:36).

A pastor must never fail to see the hand of God in his own life, and he must also avoid the sins of comparisons and criticism. We all have unique contexts to which God calls us. In times of apparent abandonment, we may interrogate if the Christ we see others benefit from is the Christ we prophetically proclaimed. It is not jealousy that is always our jeopardy. We do not always detest what another preacher has. We just want what God has for us. Because we find ourselves in solitary seasons of silence, we can become critical and bitter towards others who are boldly breaking into Kingdom possibilities while we are shackled by a sanctified suffering we fail to embrace. Thus, we must avoid looking for a new Jesus.

New and improved ministries must never be birthed from the womb of disenfranchisement with the old. That is an oxymoron for a God-called preacher. If God calls us to an assignment, it is never a mistake. On the contrary, it is a ministry. We are to receive our assignment from God and continue in that assignment under any given context we find ourselves unless God tells us to shake the dust of that assignment off our feet (Matthew 10:14). Our ministries should be constant and not in a continual state of flux. A God-called preacher ought to have a standardized way of doing ministry that transcends any prison he finds himself in. If we have a milky version of ministry developed out of disenfranchisement with the mandate for repentance, people will never have anything to spiritually eat or drink (John 6:35).

When God calls us to ministry, there is no other way than the way He called us to walk. Because Jesus is the Way, the road we tread will lead to us take penitentiary chances. Ministry is tough on all levels. If it is a God-called ministry, it is a jungle or jail. Regardless of how sparkling or successful other's ministries may look, every God-called ministry is full of trees and traps. Ministry is a wilderness, and beasts accompany every blessing. Our fellow brothers with mega-ministries battle mega-monsters. Pastors with smaller churches do not have simple assignments either. Pastors with smaller God-called assignments must battle small foxes that can destroy the vine (Song of Solomon 2:15). In smaller ministries, everything counts, and everyone is noticed. Nothing can go hidden behind the masses and mistakes can rarely be made because they will go obviously noticed.

We respect the fact that there is no room to envy or criticize the critical ministry impact another received from Christ. When John deferred to his disciples, he did not ask if *he* should look for another, but he asked: "Should *we* look for another?" John's individual perplexity gave him a false sense of fraternity. Because things were appearing to go wrong for John, he began to assume responsibility to shake the source of his contemporaries' joy. Misery loves company. John had misery, but he had no company. When the power of God flows into other geographical dimensions, it is also possible to become demographic critics of others' cures. Sometimes, others' successes are a matter of demographics. People who experienced Kingdom breakthrough in John's day happened to be at the right place at the right time. In other words, it was their season. When we lose sweet communion and confirmation of our ministries, we can miss our season. When some preachers are in a dungeon, in Jesus' eyes, they are living out their dream. Sometimes, God places us in winter seasons and trusts us to still serve Him when our jail-calling gets cold. If we miss our season, it can become us against stormy weather. Mother Nature will always win.

Since my cousin (J. C. Wade III) entered his rest to be with the Lord, I committed to communicate with his sister and my cousin, Camellia Wade-McKinley as often as possible. One Saturday morning, we were talking about churches in Dallas, Texas versus churches in my surrounding areas (Los Angeles and Ventura County, California). I was in awe at the growth of churches in the Dallas, Fort Worth metroplex since I was there as a young lad (I was born and raised in Dallas). I asked Camellia what she believed was one of the contributing factors of growth in that area. She simply said, "People are coming here from all over the nation." Sometimes, it is a demographic deliverance.

But what does a pastor do when God detains him in a demographic dungeon? In all fairness to *The Baptist* (John), he experienced a sudden shift in his demographic with no warning from Christ. Instantly, he went from the jungle to jail, wood to iron, trees to tribulation, consecration to confinement, and from preaching to prison. He went from being accepted by Christ to being arrested because of Christ. He was detained from all sides instantaneously and simultaneously. There was no way he could see it coming. He was top-sided, turned upside down, side-swiped, and bottomed-up in an instant. When persecution strikes, it reverses your spiritual compass, and you no longer know where you are until you find your center in Christ.

Persecution is not only in terms of losing our lives for Christ. In our western culture, we may rarely afford that rich privilege. In America, persecution occurs more on social, political, religious, psychological, prophetic, and demographic levels for pastors who committed to clearing their throats and telling it like it is. There is a type of psycho-social rejection that comes to pastors in our western culture who are committed to preaching Truth. Preachers with *voice* are the soundest preachers who Christians and this world could ever hear. Yet, it appears most are not paying attention to what these profound preachers are saying. With this type of persecution, a preacher's moral compass can be thrown off-kilter. He never sees it coming, even if he knows it is coming. The next thing he knows, his prophetic demographic has been disrupted, and he becomes an island due to social and even church isolation.

John was dizzied by his distress and was not thinking thoroughly. The most talented prophet in the whole world (other than Jesus) was being redlined and tormented. Religious hypocrites are deadly threats to God-called preachers. Who can blame John for raising some serious questions regarding his Redeemer? He went from the forerunner to the backburner because of the hypocrisy of King Herod. John was born before Jesus, and he came to discover he would soon die before Jesus. The beauty John later discovered was that it did not matter what position he was in while in the womb of his mother. All that mattered was the fact that he was in the womb of God's will. He was always first in the eyes of Jesus, even if he was moved to the back of the line of the chain gang. Later, John was going to see that his demographic had to shift to the back of the Kingdom line for a procession of Kingdom power to advance in violent (aggressive and forceful) possibilities (Matthew 11:12). At the end of the day, it really does not matter where God places us along the Kingdom line. The fact that we are on that line is all that matters. When we hold down the line, God will hold us down, and regardless of what naysayers say or do, if we could just get to the pulpit, we punish evil by preaching the Gospel of the Kingdom of God.

Sometimes, being in the back of the line is a position of transition and not tragedy. Many pastors will be encouraged to know transitional triumphs. God was repositioning John to be the transitional axis that would evolve the Old into the New. Unfortunately, so much of the prophetic voice has been stifled in our contexts that the concept of repositioning has been erroneously equated with moving to greener pastures. More accurately, redemptive repositioning involves God moving us to parched pastures. Sometimes, repositioning puts us in the back of the line to be more of a supportive agent that blazes the trail for someone else.

Our demographic can shift at any moment. God positions us where we will be most effective and needed. When Satan and his demons shift to different regions, God moves at least one preacher there to stand against them. The storybook of our ministries has nothing to do with a happy ending, but it has everything to do with us ending happily (Acts 29:24).

Our power comes from preaching behind pulpits that are God-sanctioned. The moment we preach behind an unsanctioned pulpit, we lose vocal power. When we lose our voice, we can no longer be heard. Then, we are nothing but a sounding brass and tinkling cymbal. *It does not matter where you stand to preach if God licensed you to preach where you stand.* You can be behind one of the most wilderness-like pulpits and still be heard in the city. On the other hand, it is possible to be behind some prosperity-pulpit God did not sanction and preach in a way that our words will not travel any further than the praise of our peers. If so, the only rewards we will receive is a paycheck, a plaque, popularity, and a pat on the back. Neither of those last exceedingly long. When you are on the line, in line, and in alignment with what God called you to do, you are standing on a long line. As a matter of fact, that line is eternal and leads straight to Heaven. If a preacher holds down the line, God will ensure he is heard because he has something to say. J. C. Wade, Sr. had a saying: *"If you have the goods and live in the woods, the world will make a beaten path to your door."*

Every pastor is not called to do the same thing the other pastor is doing. Every house on the pastoral block does not have to look like the other unless we are trying to keep up with the pastoral Joneses. It is vital for us to discern victory in our shame. John failed to realize his shame brought about his contemporaries' boldness and joy (Matthew 11:12). The prophetic power we may possess is not always for our benefit, but it is for the corporate advancement of our prophetic partners and God's Kingdom enterprise

(Matthew 11:4-5). It is when we feel least effective that we often do our best work.

In prison, John needed to realize how much Jesus could trust him with traps. His scandal was God-approved suffering that would eventually cost him his head. When a pastor chooses to be faithful, from that point on, his ministry becomes headless. In other words, he no longer has the right to make his own decisions regarding where and how he is to do ministry, and he no longer has the authority to choose his dying destiny.

Many pastors refuse to live above their level. They chose a lifestyle that compliments their ministry instead of a ministry that compliments their lifestyles. These men have the voices in the wilderness that all would be wise to hear. They are cut from a different cloth. Their cloth is a wilderness cloth. Their messages are convicting, and they give the repentant listener joy because these types of preachers refuse to discriminate. Their preaching is not prejudicial because it convicts their friends as well as their enemies (Proverbs 27:6). The greatest favor that one can give a friend is the truth. They realize that no one is above the law of repentance. Yet, they are also comforting to those who are open to a change of mind.

Because many pastors have chosen a prophetic posture, the promises of God do not have to be applied in their lives on the dimensions they prophetically proclaim them. God directs us to do His will and not ours or anyone else's will. It is never about us. Sometimes, the reward for being called is simply in having the privilege of operating in that calling. If Jesus is not bothered by our buffetings, we should not be bothered. If our outward freedom is His focus, we will experience a shaking in our cell that swings prison doors wide open. If anything happens in our lives that is so oppressive that it disturbs God, He will pull us out or give us the grace to stay in. In no way did John's misery alter Jesus' mission.

Jesus just kept healing those outside of John's prison bars because John provided a clear path for Jesus to travel to bring the tormented into triumph.

If others are delivered, what difference does it make if we are detained? An entire community can have high regard for our ministries without stepping one foot into our churches. Many pastors blessed my ministry beyond description who do not even know my name. We understand that people do not have to be members of our ministries to get our message. When we embrace vices that accompany victory for the sake of the Gospel, we are uniquely heard from the jurisdiction of our jungles. Our lives must be a voice as well as our words. What John did not know was that his preaching did not pause when he was in prison. It continually propelled. His ethics echoed. His life was a sermon in and of itself. He spent the rest of his life in prison. What a way to preach! What a way to end a ministry!

Thus, some pastors have the tremendous responsibility to turn themselves in. They are required to surrender freedoms in ministry others spend their lives trying to protect. Prophetic pastors are not as concerned about their reputation as much as they are about embracing repercussions that come from reaching the violent consciences of the unrepentant. Decades later, I believe that is a sample of what Dr. Sandy Ray was trying to get us younger preachers to understand. He was trying to teach us about the blessing of turning ourselves in. We are called to be prisoners of preaching. When we are prisoners of the Gospel, no jail on Earth can contain us, even if we lose our heads in that same cell.

Three powerful words speak loudly in my conscience: *John was beheaded.* Those three words deepen me to what real preaching is about. It sobers me to see how available our Lord will allow our necks to be on church chopping blocks. It shows me that God is more concerned about His glory than our gloom. It also deepens my understanding of the delicacy of our profession and the violence of those who refuse to repent of their own vices. Preaching and pastoring are delicate callings. A preacher can be ahead today and headless tomorrow. The beheading of John reminds me that we are pilgrims, a noble death should always be our desire, and there are repercussions for preaching the right way. Jail is not only for the guilty. Jail is also for the just. The unrepentant have a way of convicting the Christ who convicts them. Sooner or later, those who preach Christ will convict and paradoxically become the convicted.

If there is such a word as success, ***the pastor's success is within the context of what he loses and not in what he gains*** (Philippians 3:8). It is Jesus who can change minds and not freedom from cells that hold good men down. If Jesus broke the chains and set us free, that would prove little to the unrepentant. For the pastor, deliverance is seldom within an open door. Deliverance is often behind bars (Acts 16:28). Deliverance happens more from within. God is more interested in the release of the Gospel message than the release of the Gospel messenger. God-called preachers are under warrants of arrest by the gods of this world, but Truth marches on. The preacher's goal is to guarantee the Gospel prospers more than he prospers. The Gospel should always have more in its account than we do in ours (I Corinthians 9:23).

Jesus never justified those who suffered in His name by granting entrance into a material kingdom. When Jesus and John walked, they walked on grounds confiscated by the Roman Empire. Every Jewish citizen had to pay tribute to Caesar. Jesus had no intention of altering that reality during His earthly ministry. As a matter of fact, the Jews paid a high price when they revolted against Rome. Although the Jews wanted a material Messiah, Jesus' Kingdom is not of this world (John 18:36). The repeated questioning of the disciples of when He was going to overthrow Caesar teaches us that human might is a non-essential in the Kingdom of God.

Whenever a preacher has a prophetic voice, he will always be judged as one who is guilty of someone else's charges. As a matter of fact, his head may even be placed upon a charger (Matthew 14:8-11). When we have spent years in wilderness ministry, there will always be some beast in our wilderness wanderings who seeks to exalt us above measure. They are also in the audience who will put us on pedestals we never deserved. We will always be harassed by *hyena-like* hypocrites. Furthermore, we will always attract a line of fake friends and real foes who never visited us when we were in a justified jail.

Jesus' call for John to submit to the Kingdom of God entailed submitting to a mock trial under the government of Herod. Jesus was sure to send word back to John that he was in alignment with God although he was afflicted. This prophetic therapy Jesus administered seemed to be enough for John to free his chained soul. The pastor who is perplexed by pastoral prisons does not need a free ministry. He needs a bound one.

A key form of freedom a pastor needs is freedom of conscience. With freedom of conscience, we can wake up every morning, look at ourselves in the mirror, and not be ashamed of our Master, ministries, or our manhood. We can also be at peace, knowing what we gained, we gained through repentance. When a pastor has freedom of conscience, he is not afraid to confront a comfortable crowd, and it does not matter to him if they stay or go. He refuses to fall into the pitfalls of psychologically managing a mob. Contrarily, he is preaching to champion change. He is protecting his voice. He is not preaching to keep them or save his neck. He is preaching to keep his standing with God by putting his neck on the line for God. If he loses his head, it is sovereignly removed by a sanctioned sword.

If God moves the pastor to another assignment, the pastor must never lose the voice he developed in the wilderness when he did not have a decent mic or audience. Make no mistake about it, our best preaching is in the wilderness and not on mountaintops. Even an infant can shout from the mountaintops and be heard, but only a preacher with *voice* can thunder from the thickets.

How does a pastor know when it is time to move to another assignment? Of course, it is a given to exclaim, "When God says so." More practically, how does a pastor *really* know it is time to move? **One of the major signs that it is time for a pastor to move to another assignment is when he has become content in his vexation.** Before Lot was removed from Sodom and Gomorrah, he stood at the gate as a civil leader of God's people. Before the destruction of the twin cities, the people would not adhere to Lot's counsel on daily affairs and denounce their immoral lifestyles. Consequently, the soul of Lot became vexed by the indifference of God's people to God's laws for civil obedience. Lot lingered in Sodom when the angels of the Lord were seeking to pull him out (Genesis 19:16). The angels literally had to drag Lot out of Sodom despite his vexation of soul with the Sodomites. Although the inhabitants were practicing abominations, Lot was becoming content although he was vexed. We can learn from this lesson how God must drag some of us out of abominable assignments.

If a pastor has a holy dissatisfaction that refuses to become content with his vexation, that is more than enough reason for him to stay planted and not move unless God moves him. If we become content in vexation, we will eventually stop preaching on peak levels because we lost hope of any signs of change that will take place. Unfortunately, we are in a context of ministry in which we must accept the fact that some people will never change. For that reason alone, fierce preachers who are likened unto sons of Sandy Ray will discover they are chosen to be chained. When we are in the context of an unchanging generation, there is no such thing as a standstill sermon. We preach on. If God wants to move us, we must be willing to uproot and change locations of leadership. If not, God may eject us out. Not every pastor reassigned to a more fertile ministry wanted to go, but after God ejected him, he was glad God did.

Nevertheless, the context of this chapter is for pastors called to death row. Although there are rarely conventions, workshops, or conferences on the success of headless pastors, a pastor who is called to die in a ministerial prison is just as noble as one who has been set free. I am humbled by the great men of God (even in my lifetime), who remained just in their jungles. The humble beginnings and endings of their lives no longer perplexes but consoles me. I was too young to fully appreciate J. C. Wade, Sr. in his preaching prime. As a boy, all I can remember is the explosive dynamic that exuded through his preaching when I heard him preach. I had the opportunity to experience more closely who he was in his sunset years when his health began to deteriorate as I spent quality and quantity time with him. I observed the way that he lived the rest of his life in a celebrated cell.

I was too young to see the days when Pastor Donald Gardner was renowned for his radio broadcasts as his sermons went throughout the air waves of Los Angeles. However, I had the opportunity to care for him during his illness and hear what he learned when God took him through refining fires in his later years. Most saw him when he preached. I saw him when he was purged. Pastor Gardner not only taught me what to do, but he also taught me what not to do. He taught me how to avoid disqualification. He taught me not to blow smoke in God's face. Although he was a great preacher, God made sure that he became a greater person.

Both spent their sunset years in a wheelchair, but they had an unusual peace. I can say the same about Pastors Charles Dews and

Earnest Estell, Jr., the deceased husband of my cousin Dorothy Estell, and son of the great preacher and theologian, Earnest Estell, Sr. of whom the library of Bishop College was named after. I spent time with them when their bodies grew weak and weary. I even remember reading many sermons of Earnest Estell, Jr. when I would visit he and his dear wife, Dorothy Estell. He handwrote his sermons in the most beautiful calligraphy I had ever seen. Yet, what these men exuded from wheelchairs and sickbeds far outweighed what they accomplished in front of an appreciative audience. When I see how great men of God spent the last days of their ministries in humble endings like convalescent homes, ICU's, wheel-chairs, or sickbeds, it reminds me that **God will sacrifice the man on the altar of the message**.

Previously, John only knew of worship that comes through the wilderness. In the wilderness, John knew much of self-sacrifice, but in prison, he was going to become a sacrifice. In the jungle, John upheld a truth that had not crystallized until he experienced the depths of divine detainment. In the jungle, he was still free, but in jail, his privileges were stripped. Wild locusts and honey were delicacies compared to the flesh he was soon to eat and the blood he was sure to drink (Matthew 20:22; John 6:56). Human nature has never been a master of solitary confinement. There is something about *going in the hole* that plays tricks on a man's mind. From the wilderness, John prophetically proclaimed a truth that was heavier than he realized. This same principle was to be interpreted in prison to explain why the Kingdom was advancing and the bold were breaking into its possibilities while there were no possibilities for John's release. Ironically, John happened to be the boldest of them all.

The prophetic voice is crucial when it comes to leaving a legacy behind because very few appreciate preachers with *voice* in their lifetimes. One of the greatest concerns a pastor may have is that most of what he stood for will be quickly forgotten, forged, or forfeited. Preaching is usually the main reason why a preacher is persecuted unless he preaches another gospel. The unrepentant usually judge the preacher when it is convenient. If he does not say anything that convicts, he will not become their convict. We are concerned with leaving memorial stones behind for our children, grandchildren, churches, younger preachers, and the broad spectrum of people who God graciously allowed within hearing distance of our wilderness wanderings and justified jungles. When it comes to leaving a legacy, many things can be decapitated other than our heads. Our sermons can be lost, our writings can be stolen, our degrees can be shredded, our wills (inheritances) can be squandered, our programs can be vetoed, our churches can be bewitched, our buildings can be sold, our characters can be assassinated, but our prophetic voices will forever be heard.

Regardless of our human frailty, deep inside, they know a preacher with voice preached from a prophetic realm. Sometimes, that is the real reason for a preacher's decapitation. It is often because when he mounted the pulpit, he held his head up high and preached like a man. He was one of the *real preachers*. Although Herod took John's head, he could not get John's voice out of his head. Real preaching cannot entail user-friendly and seeker-sensitive adjustments to make preaching palatable to people who want to be pacified instead of purged. Fortunately, Jesus never intended on being attractive to any. If that were the case, He never would have taken on the robe of human flesh and become a suffering servant, beaten to unrecognition. When you genuinely love someone, there are times when you must get ugly to help them. Love requires a type of ugliness. Love requires taking a beating for the ones who God's heart bleeds for. The closer Jesus got to the Cross, the uglier He became to save us. He had to get ugly. He had to apologize to God for something He did not do. He knew no sin, but He became sin to save wretches like us. Real love is not pretty, and neither is real preaching.

Thus, the beauty of Jesus is seen amid our ugliness. Jesus has not called us to pretty ministries, and He has not called us to handsome ones. John had an ugly ministry. Real ministry gets bloody and gory. If a pastor does not have a good grip on God, real ministry can send him into his own private psychiatric ward. John's ministry ended in a bloody way. He lost His head. I cannot think of anyone in the Bible who had a good-looking ministry, only a God-looking one. If we are building people before buildings and preaching repentance instead of being relentless to be relevant, our ministries will be full of blood. There can be no life without blood. Ministry may be attractive in the beginning, but when the honeymoon is over, it gets gloomier and gorier. There are no such things as *golden years* when it comes to the call of God if a preacher has a prophetic voice. If he has something to say that will challenge arrogant attitudes and assumptions, his calling will call for casualties.

When we start a ministry by making user-friendly adjustments, that is how we will end. It is like make-up. Once you put it on to look pretty, you must keep putting it on. When we make-up our ministries, we will become unattractive to God as well as to the faithful followers of God. Furthermore, we lose noble disciples in the process of gaining nominal ones.

Preaching is hard work, but so is listening. The unrepentant struggle with hearing. They can talk all day, but according to them, the preacher preaches too long. We minister in an age in which people are feeling more and more entitled. People who feel entitled are not good listeners because all they have is themselves on their mind. Jesus was only cherished by those who placed value on their need for a change of mind that only He could give. If people who consider themselves Christians cannot get accustomed to conviction of their own sins and the many ways Jesus challenges their choices, they will look for another Christ-like option by creating their own Christ and ministry that confirms instead of convicts them.

Consequently, the unrepentant switch churches like they visit shopping malls, and they change pastors faster than they would change doctors. They will worship a weak-backed pastor who aligns with their whims, but they will try to break the back of a pastor who loves them enough to tell them the truth about themselves. If they cannot get what they are shopping for, they go somewhere else and pay whatever price it takes to get what they want. Accepting personal conviction as a Christian must become a lifestyle. There is a strong fallacy in the preaching circuit today in which many are avoiding preaching and hearing convicting sermons. God only convicts us because He loves us enough to tell us the truth about ourselves. This may be an elementary truth for some, but for most, it is a hard lesson to learn.

There are lessons learned from Herod's guilty conscience. *Prophetic Voice* affects the conscience and soul, which is far deeper than cognitive elements of memory. It is not a one-way issue. A preacher must never be afraid to *cut it straight*. People who curse conviction cannot face who they really are on the inside. Their conscience reminds them of that so much that it can become seared. As in John's day, they perceive the only way to rid their guilty conscience is to execute the one who reminds them of their own guilt. Herod felt the only way to remove his guilt was to get rid of John. Little did he know, when he instituted John's beheading, his guilty conscience swelled even more. After John was beheaded, Herod and all within his constituency suffered from swollen guilt. Assassinating a preacher is unlike any other assassination. When a preacher dies by the hands of hypocrites, the very same assassins wake up the rest of their mornings facing a God who will never grant them peace. Their lives are restless and reckless from that day until their dying day.

Preachers who lose their heads by the swords of people who are held captive to hypocrisy must have their heads on straight before they lose them. They must never succumb to the lie that they are at fault for preaching. *A preacher must preach until he dies and not die by refusing to preach* (I Corinthians 9:16). When a preacher is consecrated to that truth, I can at least promise one thing: He will not reach his dying day until he preached his last sermon. If he is executed, it is only because he has nothing left to say. He said enough. He has preached his way Home.

For some pastors, they must give their entire lives to the point of death before the consciences of those they lead come alive. Such noblemen are exemplifying the cost of discipleship by their poise as well as their preaching. Whatever, the case, we must avoid the aggressive trend of pastoring that has learned how to escape the prisons of preaching and pastoring. Pastors with *voice* embrace execution to avoid an uncanny way of juking jail. When Christ confines, He sometimes waives our visitation rights.

There is a strange contentment in being in a consecrated confinement, and there is a strange dissatisfaction in being in a compromising freedom. When a preacher has embraced his execution, the jail floor he sleeps on that was once concrete and cold becomes soft and warm. If his jail sentence is long enough, he becomes conditioned to abuse while refusing to be a glutton for punishment. After a preacher is in the fire for long, it no longer burns. Preachers are not called to dodge distress or trump trouble, but they are called to welcome it (II Corinthians 4:8-12).

I cannot imagine how humbling it must have been for John to prepare the bloody red carpet for Jesus and be the first to bleed. Usually, our contemporaries surround us with love when they come to know our hardships. We (preachers) are brothers, and brothers do not always like to show weak sides to one another. Yet, what enemies of the preaching fraternity fail to realize is the fact that when one preacher suffers, we all suffer. When we hear our preaching brother is in the fire, we get in the furnace with him. If we do not get in the fire with him, one thing we will never do is fan his flame. Any preaching brother who does not burn with his brother or at least hand him a cloak is a half-brother to the *true-blood* of preachers (II Timothy 4:13). Some preachers are not cut from a wilderness cloth who save their own skin, and there are others who are not accustomed to cold callings who put more coal on another preacher's fire. For the rest, we do not care how a preacher got caught in the snares of the unrepentant. All we care about is that Jesus catches him when he falls.

Recently, the Los Angeles Lakers lost a game against the Brooklyn Nets. After the loss, a little girl asked LeBron James for a selfie photo. To show you the type of man he is, he politely stopped, grabbed her cell phone, smiled in the camera, and snapped a photo with the girl. James Worthy (retired Los Angeles Laker *Hall of Famer*) made the comment, "LeBron James is the kind of man who still understands who he is, even after a loss. He realized that although he lost, she was still his fan."

Jesus wanted John to realize that although John was suffering great loss, he needed to be reminded who Jesus said he was and that there were, are, and will be many who will still be his loyal fans. Christians cannot be a friend of Christ if they are enemies of John. Many want neither John nor Jesus. John is too strict for some, and Jesus is too welcoming toward sinners for others. Jesus taught us of the Parable of the Brats. According to Jesus, some people are liked spoiled children in the marketplace who are crying because no one dances to their music. For them, either Christianity is too challenging, or it extends too much grace to people who they believe don't deserve it (Matthew 11:16-17).

Whatever a preacher loses, he must still be comforted by who God says he is, and there will be many who will forever be loyal fans. We can never forget Dr. Sandy Ray. I am his fan. He was the Hank Aaron of the Black preaching league. His preaching was too profound to delete from my conscience. His voice was too strong for me not to submit to his substance. Those who heard him can say that his sermons are still sounding in their souls. If you never heard him preach, Google him. He was a contemporary of J. C. Wade, Sr., Gardner Taylor, and many more of that era. He was a strong preacher, a straight preacher, and a sound preacher. He taught us to preach fiercely and fearlessly.

When we keep consecration to Christ in the context of our calling, no matter what happens to us from the hands of the hypocritical who are likened unto Herod's descendants, those who matter most will forever remember the *Spirit* from which we spoke, the *Power* by which we flowed, and the *Throne* to which we bowed. That alone is enough to serve anyone's conscience.

Chapter 6

THE PASTOR AND HIS SHOULDERS

∞

Bearers of Burdens
(An Excerpt from the Life of Habakkuk:
A preacher who felt God was against him)

<u>Tribute</u>: To my cousin whom I affectionately call, "Uncle Mel"; Melvin Von Wade, Sr. (Pastor Emeritus, Mt. Moriah Baptist Church of Los Angeles, CA)

"*Thank you, Sir. I am doing my best to be the best me I can be." This was the response of M. V. Wade, Sr. when I applauded him for being in a class all by himself. As my pastoral trainer, on the first day of my assignment to be his Assistant, he made three statements he wanted me to remember: "Son, first of all, I want you to know that I love you. Secondly, Satan wants to get you to a place where you can no longer hear your pastor's voice. Thirdly, I will never tell you anything wrong." There are not too many Sundays that go by that I do not mention Pastor Wade to my church. I can still hear his voice. I hear it louder as I grow older in ministry. M. V. Wade, Sr. is a classy, charismatic, and careful leader. Many were not afforded the privilege of knowing what it takes to be M. V. Wade, Sr. from Monday through Friday from 9 am-5 pm (my office hours when I served as his Assistant).* He has unusually strong shoulders, an uncanny way of shouldering evil, and he is a strategist in advising preachers about the art of shouldering adversarial assignments. In the secular world, "Take the high road" refers to taking the most ethical road to handle any given challenge. In the spiritual world, the same ideology can be referred to as, "The Low Road". The Low Road is the road of humility. Melvin V. Wade's most memorable motif is from his basic premise: "The Low Road always wins."

Little is known of Habakkuk's history. "Habakkuk" means, *to embrace* or *to comfort* as one does a weeping child. The name also has the connotation of quieting, with a calm assurance that with God's power, things will get better. The time of Habakkuk's ministry has suffered differences of opinion. Probably, his ministry was immediately preceding the Babylonian captivity, which would make him a contemporary of Jeremiah. The book of Habakkuk is unique in the fact that it portrays his experience of soul as he wrestles with the silence of God. The pastor must be conditioned to withstand loud evils amidst God's sovereign silence. God has a way of going silent when He chastises the sin of indifference. The sin of indifference is committed when we as God's people develop a distant concern for our spiritual condition.

I learned this lesson most through the death of my mother. Innumerable evils surrounded her death. The entire process of planning and preaching her funeral was a complete nightmare for me and my father. He grieved one way, and I grieved another. All I could do was watch a succession of evils occur that I had no power to control. God caused me to watch unexplainable terror throughout that entire ordeal. The passage God gave me was from Habakkuk 3:7. The title of my message when I preached her eulogy was, <u>The Discipline of Losing Everything</u>. As a young preacher during that time, I do not know how well I got the message across to the congregation, but God got the message across to me.

Often, the nature of the seed we sow in our fields of ministry does not appear as though it is producing a harvest resembling the nature of our planting. Our vineyards are unlike any other when it comes to ministry. A pastor's field of ministry is comparable to unpredictable plants. Although the law of sowing and reaping has its place, when it comes to God's sovereignty, the pastor can plant spiritual seeds and reap a harvest of wild grapes. Every God-called preacher will die scratching his head about something God allowed that he will not understand until he meets God face-to-face. No pastor is immune to the burden of unpredictable evils and God's controversial moves. We never know the fierceness of evil other pastors must contend with. One pastor's explosive growth may be his demon while it is another's dream. I can never recall a time when I assumed how wonderful it would be if I were in certain pastors' shoes when God didn't allow me to see an evil they bore that I never would have wanted to bear. Among my many sins, jealousy was never one of them. It was more of an admiration that I had for these wonderful men. Yet, God allowed me to learn a shouldering lesson: *Every ministry shoulders some type of misery.*

In ministry, it can be hard to accept fig trees that do not blossom, olives that fail, and fields that yield no meat (Habakkuk 3:17). Because most of what we do in ministry is intentional, our work is strategically implemented because we are seeking to accomplish fruitful results. I cannot think of any pastor who deep in his heart does not want to see his ministry grow in some capacity. Rarely do we preach to reap a wild harvest from seeds of indifference. When there are no fruitful vines, a unique form of bitterness, moral failure, stressful diseases, hidden anger, or discouragement can surface.

The Pastor and His Anatomy

I recall talking to Pastor M. V. Wade, Sr. months before his retirement. As he recalled previous tenures as Pastor, I asked him which church he had the most difficulty pastoring. According to him, the trouble he experienced at his first church prepared him for his second church. Then, the trouble he experienced at his second church prepared him for his last church. His following words landed on my shoulders: *"I guess you can say that each church I pastored was a succession of elevated trouble."* In no way does this demean the churches he pastored. He was speaking of the fact that when it comes to pastoring, shouldering evils had an elevated effect. Wherever a pastor goes, according to Uncle Melvin's own words, "If you preach Jesus, there will always be trouble."

I recall coming to Pastor Wade's office when I worked for him. He preached an awesome message one Sunday morning. On the following Monday, papers were all over his desk. He never said anything to me, but I could tell that his shoulders were sore. I could almost feel the weight. I asked him what I could do to help him bear some of the burden. He simply said, "Son, we need to build your muscles first." Ministry requires muscle, a whole lot of muscle. Muscle is built through God-induced pressure.

Unfortunately, I did not have that kind of shoulder strength when I pastored my first church. Yet, I at least had the strength to invite M. V. Wade, Sr.'s father and my uncle (James Commodore Wade, Sr.) to be my guest preacher. His shoulders had been tested, tried, and were true. I did so to get a feel of the type of church I was pastoring. I knew James Commodore Wade, Sr. would also know. After preaching, he said to the church, "Derrick is a good boy. I knew him when he was in diapers. He does not know what he is doing. He has only been a pastor for a few days, but he is a good boy. This is his first church. Be patient with him. You can either make him or break him." Suddenly, he shouted in merciful, pleading agony, "Don't kill him!" When he said that, the church was as silent as sleeping wolves, and I was as terrified as a lamb in the middle of their den hoping they would not wake up anytime soon. I could sense the wolfpack, but I could not see them. Some were wolves, but most were lambs. I had no fear of the people, but I feared the God in "Daddy Wade." To see a man with such broad shoulders beg a church to not kill a boy-pastor really sobered me to my assignment. It showed me how *burdensome* pastoring can be. Then, tears rolled down his eyes as he said to the congregation, "It's a shame that for many churches, it takes seven preachers to die before the next one can live." Why he chose the number seven, I do not know, but ironically, I was around pastor number six. I at least heard two things from what he said. I heard that no matter what I did, there was a strong sense in which my shoulders were at their mercy. I also heard that I did not know what I was doing. From that point on, I never purposed in my heart to ruffle anybody's feathers although I did. If I were to ever travel the road to pastoring that church successfully, *The Low Road* M. V. Wade, Sr. taught me was the way to get there.

There is a thin line between doing what you know is right and shouldering what you know is wrong. That was just a taste of Habakkuk's frustration. Young and weak at the shoulders, I chose to do what was right instead of shoulder what was wrong. All I can give is the before and after-effects of the road that I took. If I would have shouldered the evil, 2016 would have been the year the last person of that generation died because they voted me out in 2001. For me, that would have been a fifteen-year wait if I were to have remained at that church. Because Pastor Wade knew how to shoulder difficult churches, he advised me to wait it out. He knew that day would come. I later came to understand that shouldering wrong is sometimes the right thing to do.

God has ways of pinning our heads to malignant mats in ministry. His strategy of ejecting evil and purging perversion involves trusting God when the Adversary has a God-ordained advantage. In contexts of callousness, God is not defeating us, but He is deepening our trust in Him when He makes confusing calls. Like Habakkuk, God takes us through burdensome beatings to help us develop a theology for the spirit of heaviness (Isaiah 61:3). Since Habakkuk was powerless to alter his assignment, he was confused about the conditions that constituted his context. He could not shoulder the wisdom of God in how God dealt with Israel's fiercest enemy, i.e., the Chaldeans. For Habakkuk, God was adding the weight of the Chaldeans on his shoulders without explanation. God was putting muscle in his ministry and purging the prophet and people through pounds of paradoxical pressure.

Although the Chaldeans were a heavy burden, the heaviest weight Habakkuk bore was the ancient theme of the silence of God. God's word carries a lot of weight, but His silence can be even weightier. For an extensive amount of time, God would not say anything. Instead of clarifying what He was doing, God kept everything confidential. The basic equation of God's silence in the middle of the amplified prosperity of the wicked is easily solved theoretically, but it becomes an entirely different exercise when one must deal with God's silence practically. We understand the principle of how God can produce redemptive results through divine distancing and the arrogant assumptions of the ways of the wicked. However, the dimensions of these exercises can produce total chaos within when the weight is on *our* shoulders. It is hard to do the math when the books are heavy.

What can be even more baffling is our acute ability to communicate detailed oracles of our burdens, but those who we seek counsel, companionship, or comfort from are powerless to interpret indifference. If God is silent, He will ensure that our most trusted counselors have nothing to say as well. Pastor Wade was always an advocate of not being overly analytical. He also counseled us (pastors) to not bleed on the sheep. In other words, there are some struggles the people he leads will never understand. So, he must hold his peace and not try to explain himself. One of the most underestimated practices that causes much of our defeat in ministry is the practice of not being selectively strategic in learning when to keep silent.

One of the biological traits of my earthly father is his heavy hands. Although he is not a big man, he has big and strong hands. When he disciplined me, it was never abusive, but it was heavy. He would tell me to lie down on the bed. Then, he would place one of those big hands on my back and give me controlled but heavy spankings. Each lick from his favorite leather belt came with a conversation. He would explain why he was chastising me. Our Heavenly Father's hands are big, strong, and heavy. We cannot escape them. Yet, when God chastises us, He does not always give an explanation. He just wants us to trust that once He has hurt us, He will bind up our wounds (Hosea 6:1).

At the same time, Habakkuk was making every effort to stand true to the holiness of God while under the heavy hands of God. Habakkuk understood God's holiness, but he had a hard time handling God's heaviness. Systematic Theology will teach us about the holiness of God, but divine pressure will teach us about the heaviness of God. Habakkuk even understood God's eyes. He knew early in his ministry that God's eyes were too pure to behold evil (Habakkuk 1:13). Since God's eyes were too pure to behold evil, Habakkuk could not understand why God's hands were pressing upon him, forcing him to behold evil. To Habakkuk, God's eyes and hands were at odds.

How we deal with the silence of God depends upon how many pounds God places upon our perspective. We do not really know what we think we know until God pulls the shade down on our ministries and confronts us with total blackness. Habakkuk's theology was not being stretched. It was being stripped. Habakkuk wanted to preach in a way that was adversely against the Chaldeans, but God called him to preach in a way that advanced them. Everything Habakkuk thought he knew about God was being dumped in the darkness of God's sovereignty. The burden weighs heavier when we realize what we previously preached about God is being torn down by the same God who is about to reveal a sermon of Himself we never preached before. Then, we discover that we must learn how to preach all over again. We never know what preaching is until we run out of old material. After the darkest disappointments develop, our preaching evolves, and we preach with an unusual authority like never. Before Habakkuk went through his darkest days, he never had a sermon in his past portfolio entitled, <u>The Just Shall Live by His Faith</u>.

The burden Habakkuk had to endure was one that appeared as though God would do nothing to eradicate the misery of his ministry. As the years go by in pastoral ministry, we become dissatisfied with the carnal offerings of the local church and world. We grow into a weightier understanding of human indifference as we are less impressed by the religious surface of things, especially in how the overly religious address evil.

A young excited parent with his or her firstborn may experience nothing but excitement upon the arrival of their first child while a seasoned parent will look at birth from the dual perspectives of joy and pain. For seasoned parents, their joy will derive from the child's birth, but their pain will come from knowing the unpredictable evils of life the newborn must endure as the years go by. As an old deacon at my first church would say, when our children are born, they are on our laps, but as they get older, they are on our hearts. Such is the case with pastors. As we seek to satisfy the terms of our upward call, the things of this world grow strangely dim. As we grow deeper in the ministry of dark discoveries, there is not much of the Earth, the fickleness of the local church, or our finite understanding that excites us, but there is a great deal of indifference that burdens us (Ecclesiastes 1:18). We pay sober and detailed attention to what people are doing, why they do the evil things they do, and the consequences of their conscious callousness as well as our own.

Habakkuk was paying dark attention to the troubles of his world, and he was not even close to seeing the light. He was experiencing an ever-increasing evil that was stronger than his faith. He saw prosperity the Chaldeans possessed that was increasing in power, and it was God-induced. During this observation, God said nothing and did nothing except endorse Habakkuk's enemies. Habakkuk saw every arrow that pointed to his opponent, but he could not see the arrows that pointed to his lack of faith. In a sense, Habakkuk had an earned theological degree that God was ripping to pieces. Of course, that must have been necessary because nothing Habakkuk thought he knew helped him at his most malignant moments in ministry.

What Habakkuk experienced was more than God merely using evil for His glory. Most of us can understand how God can use evil for His glory. The prophet also began to realize the flipped side of ungodly prosperity resulting in the poverty of the righteous. In a much deeper sense, what Habakkuk was wrestling with was a dark side of God he never knew existed. It is unimaginable and unfathomable to the human mind to know how far into the night God can go when it comes to His wisdom in allowing evil to wreak havoc in our lives. God's capacity to endorse evil to accomplish His plan is so exhaustive that it darkens our discernment. God can allow evils to be unleashed in our lives in ways that our best defenses cannot deflect and our best perceptions cannot pierce. Our burdens are also heavy because they cannot be removed by any human agency. For me, it was disarming to go through so many silent seasons that even an M. V. Wade, Sr. could not save me from. Thank God he had enough wisdom to not play God. He would even remind me when I asked hard questions: *"Son, I am not God. Where is your faith?"*

The problem with God's people during Habakkuk's day was that they did not know how seriously God took sin. People who casually throw sin out of their equation do not understand how powerful sin is. I am reminded of a sermon of the late L. K. Curry when he said, "As you grow older, you will be sorry you sinned against a God like this." Sin is so powerful that those who learned to respect its power do not come to quick conclusions or judgments when someone has sinned. Instead, those who understand how deep sin can be learned to keep silent. Yet, Habakkuk did care. After you fight sin in your life and the lives of those you lead for an amount of time, you grow weary.

Knowing that you are going into a deadly storm can be more terrifying than the storm itself. The sound of approaching thunder can be more terrifying than standing in the thunder. What terrified Habakkuk was the fact that the more he preached, the faster the Chaldeans were coming. Nothing he could do could withstand God's weaning weathervane. In addition, the prophet could not persuade God to cause the Chaldean storm to retreat. Instead, his preaching only accelerated the advancement of the Adversary. If a preacher preaches God's way, there are times when his preaching only accelerates an inevitable evil. God places us in the vortex of evil as we watch its swirling power in operation, blown by its effects, and affected by its blows. We must not flee because God is in the center of it all. The vortex is not always where the most danger resides. Yet, it is the most frightening force to face. It is on the outskirts of the vortex that one experiences the most destructive winds. One wrong move outside of the eye of God's will, and

The Pastor And His Shoulders

we can be flung by its force. Thus, we stand in the eye of the storm, be still, and know that He is God.

When bearing burdens, we are often in God's observatory. God sees us, but we can no longer sense Him. Then, we must learn to not walk by sight, but l*ive* by our faith. In that sense, it is truly a life or death situation. Our preaching lives depend upon it. Everything turned black in Habakkuk's ministry, but there was a blessing in blackness. God could still see him in the night. Habakkuk knew nothing of God's black blessings and *The Nocturnal God*. Unlike Moses, Habakkuk could not even see God's *back*. All he could see was God's *black side*.

What does a preacher do when God puts him on blackout? What does he do when he feels as though God is betraying his every effort? God has a way of chastising indifference by giving us and our contexts something we can feel. He puts us on adverse machines that stretch us until it hurts beyond measure and challenges our inability to comprehend the meaning of it all. Muscles do not grow until they are stretched. During the stretching process, God gives more muscle to our misery than our ministry. Our misery builds, and our ministry develops atrophy. Our enemies advance as our great expectations retreat. God gives our miseries the muscle to overpower us and break us to bare trust in God. Pastor M. V. Wade, Sr. would often say that trouble is an unwanted friend.

Faith is the advocate God gives us to bear the load. Yet, God does not give us that kind of faith directly or freely. He gives it to us darkly and at a great price. God empowers His enemies while He drains all the strength out of His friends. The problem deepens when we get to the point in which we wonder if God really cares. That is how badly God can hurt a preacher, but it is also aids a preacher in the process of more greatly appreciating a more meaningful ministry. God can hurt a preacher so badly that he can think God is against him. He can unleash malware on our ministries in a way that we feel damaged. Yet, God was destroying Habakkuk's theology but not his trust. What we know is never as important as who we know. God wants us to know enough about Him to realize that whatever He ordains or allows is for our ultimate good (Romans 8:28).

All I have attempted to communicate in my finite understanding is not even a glimpse of what Habakkuk experienced. Even if our theology goes down the drain, God is still God. Plainly put, Habakkuk thought that God was his antagonist. Although we know better, God has a sovereign way of giving us an appointment with antagonistic arrangements, and He makes sure that we show up at the meeting on time. He has a way of loosening our grips on what we hold dear in a mysterious manner. God has a way of turning our worlds upside down and our ministries inside out. It is important to always remember that our ministries are not an end in and of themselves. They are not to be placed in our pockets as our possession, and they are not predictable. In ministry, anything can happen. Our ministries simply entail people who God assigned us to help facilitate His will in their lives instead of our own.

God can break His property and put it back together again. So, some of our ministries need to be torn down before God can build them up. That is also what Pastor Wade was trying to teach me. Some churches must go down before they come up. What do you do when you realize when God called you to a ministry restricted from redemption? What do you do when the fig trees do not blossom, and the fields yield no meat? My father taught me a simple lesson in preaching. He taught me to not raise questions if I did not give answers. The answer lies in the fact that we must learn to not only walk but live by our faith. When all else dies around us, we must have a faith that leaves us standing when the smoke clears.

There may be times when every "*ology*" we had about God is overshadowed by a side of God we never knew before. It is like going to seminary, and the name of one of your courses is called *Darkology*, the study of the Dark God. To this very day, I struggle with *Darkology*. I incline to want light shed on my life and leadership. I do not have the best GPA in God's divine seminary as I take His night courses in the school of darkness. Make no mistake about it, my greatest weakness is when all my mental faculties are shredded to black trust in God. M. V. Wade, Sr. knows how I can be overly analytical. When God gives me a test on black paper, I can raise all types of questions. What color ink can I use? How can I know the answers if I cannot even see the questions? During times when I realized that I couldn't figure out one iota of what dark thing God was going to do next, I found myself most vulnerable to poor decisions, especially when I was confined to contexts of the indifference of those who only cared about themselves. Yet, forces, foes, and failure are not my greatest challenges. My greatest challenge is fear. I fear getting an "F". That "F" does not stand for failing. It stands for falling. I fear that *falling feeling* more than that failing feeling. If I fell off a high ledge in the night and could not see the bottom, I would have a proclivity to die of panic before I even hit the pavement. There were times when I turned God's black exams over, walked out of the classroom and took another course with a teacher who would talk to me. Sadly, when I did that, I always learned too much of the wrong subjects.

God does not have to talk to us to teach us. In God's class of cloudiness and subjects of silence, there are times when all we know is that it is going to get a whole lot worse before it gets better. We thank God that He takes all that we learned (even in the wrong subjects) and averages our grades because sometimes, the lesson is in learning the lesson.

It takes faith to acknowledge what we do not know. Habakkuk tried to figure it all out. He was facing a puzzle that he could not piece together. No piece of Habakkuk's theology fit with the other. Pastor Wade is an advocate of the need for young preachers and even some peers to learn the discipline of sitting still and muzzling their mouths, especially when under God's heavy yoke and in the face of evil (Psalm 46:10). We are to simply listen to God's seasonal silence during times of warring wickedness and God's terrorizing and testing tardiness.

God locked Habakkuk in a dark room. When God removes us from the room of reason, everything that everyone says on the other side of the door to comfort or counsel us sounds like slurred speech. The divine door that separates us can be so theologically thick that their sentences do not make sense. They do not have much to say because it is God who ties their tongues. When in God's darkroom, He is the only one who is truly with us. Our greatest advocates can only walk so far with us on this tedious journey. Each of us has our own beaten path we must tread. On that dark path, God wants us to have dark dialogue with Him. A dark conversation with God is one in which we keep silent. When God goes silent, we must go silent as well because the Lord is in His holy temple (Habakkuk 2:20). There is strong language communicated with silent speech.

We see many unexplainable evils as the years go by. There is a brand in the ministry market that refuses to believe that there are evils we have no control over. Whether the new brand of ministry believes it or not, most evils that occur in ministry cannot be bound, exorcised, rebuked, or removed. They must be resisted (James 4:7). However, the evil Habakkuk experienced could not even be resisted. It had to be endured.

Pastor Wade has a high tolerance for enduring evil and a long attention span. Melvin Von Wade, Sr. monitors the danger of making premature moves in ministry. Rather than rebuke, ignore, or flee evil, he pays close attention to it, waits for it, studies it, and accepts it for what it is. God has a way of placing us in the belly of evil to observe its movements, notice its power, note its inventions, suffer its attacks, and pay close attention. When we think we have seen too much, we have not seen enough. Until this point, Habakkuk has not understood God's ways as he raises questions out of agony:

> *"The burden which Habakkuk the prophet did see; Oh lord, how long shall I cry and thou wilt not hear! Even cry out unto thee of violence and thou wilt not save! Why dost thou shew me iniquity and cause me to behold grievance? For spoiling and violence are before me; and there are they that rise up strife and contention* (against us).*"*
>
> (Habakkuk 1:1-2; KJV)

Notice the fact that these are the first words of Habakkuk in the very first chapter. The burden is so heavy that Habakkuk does not have time for a salutation or some soft introduction. Habakkuk had a hard time looking at what was happening before his very eyes. Evil was raising up contention. While God was chastising His people, Habakkuk's prayers were enabling them. God was virtually saying, "Look at the damage my people caused me to deliver!" God wanted Habakkuk to detect the darkness of God's discipline. That was Habakkuk's struggle for a silent season. Habakkuk was called to a ministry of watching and *weighting*.

It is hard to bear indifference because it weighs hellish pounds. It weighs heavy on the shoulders of a preacher who cares. So many people do not care about anything or anyone but themselves, and they are not doing a great job at that either. The only pain they feel is their own. There comes a time when God is downright fed up with selfishness. God has a dark way of disposing of the sins of carelessness and callousness, especially if they are within the hearts of His people. God does a nocturnal work that demands trust in Him when everything around us is lost in silent space.

Habakkuk's struggle was compounded when he was caused to observe the chilling of the law. Dedication to sound doctrine can produce perplexing perceptions for the doctrinal preacher. It is baffling to see how the cold-hearted have a skilled way of doing away with Truth. One would expect the more qualitative the product, the greater the chances of increases in market share. Unfortunately, the best way to make a profit in the business arena is to give people what they want. Sometimes, people will spend more on vices than virtues. Any businessman knows that. Give people what they want and not what they need, and you can grow rich overnight. This must never be the case when it comes to ministry and spiritual indifference. The God-called preacher can never be approved of God if he gives people a poor quality of preaching by giving them what they want. Give people what they want, and not what they need, and we will find ourselves in a state of spiritual bankruptcy with God. Give them what they need, and many will often think it is cheap and not worth buying into. When we experience the numbness of long winter seasons, we may undergo a psychological warfare that resembles a successful entrepreneur preparing for bankruptcy. Nobody is truly buying into our Bible, and it appears that our ministries are going out of business. Sometimes, they are (II Timothy 4:3).

The old folks in our family had a saying when we as children had a bad attitude. They would say it exactly like this: "If you get an attitude with me, I will get one right along with you!" At times, God must match indifference with indifference. God's people were not the only ones who could grow cold. Not only did Habakkuk know *The Dark God*, but Habakkuk would soon know *The Winter God*. Habakkuk stood between two winters. As God's people grew cold to His ways, God grew cold right along with them. Habakkuk observed evil at work, but he also observed God's word being systematically disposed of by God's own people (Habakkuk 1:4). The pastor is not beyond Habakkuk's frustration if he is called to a chilled church and context. All a pastor's chills do not just occur within his church. If he is going through a winter season, his life is cold everywhere he goes. Habakkuk had to learn how to develop a faith that would keep him from freezing to death.

Indifference breeds a strange ministry context for the pastor. If we become numb to sin, God gives us something we can feel. The only thing we can feel is pain that is God-induced. God-induced pain is like no other pain. When God injects pain, it feels as though it will never go away, and it grows the longer it is with us. God knows exactly where to hit us where It hurts. Not only are our arms too short to box with God, but our arms are too weak to block God's blows. When God hits, there is no defense to withstand His blasting beatings.

Habakkuk's ministry was born out of the context of the selfishness of God's people when God did not appear to be enough in their eyes. In the 21st century, what most define as *ministries* are segmented and specialized areas of service reserved for people who cannot contain God in their thoughts without intensive care. There is a rich truth behind an ancient tradition that once existed in the strongest of churches. At one point in time, people just *came to church*. They came to church to contribute rather than take.

When individuals accept Christ as their personal Lord and Savior, there is so much residue collected that some form of *self* must be denied (Matthew 16:24). Pastor M. V. Wade, Sr. would call this the need for people to be "deprogrammed". At this point, people are confronted with their own indifferences. When God's people make the right choices and desire wholeness, the demand for ministries that pound tremendous amounts of pressure on pastors' shoulders will be removed. Then, pastors will have more responsible congregations who can take up their own beds and walk rather than develop codependent ministries that do for people what they can do for themselves (John 5:8).

Pastor Wade has a unique way of grooming ministers to accept their churches for who they are and learn the art of staying with that assignment. His main thesis in pastoring churches is to love the people and shoulder whatever comes along with being called to that church. He has no middle ground or contingent clauses. If God called us to that church, we were expected to stay there unless God moved us elsewhere. Everything that happened in between was either irrelevant or secondary. We were taught to not do anything that would provoke indifferent churches to vote us out. He also pounded in our heads to not become indifferent to God's sovereign will. If they were to vote us out, it would only be because we preached Jesus. The only thing Pastor Wade permitted us to be guilty of was preaching, praying, and loving the people.

Yet, Habakkuk was not affected by an indifferent congregation. Sin should have disturbed him more than the silence of God and volume of his enemies. To further add to the equation, Habakkuk had problems with the Chaldeans because of their dreadful nature. However, he forgot to consider the dreadful nature of the indifference of God's own people that brought about such chastisement. When God chastens us by allowing our enemies entrance, it is hard to have a faith that welcomes wickedness. If we did, that

The Pastor And His Shoulders

would be the least we should do if we brought God's chastisement upon ourselves.

God does not just go around inducing consequences upon people. When bad things happen in our world, it is because somebody made a bad decision. Although Pastor Wade protected his preachers, he never excused our behavior. Make no mistake about that. He is the kind of leader who would tell us to our faces if we had anything do with it. If we brought it upon ourselves, he did not bite his tongue, but he let us know, and he would only say it so many times.

The Chaldeans were more than mere men who opposed Truth. They also consisted of troops and ranks of officers who constituted an army mobilized by the powers of darkness. They were a human army possessed by a demon army under the sovereignty of God's arm. The Chaldean army battled for the supremacy of a Babylonian system that was enforced by the kingdom of darkness. Every facet of their idolatry revolved around demonic beings. Consequently, the Chaldean men opened themselves as channels through which the spirit of Satan could flow. When their invasions are studied, they are described in demonic detail, demonstrating that their horses, chariots, and soldiers moved with a dark terror that psychologically shocked and awed their victims. When Habakkuk thought of the Chaldeans, he was well-aware of their demonic disposition of destruction. When he felt the approaching hoofbeats of Chaldean horsemen advancing into the city, he was watching an invasion of demons as well. His lack of faith blinded him to the reality that God had these demonic dogs on a leash. Although ravenous, God used them as a redemptive resource. God had to allow the fangs of the Chaldeans to rip through the skin of pride and idolatry that His people developed.

Habakkuk was a prophet who had hindrances within his anatomy that ignored points of bondage that evil would induce.

No matter how dark the night, when we consider the source of evil, it is always a battle for the soul that is the issue. As in Habakkuk's times, God must do His deepest work to sanctify and satisfy our souls. When sin abounds, Satan becomes a greater force to reckon with, but he is never outside of God's sovereign hand. The pastor's shoulders must be strong. Because we are usually trained to combat evil and not condone it, we are trained to war against the powers of darkness. What Habakkuk experienced overturns most of our traditional training. Habakkuk was called to exercise a discipline unfamiliar to a true soldier. Habakkuk was called to embrace the enemy and shoulder the satanic. Habakkuk was called to put his arms around Hell for a season. No other "ology" teaches us that but *Darkology*. Demonology does not even teach us that lesson. *Darkology* is nothing more than the doctrine of God's sovereignty.

Ambitions must be distinguished from an assignment. There are many things we may want, but our assignment is to do what God wants done. When it comes to the will of God, we will experience casualties of all kinds, even among the ones who we hold so dear. A pastor who ministers in this age of a new brand of Christianity that believes we can't control the inevitable will be a pastor who is cutting against the grain, but in the end, his ministry will have more of a salvific effect where it matters most. Not much that is new lasts exceedingly long. Usually, it is only that which has stood the test of time that has the most value.

Although he shrugged his shoulders, Habakkuk positioned himself to straighten them and hear from the Lord. Through intense agony of what he saw, Habakkuk was soon to learn the keys to life and death, i.e., the just shall live by his faith. Habakkuk was to later understand the fact that the Lord has set a limit to all evil. Although God uses evil to purge us, He also chastises the same evil that He uses. God uses our enemies to strap us closer to Him. Then, He destroys them and sets us free. Evil has restrictions and is never permitted to flow with unhindered power. Thus, God assured several acts of judgment would be placed upon the Chaldeans.

The first woe was a judgment upon the Chaldeans because of *impunity* (Habakkuk 2:5-8). The second woe was judgment upon the Chaldeans because of *covetousness and pride* (Habakkuk 2:9). The third woe was judgment upon the Chaldeans because of *tyranny* (Habakkuk 2:10-13). The fourth woe was a judgment upon the Chaldeans because of the *shameful treatment of weaker neighboring nations* (Habakkuk 2:15-17). The fifth woe was judgment upon the Chaldeans because of **idolatry** (Habakkuk 2:18-20).

These judgments gave Habakkuk the renewed endurance to shoulder the load a little while longer. The Chaldeans knew of nothing but oppressing, killing, and destroying. God knew what the Chaldeans would do if they could perpetuate their evils. He understood that the Chaldeans would accredit dominance to their demons. This would invite God's judgment also upon them. God was also to punish the Chaldeans once their iniquity was fulfilled. God can kill two birds with one stone because He never throws small stones.

As a trainee, I had an extremely difficult time learning the lessons Uncle Melvin was trying to teach me about shouldering the satanic and learning to keep silent. I just could not wrap my mind around how spiritual leadership had extraordinarily little to do with desired results. I failed to realize the fact that it was not a mental issue. It was a shoulder issue. While I was trying to figure things out, M. V. Wade, Sr. was trying to teach me to *faith things out*. I watched a man stand up in a worship service on a Sunday morning and challenge Pastor Wade. I have seen people write books in attempts to destroy his credibility. I watched a man barge into his office and threaten him. I watched him endure scandals, and he would keep silent. I watched Pastor Wade fight fire with water, hate with love, the schemes of his enemies with silence, serpents with the spirit of a dove, ambition with patience, wolves with wisdom, people with prayer, and his ego with humility. Melvin V. Wade, Sr. is a survivor. He has survived the satanic. He has outlived his opposition.

As I was released in pastoral ministry, whenever I failed to take a lower road, God made sure I paid a high price for it. Finally, I had to realize that my lesson is to not focus on winning. Instead, I had to focus on worshiping. Melvin Von Wade, Sr. taught me the need to lose battles to win wars. If we take ministry personally and demonstrate to our enemies that we will only take so much, we can develop slick and glossy ways of going in survival and attack mode. They may back up and leave us alone, but God will not.

The bearing of burdens is an art developed through contending with God on reverent theological platforms. As the late T. M. Chambers, Sr. would say, "It is okay to question God, but we must remember who we are talking to." For Habakkuk, he would stand upon his watchtower and contend with God until he would be reproved by God. The building of shoulder muscle is an exercise of reverent questioning, realizing that rebuke will also thunder from the throne of God to threaten and thread our theology. At the heaviest points of Habakkuk's burden, God uniquely placed a calmness within his soul to still his trembling knees as they buckled under the pressure of the Chaldean invasion. It was not until Habakkuk had a complaint to be corrected that he began to see a side of God he had never seen before. Listen to his willingness to be corrected:

> *"I will stand upon my watch, and set me upon the tower, and will watch to see what he will say unto me, and what I shall answer **when I am reproved.**"*

(Habakkuk 2:1; KJV)

Habakkuk knew that although he stood for righteousness, he needed rebuke from his Redeemer. In the second chapter, God broke the silence and checked Habakkuk with reasons behind it all. God rumbled his final words to Habakkuk that He was in His holy temple, and all the Earth was commanded to keep silent before Him (Habakkuk 2:20). What do we do when we are in God's divine dark room? We keep silent as God develops the film for our faith. When God finished thundering a new theology, Habakkuk developed a trembling trust that God was still on the throne.

The third chapter reveals how Habakkuk was calmed by God's power. Habakkuk cataloged a series of revelations of God's power at work in the past. Descriptive language is given as Habakkuk sees God's power in operation with an even greater clarity than beholding the evil around him. God came down from Teman and Mount Pa'ran in such splendor that His glory enveloped the skies, resulting in the praise of the Earth (Habakkuk 3:3). The horns of God erecting from His mighty hand revealed God's power that was previously kept private (Habakkuk 3:4). Burning diseases afflicted the land as the flaming feet of God pranced plagues throughout disobedient lands (Habakkuk 3:5). The hills worshiped God as they bowed down to the entrance of the King who was advancing in furious judgment against rebellious nations (Habakkuk 3:6). Even Africa trembled at the furious feet of the Lord (Habakkuk 3:7). The rivers and mountains trembled and began to overflow the lands out of haste as God approached the nations (Habakkuk 3:8-10). The sun and the moon stood still as they were struck with awe and reverence when God passed by (Habakkuk 3:11). Upon arrival, the ancient civilizations who refused to worship God were smitten as He *tornadoe*s through the villages in whirling anger and destruction (Habakkuk 3:12-14). God treaded the seas with His army, demonstrating His unhindered thrust of destruction, perhaps even referring to the miraculous devastation of the Egyptians as they attempted to pursue Moses and the children of Israel (Habakkuk 3:15). Pharaoh's horses drowned in the sea while God's warhorses gallantly pranced through waters. The waters gave way for the angelic thoroughbreds to gallop under the reigns of God's glory.

Habakkuk began to tremble in his belly and quiver in his lips when he realized how God would move upon such evil (Habakkuk 3:16). God's visitation upon evil was no longer something Habakkuk desired, but it was something he dreaded. No righteous soul would dare desire to be present to visualize the fierceness and wrath of Almighty God, not even upon our worst enemies. Powerless observance must submit to prayerful and praiseworthy obedience. Habakkuk's observance of the march of the Chaldeans was overcome by his obedience to the might of the march of the armies of the living God. Seeing God's Nocturnal Navy at work among the seas, Habakkuk no longer strains his soldiers. He begins to straighten and strengthen them. He also resumed the line as a soldier in the armies of the Lord. When God marches, all opposing forces in the Earth below must retreat or be ravished. Once that realization penetrated Habakkuk's anatomy, he knew he could trust God and shoulder fig trees that would not blossom, fields that would yield no meat, fruitless vines, failing olives, flocks cut off from the folds, and empty cattle stalls (Habakkuk 3:17).

Like Habakkuk, it is not until we come into a major update of God's majesty that we realize how God will judge sin wherever it is found. Then, Habakkuk could bear it all, realizing the same God who regulates the wicked will rescue the righteous. Not only will He rescue the righteous, but He will establish their goings, make their feet like hind's feet, and set them on high places (Habakkuk 3:19).

We worship His majesty, even if we are bearing baffling beatings. While our shoulders may tremble under the trouble, we

The Pastor And His Shoulders

command our souls to be still. If we do not, God will. The same God who judges the world will be the same God who removes heavy burdens, but in God's own time. M. V. Wade, Sr. knew that timing is everything. In time, God weakens our worries and fortifies our faith. A strong minister will always outlast a successful one. No matter how heavy the burden, the greatest burdens are upon God. Although the preacher is in the middle of a malignant ministry, he will stand correctively comforted. Because God is greater than our greatest knowledge of Him, there is always more room to trust Him than test Him. Once God reveals new sides of His sovereignty, our souls humbly bow before Him, and we find trembling peace. It is not until we learn to bear burdens that God will permit us to lay our burdens down.

The theme of M. V. Wade's ministry is correlated to learning how to shoulder heavy loads and trust that God has the heaviest end. His premise for pastoring is losing ground in today's methods for ministry. Learning how to take the lowest road is a theme of ministry that is being thrown out of many church windows and many pastors' offices. Living by faith guards us from trading humility for a ministry that protects our pride. God does not appreciate when pastors with strong shoulders are shunned. So, he brings veterans with victory Home, rewards them for their shoulder strength and leaves the rest behind with shaking shoulders because of failure to learn from the heavyweights of the Gospel.

As far as I am concerned, Uncle Melvin promised that he would not tell me anything wrong, and he kept his word. I am a load who he had to shoulder. He saw Chaldeans coming in my ministry long before I ever did. He braced me for blows that were sure to come my way. There were times when I did not give him much to work with. I put some heavy things on his shoulders. Yet, his shouldering has not been in vain. If success is defined by who you are and not by the material things you have, I can say that I made it to the top. There is not much that I know, but there are two things that I do know: I am saved, and I have been called to preach. I never would have been the man who I am today if Melvin Von Wade, Sr. wouldn't have allowed God to place me on his shoulders.

There are some things a preacher cannot talk about. He must faith it out. Only God understands dark dialect. When God is fed up with evil, He will pull the hounds of hell off the preacher's trail. In this context, nothing can kill a preacher but a lack of faith. No disease, no demon, no disaster can take the God-called preacher out who lives by his faith. When God moves, we muzzle our mouths. When Satan moves, we stand still and see the salvation of the Lord. With broad shoulders, God packs pounds of purposeful and purging pressure on the preacher, but if God's preacher could just get to the pulpit, the pressure is released as he preaches, "The Lord will make a way, somehow."

Chapter 7

THE PASTOR AND HIS HEART

∞

An Affair of the Heart
(An Excerpt from the Life of David: A preacher who did it all)

Tribute: To the godfather of preachers in our family, James Commodore Wade, Sr., Pastor of Salem Baptist Church of Omaha, NE (1944-1987)
Sunrise: 1909; Sunset: 1999

J. C. Wade, Sr. was the total preaching package. There was something extra about "Daddy Wade". He was different. Other than Jesus, he was my favorite preacher in the world. I will never forget the Sunday when I was to preach for "Daddy" at Salem Baptist Church of Omaha, Nebraska. I was spending that Saturday night at his home and heard muttering as I awakened that Sunday morning. I began to slowly move toward the muttering, it sounded as though it was coming from his room. I peeked in and saw him sitting on the edge of his bed. His wife, Mary Wade ("Big Annie") was on the other side of the bed in silent prayer with her eyes closed. With closed eyes, they knew I was watching, but they did not mind. They were teaching me how to seek God's face. With his back turned, he was chewing the cud of the Psalms of David slowly, powerfully, passionately, and prayerfully. Anyone who knew

James C. Wade, Sr. could tell you that he had a sweet but thunderous tone to his voice and an impeccable memory of Scripture. Not only his voice, but his spirit was also sweet but thunderous. You would have had to have been there to not only see but feel the power that exuded from that room. Although "Daddy Wade" was gracious to allow me to preach for Salem that morning, God wanted me there to witness his worship. Because of what I experienced that morning, every now and then, I sit upon my bed and mutter, "The Lord is my Shepherd, I shall not want…"

It sounds too raw for most Christians to believe, but David was far from perfect. Even more unpopular is the understanding that David was also a prophet. In Hebrews 11:32, he is listed among the group of prophets. In Acts 2:30, Peter specifically names David as a prophet. In II Samuel 23:2, David says God's word was on his tongue. If David was a prophet, that automatically means he was a preacher. Look at the sins of this preacher. He committed adultery. He had a sexual weakness for women. He had a man killed to have his wife. He contracted a sexually transmitted disease. He had anger issues and gangster tendencies. He misled a man under his leadership in a way that got that man killed. He had a highly dysfunctional family. He was vengeful. He married an insecure, controlling, vindictive, and competitive wife who turned on him. He suffered anxiety and depression. He lied. He had such pride in his mega-ministry that he trusted in the number of his men more than he trusted God. His child was aborted. His sins created havoc in his family, and the list goes on.

About all you think a man could do that is sinful, David did it. However, what he did right, very few men and women do. David took every one of his sins to the Lord. He loved the Lord more than he loved his lusts. Make no mistake about it, David paid a high price for every sin we know of, but he profited from God's grace and was one of God's greatest leaders of all time. God even kept David's secret sins out of *The Book* (Psalm 19:12). They were not for us to see, and neither are yours or mine. Certain sins are between us and God. It is a *heart* thing.

I sit in a juvenile posture as I listen to how far the Lord brought many great pastors. If people can handle the fact that they are far from perfect, they will be blessed by the ministries of these big-hearted men. God-called preachers have sins and flesh wounds, but they respect how the altar is to be approached. They do not take worship lightly. Worship involves a realization of our sinfulness and God's holiness. H. B. Charles, Jr. put it something like this: "Our job is to do the sinning, and Jesus' job is to do the forgiving." Of course, no such theology is so shallow that we would dare justify sinning. God knows our frames are dust (Psalm 103:14). The greatest men of God failed miserably, but the Lord fixed them.

Seasoned shepherds young and old learned to cherish their challenges and journalize their journey. When we read the Psalms, they are the diary of a psalmist. David lived a passionate life. He went at ministry hard. He worked hard, and he played hard. It appears everything David did, good or bad, he put his heart in it. The preacher cannot always accurately identify his cardiac capabilities (Jeremiah 17:9). We are not always certain when we need an inside job. We are not as skilled as we would like to be in releasing or realizing the power of our inside options. Our emotive processes are some of the strongest dynamics that operate within. Pastors are passionate people. Sometimes, passions pose problems. On other occasions, passion promotes. When we lose passion, something has gone passionately wrong, and somewhere along the line, it is evident we are experiencing heart failure.

When we mention the heart, we are speaking of *the motivational drives within that provide a channel of intimacy with God that supersedes anything wrong we have done or the pain experienced from broken hearts by what others have done to us.* With a passion for God, we are unstoppable regardless of our issues internally or externally.

No matter the situation, David appeared to rise to the occasion due to a heart that God would not ignore. God was pleased to watch David passionately penetrate his problems and perversions through a pursuit of God that gave God ultimate pleasure.

David teaches us the art of intimacy with ourselves and God. David's intimacy with himself often surfaced as he had deep conversations with his soul (Psalm 43:5). Learning how to be intimate with God touches a part of us that we cannot resist. Learning how to be intimately honest with ourselves touches a part of God that He does not resist. When we passionately pursue God above every other pursuit, we are connecting to a part of God that will move Him to do virtually anything to protect that intimacy.

Unlike David, the people he led had hearts that grew hard. God was fed up with Israel's rejection of Him as King (I Samuel 8:6-8). Their rejection gave way to idolatry as the King of Glory was not welcomed within Israel's gates (Psalm 24:9). So, God prepared a man for Himself who would not reject Him. Israel would be greatly mistaken if they believed David was anointed to be king *for them*. Some people who we lead or have led assumed a level of ownership over our lives that God never sanctions. The fact that David was provided by God and for God reveals that David was God's answer to God's own problem. The God-called preacher is God's property. If he errs in any way, He is God's problem. God knows how to solve His problems, and He knows how to take care of His property. God emphatically said that David was primarily *for Himself*:

> "...for I have provided Me (God)
> a king among his sons."
>
> (I Samuel 16:1b; KJV)

It is easy to confuse externals with intimacy. Externals can never do what intimacy can accomplish. It is not the leader who has *the look*, but it is he who can touch the heart of God who is sanctioned by God. David had an external appearance that in no way resembled a man who would be considered the next king. David's appearance was so unremarkable that none of us would have targeted David to be the king, not even Samuel.

> *"But the Lord said unto Samuel, Look not on his (Eliab's) countenance, or the height of his stature; because I have refused him: for the Lord seeth not as man seeth; for man looketh on the outward appearance, but the Lord looketh on the heart."*
>
> (I Samuel 16:7; KJV)

While extensive emphasis has been directed towards the shallow judgments of common people, prophets fall guilty of the same thing. Notice how God told *Samuel* not to look on Eliab's outward appearance. Samuel preferred Eliab and completely overlooked David. Instead, God chooses men who are *lion-hearted* and *bear-handed*. Pastoral *Davids* display unusual courage by killing lions and bears with regularity while the *Sauls* of our day are parading easy kills:

> *"David said unto Saul, Thy servant kept his father's sheep, and there came a lion and a bear, and took a lamb out of the flock: And I went out after him and smote him, and delivered it out of his mouth: and when he arose against me, I caught him by his beard and smote him, and slew him. Thy servant slew both the lion and the bear: and this uncircumcised*

Philistine shall be as one of them, seeing he hath defied the armies of the living God."

(I Samuel 17:34-36; KJV)

It is accurate to say that slaying Goliaths only comes through a succession of previous battles that testify that one is a shepherd fit for combat. David was known as a mighty valiant man who succeeded in battle before he killed Goliath. David was a warrior of the wild. His resilient resume' was full of success stories of battling beasts. David was already tested tried and true, battle-proof and beast-proof. Pastors who defeat Goliaths are those who have a previous history of going in beast mode. Be faithful in beast mode. Be it known, there is no day of our lives that God is not allowing to mold us for momentous ministry. When God prepares a man for ministry, every moment is relative. Idle time delays our destiny. There is no such thing as a fleeting moment when a man has *heart*.

If there is such a thing as success in ministry, those who have succeeded have testimonies of successions of seized seasons. Such shepherds share the fact that the promotions of which they gained today are nothing but the accumulation of agonies, defeats, lessons learned, and gracious interventions of God from the contested struggles of their yesterdays. If a passion for God is practiced, we unknowingly ready ourselves for gargantuan experiences that will be the defining moments of our ministries.

We humbly bow to pastoral predecessors such as J. C. Wade, Sr. who blazed the trail for us to realize that much of the pathway to greatness is loving the Lord with all your heart. We are grateful for pastors present and past who divested their hearts in the daily grind of life, testifying to each anxious soul that it pays to bloom where God planted you. J. C. Wade, Sr. warned me of what he called, "hankering." Hankering is getting to a point in which a preacher politics in a way that he becomes ambitious for ministry opportunities God has not sanctioned. So, I stayed off that type of radar. His son, Melvin Von Wade, Sr. would say to gifted preachers who were in rural assignments that they did not want to be guilty of being major prophets in minor lands. David struck that balance. Although he was a shepherd, his heart positioned him to be a leader in a larger land.

On April 03, 2015, Palestinian children used slingshots against Israeli soldiers outside of Ofer (an Israeli military prison camp). Children posed a threat to men with guns due to a protest that erupted because of the death of prisoner Masara Abu Hamdiyeh who died of cancer while in prison because he was neglected treatment. This is one of the closest historical depictions of David's day to hint of the power of a sling and stone. Shallow interpretations of David's battle with Goliath canvas David as a kid who had never known battle before. It is almost as if David is pictured hurling stones at Goliath with youthful vengeance. Yet, a boy-David is far from the truth.

Not only will opportunity reveal the condition of our hearts, but adversity will also. It does not take long before tall trials come to reveal how tall we are. David was young, but God described him as a man. There was a giant who David took down who was much taller than Goliath, lions, and bears. The most difficult giants to take down are not physical but spiritual ones. David was not only a warrior of the wild, but he was also a warrior against witchcraft. David praised an evil spirit away that visited King Saul. Notice the text as David is being recruited to exorcise a demon from Saul. Notice the battle with the Philistine giant (Goliath) has not yet occurred:

> *"And Saul said unto his servants, Provide me now a **man** that can play well, and bring him to me. Then*

answered one of the servants, and said, Behold, I have seen a son of Jesse the Bethlehemite, that is cunning in playing, and a mighty valiant **man**, *and a* **man** *of war and prudent in matters, and a comely person, and the Lord is with him."*

(I Samuel 16:17-18; KJV)

It takes a man to slay satanic spirits. They are not slapping people on the forehead with oil, hurling holy water at the demon-possessed, waving crosses at evil spirits, and shouting at Satan as if volume is a virtue of victory. On the contrary, they are worshipers. They are men who have such an intimate relationship with God that their methods of ministry are ejecting evils in wondrous ways. When a pastor has *heart*, there are one hundred ways (figurative number) to defeat a demon. It was not specifically the instrument that shunned the spirit, but there was something about the way David played. He had skill. He meant every melody. He played songs in the key of God's heart. As David was pulling the harp strings, he was also pulling God's heart strings. It was an affair of the heart between David and the Lord that served as a combination strike against the evil spirit.

Because of David's passion, he was prepared for promotion. The battle with Goliath settled the issues of the nation to prepare them to receive David's anointing as future king. David was determined to slay the Philistine giant because of the offenses of which Goliath was bringing against the God who David loved. David appears to have previously left the battle to Saul and the armies of Israel until Goliath made a faulty move by pushing David's cardio-envelope. Previously, David was untouched by the taunts of Goliath, but Goliath began the process of pushing David to his limit, but not yet:

> *"And the Philistine (Goliath) said, I defy the armies of Israel this day; give me a man that we may fight together."*

(I Samuel 17:10; KJV)

In the very next verse, we discover Goliath was demoralizing the army of Israel, including Saul. Yet, we hear no mention of David. David is somewhere taking care of rural responsibilities, tending his father's sheep. In the spiritual realm, David was in God's incubation hold being groomed for a mega-ministry. Goliath's taunt continued for forty days. David was previously unaware of the scope of Goliath's threats but happened upon the Israelite camp and became a leader in transition to protect God's sheep (Israel). Goliath championed a challenge once again. This time, David *hears* Goliath:

> *"And as he (David) talked with them (the army of Israel), behold there came up the champion, the Philistine of Gath, Goliath by name, out of the armies of the Philistines, and spake according to the same words:* **and David heard them.**"

(I Samuel 17:23; KJV)

A pastor may not be called to get involved in specific battles unless he hears something that pertains to his purpose in life. The Israelite soldiers flee from Goliath out of fear, but David enquired who he was. David's concern was not with Goliath's stature and appearance. David was more concerned about Goliath's statements and accusations. Goliath was implying the armies of the living God were helpless against the Philistine army. The *armies of Israel* may have been helpless, cowardly, and afraid, but David knew of another army who was being reproached, i.e., *the armies of the living God* (I Samuel 17:36). While Goliath saw the armies of the living God as a human army, David was aware of spiritual ones in angelic dimensions. David previously may not have been allowed to be a soldier in the armies of Israel, but he was a true soldier in the armies of the Lord. Not all pastors are approved by their peer pastoral army, but they are approved as true soldiers in the army of the Lord. Soldiers of the army of Israel may flee, but soldiers in the army of the living God fight.

David realized what was at stake. The God he loved deep in his heart was being insulted. David knew God could fight His own battles. That is precisely the point. David's heart for God was pulsating according to God's purpose. When intimate in worship, the lines that distinguish our business from God's sometimes disappear. Thus, David took Goliath's threats upon God as threats upon himself. If it were a *god* who was insulting God, perhaps David would have left the battle for the immortals to fight. However, it was a mere mortal challenging the Immortal. It was flesh against Glory. If David previously had slain an evil spirit, he was qualified to slay a mortal. David's heart was beating for God in a way that he knew this battle was within his mortal reach. Goliath was tall, but he was still temporal. Goliath was strong, but he was not mighty. People with pride have no might. They have not been battle-tested, and they are not beast-proof. Thus, they have a false sense of invincibility. At the core, it was the Dark One (Satan) challenging the Divine One (God). The manifestation of spiritual wickedness in high places was evident through mortal bodies. Goliath was Satan's man, and David was God's man. Goliath had a height advantage, but David had a heart advantage.

Christianity is being challenged in this age like no other in human history. Much is being said about the Coronavirus, but not much is being said about Christ. Discussions of racism are rampant, but not much is being said about righteousness. Satan is possessing individuals who challenge the Church to welcome their demonic rights that they call human rights. The legislation of new moralities is an attack upon the Church and an encroaching evil. Our legislation reveals that as laws are being passed that are abominable to God. Pastors with *heart* lead congregations to realize why a new morality must never replace God's law. The killing of a baby in the womb of a mother has been exonerated by the right of a mother to have an abortion. These and many more are also the new giants of our day.

David was not declaring war against Philistines as much as he was defending Holy Ground. Often, the world will call Christians aggressive when they are only defending Holy Ground. When the world stands on God's ground, they must take off their shoes (Exodus 3:5). With *heart*, we defend the grounds that protect us from being slain and from falling upon our own swords.

Too many laws of our country trample upon the grounds of the Christian faith. We hear about them all the time. Satan strategically imposes these laws and orders to weaken the fabric of the family, preservation of human life, and God-ordained roles in the Christian Church. Of course, we are never to attack civil or human rights. The Spirit of David does not attack human rights, but it does defend life. When human rights threaten human life, human rights become human wrongs. These practices can abort an infant, including new laws proposed to abort an infant at nine months old. Today's new moralities can divide a nation, destroy the foundation of the family, and compromise a church. The legalization of such practices is a national issue. The consequences of Goliath's attack upon Israel would have meant the death of a nation as well as God's promise to bring the Lion out of Judah (Hebrews 7:14).

The Goliath's of our day are national in scope. They have little to do with overcoming the overhead of a church project or personal issues. Christianity and the God of the Holy Bible are being taunted by nations and heads of nations who are legalizing a new morality that wants nothing to do with righteousness and justice. Furthermore, they want nothing to do with mercy or truth (Psalm 85:10). Instead, this new morality wants what is acceptable. Of course, we all have sinned and come short of God's glory. For these reasons and more, we come to terms with acknowledging our transgressions as David always did. His adultery cost him his family (II Samuel 12:10). David had so many sins in his life that he could not even number them (Psalm 40:12). Most were committed during his ministry and not before. However, David was better on his worst day than the entire nation of Israel on their best day.

Yet, Goliath and Israel committed sins David never committed. Goliath was challenging how God governs the universe, and Israel was too afraid to defend how God governs the universe. Christians do not have to be silent soldiers in a society that shouts against the fundamentals of our faith. We cannot use Saul's armor because we will not survive unless we do what we do best. Our slings and stones are the God-given methods that have been most effective throughout the humbling inauguration of our ministries. Although the giants are strong and tall, our God is stronger and taller. ***Our slings and stones are the amazing graces that brought us safe thus far.*** God is not depending upon us to use new inventions we are unfamiliar with. Our slings must be harnessed in the effective methods of biblical history to bring down the giants of our day that involves having a heart for the Gospel with all its implications.

James Commodore Wade Sr.'s reputation reached the respect of governments in Omaha and Nebraska because he remained a Gospel preacher and pastor instead of becoming a political one. Many sages believe they have holes in their shepherd's bag. They feel as though they are no longer relevant to bring down the giants of our age. Relevance has never been the key to redemption. Sometimes, a shepherd's irrelevance is a weapon to bring down the giants of our age. Much of what is happening in our age is beyond relevance because it is beyond redemption (Romans 1:28). Many abominable practices and laws are being established that refuse God as King. When our contemporary age of reason and religion in our churches refuses to appreciate the faithful stance of pastors of our past, they are left to face the giants of their day with rugged stones instead of smooth ones.

Goliath's defeat gained David new drama that would send his life on the journey of a conqueror. The defeat of Goliath was the turning point for David as his passion for God was deeply needed for the tests sure to follow, beginning with the shallow shouts of the daughters of Jerusalem to the evil spirit of jealousy that possessed King Saul (I Samuel 18:7). Defining moments are also deepening moments when we are shaped from mere warriors to worshippers. At the heart of worship is coming to know God and ourselves intimately, keeping our lives sanitary by praying for a clean heart, allowing our hearts to be beaten into a tenderized passion for God and developing tough skin concerning jealous spirits that threaten our thrones. God wants us to reign victorious. Yet, there are vengeful spirits that seek any means to prevent that from happening. God has an art of war that He wants every pastor with *heart* to develop to ward off jealous wars.

For at least a succession of twenty-one times, we must not allow jealous spirits to give us a *heart* attack. Saul attempted to kill David at least twenty-one times, due to jealousy. It can sometimes be disheartening to deal with people who have an evil eye on you. The psychology of a jealous person is a strange phenomenon and a baffling battle. Jealousy is nothing to play around with.

Sometimes, a preacher's enemies know him better than his friends. How a person can become so intoxicated with destroying another person is a mystery to me. Jealous people would kill you if they had the chance. Although Saul was David's next giant, Saul was not to be slain. Saul served as a jealous lesson to remind David of the king he was to never be if he were to maintain his heart for God.

Concerning the shouts of the daughters of Jerusalem, those who doubt the heart of their leader are the same people who wield vain shouts of praise when he wins battles significant to them only. The praises of women singing how David had slain his tens of thousands while Saul had slain thousands is an admiration a leader must not fall prey to. For pastors, the applause of men is a dangerous, but the appeal of vain women is even more dangerous. Usually, our rise or fall starts or ends with sexual aggression.

Dr. Manuel Scott used to say, "**Power is the ultimate aphrodisiac.**" Pastoring is a powerful position, and certain women are addicted to men who have that type of power. When all men speak well of us, we must beware, but when certain women have admirations, we must be watchful. Like David before he was king, we rarely suffer temptations to glory in ourselves when we have spent major portions of our years in rugged assignments. However, on pinnacles, in palaces, and thriving on thrones, our defining moments can give us a recognition we have been deprived of for so long. Pastors and preachers cannot glory in the praises of people, male or female. There are many tactics Satan uses to stroke our pastoral egos. Any man in a relatively powerful position faces ego challenges, and Satan wishes to send such a man on a power trip that will take him to the land of reproach or resignation. If his battle is not sex, it is a battle with success. If his battle is neither of the above, it is a battle for significance on the ego-level.

Although David had a weakness for women, he did not fall for most of them. David turned away more women than he received.

David recognized the glorying of one man meant the shame of another. As women gloried in David's accomplishments, Saul was being shamed. A wise man once said, "When two powerful men get into a fight, it is often over a woman." A leader must lead in a way that does not instigate jealousy. If you *got it*, you *got it*, but we are not to gloat in it. David had such passion for God that he did everything in his power to turn their praises toward God to keep Saul's jealousy at a minimum and God's glory at a maximum. Unfortunately, Saul's jealousy was so severe, and the women's shouts were so surprising that David did not have enough time or space to close a severe and sudden gap. Saul's jealousy was growing faster than David's praise, and the evil spirit that came upon Saul praised the process.

Because of Saul's jealousy, David was successful at playing the harp in a way that chased Saul's demons away because Saul requested David to play his demons away. When Saul refused David's music, Saul's demons danced to another tune. Without a spiritual song, Saul was susceptible to ghost music. From that point on, all David could do was hang his harp on the willow tree and run. Usually, retreat is not an option. However, whenever there are two kings and one throne, the true leader may have to leave. A throne is not big enough for two kings. David's glory was radiating, and Saul's glory was being removed.

It is sad and scary when a protégé must run from his predecessor or a minister must run from his mentor. Saul was the man who felt the impact of displaced recognition because he was overtaken by the praises of people and a satanic rage for relevance. When a predecessor is on his way out, his mind can play tricks on him, and his ego can become edgy. He becomes vulnerable to many vices. He becomes hyper-sensitive to the slightest things because breaking up is hard to do. He is breaking up with a ministry he dedicated most of his life to. More than that, he is vulnerable to over-reacting. If so, he lives by what is in his head rather than who is in his heart (God). Saul fell victim to the vain need to know if he still *had it*. Unfortunately, he did not *have it* like he used to.

Here is where successors must learn a valuable lesson. A successor is playing the fool if he thinks he has something so special that people love him more than his predecessor. Sooner or later, he will learn the biblical or hard way. When a succeeding pastor is down for a cause, he will soon discover who is for and against him. The very same people will also break rank if a pastor is marching for a cause greater than the people who he leads. People of that sort can be in your parade, but the same people will not march to the beat of God's drum.

When the women were shouting David's praises, it was nothing to shout about. David's installation service was not supposed to be a celebration. David may have been young, but he was not stupid. He was not so foolish in his youthfulness to be anxious to assume Saul's seat. In God's eyes, Saul had fallen, and Saul's spirit was not right. David's anointing as king was a sobering statement to Israel that they refused God as King. David was God's replacement for their rebellion. David was inheriting a congregation full of wild women and misguided men. Besides, David had his own sins to worry about. Leading Judah was not something David signed up for. God-called preachers did not sign up to preach or pastor. God signed them up.

Yet, David was down for the cause despite his sins and even Saul's sins. David was wise enough to know that Saul's dirt did not make him any cleaner as the new kid on the block. It is low down and dirty to praise one spiritual leader and curse another. In this context, every God-called preacher is cut from the same cloth, even if we are woven with the fabric of different denominations and doctrines. David had enough *heart* to not let fickle people get between his relationship with a leader whose ministry was fading:

> "*The women answered one another as they played, and said, Saul has slain his thousands and David his ten thousands. And Saul was very wroth **and the saying displeased him.**"*

(I Samuel 18:7-8; KJV)

When people appear to be devoted to their leader beyond measure, those same people must be severely screened. Devotion is more than a notion. True devotion must be based on more than one single success and one sentence. A leader must be aware of people who are vulnerable to the Halo Effect. The Halo Effect is a mental bias in which someone's overall impression of a person influences how he or she feels and thinks about someone's character. As spiritual leaders, most people usually give us more credit than we deserve while simultaneously failing to give us credit we do deserve. One major deposit happened in these women's lives, and they praised David as if he were a god. In the same sentence, they shamed Saul as if he was a worthless man.

No pastor is immune to Saul's sins. A sin often unaccounted for in spiritual leadership is the lust for power. The overindulgence in power is developed when we personalize our position. If we take ownership of the position God graced us to be temporary stewards over, our sense of ownership transfers from God to ourselves. When God strips us of our seat of leadership, turf-guarding can be a sign that we have a problem getting up from that seat. We as pastors must sooner or later get up from our seats as quickly as we first sat down in our seats. When we slowly and soberly sit down in our seats we are assigned to lead, we can more quickly and soberly get up from our seats when we are assigned to leave.

We can never fall in love with songs angels dare not sing. The angels denounce worship of any being other than God. In no way would an angel give another praise, receive praise, or sing a song about themselves. They see too much of God's glory to be foolish enough to forget there is none like Him. Heaven's angels are so reduced by God's throne that they would never receive glory and honor due to God alone (Isaiah 6:3). Even Hell's angels tremble at the name of Jesus (James 2:19). Neither in time nor eternity will our worship match that of the angels toward God. When we grow fond of the praises of people, we lose sight of God's majesty.

We cannot afford to fall in love with the mic. When we love the sound of our own voices, we become devoted to our own vices. When we start to love the sound of our own voices, all Heaven can hear is a recording played backwards. It is an evil sound. The sin of narcissism is a backwards practice. When we preach from the heart, it is all about God. Narcissism preaches, *it is all about me*. When we hold the mic, we hold it toward Heaven for the people to hear from God as He thunders thick Theology from His throne. There will always be some spirit who will try to convince us that we are *all that* over and against the grace of God. David avoided this trap while Saul had fallen privy to it.

Even if God disqualified Saul from office, he lacked the wisdom to resign gracefully. Now, Saul has such a strong ego that he is too proud to step down, step aside, or step back. If he cannot step up, he refuses to step out of the way. He just keeps on stepping on David's toes, going in the same direction, nowhere fast. Saul does not know how to stop showing up. Now, Saul is caught in the cycle of being seen and the cycle of repetition. He is predictable. Saul has lost the element of surprise. Saul should have showed up so infrequently that David would have been overjoyed by a surprise visit from Saul.

A transitioning leader from service must learn the art of blessing the people who he served and the new leader by his absence. Instead, David knew Saul could show up any day because he never really left. Saul was always somewhere around David's throne. Everywhere David turned, he ran into Saul. David knew what Saul was going to say before he even said it and how he would react to any given situation. Saul became a dead target. To David, Saul was no surprise. Yet, he dared to keep going after David's life. He kept making selfish attempts to prolong the inevitable, doing the same thing, expecting different results. If stupidity is doing the same thing over and again, expecting different results, Saul stooped to that level. Sometimes, the most anointed thing to do is get as far away from stupidity as possible. From that point on, David knew he had to get on the run and disappear out of Saul's sight. Whenever David did see Saul, he was always reminded of why he ran from him.

If David would have fallen in love with the externals, he would have stopped running and slain Saul out of self-preservation and ambition. This brash act would have given David spiritual heart failure. David knew he was in danger of heart disease if he were to retaliate against Saul's jealousy. God wanted a man after His heart and not after His hand. If David were to be involved in the assassination of Saul, that would have meant the assassination of his passion for God and his calling. Then, David's passion would have been for power and not God's purpose. David's passion for God only increased as Saul's power decreased.

A preacher never has to jockey for position. When God has a man in mind, no one can stop God's plan for that man. The two most important things a preacher must be willing to do if he is to assume the position God ordained is to *wait* and *run*. He must patiently run. He must run the waiting game, and he must wait out the running game. If no one is jealously pursuing him, he must run the waiting game. If he has jealous spirits on his trail, he must wait out the running game. He must learn to walk away and not come back unless God brings him to his rightful position. Sometimes, people cannot appreciate a good man's presence until he gets out of their sight. As he runs, the only thing he should seek is the heart of God. He is to be a God-chaser and not a glory-chaser.

There are countless pastors who would not be in the elevated positions they are in today if they had not learned the discipline of disengagement and righteous running. While they may have been criticized for being anti-social, they knew they were on the hit list of jealous spirits. Every great pastor and preacher who I know is peculiar about who he associates with. They learned to wait on the Lord, stay off the radar, and avoid bad company. The same assaults jealous spirits hurled to assassinate these men became the stepping-stones for the success of pastors who were next in line for promotion.

Hanging around the throne threatens the insecurity of men with a Saul-spirit. It also puts men who are like David in danger. James C. Wade, Jr. taught me early to never fool around with a preacher who has nothing to lose. He reminded me that my best friend would be a preacher, and my worst enemy would be a preacher. One of a preacher's worst enemies is a gossiping preacher. Since the days of Early Church history, too many bishops considered for a position stayed too long, arguing, fighting, and politicking, trying to convince the wrong people that they were the ones qualified for the wrong position. All that did was assassinate their anointing. Sometimes, running is the anointed thing to do. If a pastor is passionate about position more than what he is predestined to do, once he assumed that position, the nature of the seat would have switched. The oil would have dried up. It would have no longer been an anointed assignment because God did not appoint that man to the seat. At that point, he has maneuvered his way into a political seat instead of a spiritual one. From then on, he is bound to operate politically instead of pastorally. The same way he got the position will have to be the same way that he must politic to keep it. A pastor with a strong anointing will always be frustrated in a political seat.

A difficult root of truth to come to terms with along this context is in realizing the lust for power is predominately self-centered. Once self-centeredness enters the picture, it becomes satanic. What happens to a leader who is addicted to power is the same thing that happened to Saul, i.e., *he falls upon his own sword* (I Samuel 31:4). Some get themselves before someone else gets them. They carve their own valleys of death. By the time a man caught up with an Adolf Hitler, Benito Mussolini, Richard Nixon, or Osama bin Laden, they already fell upon their own swords.

However, David must not leave in a lying way. David lied his way out instead of just flat-out leaving. He lied and told Jonathan (Saul's son) to also lie to Saul at a table feast. Saul had a reserved seat for David at the feast, but David went AWOL (I Samuel 20:4-10). Out of fear, David continued along lying patterns. As a fearful fugitive, David lied before the priest (Ahimelech) and requested two things that were not his to have. Due to hunger, he asks for holy bread that was only to be used for temple purposes. He also requests Goliath's sword to defend himself against Saul or any of Saul's men as he is on the run (I Samuel 21:1-9). Whenever we flee out of fear from a God-ordained position, we run the risk of asking for things that are not ours to have, tampering with holy things, and lowering ourselves to the level of past enemies by relying on the same weapons of our enemies who we previously defeated.

David is not done with his flight of fear. David dumbs down and pretends to be insane before Achish, king of Gath (I Samuel 21:12). No one wants a mad man who is ordained to be a minister, even if he is pretending to be someone who he is not (I Samuel 21:15). So, Achish coughs him up, and David escaped to the cave Adullam. When a minister is on the run from threatening spirits, he must resort to his maximum level of intelligence and not downplay it because intelligence grows from integrity.

There is so much within these verses that describe David's paranoid posture. The profound truth is that David was scared out of his wits, and he resorted to any means necessary to save himself from Saul skinning him alive. There are preachers, presidents, pastors, and professors in the Christian realm who can skin their peers alive if they do not align with their agenda or be devoted to their denomination or doctrine. They have a way of shutting another preacher down and shutting him out. That is not only a lesson of David's fear, but is also a reality of how frightening it can be to be under the yoke of a leader or preaching league who has serious insecurities and severe ego issues.

David was dealing with reality. It was what it was, and it is what it is. As a result, God has a way of hiding men after God's own heart and allowing them so surface later, but it is not until such men come to terms with who God called them to be. God allows a preacher to be pursued as a pathway to discover, develop, and deepen his true definition. When God has a plan for a man, the years he lost running from those who delayed his destiny can be recovered with a single shot.

As David flees to the rocks (the cave of Adullam), he begins to establish his headquarters. Adullam means, *a place of squeeze*. Although God allows David to be in a squeeze, He is not squeezing the life out of David. On the contrary, He is squeezing any signs of jealousy out of him. Out of all of David's sins he committed while on the throne, jealousy was never one of them, neither was he threatened by any of his mighty men who had skills he didn't have (II Samuel 23:8-39). God was molding him into a faithful and just leader (II Samuel 23:3). Confined contexts create leadership developing skills for men who have *heart*. They shape our perspective of ministry, and we attract *cave-members*. Many pastors who have thriving churches have loyal members who were with them in the trenches many years before their glory days. Caves are representative of places of refuge while God battles on our behalf and prepares us for our ultimate unction. They are detained developments that train us to be trusted. Cave-members are quality people who God sends our way who are sensitive to our struggles. They are loyal people who have a passion for faithful objectives beyond themselves. Pastors who are in tight places have ministries with headquartered characteristics, and their churches become citadels for breeding a new army of tender warriors who are distressed with a vengeful form of victory. There are countless *cave-ministries* today that are not on the radar but are being reformed as instruments of revival in our cities. Pastors who minister in contemporary caves of secluded but strong sanctuaries are reminded that God has not forgotten them.

There is an authentic Chinese restaurant I love to visit frequently in Oxnard. I usually order an entrée entitled, "*The Three Ingredients*". There are three ingredients that constitute a quality entrée for a church:

> "*David, therefore, departed thence and escaped to the cave Adullam: and when his brethren and all his father's house heard it, they went down thither to him. And everyone that was in* **distress**, *and everyone that was in* **debt**, *and everyone that was* **discontented**, *gathered themselves unto him; and he*

became a captain over them: and there were with him about four hundred men."

(I Samuel 22:1-2; KJV)

This was the beginning of David's new congregation. If he had a building, it would have constituted 400 men. That is a mighty good start for a church plant. When a pastor maintains a heart for God, people who are in distress, debt, and discontentment are attracted to the integrity of their leader's heart and not the tens of thousands who has slain on his resume'. Although these may not appear to be attractive qualities of a congregation, they are some of the best ingredients any congregation could have. Consider a congregation the opposite of these three ingredients. The opposite of *distress*, *debt*, and *discontented* would be *unconcerned, wealthy,* and *comfortable*. Have you pastored a church full of unconcerned, wealthy, and comfortable members? Have you tried to disciple even one person who was an unconcerned, financially fortified, and comfortable Christian? It is a headache, to say the least. What if a pastor was unconcerned, wealthy, and comfortable? Would you follow him? This type of church has no *heart*. Therefore, this will constitute a *heartless* church.

There are noble reasons why good members follow leaders with *heart* despite their failures. People who have Kingdom needs are not attracted to many of the things some tend to covet in ministry. Cave-members are dedicated because their pastor is transparent enough for them to see what his heart throbs for. He even has integrity amid his iniquities. If he makes a mistake, they know how to charge it to his head and not to his *heart*. When we are willing to maintain *heart*, we will not stay in a cave for too long. *Heart* propels us to move to levels of ministry with Kingdom dimensions, and God will see to it that we do:

*"And the prophet Gad said unto David, Abide not in the cave any longer; depart, and **get thee into the land of Judah.**"*

(I Samuel 22:5; KJV)

Although cave ministries can be a place of repositioning, refuge, and replenishment, we move when God says move. Sometimes, the move is geographical. Most of the time, the move is spiritual. God invested too much in us to stay confined to an antiquated assignment. God has not called men with *heart* to continue to shrink to fit tight places. Their hearts are too big to be put on hold for too long. The cave is just a temporary hold that God places them in to roll their stones away. David had to be ready to move to Judah. Judah means, *"praise"*. The Psalms are full of David's praise. It was not a shallow praise that can be faked, imitated, or a trendy style of worship. His praise was unpredictable and unprecedented because He constantly came into new encounters with God. David's praise pulsated from a heart that was in love with God. When David went to Judah, he fulfilled God's purpose, and God repositioned him to a place of power. Judah was a powerful and purposeful Kingdom. It was the place where God would do His most efficient work in generations to come (Revelation 5:5).

To receive a promotion, preachers with big hearts learn to survive henchmen. They experience jealous assaults from Saul-like contemporaries who would make the mafia look like toy soldiers. Jealous contemporaries often try to stay in close communication with men of passion with a hidden motive to keep them in striking distance. Sometimes, they only surface to see if the men who they envy have failed yet.

When a pastor has *heart*, nothing and no one can hold him back, not even his greatest failures. To those who are on a righteous run and faithful flee, there are so many valuable lessons to learn from David. God is responsible for the outcome, even if His Kingdom is suffering civil war among brethren. The more we love God through the turmoil of a divided pastoral fraternity, the more we can be trusted in future leadership when our seats become stabilized. David's son (Solomon) would come to teach us through his wisdom sayings that one of the most *disheartening* things to see is a fool in power. God's Kingdom is advancing, and He has a way of replacing fools with the faithful. The faithful are those who gained victory over pride, arrogance, self-preservation, and have proven that purpose takes priority over the praises of people and politics. A purposeful ministry supersedes a political one.

J. C. Wade, Sr. did not pastor people or relate to his peers with a political paradigm. He had a servanthood mentality. He respected the choices of others, even if he disagreed with them. There were countless times when he had the power to veto those who he led. Yet, he did not insist on having his way. He also loved his fellow-preachers regardless of some of their jealousies toward him. The last years of J. C. Wade, Sr.'s life were humbler than when he first began. He was far from perfect. He shared with me countless soldier's stories he couldn't have told while he was a pastor. Yet, he found solitude in a wheelchair or walking on a cane. When I would push him in his wheelchair, I learned things from him no seminary could have ever taught me. Around a group of the most respected preachers, I could not help but notice how much he was in a class all by himself. When he walked on a cane, he would whistle songs of Zion. He never wanted to be a burden to anyone or his own family. He told me exactly how his funeral would be, who would be laughing, and who would be crying. James Commodore Wade, Sr. brought life to any hospital room he was confined to. As a matter of fact, in his convalescent room, he laid his hands on me and blessed me. I never will forget his words:

"Come here boy, let me bless you." He could have retired from pastoring in royal fashion, but he left everything in the hands of God. He suffered shame, but he was not ashamed. He was a proud man. He was proud of his calling regardless of where it led him. He refused to fight the unrepentant who he preached to. J. C. Wade, Sr. told me how his enemies tried to trap him in his sins. Yet, he loved them because he loved his calling, and he loved his Lord. His response to rejection was not in securing royal garments for himself. He believed the only ones to wear such garments were either Jesus or the ones who he suffered to help save.

It does a world of good for a young preacher to have a heart to heart conversation with a man such as J. C. Wade, Sr. whose service synced with Scripture. He did not have a polished, political, and glossy way of leading people. He did it the right way. He pastored from his heart and not his head. He died behind the bars of some cold-hearted people, but his ministry was free. Much of what Salem Baptist Church is to this day is because J. C. Wade, Sr. had a big *heart*. His life and ministry were exponentially larger than the church he pastored. His church was without walls. The new Salem Baptist Church is not just a mega-building in Omaha, Nebraska. Salem Baptist Church is all over the nation. *I am* Salem Baptist Church along with countless others.

Men with *heart* do not wait for inheritances. They leave their own. Saul eventually dies, and David refuses to dance over Saul's death. David refused to politic for the throne and use Saul's death as a platform to become popular. In my opinion, every God-called pastor who retires from pastoring should have an honorary seat in a seminary to teach young ministers how to sit in Saul's seat. It is a dangerous sign for a protégé to become anxious for a promotion. He should show a slowness about his succession. Succeeding Saul is nothing to be excited about. It is a sobering succession. A man after God's heart weeps when Saul resigns. David recognized what

God knew. He knew Saul was still God's man although he was not always a good man. He recognized how Saul accomplished a substantial amount of victory for Israel. God is more committed to His purpose than He is to personalities. God can use any human agency to accomplish His will, including Saul and Saul's of our day. In no way would God allow Saul to destroy or turn over the chair of Judah. Thus, Saul was still a vessel of the Lord, even if he had the capacity to be careless and the disposition to be demonic. He won battles in the name of the Lord, and he was known by God as a "weapon of war".

I always believed I was a better right-hand man than the lead man. I took joy in being loyal to my pastors. As a former armor-bearer for my pastors, when it comes to understanding a man of God, it has nothing to do with his faults, but it has everything to do with focus. David had the right focus regarding Saul. Therefore, he refused to demonize Saul. Knowing Saul tried to kill him, Saul still had Israelite and not Philistine or demonic blood. David recognized when the overall glory of God in having Saul on the throne had to do with blood. It was about Judah and the blood of Jesus (Hebrews 7:14).

One of the honorable descriptions David attributed to Saul was in calling him "The Beauty of Israel" (II Samuel 1:19). A preacher who has *heart* honors previous pastors who no longer have their previous power. There is still a beauty about them although they are no longer with us in body or spirit. The most heartless thing to do is undermine them. The best thing to do is to honor them and never forget that leading God's people is no easy task. There is no way a pastor can spend decades serving a congregation and his successor come in and develop a genuine rapport with people in a few years. He may develop a rapport in a short amount of time, but it is not genuine. It takes time for people to truly trust the heart of their leader. Sometimes, people will prop up the successor to undermine the predecessor. Leaders who are eager to have Saul removed must be patient, and God will ensure their turn to succeed and fail at the throne. A man must be careful what he asks for because he just might get it.

A lesson arises when we address the civil war amid ourselves. A heart of God will relinquish personal issues that divide pastors from one another for the benefit of the Kingdom of God. David not only loved to play, but he also respected the game, even if he was not in the line-up. He also respected other players. He was true to the game. Therefore, it was not his style of play to resort to competition. A preacher with *heart* is not responsible for those who are jealous of his spiritual swagger. God assumes responsibility for our haters and makes decisions best for His Kingdom agenda. When we stop running and begin to fight back, we may be defiantly interrupting a closure God is bringing that will prevent us from transitioning gracefully to the next chair, even if it means a tearful transition. Listen to David as he tearfully transitions to the throne as Israel's next king:

> *"**The beauty of Israel** (Saul) is slain upon thy high places: **how are the mighty fallen**. Tell it not in Gath, publish it not in the streets of Askelon; lest the daughters of the Philistines rejoice, lest the daughters of the uncircumcised triumph. Ye mountains of Gilboa, let there be no dew, neither let there be rain, upon you, nor fields of offerings: for there **the shield of the mighty** is vilely cast away, the shield of Saul, as though he had not been anointed with oil. . . **Saul** and Jonathan **were lovely and pleasant** in their lives, and in their death, they were not divided: **they were swifter than eagles, they were stronger than lions**. Ye daughters of Israel (the same ones who*

shouted that Saul had only slain thousands) **weep over Saul, who clothed you in scarlet, with other delights, who put on ornaments of gold upon your apparel... How are the mighty fallen, and the weapons of war perished!"**

(II Samuel 1:19-21; 23-24; 27; KJV)

The beauty of Israel, mighty, lovely and pleasant, swifter than eagles, stronger than lions, the man who clothed women with scarlet and other delights, the man who put ornaments of gold upon the clothing of women, and a weapon of war are all descriptions of the same Saul who fickle women had quickly forgotten. No matter how impactful a leader can be, people tend to forget his accomplishments when they identify a better prospect who tickles their fancies. Somebody must guarantee the pastor whose glory fades is not forgotten. One day, all our glories will fade, our lights will dim, and we must die. God has a way of making sure He is the only one who writes a true narrative of His men.

Any man who is anxious to see Saul removed or thinks he can do a better job has a sick heart. Whenever a man anxiously awaits an inheritance of another, he will always inherit more than what he bargained for. When his efforts fail while on the throne, he must understand how much of his failure is God-ordained because God will never bless a church who buffeted the previous pastor until they learned a lesson about God's leaders. In addition, God will not bless a preacher who believes he is a better man than their previous pastor. Even if he is doing well now, it is only because the fall from pride is a long way down. Sometimes, it takes years to hit the bottom from the fall of pride.

Between David's weeping for a night due to his sins and the joy that came in the morning through God's forgiveness, he catalogs one of the reasons for his failure. David learned humility because he had to hit the bottom before he could rise to the top. In his prosperity, he began to feel invincible. His faith was in the mountain God blessed him to inherit instead of the God who could move mountains (Psalm 30:6-7).

It always amazed me how great of a man James Commodore Wade, Sr. was, but he esteemed others higher than himself. Trust me, he was human. He had a way of laughing at himself because he learned not to take himself too seriously. The only other preacher I know who had that quality was his grandson, J. C. Wade, III. Believe me, I have rubbed shoulders with some of the best of them. Yet, J. C. Wade, Sr. and his grandson, James C. Wade, III were so gifted, but they almost admired the giftedness of others more than their own. In other words, my uncle (J. C. Wade, Sr.) and my cousin (J. C. Wade, III) had humble hearts.

David's heart for God was all that mattered. The kingdom was secondary. We can never develop a bad heart rate that beats as though we cannot live without a church to pastor. Even if the hearts of our churches we lead don't beat a certain number of beats per ministry-minute, we can still survive, but if our hearts fail to beat according to the minutes of maximum manhood, we are dead men.

David guaranteed that even though Saul no longer had his position, his oil would not be wasted (II Samuel 1:21). Sometimes, a senior pastor who loses his anointing gets it poured back upon his head when he dies. He may have faded off the scene, but his death became a rich testimony of the forgotten good he accomplished. While it was publicized how much Saul hated David, David held his peace, refused to demonize Saul, and made known how much he loved Saul. Before David embalmed Saul, he eulogized him. Little did David know that he was investing in the covering of his own credibility when he protected Saul's name. *When our ways please the Lord, our calling will always survive those who seek to assassinate our characters.* We may even live to see the day when life catches up with them. It will be a day when we experience God's faithfulness to His purpose by propping us up and laying our enemies down. However, it will be a tearful transition. Something or somebody must die while His grace keeps us alive. Their hearts stop, but ours keeps throbbing on a God-ordained throne. It will not be a joyous day when God kept us and took them. It will not be a happy day when they fall out of their seat while we remain in ours. On the contrary, it will be a sobering day of God's faithful hand upon our lives that brings us into a heartfelt existence, reminding us that God loves a man who has clean hands and a pure heart (Psalm 24:4).

After lamenting Saul's death, David asked God if he should even go to Judah. He placed God before his throne and not his throne before his God. At the throne of God, David was humble enough to bow to the will of God. Yet, Saul's seat was not an easy seat to assume. It had its evils.

Later, David was going to experience that by going down a pathway that would cause those who he led to question his credibility. God was going to make sure David learned his lesson, even if he must learn the hard way.

David began to take another journey with God as Israel's new king. As a matter of fact, the challenges of leadership can cause love for God to wax cold if we are not careful. David began to sample many of the same sins Saul swallowed. Now, David is sitting in Saul's seat. The seat of Saul is different when you are sitting in it yourself. When we assume Saul's seat, we must not succumb to Saul's sins. David wins major feats for the Lord, but somewhere along the line, success and too much experience get the best of David, and he begins to take subtle drifts in the wrong direction that led to a moral failure he would live with for the rest of his life.

The murder of Uriah the Hittite and his adultery with Bathsheba did not happen in the heat of the night. ***No pastor who falls from a high seat of trust does so in the heat of the moment.*** There are subtle flames that flicker early in the fire. This is also another reason why people should be careful to not judge the conduct, character, and consequences of a pastor who failed. They rarely know the preceding events that led to his fall out of his seat. Every man who sits in the seat of leadership is constantly being pushed by something, someone, or both. Yet, he must learn to not perish when he is pushed. Most of David's sins were reactions to significant events beyond his control. Of course, he could control his actions, but he had no control over the painful circumstances that preceded his reactions. In other words, David lived a hard life. He faced a lot of unfair and hard challenges that were much more than our minds can truly imagine. Yet, God had to teach him that he was not a victim.

When intimacy with God becomes a routine, the demons of presumption can sliver through the cracks. Sometimes, some of us can lead for so long that we become lethargic. We become so accustomed to pastoring that we make careless presumptions rather than follow standard principles that honor God's prescribed order of how we are to do ministry. David's heart for God was so intricately woven into the fabric of his relationship with God that he began to assume God would sanction his sophisticated ideas and strategic plans. Instead of keeping the heart of a child-like worshiper, David became too smart for his own good. Consequently, David carelessly overlooked a principle that also applied to him in how the ark of God was to be carried.

David had a shot at doing things God's way. As difficult as killing lions, bears, and giants may be, leading God's people is even more difficult. Running from Saul was a lot easier than staying on the throne. After a severe period of the absence of the ark, David rejoices like a kid in a candy store as he finally recovers the ark of God. Little did he know that he was later going to face a wife (Michal) who was so controlling and jealous that she wanted him all to herself. She had a possessive kind of love. She was just as temperamental as her father (Saul). The saddest thing about the second time when David got it right and brought the ark home is that Michal was resenting him instead of rewarding his new success. She would stand next to him on the throne, but she would put him down at home. She did not resent his failures. She resented his successes because she could not claim credit for what God had done for David. Because she saved his life in the past, she felt he owed her his life in the future. Michal's controlling love for David caused a God-ordained breach in their marriage. While it may appear as though David caused his wife's bitterness, it was actually God who struck her with bitterness and barrenness because she failed to realize David was God's property and not hers (II Samuel 6:16-23). Michal had a vindictive way of assuming responsibility for David's actions. When she was in his corner, she helped him (I Samuel 19:12-14). When she was not in his corner, she harassed him (II Samuel 6:16-20).

Yet, on the first go-around, he commands two of his best men to carry the ark back to Jerusalem. As they carry the ark on a new cart, the ox stumbles, and the ark slides. Uzzah thought he was protecting David's plan and reached to catch the ark. As soon as he touches the ark, he is struck dead. It was not the ark that killed Uzzah. It was the Almighty. David is floored by the death of Uzzah and throws a major tantrum with God. David is so bent on being angry with God that he does not take time to realize God was angry with him for not consulting Him about how the ark was to be carried (II Samuel 6:8). The sin of presumption can cause us as leaders to feel as though we are entitled just because we have a title. The only thing we are entitled to if we make presumptions is a casualty. If anyone deserved to die, it was David whose careless leadership cost a good man his life. Uzzah was not the only best man David got killed. David later got Uriah killed.

The loss of our best men has a long line of consequences, even if they were unintentional. God called us to lead and not lose good men. He called us to keep them alive instead of getting them killed or in trouble with the Lord. Our best men are not to be used as tools to execute our private matters. David finally cools down long enough to learn an important lesson. Although David had a unique place in God's heart, he was not above the law. Through Uzzah's death, God reinstates something in David's heart that he should never have let slip away, i.e., the fear of God (II Samuel 6:9). The fear of the Lord is the beginning of wisdom, and the lack of fear of God is the beginning of foolishness. Because David's presumption intercepted his fear of the Lord, he made a foolish move by assuming the new could take the place of the old by building a new cart to carry the ark of God.

Boards and big wheels are not even enough to replace the Bible. The Law required for priests and Levites to be the only ones to carry the ark. This was an old standard overlooked. Some things may be expedient, but not all things are lawful (I Corinthians 6:12). David had a habit of inquiring of the Lord on the simplest of details. Had he inquired of the Lord on this issue, a life would have been spared. God is no respecter of persons. Whoever respects God's laws prosper. When God's laws are presumed to be non-existent, we can rest assure that casualties will occur, even among the best of us. If we do not get it right, God always has somebody in our stead who will do it the right way, and they do not even have to be on our level to get the job done. He can entrust His purposes in the hands of a common man if He cannot trust a called man. It is sad that at that moment, God could trust the ark in Obed-Edom's home more than He could in His own house under King David's leadership (II Samuel 6:11).

After Uzzah's death, Obed-Edom housed the ark for months, and his house prospered because he handled the ark according to the Law (II Samuel 6:11-12). Although David repented, the loss of a good man cannot be swept under the rug or removed by mere repentance. When a life is carelessly wasted due to our laziness in leadership, God has a strange way of chastising us by literally letting us know how the lives of who we lead are in our hands. When we lose sight of the fear of God, the gravity of the consequence has a stronger pull than the gravity of the confession. Saying "I am sorry" can never bring a dead man back to life. **Although God's grace keeps us in ministry, sins on the leadership level have a long line of consequences that are irrevocable.** This is the part of leadership people do not always know. God allows many leaders who led lethally to remain in leadership. He does so because he inflicts us with life-long afflictions to get the best out of us. I would not be surprised if every man of God does not have at least one regret he has to carry with him all the way to his grave. For the rest of David's life and leadership, there was no way he would forget the lesson learned from the death of Uzzah, i.e., no one is above the law.

Although David learned *his* lesson, he had not learned *the* lesson. The seeds of power continue to develop in David as he abused his leadership privileges by succumbing to presumption. Please take a closer look in retrospect at what David did that looked good on the surface but was deadly in its depth. In II Samuel 6:1-5, David has an elite group of men organized for ushering in God's presence. David presumes he is top of the line in organizational administration, strategic planning, and implementation. He has new technology, a new cart, two new officers designated as heads of internal affairs (Uzzah and Ahio), and an elite staff of chosen men. A strong fanfare of praise and worship is stirring by the thousands as the entire nation is celebrating this national day of thanksgiving. David has established his brand and praise band. David chose surfaced praise over solemn worship. He chose administration over the anointing. All seems to be well and in order. However, he is sinfully bent on doing a new thing. David has organization, specialization, precautionary measures, branding, technology, and a strong praise and worship team. Yet, a good man gets killed.

God is not interested in our programs, methods, or ingenuities. God is not even interested in the beat we march to in praise. God's heartstrings of operation for our lives and churches are outlined in His word. True worship is Word-based. God cares about what we passionately believe will advance His purposes, but He is more concerned about what *He* is passionate about. God was not a God after David's own heart, but David was supposed to be a man after God's own heart. The order should never get twisted. Presumption is a sin committed on experienced and sophisticated leadership levels.

Another pattern of behavior corroding David's heart happened prior to his ascension to the throne. *David's heart was hardened in how he dealt with the challenges of fools.* A fool can tempt us as leaders to forfeit our future. A pastor must be careful how he deals with fools. Inexperienced leadership can blind a man from seeing fools in proper perspectives, but experienced leadership can cause us to become numb to the naughty nature of a man. In other words, experienced leadership makes us men of tough skin who cannot be easily offended. As a young leader in the making, David had soft skin when fools scratched him. A fool could cause David to snap at the drop of a dime. When David dealt with Nabal, he was not a seasoned leader. He was too sensitive to scrapes from those who disrespected him.

Nabal was a sheep master who led his flocks near the village of Carmel in the land of Judah. Remember, David was soon to be King of Judah. While on the run from Saul, David had special agents guard the area to protect it from raiders. David sent ten men to ask Nabal for assistance, and Nabal sends a harsh response that insulted David. David reacts in a fit of rage and initiates a contract against Nabal for him to be killed along with every male in his household. David organizes his four hundred cave men and starts after Nabal in foolish fury. Once again, David is misleading his most loyal men to execute his private and personal matters.

Pastor L. A. Kessee would often say to me that women are smarter than men. If that is the case, Abigail (Nabal's wife) had a higher IQ than David. Abigail was blessed with beauty and brains. The content of her conversation with David reveals acute signs of David's negligence as his rage completely blinds him to the greater issues of the Kingdom that an overgrown ego ignores.

Patterns of abused power cause a leader to take insignificant matters personally. If a leader assumes a matter is personal, it can be the launching of a power-trip he is about to embark upon. When we are called to move according to God's heart, our lives are in His hands as He uses various means to sober us from being intoxicated by our own egos in a power-drunken frenzy. My father would call this, "ego-tripping." While David was on an ego-trip, Abigail was in the business of *ego-trapping*. She knew she had to lay a trap for David's ego so that His pride would not get out of hand in a way that God could no longer use him. In I Samuel 25:26-31, Abigail had to stroke David's ego to calm him down. This is how a wise woman must put a plug in a man's pride. When David is about to cause injury, she does not inflict more injury upon him. Abigail was not a selfish woman. She was a spiritual woman. If David would have killed Nabal, Abigail would have been a widow. Yet, that was not her major concern. She was not concerned about how much his sin would cost her. She was more concerned about how much his sin would cost *him*. David recognized he would later need a wife like that. After Nabal died, it is no surprise that he married her.

As much as many may hate to acknowledge, men who have not been delivered from power sins can only be persuaded with a little ego-stroking. Abigail does not cut against the grain in a way that will invite resistance from David. She had enough sense not to challenge him if she was trying to change him. Instead, she diplomatically shuts down his mind and opens his heart. David's heart was his strength. His mind was often his weakness. David had some bad thinking issues, but he had good intentions, and Abigail was mature and spiritual enough to recognize that.

It is striking how David could quickly hunt down someone else's life while Saul was presently hunting for his. Donald Parsons, Pastor of the Logos Baptist Assembly of Chicago, Illinois would say, *"Proximity determines destiny."* How we handle what we deem irrelevant in our present can determine the direction of what is most important in our future. When we see how David responded to Nabal, we can also see why it was somewhat beneficial for the development of David's character to be on the receiving end of Saul's pursuits.

Whenever God's men are between a rock and a hard place, they must bend a little. David had a little killer instinct in him as well that almost brought about his downfall. Although David's anger was derailed by Abigail's wisdom, David's gangster tendencies followed him all the way into the kingdom. Like a mob boss after one of his best men's wives, he would eventually have Uriah killed to lay with Bathsheba. David's pride blinded him in a matter of moments. In seconds, David was about to risk everything he was running for and become who he was running from.

Men with passionate hearts must pay attention to detailed matters that can destroy godly affections. It is often the small fox that destroys the vine (Song of Solomon 2:15). The Devil is truly in the details but so was Abigail. She made David bend toward the details and pay attention to how he was acting apart from his God-given anatomy. Vengeance must never flow through the arteries to the hearts of God's men. For most of David's life, he fought for noble causes. If he were to kill Nabal, there would be nothing noble in shedding a fool's blood. Basically, Abigail was telling David that it was not worth it. There will always be certain people who can push a pastor's buttons if he allows. Our humility must tell our pride that it is not worth the fight. Fortunately, Abigail's intervention was more out of her deep concern for the Kingdom of God than Nabal's stupidity and stubbornness. This is the heart of a wife who is truly down for the cause. She feared the Lord and was used mightily of God to break up a tragic death because of the pride of *two* fools instead of just one. Nevertheless, David is developing a subtle foolishness about him that would infect his integrity in the future.

Let us get back to the throne. After a succession of battles, David is now a skilled veteran of victories who is comfortably sitting in Saul's seat with years of experience. As a matter of fact, he has too much experience. Yet, he is new at kingdom leadership. He has the thread of an alter-ego inside. He is sitting upon the throne like a leader who has little left to learn, so he thinks. He has some anger and aggression issues that were tendencies he previously had with Nabal. He also has a tinge of presumption. Furthermore, he has some ego and power-trip proclivities. To make matters worse, he has an aging weakness for women. He also tends to see what is in front of him, blind to the consequences that follow if he moves in the heat of the moment. Finally, he is careless in how he handles men who are loyal to him. He had an acute tendency to take

The Pastor And His Heart

his right-hand men for granted. He tended to treat them like slaves and boys. He not only had godly experience, but he also had sinful experience. Yet, God still chose him for the job. This would have meant David had to learn the true meaning of accountability. With an absence of accountability, David resigns from battle, and the foolish power-trip demon dormant in his heart awakens and begins a new saga with Bathsheba…and the rest is history.

One cannot dismiss David's adultery from murder. It was not just sexual lust that had overtaken David as much as it was power and borderline extortion. It is possible to get bored with sex sins or not even be affected by sexual temptation, only to upgrade to power perversions. To bring a weaker person into subjugation turns a man on if he climbs the ladder of power-lust. To have Uriah killed resembled tendencies he had with Nabal and Uzzah. David had some serious control issues. Each involved violating known laws that involved governing the nation and preservation of human life. Presumption caused him to neglect the costs of making rash decisions. David was not an impulse buyer, but he was an impulse spender. He consumed things he could not afford. He was so conditioned to purchasing things that did not belong to him that he did not even save the receipts. Whatever he no longer wanted, instead of returning it to where it came from, he just threw it away. He tended to order more than what he could eat. He wanted everything he saw on the menu. His eyes were bigger than his belly. David wanted things he was not sanctioned to have. The price he paid for Bathsheba was way too high. He loved items in the window and quickly got bored with them once he purchased them. God could not use a king who became a glutton.

After he suffered life-long consequences from his sin with Bathsheba and the murder of her husband and his loyal soldier, David discovered that a leader who rules over men must be fair and just (II Samuel 23:3). Therefore, God ensured David would live the rest of his life purged from the sin of lusting for power. David would learn that he did not own anything, only God has all power, he was not sovereign, and he was not entitled to anything, especially another man's woman. The kingdom God gave David was not to be spent on womanizing. He was not to convert his palace into a harem or become a ministry mob boss instead of a man of God. David confused lust with love. Lust wants it all. Love wants nothing in return. Lust takes, and love gives. David became a taker instead of a giver.

Make no mistake about it, there were years of sweet communion David held with God, existing between Nabal, Uzzah, and Bathsheba. The dangerous truth is that communion with God does not make sin easier to defeat or detect. The greater fellowship a man has with God, the subtler the temptation from the Evil One becomes. As a matter of fact, David was in denial when he got Uriah killed to have Bathsheba. It took Nathan to use picture therapy to open David's eyes to see his sins. Because of his pride, words were not enough (II Samuel 12:1-7).

When we are on the mountaintop with God, we can overlook demons in the valley (Matthew 17:4-15). The issue is not about what we accomplished throughout our mountaintop years of ministry, but the real issue is what have we done for the Lord lately? If we do not maintain fresh communion with God, we will make the mistake of eating stale bread and repeating broken formulas. We will start to repeat ourselves in everything we do and say. Our sermons will be nothing but repeats, our lives will be predictable, and our sins will become repetitive. Just as Saul started to repeat himself, so did David. David is now guilty of the sin of stupidity. You would think the privilege of being called by God would be enough for some of us to steer clear of stupid sins. Yet, God's grace can be taken for granted. Thus, God has a way of chastising us for stupid sins and giving us a better IQ in the school of integrity.

Yet, David's heart placed him in position to overcome senseless, strange, and stupid sins. David overcame some of the strangest struggles. David's senseless and stupid sexual failures were evident as a disease was one of his consequences of sexual immorality. When he could have any woman he wanted, little did he know that he chose at least one who was an infected woman. His passion for God somehow touched God's heart in a way that God sustained him as he contracted some type of sexually transmitted disease. Listen to the diary of his disease:

> *"My wounds stink and are corrupt because of my foolishness. I am troubled; I am bowed down greatly; I go mourning all the day long. For **my loins** (sexual organs) are filled with a burning disease: and there is no soundness in my flesh."*
>
> (Psalm 38:5-7; KJV)

Often, he could not understand why he was so depressed (Psalms 42:11). At times, David was engulfed by his sins. David was painfully real with God, and he poured every issue of his heart to God regardless of the offense. Mind you, this is not some little local pastor at a church. This is a man who was the king of the most important and powerful nation in the world who God had chosen. Yet, David talked to God about everything he did. He did not give cover-up confessions to God. David gave God careful confessions. If you have ever been in a position in which you genuinely loved someone, but you kept letting them down, you may get a glimpse of what David's relationship with God was like. David really loved God more than anything and anyone, but he kept letting God down. So, when he confessed his sins, he was not confessing because he was caught. He confessed to God because he cared.

David's long line of sins thread throughout the Psalms and we see most of the fabric of his failures in First and Second Samuel. Yet, he succeeded in a dimension known only by few. There is a secret place in God to those whose passion for God outweighs their passion for sin. God knew David loved Him more than anything or anyone. God cannot say that about everyone. David's life proved it. It was not a life of perfection, but it was a life of passion. David was not so engulfed in any of his pursuits that he was willing to do anything it took to protect his alternative lifestyle.

Regardless of how much David sinned, he never resorted to making a career out of being a professional sinner. David would let go of whatever or whoever jeopardized his anointing and hardened his heart. If his anointing and communion with God was threatened by anything he did, God had David exactly where He wanted him because God knew that David would not trade God's presence or Spirit for anything or anyone (Psalm 51:11). If you tell a God-called preacher that he will lose preaching and standing power with God if he holds to certain sins, he will usually turn those sins lose. In other words, sin was never David's priority. God was always David's priority deep down in his heart.

Nothing fit David well but God. God looked good on David. Sin never looked good on David despite the countless times he committed it. When he sinned, he was not at himself. Murder did not look good on David. Adultery did not look good on David. Rage did not look good on David. Venereal disease did not look good on David. Power-trips did not look good on David. Gangster gear did not look good on David. The wicked could wear sin so well that David was tempted to put their sins on too (Psalm 73:2).

Many people believe that a preacher gets away with murder. So, they try to indict him if God does not place him on Death Row.

Because they never keep an honest journal with God about their own transgressions, they cannot appreciate the process of prosperous purging. Thus, they fail to embrace consequences for their own afflictions as blessings in disguise. However, a preacher with *heart* learns to live and love the lessons he learned from the school of hard knocks. David's shares his sentiments that it was good that he was afflicted, that he might night go astray (Psalm 119:71).

David's life was a string of a long line of consequences because of his most significant offense regarding his sin with Bathsheba. It was not as much the fact that David committed adultery as it was in how he committed it. He got a man killed and deceived an army and nation to get it done. He committed pre-meditated murder. It may sound contradictory, but He had no ethics about how he went about doing wrong. Whenever we are bent on doing wrong, it becomes a paradoxical obligation to make sure we minimize our mistakes and have a level of integrity about our iniquities. ***There is a such thing as having a level of decency during our depravity.*** David made a mess out of his mistakes. No one took the evil responsibility to publicize his perversions. His sins spoke for themselves. David's sins with Bathsheba were so obvious because it was God who exposed them for all to see. God did not need anyone's help to play God and take David's sins into their own hands. God did it Himself:

> *"Thus saith the Lord, Behold, I will raise up evil against thee out of thine own house, and I will take thy wives before thine eyes, and give them unto thy neighbor, and he shall lie with thy wives in the sight of this sun."*
>
> (II Samuel 12:11;KJV)

Herein lies a powerful truth in relation to sin and who it affects. The question is not always about how much our sins will affect someone else. The real question is, "God, how much is my sin going to affect You?" Yet, in the above-mentioned passage, David's sins appeared to cost his wives and family much harm and damage. However, David almost makes a seemingly contrasting confession to God:

> *"Against thee (God), thee only (God), have I sinned, and done this evil in thy sight: that thou mightest be justified when thou speakest, and be clear when thou judgest."*
>
> (Psalm 51:4; KJV)

How can we harmonize two seemingly contrasting truths? We discover that the neighbor to have his wives would be his own son, Absalom:

> *"So they spread Absalom a tent upon the top of the house; and Absalom went in unto* (had sexual intercourse with) *his father's concubines in the sight of all Israel."*
>
> (II Samuel 16:22; KJV)

When David's wives were to be given over in sexual intercourse, did Absalom have a choice, or was he forced by God to have sex with David's wives because of David's sin and murder? Yes, he had a choice, and God did not force him to have sex with David's wives. When David's son (Amnon) decided to commit incest with his sister (Tamar), did Amnon have a choice? The answer is, yes. God did not put burning lust in Amnon's loins for his sister and neither did David's sins. When David's son (Absalom) decided to go against him to usurp the throne, did Absalom have a choice, or was he somehow possessed because of David's sin with Bathsheba? The answers are, yes and no. Yes, Absalom had a choice to not attempt to usurp the throne from David, and he was not possessed with hatred for David because of David's sin with Bathsheba. God did not cause his family to become dysfunctional because of David's sins. Because of David's sins, *God was saying that David would no longer have power or control over his family's already existing dysfunction.* So, when David saw his family commit evil, there would be nothing he could do about it.

Thus, no one else had the right to punish David for his sins. It was not their business. That was between David and God. David was not their king. David was God's appointed king who He chose for Himself. However, God had to remind David that God was truly on the throne. The man who God loved had temporarily fallen out of love with God. David broke God's heart when he got Uriah killed. Uriah was a soldier in the army of the Lord. Therefore, God hit David where it hurt him the most, i.e., in his own house. Because David tampered with the way God's house (Judah) was to be governed, God made sure that David would no longer be able to govern his own house. His family was divided for the rest of his life because David no longer had leverage to bring them together. When David's heart was right with God, he could expel evil spirits from the hearts of people. Now, God was going to strip that power from him when it came to the evil within the hearts of those of his own family. When his family practiced evil, there would be nothing David could do about it. In other words, it was not David's fault that his sons sinned, but it was David's fault that he could not save his sons from their sins.

The most publicized truth God wanted all to know was not some juicy news about what David did in the dark that was brought to light. Only people with bad hearts and parasite personalities feed off that type of perverse publication. Thus, God kept him on the throne because a leader whose sins draw him nearer to God leads with justice and mercy.

When I was a little boy, my parents would encourage me to go outside and play. We grew up in a culture and age in which our parents put us on punishment if we were disobedient. Part of our punishment was that we were restricted from going outside to play. Sometimes, we would look for one of our friends, but he would not be outside as he usually was. Then, we would ask each other where he was. There would often be a reply in these exact words, "He is on punishment." Sometimes, I was that little boy. When outside, my friends would ask, "Where is Derrick?" Then, one of my friends would say, "Derrick is on punishment." Although our parents put us on punishment, we realized why they did so. They placed us on punishment because they loved us. God-called preachers with *heart* realize the fact that God is their Father. Thus, they do not have a problem acknowledging when God puts them on punishment. They do not curse God when He punishes them. Instead, they bless God when He does. Preachers with heart realize punishment is not a sign that God has left them. Instead, being put on punishment is a sign that God has not forgotten them. Christians who have hard hearts have a problem with a God who puts them on punishment, but they do not mind putting other people and preachers on punishment. They feel entitled and only serve God to an extent. If God punishes them, they will no longer honor God. Instead, they will curse Him because they do not understand what it means to be a true son or daughter.

After David sinned with Bathsheba and accepted the punishment, he learned to be devoted to God *amid* the dysfunction instead of being devoted *to* the dysfunction. When God killed their first-born child, he wept for a moment. Then, he worshiped. When we are devoted amid the dysfunction, we are committed to accepting the damage we caused ourselves and God, and we learn to live with our losses. Yet, it all draws us even closer to God. Although we affected others, we know we infected ourselves and offended God the most. In this sense, it is against God and God only have we sinned. We also know that only God can tell us what to do and where to go from that point on. Then, our lives are in God's hands.

On the other hand, when we are devoted *to* the dysfunction, we place ourselves in positions of indebtedness to those who were damaged by our depravity. Although we injured ourselves, we may feel as though we injured others even more, or they may try to trap us into believing that we owe them more than an apology. Then, our lives are in their hands as we are devoted to them out of a shameful sense of guilt. Consequently, we relate to who we offended based on a guilt-trip because we know that we can never repay them for the pain we caused them. When we are devoted *amid* the dysfunction, God reigns over our lives, and there is also a level of accountability those who have been offended must also have with God. They must learn to put our sins in God's hands and take them out of theirs. In addition, they must learn to be accountable for their own actions that may have contributed to the conspiracy. If not, those who were offended never realize their responsibility in the equation. After all, David did not rape Bathsheba, raise Absalom to be covetous, raise Amnon to commit incest, or teach his family to be dysfunctional. The sin that the offended must come to terms with is the sin of playing God and using leverage tactics to keep the offender obligated to them for a lifetime.

Although David failed beyond human comprehension, God allowed him to stay on the throne of Judah. Because God prepared

David for Himself, God was going to have David one way or another. Yet, God did not force David to love Him. David realized his love for God more than anything or anyone else, even more than he loved his own family. Therefore, if he had to lose his family to keep God, that would be the painful but purging price he was willing to pay.

There is a thin line that exists along this type of family dysfunction. Regardless of our sins, it is vital for us to not worship our families at the expense of worshiping God. Our families must be as accountable for their own sins as we must be of ours. If not, we can die in the process of trying to save them. When it comes to dysfunctional families, very few members of our families genuinely want to conquer codependence, including ourselves. This type of family dysfunction takes place on several dimensions. During times of dysfunction in families, lives can be lost in the process of trying to be devoted to dysfunctional families. Only families who have a heart that is totally devoted to God can truly survive family dysfunction in a way that pleases God.

God extended grace and chastisement to David in a way that he could not have the audacity to resign from rulership. When our heart is for God and we have sinned greatly, that does not always mean that we have fallen out of our seat. What it does mean is that we fell out of our standing. A long line of consequences is sure to follow. Make no mistake about that. Those consequences will trail us to our graves. Yet, our heart for God will constrain us to be devoted to God *amid* the dysfunction. God can use our mistakes to make us into meaningful ministers. Leaders are not born, but they are made. God will ensure that a man whose heart is right with God will become a great leader through the process of falling at least seven times (Proverbs 24:16). To regain standing with God, we must sit in our seat uprightly with accountability, integrity, and humility (Psalm 25:21). In regard to people, God will then deal with them accordingly and give them the same heart He has if they desire, but He will never sanction their vengeance if they make heartless attempts to push a pastor or preacher out of a seat of ministry that God sanctioned.

There is a strange peace that accompanies a man after God's own heart, even after years of the moral agony of defeat. There are certain things in our lives that will never grow because our sins cut them off at the roots. When we have crossed heavenly lines, we must humbly adjust to the times when God says, "No!" There are some things we can no longer have regardless of how clean our hearts have become. What we can no longer have becomes a painful reminder that keeps us sensitive to having clean hands and a pure heart (Psalm 24:4).

When a pastor has *heart*, he not only praises God for growth, but he also praises God when there is no growth. He not only worships God for what he has, but he also worships God amid what he no longer has. God told David that the sword would never depart from his house. When God sends a sword to divide our interests because of our immorality, our worship can still be whole. The critical place to be positioned during great moral failure is at the foot of God's throne. We place all our dirty linen in the throne room of God. Somehow, our Heavenly Father takes more pleasure in our purging despite our pain. Although David hurt God and others, God knew David injured himself the most. Thus, God also knew what would get the best out of David.

You see, David rarely had a problem acknowledging his transgressions once he saw himself through God's mirror. He did not get amnesia about the sins he committed (Psalm 40:12). He was constantly conscious of them. When God matched David's sensitivity of his sins to God's mercies, he knew that would incite David to serve Him with his whole heart. God knew that His goodness would lead to David's repentance (Romans 2:4). Not everyone grows in God's grace (II Peter 3:18). They do not believe they are sinful enough to even need God's grace.

I pray that everyone who sees David's sins will recognize the strange grace in the fact that David deserved to live. Everyone who has been forgiven by God deserves to live the life God allowed them to live. It is no one's right to try to destroy a preacher's life and ruin his reputation. Regardless of whether one is a preacher or not, none of us have that right to do that to one another. If David were to appear in our churches today, no real Christian would inflict any more punishment on David than he already suffered. Why many Christians do that to men outside of the Bible who failed in a *David-kinda'* way is a mystery to me. The best explanation I could give is that they would overlook David's sins because they are not affected by David's sins. They have no *beef* with David. Christians who have cold hearts tend to only care about the actions of the person who affects them. Some people must be careful who they justify and who they condemn. The very man who people condemn could be the man who can save them. The same person who people reject could be the very person who God accepts. David was not always a good man, but He was always God's man. Only people who have hearts for God understand the difference.

David's unordered private world so damaged his household that there was little he could do to maintain leverage. He could do nothing to bring Uriah back to life. He could do nothing to bring his dead children to life. Yet, David could praise God during his pain. David was not arrogantly excusing himself of the consequences that came from violating another human. David just had a way of realizing that it is always a safer risk to fall into God's hands than the hands of humans (I Chronicles 21:13). People can be merciless, but our God will be merciful. People can be judgmental, but our God will be just.

We are reminded of the verses of David's last song as he suffered the consequences of the sword that divided his household because of his sins. David learned to accept what he could no longer have and appreciate what God would never take away. He could no longer have a happy home, but he could always have God's heart. David learned to be a real lover and leader. J. C. Wade, Sr. had a way of leaving people with God's word as the last word, and I will do the same:

> *"Now these be the last words of David. David the son of Jesse said, and the man who was raised up on high, the anointed of the God of Jacob, and the sweet psalmist of Israel said, The Spirit of the LORD spake by me, and His word was in my tongue. The God of Israel said, the Rock of Israel spake to me, He that ruleth over men must be just, ruling in the fear of God. And he shall be as the light of the morning, when the sun riseth, even a morning without clouds; as the tender grass springing out of the earth by clear shining after rain. Although my house be not so with God; yet he hath made with me an everlasting covenant, ordered in all things, and sure: for this is all my salvation and all my desire, although he make it not to grow."*

(II Samuel 23:1-5; KJV)

VOLUME II
Chapter 8

THE PASTOR AND HIS RIB

∞

The Pastor's Greatest Helper
(An Excerpt from the Life of Eve:
A wife who was too smart for her own good)

Tribute: To Mary Wade ("Big Annie", deceased Wife of the late, James Commodore Wade, Sr., former Pastor of Salem Baptist Church of Omaha, NE)

Who can find a virtuous woman? Our family called her, "Big Annie". Her grandchildren called her, "Big Mama". Big Annie was no Pragmatist. Neither was she a Universalist. She was a Specialist. Mary Wade specialized in staying by the side of her husband. She was comfortable in her own skin as a wife and shunned any title that would suggest anything other than being the wife of her husband. When I was informed that her heart rate slowed to 38 beats per minute, I stayed up night and day, pushing to publish this book before she passed. I wanted her to read this chapter and the preceding chapter in honor of her husband, J. C. Wade, Sr. Yet, on April 11, 2016, I received a text message from Florence Kilgore stating, "Mama went home this morning." Big

Annie only has one home. Her home is Heaven. I was pinning the finishing touches on this chapter, writing with a fury to get this book published and placed in her hands before God called her Home, but I did not finish in time. Although I wanted this book to be a blessing to my family, friends and foes, I wasn't as motivated to continue editing this book after she died, but I knew she would want me to keep writing until God was finished with me. While everything in me wants to believe I could have finished in time, she taught me to never make assumptions, and that we cannot hurry God. She would always say, "We will do this, and we will do that…if the Lord says the same."

The duties, privileges, and calling of a pastor are seen throughout the Bible in detailed print. Yet, nowhere in Scripture is his wife mentioned in major detail. My biblical deduction is that *Pastor's Wife* is a title, function, and office that does *not* exist in the Bible. However, we do find the Bible filled with the beauty of examples and help for who God called the *Wife* to be. She is *Wife* and does not have any other role to distinguish her. Her role speaks for itself and needs no adjectives to enhance her anatomy. Her role is *Wife*, and her title is her name. Aunt Eloise Temple, who is responsible for much of my spiritual development to this day, has a saying when someone identifies the pastor's wife as *"she"* or *"her"*. Aunt Eloise would say, "*She* has a name. Please call her by her name."

I always heard J. C. Wade, Sr. call Mary Wade, "Mrs. Wade" at home and church. He even had a nickname he called her at home, i.e., "Mae" (short for Mary). I heard Big Annie call James Commodore Wade, Sr., "Reverend" at church and home, not just because he was a pastor but because she honored him as her husband. She reverenced her husband as her pastor, and she also reverenced her pastor as her husband. When J. C. Wade, Sr. was at church, he saw her as his wife. When she was at home, he saw her as his wife.

The wife of the pastor has a function within the local church that is always under the process of evolution and scrutiny. The ministerial context from which she finds herself often falsely defines her responsibilities. She has one of the most confusing positions in the local church and home. God elevates her beyond the role of a victim, even if she is often unprotected and left alone to deal with the snakes in her garden. Just as the pastor's organs possess God-given ability, his *rib* is no exception (Genesis 2:22). She has an exceptional ability to *help* her husband as a man more than a minister. God is responsible for his ministry. The wife of the Pastor has a responsibility to support his manhood.

A title that attempts to honor her in some denominational circles is the title of First Lady, especially in the Black church. So many pastors' wives held their positions of *Wife* in such high honor that they inherited a type of royalty with their position they did not ask for. These women earned the right to be honored on so many levels that sincere Believers sought to maintain her distinction above all women in the local church. Thus, the title of First Lady evolved to compliment faithful wives who stood by their husbands, who were their pastors. *First* can also depict preeminence. Preeminence means, *to surpass all others*. Sincere churches struggled with a title that would make known how she surpasses all other women in the church.

Historically, the title of First Lady originated in the United States to describe the spouse or hostess of an executive. Not long after, the title of First Lady began to develop in the White House as an honorable description of the wife of the President. Before then, there was no official title for the wife of the President. Wives of the President even had their preferences of who they were to be called since there was no official title for them. It was not until 1877 that Lucy Webb Hayes, wife of former President Rutherford B. Hayes, earned the title of First Lady of the Land. From that point on, the title of First Lady began to get national attention and spread to other countries.

I may grammatically capitalize *Wife* in this chapter because she needs to be capitalized in her church and home. In the ideal sense, when the pastor looks at his Wife, he is beholding a part of his anatomy and not a *rib* of church politics or practice. Thus, a Wife needs to be an actual rib of the man who she marries. In other words, their marriage must be God-ordained. The Wife who God made for Adam came out of Adam's rib. In contemporary application, only the Wife who God ordains for the man can stick by his side. If she is not called to the man, she can never be called to be a ministry unto him. She will always feel strangely out of place and insecure. In a God-ordained marriage, out of all the ministries she may have, *he* is her number one ministry. Only a God-ordained Wife can understand and accomplish that supernatural challenge and opportunity. Yet, her ability to be successful in service to her husband does not come automatic. It is hard work, to say the least.

In a God-ordained marriage, the pastor's Wife is tailor-made for her husband. When a pastor has the right woman by his side, she is the one who will stand by him when all his other organs fade. Mary Wade was the last organ of J. C. Wade, Sr.'s body that remained. She outlived his heart. His heart stopped beating before hers did. She stood by him till death did they part.

A broken rib has something to do with a broken marriage. The danger of having a broken rib also has much to do with the damage it can do to the lungs. A broken rib can puncture a lung. When a man has a Wife who was not ordained for him, it takes the life out of him because he can't breathe. Then, he is no longer inspired to do marriage or ministry. The right woman by his side enables him to breathe again. The woman was made for the man instead of the man being made for the woman (I Corinthians

11:9). One reason why the woman was created *for* the man is because she is *of* the man (I Corinthians 11:8). God took a rib from the man and made a woman. She is for the man because she is an organ of *his* anatomy. She is one of *his* ribs. Every organ a person has is for *that* person. Adam's heart was *for* him. Adam's lungs were *for* him. In like manner, Adam's rib was *for* him. When a man has a God-ordained Wife, he has an anatomical advantage.

The Wife is not the husband's feet. Therefore, she is not to be stepped on or below him. She is not his hands. Therefore, she is not to do what he is supposed to do. She is not his head. Therefore, she is not to do his thinking for him. She is not his eyes. She cannot see what he is supposed to see. She is not his back. Therefore, she is not to be the backbone of the family or marriage. She is not his mouth. Thus, she is not to do his talking for him. She is his rib, ordained by God to be by his side and a part of his side. She is bone of his bone and flesh of his flesh. She is part of his side-structure. She is his helper.

The order of the woman's existence does not place her in positions *below or inferior* to the man but *alongside and interior* to the man. For the pastor, his Wife's greatest ministry has more to do with what she can do *in* him. Having the right Wife provides the pastor internal relief. Nothing said suggests a Wife cannot assist her husband in administrative functions of ministry. However, if that becomes priority, something will still be missing *inside*. It is difficult for the Wife to be internally satisfied with being connected more to ministry than her marriage. A husband must let her help *him* as a man more than his ministry as a minister.

The Bible says that it is not good for man to be alone (Genesis 2:18). It is hard for a man to do ministry with an unhealthy sense of aloneness. If he does so, he will minister from the context of his insecurities and incompleteness. He will also be vulnerable to others who have no problems codependently confirming him.

Affairs also develop out of this type of dysfunction as husbands begin to gravitate to other women who are *into* them. If that is not the case, couples in ministry begin to develop a codependence that becomes a form of ministry addiction. When a woman is by his side, she restores *his* confidence in what *he* does because she enhances who *he* is.

No couple plans to divorce as soon as they get married or become addicted to the local church. Understanding the root causes of marital and ministry dysfunction will bring healing that helps couples know that life goes on after divorce, marital competition, and church addiction. For those who are married and addicted to the local church, following the biblical paradigm for marriage allows couples to develop new dimensions of wholeness of which the local church could never give because the local church was never intended to be the antidote for mistaken identities. Such mistaken identities in marriage are often inherited by the children.

Please allow me to express some hard sayings. Regarding the pastor's family, when the ministry overpowers the marriage, the Wife or children may resent the church. If the children do not resent the church, they often conform to the church. They are unfairly stigmatized as preacher's kids (PKs). Because the church has occupied their childhood lifestyle, they were not afforded the nurturing to fulfill healthy roles in their future families as adults. Most must combat becoming narcissistic. By the time they become adults, because they were denied proper nurturing, they may be underdeveloped and crave abnormal amounts of attention because the church as demanded their attention. After all, that is where their father is most of the time. If the Wife sticks by the father, the mother (Wife of the Pastor), spends most of her time at church also. Many of them grow to be adult children who are not far from home, even if they live miles away.

In the year 2017, it had been statistically said that more than 70% of the children who grew up in the local church never become faithful attenders of the church when they become adults. If that is true, what happens to the pastor's children? Either they no longer attend church, or they are left among the remaining 30% who stay in the church. I must be even more detailed than that. Those who remain are usually out of touch with their generation because they lived sheltered lives. It was not just the parents who sheltered them. Many times, it was also the church who sheltered them because that is where "PKs" spent most of their time while their friends were at home living normal lives. PKs are often forced to grow up too fast. They must learn church politics at an early age because they live in glass houses. This will also constitute the decline of church attendance and the decline in the quality of church life in succeeding decades as they may develop a new morality for ministry and marriage.

I wonder if too many of us have not made a grave mistake by thinking that just because a pastor's family is at church or in church, that church is the best environment to raise a family. I will supply another hard saying. ***The local church is usually the worst environment for the pastor to raise his children.*** The local church is like a hospital full of sick people with all types of dysfunctions and maladies through living in a fallen world and having a sinful nature. Thus, many have warped psychological understandings of the pastor and his family although they may not intend to do so. The local church often has a built-in system that expects the pastor, his Wife, and family to be void of the same dilemmas they face because they have a disillusioned understanding of the Bible and human nature. If the husband (Pastor) does not put home first, he may be under that same unrealistic expectation.

A hospital is not a healthy place for a doctor to raise his children, but it could be one of the best places to heal a child. A psychiatric ward is not the best place for a psychiatrist to raise his family, but it could be one of the best places for his family to receive therapy. Unfortunately, pastors' families and children are rarely allowed to be healed at the church they serve. If the pastor's family comes to a church who understands that his family also needs healing just like everyone else, miracles can happen. Sadly, the average local church usually will not allow the pastor and his family to be transparent enough to admit the fact that they have sicknesses too. The pastor's house is a glasshouse while many members live in brick houses with window shades pulled and doors locked. Too many local church people are constantly peeking into the pastor's home. The pastor, his Wife, and children are often condemned for getting mentally, emotionally, physically, or even sin sick. God forbid if the pastor and his Wife are going through problems also. Too many in the local church are acutely observant of what goes on in the pastor's house, but many do not want the pastor to know what goes on in their houses. They may have an idea of what is going on in the pastor's house, but they rarely have an idea of why it is going on.

The only scripture most are familiar with is I Timothy 3:4-5. This scripture teaches that the pastor must ensure that his home is well-managed, but God never gave the mandate for pastors and their families to live in glass houses where people are constantly throwing stones. Thus, the pastor and his family spend most of their time deflecting rocks thrown by hypocrites.

Mostly, the local church affords the pastor and his family little or no privacy to truly process their problems. The local church places high demands on the pastor, his Wife, and his family, even if they do it unintentionally. Most of what the pastor and his family does is under the scope of people who do not understand unconditional love. Too many members of the local church see the pastor's family on a warped and unbalanced pedestal. Thus, the pastor, his Wife, and children are under unrealistic pressure and scrutiny, and they usually slide off that pedestal quite quickly. As a result, many pastors and their families pretend to not be sick to avoid the slide. If the pastor's daughter gets pregnant before marriage, she has been known to have to stand before the entire church and confess. If a member's daughter gets pregnant before marriage, nobody notices, and if they do, nobody cares. Pastors must avoid portraying perfect images of their families because they are trying to defer defamation bullets people can throw at their glassy homes, especially pastors who have a board who pays them who they must answer to.

With the explosion of social media, the pastor's family learns to live with the limelight instead of paying needed attention to their private world. Other pastors and their families learn to protect their pain or submerge their sorrows. Some members of churches have good intentions and not harmful ones. Yet, there are other stories pastors cannot tell while they are the pastors of those churches.

Mary Wade learned how to balance the scales of home and church. She said a lot of things I could not put in print. The dumbest thing a Christian can do is write a *tell all* book. She would counsel pastors (including myself) in this manner: "If your Wife is ever absent from church and somewhat asks you where she is, just tell them, she is not here." While that may sound rude, she was teaching us how messy some church people can be. She wisely recognized through half of a century of church experience that people who usually have the audacity to ask are those who really do not care. If they do care, they do not care for the right reasons. In my experience, the people who usually ask are the ones who are simply trying to be what we called in the Black culture, "nosey". In other words, they were simply trying to keep their noses in our family business.

For these reasons and countless more, many pastors, Wives and children are almost forced to fit into a church picture frame and put on church smiles. For this type of pastor, it is vital that his family looks good on the portrait or he knows he will be out of a job. The local church can have a strange way of threatening many pastors' sense of job security and credibility. They will vote pastors out or leave the church for some of the ficklest and most hypocritical reasons. Therefore, the children of many pastors who are in church are raised in a protective bubble by one or both parents. If many pastors were not in certain churches they held in such high esteem, I am not sure if many of them would be so driven to ensure their Wives and children walked such a straight, narrow, and unrealistic local church line. What makes matters even more challenging for the pastor and his family is that God often calls pastors to these types of churches.

Although the church is a religious entity, it is not immune to the perils of people. Notice how these same psycho-social dynamics exist within royal families, President's families, famous movie star's families, famous sports star's families, etc. It is not as much of a spiritual issue as much as it is a human nature issue.

No matter how important our local churches may be, our children are never to be sacrificed on local church altars, and neither should the pastor's Wife or his children sacrifice him on local church altars. If someone mischievously discovered my son's issues, I really do not care what people think. My sons should have the same freedom to fail and opportunity to succeed that I give my members. I have too many issues and sins to seek healing and cleansing from that only Jesus can give than to get bogged down by critics who mean more harm than good. I placed my sons on the altar of God and not the altar of religious opinion a long time ago. Presently, they still live with me, and they come first. I do not apologize for that.

Please understand, the motives that incite many of us as pastors to fall prey to this subtle type of hypersensitivity are more than understandable. Any vocation that involves people is a challenging vocation, to say the least. Marriage and ministry are tough for anyone who would be honest and remaining married and in ministry is even tougher, especially if you were in a marriage or ministry God never sanctioned. I do believe it far better for a couple to genuinely divorce, wish each other the best, and try their best to make something out of the rest of their lives than to hypocritically stay together in a church cover-up game or seek confirmation from people who are carnal, anti-family, anti-Christ, or those who use the failures of the pastor or his family to defend or deflect their own dysfunction.

Ministry marriages consist of pastors and Wives who simply care about ministry and people in a supernatural way. Even in a marriage God did not sanction, I am certain that most couples did the best that they could with what or who they were working with. Yet, the hurt at home can never be resolved by creating an ecclesiastical extension of marriage in the church that never addresses biblical manhood and womanhood.

Regarding the sexes and role-reversals, there are over 6,400 genetic differences between men and women outside of their sexual organ distinctions. Thus, a man will still be a man, and a woman will still be a woman, even if they get a sex change. A man may act like a woman, but he cannot think like one. A woman may act like a man, but she cannot think like a man. A male brain is completely distinct from a female brain and so are the emotions. The plethora of distinctions are deal points in God creating a woman for the man. No man can do for another man what the right woman can do for him. No woman can do for another woman what the right man can do for her. The beauty of the relationship between men and women is exponentially enhanced when those differences are respected, appreciated, and encouraged. When God created Woman, he made her a distinct human being, but this female human being would be fearfully and wonderfully different from the man who He previously created. When God created Adam, that was one thing, but when He made Eve, that was quite another. She was more than just another human with a womb as an attachment. One creation of one human (Man) was from the dust of the ground. The other creation of another human (Woman) was from the rib of the man.

If God would have created another man for Adam instead of a woman, the last thing that would have occurred between the two was a sexual attraction. They would have just been two lonely men in the Garden (Genesis 2:18). If God would have only created two women, they would have just been two women desperately trying to help each other out.

You would have had to have been there to understand the complementing chemistry and differential dispositions of Mary and J. C. Wade, Sr. in marriage. When I speak of James C. Wade, Sr., I am speaking of a preacher who was one of the most well-known preachers in the Black preaching context of the 20th century who all great preachers of that era knew. He was a legend in the Black preaching league. I do not believe any of us as preachers in our family will deny the big shoes of J. C. Wade, Sr. that none of us can fill. He was not just a great minister. He was a great man. Beside that great man stood a great woman (Mary Wade). Looking and listening to Mr. and Mrs. Wade as they sat side-by-side and converse spoke volumes of what marriage is about. Like any marriage, they had problems, but unlike most, they turned those problems into opportunities. You could bring up a subject, and Mary Wade would speak on that subject with feminine language while James C. Wade, Sr. would speak on that subject with masculine language. After they finished saying what they were saying, they formed a complete sentence. J. C. Wade, Sr. formed the subject of the sentence, and Mary Wade formed the predicate of the sentence. What James C. Wade, Sr. said was subject to what Mary Wade said, and what Mary Wade said was predicated upon what J. C. Wade, Sr. said. They never got their roles reversed.

A marriage and ministry that upholds role-reversals is the by-product of one or both parties privy to a faulty hermeneutical system that misinterprets God's word. I remember pastoring my first church some time ago. James Commodore Wade, Sr. was my guest preacher, and Mary Wade accompanied him. We had Sunday School before the morning worship began. Mary Wade attended one of our Sunday School classes. Instead of teaching the lesson, the teacher would ask everyone their opinion of a passage of scripture. Of course, that was a dangerous practice because people would go off on all types of tangents. Well, it was finally Mary Wade's turn to give her interpretation. Anyone who knew Mary Wade knew she had a heavenly mind and a keen sense of humor. When it was her turn, she said something like this: "Since everyone is giving their opinion, I might as well give mine." On the outside, I kept a poker face, but on the inside, I was rolling with laughter all over the floor. Mary Wade might not have gone to Bible college, but she knew her Bible forwards and backwards. She not only knew the truth of the Bible, but she also knew the tone of the Bible. She knew when someone said something regarding the Bible that did not sound right. She even used to say, "I may not know how to preach, but I know good preaching when I hear it."

Satan presented everything to Eve in the tone of what sounded like a biblical opportunity for more Truth (Genesis 3:1). Satan and his demon workers camouflage their agendas for women under the cloak of freedom, independence, opportunity, and equality. These are the snakes in the garden of our culture to smear lines that biblically define the differences between men and women. Although

Eve did not notice the Tempter's snare, there was a Snake in her garden hissing an offering to her that she believed was the opportunity of a lifetime. When she offered it to Adam, it came under the guise of a new marital and ministry proposal. She possibly wanted to go to another level with Adam and not without him. A Wife on this level may consciously believe she is only making extramarital moves on behalf of her marriage, but Satan knows subconsciously she is only making such moves for herself.

Once the Snake arrives in the gardens of marriage and ministry, some women may only see an apparent opportunity for personal deliverance from the yoke of submission and interiority. This principle has nothing to do with depreciating the discerning capabilities of a woman, but it has everything to do with respecting the deceptive powers of Satan. Satan is crafty. He is so subtle that it takes a man and woman with an impeccable desire to obey God's order to defend their marriages and ministries from the satanic infiltration of role-reversals and battle of the sexes. Women have the daunting challenge to learn the art of defending themselves against deception, and men must defend themselves against disobedience.

As long as Eve remained in submission to God's authority, she was covered from satanic seduction. The freedom she was seeking was a freedom Adam was also forbidden from seeking. To further break down the defenses of the Wife, the Serpent does not want her to recognize she is in spiritual warfare. Once Satan lets a good woman know what is at stake, she will align herself with God and her better senses. A good woman can figure her way out of a situation in a much more healthier way than talking to third party vendors who are only selling her advice that will draw her further away from her Lord and God-ordained lover.

To prevent Eve from resorting to her better senses, he talks the sense out of her that God talked into her. Satan sets the stage of reason and subjective experience. Satan knew Eve found no fault with her own reasoning, and he knew her perception would be her reality. The Devil also knew Eve would argue with him if she detected an antagonistic spirit. So, he set the stage for her to argue with herself. Thus, she would feel as though she had a right as a woman to change her mind. He seduced the Wife to look at the fruit for herself rather than from God's eyes.

As Eve's curiosity was aroused, Satan placed her on a platform he suggested was equal to God and isolated her to use her own judgment instead of better judgment. Only God is sovereign and at liberty to rely on His own judgment. Neither Male nor Female can ever pretend to exercise sovereignty. Satan was tricking Eve to exercise sovereignty she did not have. All of God's creation are forever under His accountability. None of us can make personal decisions apart from God's prescribed principles without paying a high price. We pay a price when we invent or welcome suggested revelations for ministry and marriage outside of God's ordained standards. If we do so, we complicate our roles and relationships to the extent that we cannot explain who we are in one sentence anymore. We should be able to simply say that we are Husband and Wife. Unfortunately, in our times, being *"Just Married"* comes with a variety of bells and whistles. **When supremacy and spirituality are satanically craved, ministry, and marriage become satanically complicated.**

The Snake seduces Eve to believe she should not have limitations and coerces her to not acknowledge those limitations (Genesis 3:5). To Eve, suggestions filling her mind appeared to be liberating and logical in a way God would condone. It is hard to keep your mind when the Devil has his hand on your heart. Satan was touching Eve in areas she was deeply affectionate about. He was delving into her definition of what it meant to be a woman. So, she was not thinking clearly, but she was starting to feel really good. Satan made it sound reasonable that there was more to life than her apparent limited role as Wife. Independence became a desirable option for her, especially if the road to independence was within the framework of her own choices and perception of God's word. Little did she realize, the one imposing warped definitions of a real woman was Satan, and the woman who doubted who she was happened to be her own self.

Love is often powerless when it is pitched against human will. God infinitely loved Eve, but somewhere along the line, Eve did not value God enough to stay virtuous. It is important to remember Eve's good intentions. Adam had a proclivity to compromise. Yet, it was Satan who knocked on Eve's door to induce her to welcome Satan into her home as her disguised, distinguished, but devilish guest. Eve was not trying to hurt her husband. After she bit off more than she could chew, she was no longer her normal, God-ordained self. She hellishly thought she was helping. After she dined with the Devil, she offered Adam something to eat also.

We do not know what the fruit was, but we do know what was in it. The content of the forbidden fruit was knowledge of good and evil that would give greater access to spiritual enlightenment. Thus, Eve believed she could offer Adam a better revelation than the one they had. Satan wants to make some women too smart for their own good, their husband's good, and God's glory. Wisdom teaches us that there are some things we are better off not knowing.

From Genesis 3:5, we understand that Eve wanted to be a *knowing one ("…you shall be as gods (God), knowing good and evil")*. Sometimes, knowing is evil. The wisest women do not want to know too much. There is a malignancy in knowing certain things regardless if one is Male or Female. You can see in a man and woman's eyes when they have bitten off more than they can chew. When we bite off more than we can chew, we know too much about deadly subjects instead of life-giving ones. Then, women know how to give their husbands deadly assistance, and men know how to blame the woman for it instead of themselves for allowing their Wives to dominate them by reversing roles.

In Genesis 3:5, the Hebrew word for "gods" is, אֱלֹהִים ('ĕlō·hîm). Even though the word is in the plural sense, it has a singular meaning. The New American Standard Bible along with several translations has the phrase, "…you shall be like God". Other English Bibles may have the phrase, "…you shall be as gods". I agree with the New American Standard Bible. Eve did not want to be God, but she wanted to be like God. Being like God should be all our desire. We all should want to be like Him. Yet, we can never be God. Therefore, submission to God is the element that Eve allowed Satan to deceptively erase out of the equation.

The sinister nature of forbidden fruit was in gaining a heightened sense of identity and spirituality apart from God's prescribed commands. Thus, Adam knew it was a fake fruit because of who offered it. In other words, he knew the Tree was not real in the sense that it would not make them like God. Satan was proposing to Eve a false claim. Instead, the forbidden fruit on the Tree would make them ungodly. This temptation was not the fickle dangling of devilish and delicious fruit before Eve's eyes. She was much too godly for that. What she saw was something deeper. To her, the fruit was a gateway to God. She was not hungry for food. She was hungry for fortune. Satan was offering her a new religion, revelation, realization of herself, and a new relationship with the supernatural. Satan was helping her develop a ministry and marriage on her own terms. To her, she was deceived into believing her eating would be on terms God would make an excusable exception for.

It would have been understandable if she would have fallen to a temptation that would have deceptively promised she would only *know good* if she were to partake of the fruit. *Knowing evil* was an addendum she could not resist. She felt that if she knew evil, she could better avoid it. In no way could she avoid evil because she was with the Evil One and did not even know it. Satan crawled upon the branches of that tree night and day. Eve's innocence was no match for her inexperience with iniquity. She allowed her virtue to evolve into a vice. She did not want to be left in the dark and thought *not knowing* was to her disadvantage. Knowing evil was not a temptation Eve would avoid because she had never known evil before. Therefore, she did not understand how bad of a predicament she would be in by succumbing to evil. However, knowing evil can be good. What good is evil if you have never known evil before? Evil can be good because it can teach you to stay as far away from it as possible. Evil has only one positive lesson to teach us, i.e., *to leave it alone.*

Eve had limited knowledge (innocence), and Satan drew Eve out of the interior anatomy of her husband and placed her in a position in which she relied on her innocent anatomy. She was a rib, standing alone. Innocence produces poor judgment of character regardless of one being Male or Female. Now, she can justify her actions in a way that she does not feel shame in doing what she is about to do. Satan loves preying on naïve women and naughty men. He loves destroying curious women and compromising men. From the premise of innocence, nothing appears to be harmful; not the Serpent, knowing evil, or forbidden fruit.

Disobediently, Adam was co-signing for the deception of Eve. After eating, she gave the fruit to her husband *who was also with her.* When Satan can divorce God-ordained husbands and Wives from one another, nobody wins. Yet, divorce can also happen *within* the context of a marriage between two partners who are together but living single.

"And the Serpent said; hath God said; ye shall not surely die; your eyes shall be opened; you shall be as gods, knowing; make one wise" (Genesis 3:1b; 406b); these are satanic suggestions designed to

break up any happy home. Third-party interferences *("and the Serpent said")*, apparent concern from a third party for the woman's personal relationship with God *("hath God said")*, pushing the envelope against a literal interpretation of God's word *("ye shall not surely die")*, opportunities for the woman to be liberated *("ye shall be as gods")*, and appeals to the woman's intellect and intuition *("make one wise")* are all snakes in women's gardens to this very day. Homes are being ripped apart, and ribs (Wives) are being torn from the man, ending in *rib-less* relationships and *man-less* ministries.

Prior to succumbing to the Serpent, it is evident Eve had a viable relationship with God. She was as spiritual as any woman could be. She was the first and heightened sample of the total woman. No woman was ever as wealthy and worshipful as she. Eve shared the entire Earth-world with her husband. She had intimate knowledge of what God said, but she had limited knowledge of what Satan meant. No woman was ever as innocent as she. Eve had never known sin. What Satan meant could only gel in her soul as she continued to heed to it. She would have had to bite to utterly understand where Satan was coming from, and she had to stay away from the fruit to utterly understand where God was coming from. She did not harness the fact that God says what He means, and He means what He says. Eve did not realize that any alternative apart from accountability is dangerous despite how spiritual it looks and what it promises. Everything she had was from God and with her husband, and Satan made sure that became a problem for her.

Of course, the husband had a deficiency as well, to say the least. His deficiency would soon be discovered by eating also. Yet, God and her husband were all she really had to be accountable to. A woman, man, and God are all who are needed to make a happy marriage. As long as that three-fold cord is tight, a happy home is in the making. When couples let other people, parents, priorities, and passions in the relationship, things can get satanically seductive and sinful. Eve was seduced, and Adam was sinful. Men sometimes allow passions to disrupt the marriage, and women sometimes allow other people to disrupt the marriage. Sometimes, men play too much, and women talk too much.

It was easy for Eve to not be accountable to Adam because he did not man-up. However, she was without excuse because there was no failure in God. Satan made sure both options were removed from her equation. Therefore, she saw no reason to do the math. Although she had some major restrictions before her fall, she fell prey to the permanent paralysis of taking what God ordained out of the equation. She did not realize how good she really had it until it was gone. Staying where God placed her would accentuate her advantage and polish her personality. God placed her beside her husband, but she decided to stand alone. A man and woman who are made for each other look better together than apart. Only those who are not made for each other appear to do better on their own. For once, she wanted to achieve something on her own. Satan knew how getting Eve to examine the possibilities would be the introduction to his ultimate target of getting Adam to conclude to eat. It never was all about Eve. It was all about Adam. Satan was after the man the whole time. Notice the order. The break-up of a happy home started with Satan, trickled to Eve, and finally influenced Adam.

The poisoned chemistry of the marriage of Adam and Eve has spilled into marriage and ministry to this day. There are no more trees, forbidden fruit, and gardens to access, but Satan is present. The world and local church have become Satan's new garden. The Serpent is no longer crawling. Something sinister is in the air. A literal interpretation of God's word is being replaced by a false matrix of revelation and experiential knowledge within the local church and home. Too many are no longer studying the scriptures, but they are staring at the scriptures, looking for a new revelation. Marriages and ministries are only appreciating scriptures that are liberating instead of those that are restricting us from doing what is right in our own eyes. The increasing movements in ministry are not only about the lethal liberation of women, but they are about the deceptions of Satan and the disobedience of men. We are losing value in marriage and ministry because many of us disobeyed God on marital and ministerial levels. We are prone to co-sign for compromising relationships and biting into things that are not ours to chew. Men are indicted by some women for a lot of things. However, I am not sure if some women would indict a man for letting them usurp their authority, but God will. Each time a man disobeys God, he loses leverage with his God-ordained lover.

Our disobedience as men weakens our defenses against the consequences of playing with fire. We know it is hot, but we do not know how hot it is until we get burned. Some of us must touch it to believe it. By then, it is too late. Once a man experiences literal third-degree burns, there are other complications that occur in his biological anatomy for the rest of his life that we rarely hear of. Men with third degree burns usually do not have as long of a life span as they would have had if they had never been burned. In like manner, ministries and marriages are filled with burned men and bitter women. Satan knew how much Adam loved playing with fire. If Satan could get Eve hot enough, Adam would fall for her fire. Adam was attracted to a hot Wife who broke the rules, and he was desirous of everything that accompanied her except for death. Eve did not think about it until Satan put the thought in her mind. Remember, *men and women are more different than alike*. The only thing Adam and Eve did the same was eat of the forbidden fruit. Yet, they chewed for different reasons (I Timothy 2:14).

For the woman, the bondage was in what she did not know and what she did not want. If she would have known it was evil, she would have spit it out of her mouth. What she did not want was to miss out on more if she felt more was better. Therefore, instead of spitting it out of her mouth, she swallowed.

After they had eaten, they both ran and hid. By now, I can imagine Eve picking every piece of the fruit from her teeth because she could taste the bitterness of sin. Sin usually feels good with the thought of doing it and while we are doing it, but it never feels good after we do it. There will always be that empty feeling of godlessness and emptiness when we wake up from long nights of deception or disobedience. I can see Eve scrubbing herself, frantically trying to get clean again because she felt spiritually raped. Yet, no matter how bad she scrubbed, she could not wipe off the filth of her own sin. On the contrary, I can see Adam licking his fingers with an insatiable lust for more. Eve became a deceived mess, and Adam became a disobedient monster.

Eve's conversation with the Devil lasted way too long. She should have ended the conversation with Satan's first pick-up line. She gave Satan time to appeal to her senses and touch every sensitive spot in her soul in a way that left her defenseless. He appealed to her mentally ("What do you think?"), emotionally ("How do you feel about the issue?"), spiritually ("What is your view on what God said?"), and physically ("See and taste for yourself.").

Satan uses the very same principle to dupe women and dominate men to bite into the forbidden fruit of role-reversals. Whenever roles are reversed, a pride that seeks to exalt itself above God's design for gender is developed. Thus, men and women begin compromising and competing in roles for the sake of more and an enlightened brand of spirituality within the local church setting. As the drama plays out, the local church is becoming more populated with *spiritist* people rather than spiritual people. The angels of God in Heaven are the very opposite. They fear God and denounce self-exaltation.

Satan was conforming Eve more to his image over and against her God-given image. He was not only seducing her to sin, but he was also seducing her to become hyper-spiritual, and he told more truth than lies to get her to do so. A woman who has sinned on this level can lie, but you can see the truth in her eyes. In her eyes, you can see that she has been poisoned by too much knowledge. The truth may hurt but lies kill. Now, Eve is dying on the inside. The fact that she would not die was a lie, but the fact that it looked good, tasted good, sounded good, and that she would be a *Knowing One* was no lie.

Instead of being like God, Satan desires for us to be little gods who seek to be masters of our own little universes. If we continue in Adam's disobedience, Eve's deception, and Satan's devices, the local church will be more populated with *gods* in ministry and marriage. Satan wants the local church to become infiltrated with gods and goddesses in pews and pulpits. In addition, he wants to continue to birth a strange breed of preachers, prophets, prophetesses, pastors, and parishioners who will invade the local church with a lack of biblical accountability and heightened sense of existentialism. As the local church, Satan wants us to become too high-minded to be of any earthly good. The Devil's desire is to turn our praise and worship songs into ghost music and transcendental meditations. The Tempter seeks to give people the skills to have a keen way of dodging Truth and seducing men and women to preach sermons that are strangely spirited, full of strange revelations with no real redemption or responsibility. The Devil wants the local church to have a form of godliness but deny the power of God. It is Satan's goal for the local church to have revelations, demonstrations, and manifestations of the supernatural as motifs for ministry and membership while the sober discipline of the scriptural is thrown out of local church windows. Yet, there is none *like God* (Psalm 113:5)

The Serpent's strategy is to tempt us to bite into forbidden fruit of modern-day ministries and marriages that consist of major amounts of Truth mixed with a minor number of lies. There is more right in ministry than wrong. That is the way Satan wants it. That way, we can gloss over the devilish details and sweep them under rugs that haunt us later. In marriage and ministry today, things look good and right on the surface, but something sinister can be hissing. All the church paraphernalia is present. The husband and Wife are co-laboring in ministry, but the home-life is competitive, codependent, confrontational, and compromising. One little lie can send a ministry or marriage in an entirely different direction within a matter of years, months, days, and minutes. *Adamic* men are remaining silent, overlooking a few lies at the expense of major amounts of Truth. When it comes to Truth, the slightest lie distorts the whole Truth, thereby producing total lies. Sometimes, if good seems to outweigh the bad, we can dismiss the bad and think it is all good. Most men see the discrepancies, and we as pastors must not develop an Adamic way of hiding from God, covering ourselves with pseudo-spiritualities that are leaves that hide our masculine shame.

We must avoid flirting with the God-realm, falling under the temptation to be *as gods*, arrogantly believing we are above certain evils. The worst evils can happen to anyone if he or she is not careful. Women must avoid spiritual deception, and men must avoid disobediently allowing revelations that are a futile effort to exalt the mortal state of consciousness. It is almost as if we are attempting to move from mere mortals to immortals before our time. We are in such a hurry to elevate that we sell our souls to the Devil to levitate. Instead of being so ambitious to come up, we need to come down. A little common sense will take all of us as members of the local church a long way. Doctrines are being taught that lead people to believe they can control too much of the inevitable, know too much of the unknown, and demand too much of the restricted. We cannot have it all in this life. We will have more than our eyes have seen, ears have heard, and minds have imagined in the Afterlife (I Corinthians 2:9). People who lose patience with God want too many powers and perks. Mary Wade had a saying. She would say, "It don't take all that." We must want more meaning than miracles. We must embrace suffering and denounce success. Many want a *yes* from God and are not submitting to God's *no's*. Too many want too much supernaturalism.

We are in a serious, supernatural, and serpent-like storm. Yet, nothing is beyond God's saving scope. He has a painful but purposeful way of grounding us as Earthlings. It is also important to note that after God chastised Adam, Eve, and Satan, he kept Adam and Eve together. He reunited and restricted them with new revelations of their roles. Although they failed each other, divorce was not an option. They had to learn to live with their failures and submit to God's order for a man and woman. Until we do that, none of us win.

There are pastors who fell into the snares of the spectacular who can remind many that the chase is not worth it. ***There is a thin line between witchcraft and worship***. The practices are distinctly different, but the lines that distinguish them are thin. The Serpent was more cunning than any beast of the field, and we must never forget that he once was one of the chieftains of worship in Heaven before his fall. When you bite into this type of pseudo-spirituality and hyper-holiness, you never get full. That type of magic never truly ministers.

Now, there is a dropping of the guards because of a lust for a new and improved spirituality. Many of our worship services are too high and are looking for too many shifts in the atmosphere instead of appreciating the fact that the ground we stand on is Holy Ground. We are called to come down, turn it down, bow down, and lay our man and woman-made crowns at the feet of Jesus. Much of our worship is loud and lethal. We are infatuated with the art of noise instead of sobering silence and solitude by being still and knowing He is God (Psalm 46:10; Habakkuk 2:20).

Much appears to be geared toward *another level, a new season,* and *another breakthrough.* In the words of Pastor Prentiss Lewis, "We have compromised integrity for new levels." Now, there are flaming swords of angels guarding the Tree. Perhaps the Tree is hidden on our planet. One thing we know, i.e., we will never have access to that tree again. Now, our tree is the Cross. When we examine what Jesus provided at the Cross, there is no greater level or breakthrough that we can experience other than breakthrough-forgiveness and a second chance to do marriage and ministry the right way. Because both Male and Female ate, we are living souls trapped in dying bodies; spirits living in a material world.

How wonderful it would be if we appreciated what we already have and who we already are. Too much in the local church is a prophesy of a new thing God is going to do instead of appreciating the things God has already done. When we truly examine what was in the Garden, they already had it all. For Adam and Eve, Heaven would not have been any better than the Garden if they would have followed God's ordained order for dominion. They had Heaven on Earth. They were only human, but Satan wanted them to come out of their skin and believe they could be *like God.* That was a prideful poison Satan duped them into drinking. The Garden was an earthly paradise, a human heaven, and a tangible oasis. God originally created a planet called Earth for humans to inhabit forever. The original Earth was an organic utopia that humans could have enjoyed for eternity. Whenever we pause and take a good look at nature, we see glimpses of glory that reveal mind boggling truth that there must be a God somewhere. We also see decay all around us that reminds us that even the Earth groans for a redemption that is necessary because both man and woman caused deceptive and disobedient damage (Romans 8:22).

If we get too quiet in sober and silent worship, too many in our churches will fall asleep. If we get too loud, no one can understand what we are saying. We are to guard ourselves against trying to be too much, and we must refuse to live like gods when our God has placed us in temporal temples (I Corinthians 6:19). We cannot move from edification to exaltation and fail to be satisfied with being human. Men are looking for wonder women, and women are looking for super men. Of course, there are some who do not need another hero. They become their own gods. Too many cannot handle the fact that we all are subject to sin, and we all make malignant mistakes. Marriages with unrealistic expectations are the ones subject to the greatest sins. Usually, neither the man nor woman took full responsibility for their own actions. If we fail to take personal responsibility, we will spend the remainder of our lives stuck in a deceived and disobedient past.

Whenever we have been scarred by our own sins, there is never enough time in even one of our days to focus on the failures of the opposite sex. God comes to us individually. Many forget that while we stand on Earth accusing the other person or playing the victim, when we get to the Judgment Seat of Christ, the other person will not be standing next to us to condemn or defend us. We all must stand before Christ the Judge alone and give accounts.

I agree with my father in the ministry, Pastor Derek L. Winkley. We tend to think Eve blamed the Devil and Adam blamed Eve. Yet, when we read the passage, both Adam and Eve answered God's question directly when He asked them what they had done. In other words, they gave God an honest confession. When troubled marriages acknowledge their own sins before God, there will not be enough time in the day for husbands and Wives to be bitter with one another. Nothing was false regarding what they said. Notice again:

> *"And the man said, The woman whom thou gavest to be with me, she gave me of the tree, and I did eat... And the woman said, The serpent beguiled me, and I did eat."*

(Genesis 3:12b-13b; KJV)

God takes role-reversals seriously. When God disciplined Adam and Eve, He disciplined the sexes from then until this very day. Consequently, even the best marriages have at least a tinge of tension and a dose of divine discipline. Women have the tendency to raise their heads with pride, and men tend to lower their heads with shame. The height of a woman's deception is real, and the depth of a man's disobedience is just as real. Too many women do not know they were wrong, and too many men know they were not right. None of these dynamics should come as a surprise when we get married or divorced. Mature marriages that many admire have already grazed those gardens. If they told their stories, their truth would be unbelievable. So, they are wise enough to say less because they had their longest confessions with God. After you have a long talk with God, there is not much else to be said. So, healthy couples talk less and pray more.

It is satanic to believe marriage and ministry can thrive when there is a compromising of roles. When men do not want to lead and Wives do not want to follow, the consequences are deadly. When roles are reversed and couples take the smallest bites out of marital crime, godly boundaries in marriage and ministry are removed, opening a gateway of evil that forces God to place flaming swords in our gardens to ensure we are ousted from His optimum for our lives. For these reasons, many marriages and ministries are beyond recovery. The wage of sin is death. Thus, we have dead marriages and ministries regardless of how lively they look. Many remarriages are adulterous relationships, and many worship locations are witches' temples. When we have committed these spiritual crimes, our hope is in turning our ministries and marriages in and praying for God to give us a Christlike chance. Our only hope is at the Cross, where we first saw the light. Yet, when we get to the foot of the Cross, the only way we know that we are at the same cross where Jesus died is when all we see are our own sins more than someone else's.

All the promises of Satan were true regarding the forbidden fruit of the Tree except for one lie. He promised Eve that she would not die. Unfortunately, the *Adam* in every man has the propensity to gamble. At least Eve finally came to realize the Devil deceived her to do it. Remember, in Eve's eyes, she was not talking to Satan. All she saw was a serpent-like beast with legs on or around a spiritual tree making a lot of sense to her. Women must not only pay attention to spirits, but they must also pay attention to those who have legs. Some women must also beware of other women with beastly beliefs who crawl around their marriages and send seemingly sensible suggestions that are subtly satanic. Satan can use anybody. As a matter of fact, he can use the ones who are creeping around your family tree.

Although women have been known to be wittier and smarter than men, they are not inherently designed by God to be as logical. While that may sound insulting, it is not. Men and women (by nature) operate on two different levels of intelligence. Biologically, it is proven that men and women's brains function on two totally distinct wave lengths. Logic and wit are not always the same. Men are more logical. Satan did not resort to wits to deceive Eve. If

Satan relied more on wit, Eve would have immediately sensed something that was not right about his indecent proposal. On the contrary, Satan resorted to logic. He presented the facts in a way that did not add up in Eve's mind. He was keeping her from thinking like a woman. Instead, he was trying to get her to believe she could think like a man. Thus, she wanted to know so much that she could not say, "I don't understand."

In another sense, Satan made it all about Eve. He was confirming what Eve was subconsciously believing. It is so easy for Satan to deceive a Wife who wants to be the center of attention. He gave her an almost irresistible amount of attention. Instead, it should be about how much attention God can get. If we are content with the level of spirituality, marriage, and ministry God entrusted to us, God can trust us to keep the glory off ourselves and unto Him.

Those who open the gate for role-reversal ministries and marriages will be wise to better understand the schemes of Satan, psyche of women, and duplicity of men. A pastor can never underestimate either. Some debate what the Garden has to do with same-sex ministries. The issue involves role-reversals between a man and woman, anxiety for new levels of spiritual enlightenment, supremacy, and a demonic, deceptive, and disobedient depreciation of the opposite sex. The apostle Paul explained to us that the major premise of what happened in the Garden was about role-reversals, women usurping authority, and men who refuse to lead. Thus, Paul instructs young Timothy on several fronts in the context of local church polity:

> "[11] *Let the woman learn in silence with all subjection.*
> [12] *But I suffer not a woman to teach, nor to usurp authority over the man, but to be in silence.*
> [13] *For **Adam was first formed**, then Eve.*
> [14] ***And Adam was not deceived**, but the woman being deceived was in the transgression.*"

The Pastor And His Rib

(I Timothy 2:11-14)

I always experience many women cringe over this scripture because they have much to say that should be heard. I totally agree that a woman should be heard. Yet, godly women do not have to talk to be heard. Talking too much is a curse. Talking was never God's avenue for a woman's voice to be heard. Instead, Eve was designed to touch her husband and not touch the forbidden fruit in any form. When God rebuked Adam for hearkening to the voice of his wife, God was rebuking Adam for allowing her to dominate him by her words. Her voice was designed to be heard by learning how to partner with the man in an interior way and under the authority of God. Paul is not implying that men should not listen to or be educated by women. He is simply stating that men should not allow women to usurp authority through any venue, even if it is within the teaching arm of the Church.

Believe me, I have heard all the jargon regarding the cultural reasons why women were to keep silent in that day as a defense of why women can speak in church today. Although shifts are made regarding the interpretation of these scriptures to the historical context to defend arguments, Paul gives the literal reason why women are to learn in silence. It has more to do with the science and art of biblical interpretation than the mere culture of that day. The reasons are inherent within the text itself. The best interpreter of Scripture is Scripture. The reasons why women are to learn in silence are timeless principles, even for today.

The first reason is that ***man was created first***. Because man was created first, there is order. The woman should not go before the man. In other words, she must not lead the man. She was not created to do that.

Secondly, ***the man was not deceived, but the woman was***. Eve was prone to deception. Eve was not built by God to defend herself on a satanic stage. Thus, Eve's only defense was to stay away from the Tree and Serpent. Once she entered temptation, there was no way she could have been delivered from evil because she had already gone too far (Matthew 6:13). Adam knew exactly who was lurking among the Tree. Paul is not trying to get the Church to depreciate the discerning disabilities of women.

Any woman who studies the Bible for herself can come to an accurate interpretation of the scriptures if she follows the laws of biblical interpretation. However, when Satan intervenes and attacks the woman in her interpretive faculties, he is attacking a weaker vessel who must protect herself from believing she has the right to change her mind (I Peter 3:7). Therefore, Paul gave instructions to not place the woman in a headship position of this nature in the local church because leadership on that level brings indefensible temptations to women in the spiritual realm of demonic and deceptive revelations. She needs to be protected more than promoted or pacified.

The idea of usurping authority in Paul's address to Timothy is exactly what happened in the Garden. When Eve gave the fruit to Adam, she usurped authority over Adam regardless of whether she was doing it intentionally or not. When a man succumbs to a woman on this level, he gives his authority to her. The apostle Paul gives us the psyche of Adam and Eve in the Garden. Paul tells us that Adam was disobedient, and Eve was deceived (I Timothy 2:13). It takes more time and processes to be deceived, but disobedience can happen in a split second. Adam did not need a long conversation with Satan. He would never have taken the fruit from Satan, but he would have taken it from his Wife. This proves how a man *does* value a woman. As a matter of fact, a man tends to overly value women on this level. There is always at least one Wife in the world who can make her husband weak at the knees. There was something significant about Eve's proposal that weakened Adam and caused him to bow. Sexy and seduction had a lot to do with it.

A truth that is a mystery to some women is the fact that there are certain sins the Devil cannot tempt men to commit, but certain women can. It is quite possible Adam was somewhere in the cut viewing this episode. Grammatically, it is most probable that Adam was close by lurking undetected in the thickets of the Garden observing the dialogue between Satan and Eve. According to textual and grammatical analysis, the Hebrew text could possibly be interpreted:

> "Eve gave the fruit to her husband with her (**who was also with her**) and he did eat..."
>
> (Genesis 3:6; KJV)

For even a better elaboration on this text, I encourage all to read a book entitled *The Silence of Adam*, by Dr. Larry Crabb. Whatever the case, Adam was close enough to be highly involved in this Devil's triangle. Adam reveals his true colors when Eve comes with a change of heart. Although Adam fell for the fruit, he only fell for it in Eve's hands. As far as God was concerned with Adam, the Devil had nothing to do with it. God condemned Adam for listening to his Wife. After biting of the forbidden fruit, Satan could possess Eve's God-given ability to influence Adam to do something forbidden with her. After partaking, she was more seductive than ever. After Eve partakes, it is the fruit *in* her that he also craves. The fruit created a combination of the supernatural, sinful, and the sexy. It looked more appealing dangling in his Wife's hands than on the Tree. She possibly could have been sensually chewing and suggesting that he eats also. This may appear vulgar, but we cannot underestimate the fact that Satan used Eve to seduce Adam in every sexual, sinister, and satanic way possible. The scene in the Garden was a highly satanic pornographic display of a husband and Wife.

She even knew how to be evil because she swallowed it. She had the Snake's venom in her veins that poisoned her virtue. For Satan to get Adam, he needed a woman's body to do so. Men are not attracted to four legged serpents, just two legged ones. A serpent's body was not enough, but Eve's was. Now, she really does know good *and evil*, and she is as a god. Unfortunately, the god she is more resembling is a demon. In a strong sense, Eve was a woman demonized.

We can never minimize the darkness that filled that Garden. Once she ate, she was an interplay of a woman acting like a demon and a demon looking like a woman. None of us are the same after we have dined with the Devil, and no man is the same after he has dined with a Wife who prepared for him a sexy supper. Her countenance has changed, she is a sinner, and she is sexy. She is no longer innocent, but she is iniquitous. She is no longer simple, but she is seductive. She had no name before she sinned. She was just called, "Woman". After she sinned, she made a bad name for herself. Now, Adam named her "Eve", the Mother of all living (Genesis 3:20).

She is now the mother of all who will one day die. After taking a bite out of Evil, Eve was complicated and hard to explain. She had no idea what she was capable of and neither did Adam. She had a demonic mystique wrapped in a woman's body. Adam knew, but he did not fully know. All he knew was that he wanted more of what he saw. He never had his Wife that way before. She had a total make-over. There was no way Adam wanted to be without Eve at that point regardless of what she had done. Whatever her new issues may have been, it was a turn-on for Adam that would eventually turn him out.

There are several things the text teaches. In Adam's eyes, she was strong-willed, sexy, and seductive, but she was no longer spiritual because she was not like God. Instead, she was cunning and crafty, mysterious, and manipulative. Remember, this was not some other woman. This was his Wife. Even today, *sexy* has been portrayed as a combination of sin and seduction. It is used in commercials to get men to drink more beer, buy more cars, have more sex, and buy into whatever the market is selling. As men, we do not always have a deceptive reason or complicated answer for why we did what we should not have done, just a disobedient one. To some women, it must be more than that. Men are simple beings with only about five basic needs. Sex and female companionship are two of them.

Again, this was his Wife who dominated him. Domination is even more demonic than divorce. All these things happened within the context of their marriage. This is one of the reasons why it is wise for people to not judge what happened in the failed marriage of someone else. It is also wise for failed marriages to spend more time analyzing their own individual actions rather than accusing the other partner. Adam did not want to lose his Wife and companion, even if she made a grave mistake. Once a Wife goes to this level, a husband must learn how to turn her loose before she turns him in.

Regardless of Eve's deception, that is not the central focus of the narrative. The root of the problem was the silence of Adam. God chastises Adam for *hearkening* to her voice. Adam should have been the one doing all the talking. Yet, there is no mention in this episode that Adam ever said a word. He just compromised his position with God at the expense of his passions for the woman who God gave him. He did not listen to Eve with his love. He listened with his lusts. He *gave in and consented* (שָׁמַע – shama) to her voice.

Most men get tagged with getting involved with women outside of the marriage, but many never identify men who get wrongly involved with their Wives inside of the marriage. Inside evil is just as deadly as outside evil. As a matter of fact, that is where it begins most of the time. Domestic and demonic domination is even more dangerous. Domestic demonization occurs when a God ordained couple becomes unfaithful to God. Eve was unfaithful to God by allowing Satan to deceive her, and Adam was unfaithful to God by allowing Eve to dominate him.

Eve was satanically getting under Adam's skin. As his rib, she had not lost her interior power. She was sticking him from the inside-out, and she had help from what she learned in Satan's school of seduction. Eve went from simplicity to seduction, and Adam when from simplicity to stupidity. Adam had more of a weakness for his Wife than he did for wickedness. Under this context, a man cannot always compliment himself if he is faithful to his Wife because he could be faithful to her for the wrong reasons. He could be faithful out of fear and codependence instead of courage and dependence upon God.

In some demonic way, after Eve had eaten, she developed a strength foreign to Adam's defense mechanisms. God hates it when men allow Wives to dominate them. When these things happen in the home of a pastor, it affects his ministry style in the local church. The husband no longer pastors the church. His wife does, even if she does not have the title of Pastor. Also, the husband no longer heads the home. Instead, his Wife does. When that happens, couples are on the borderline of blasphemy (Titus 2:5). Weakness for our Wives must not be one of the major reasons why we bite into the fruit of Spiritism that sexualizes ministry and opens gates for role-reversals.

The Bible describes the Serpent as subtle or crafty. Now, Satan has influenced Eve to be a crafty little goddess. A crafty little goddess will never rebuke her husband for allowing her to dominate him to make dumb decisions, but she will rebuke him for letting another woman dominate him. In her eyes, it is okay for her to control him, but another woman cannot. The part that amazes me is how many of us who are or were under this type of controlling relationship rarely do the math.

To curtail this curse, God commanded women to submit to their husbands, and men are commanded to love and lead their Wives (Ephesians 5:22-25). Because God's commands cut against our sinful nature, men intrinsically do not want to lead with that type of love, and Wives do not intrinsically want to follow with that type of faithfulness. Previously, Eve was a helper. Now, she is a hindrance. Previously, Adam was a man. Now, his Wife is his manager.

If Adam was going to eat, Satan had to make it a sexual issue. Then, he could develop it into a submission issue. The sexual issue is not just physical, but it is also spiritual. Adam sees his woman as a different type of female; one he has never known before. She has too many issues going on after she eats, but Adam is attracted to every one of them. Her issues are filled with iniquity. She knows how to adjust the tone of her voice in a way that gives a subtle whisper that wears down the will of the strongest of men. She knows how to look at him in a way that reveals mystery in her eyes that excites his stupidity. She is no longer a simple, God-fearing woman. At this point, she is the kind of woman the sinful nature of a disobedient man could easily fall for.

If God would not have intervened in the Garden, Adam and Eve may have continued sensually eating themselves to death in a rebellious and religious way, devouring the fruit in heated lust. Hell is also a place where the souls of people will have eternal lusts, tormented with what they can never have but will forever want (Luke 16:24). If God would not have put flaming swords to guard the Tree, Eve would have been eating in fits of power, and Adam would have been eating in fits of perversion. The power of the woman and perversions of the man are often the deadliest viruses in a God-ordained marriage.

God had to put boundaries between the man and woman to keep them accountable and together along with keeping them from codependently taking advantage of each other by vomiting up their God-ordained roles. God gave them male and female roles. God-given roles keep a man and woman from overpowering each other with senseless demands, no boundaries, and a battle of the sexes. A man takes advantage of a woman if he allows her to have her way all the time. At that point, he is aggressively passive. A woman takes advantage of a man if she seduces him to have her way all the time. At that point, she is passively aggressive.

When married and in ministry, we must decide which paradigm we are to govern our marriages by. Are we going to go by a Pre-Fall or Post-Fall paradigm? A Pre-Fall paradigm is a one in which a man looks for his Wife to be his partner and helper for life. He sees himself sharing dominion with her (Genesis 1:28). Prior to their fall, God wanted partnership in a marriage. Eve was not a lot of work for Adam, and Adam was not a lot of work for Eve. At that point, marriage was not hard work. It was God's work. They were innocent of any infections of evil that would cause a man to be compromising and a woman to be conniving.

A Post-Fall paradigm develops after the fall of Adam and Eve. Now, God wants priorities to be established in the marriage. The man is now the head of the woman and both parties must accept and operate within that principle. It is one in which partnership can only be accomplished through godly submission and loving authority. With this paradigm, the couple must work. The best marriages require the hardest work. The woman must lovingly submit to the man, and the man must lead the woman with loving authority (Ephesians 5:22-25). All of that is hard work for both partners. It takes a committed decision for both parties to *work* those roles as husband and Wife. It does not come naturally. Love must be a choice.

Subconsciously, when a man looks for a woman to marry, he usually sees her as his *partner* for life. He has a built-in Pre-Fall paradigm. He is looking to share everything he has with her. Although he knows there will be ripples in the water, for the most part, he still believes his marriage will be smooth sailing. As a matter of fact, whatever he has accomplished before marriage, he is rarely able to enjoy alone (Genesis 2:18). Unfortunately, a Pre-Fall paradigm is no longer a reality. Those days were dead and gone after the fall of Adam. Now, marital equality and partnership must come through authority and submission. That is the road to shared dominion.

Satan seeks to influence the Wife to draw her husband closer than he should be to her or drive him away from her. It does not matter to Satan if the man compromises his calling and loses his leverage from the Lord. The same mistakes are made to this day, and I have made my share of them, to say the least. Strange fruit is sexy to men who opened this new gate of an imposed equality. I am referring to *sexy* in the sense of being overly gender conscious. In efforts to silence the differences between men and women, they are only amplified even more. When men do what women should do and women do what men should do, it becomes loud. The local church must defy an amplified arrogance that forgets how fragile and sinful we are. Sin is being compromised because our actions are no longer called sins. For these reasons and more, Christians are surprised by sins of others but comfortable with their own. On the other hand, when a person's sins are noticed, many members of local churches act like they are surprised. Then, people call it a scandal. *The first scandal in the Bible was when a Wife was deceived and dominating and when her husband loved every minute of it.*

Mary Wade had a saying. She would say that she learned not to put her trust in people because they will let you down. Later in life as she was well within her eighties, she had another saying. She would say that she came to learn to not even put trust in herself. Today's brand of ministry and marriage is asking for too much trust. Men are asking Wives to trust them, and Wives are asking husbands to trust them. We cannot trust each other to do ministry or marriage however we want to do it. Much of today's brand of Christianity is marketing a product of ministry that tries to sell us the idea that what they have is enough. None of our ministries or marriages is enough.

Only a small remnant of marriages in ministry can attest to the fact that marriage can work if it is done God's way and according to God's word. The absence of healthy marriages attests to the fact that something has gone drastically wrong in our gardens. I cannot help but think of that secular song, "It Takes Two to Make a Thing Go Right." However, staying in a marriage with confused priorities can be worse than being divorced. There are countless episodes when either the husband or Wife is obligated to stay with the other partner while staying married is killing that person softly. Staying in a relationship to save face with critics who do not love them for who they are is not worth a man and woman jeopardizing their wholeness for.

As long as such men or women are running to the Cross for healing, let them run, even if they have to run away from a toxic relationship. There have been many toxic relationships and ministries God delivered me from. In all of them, I could have stayed longer if I wanted. As a matter of fact, I would be much further today if I never got in those relationships or if I would have left a whole lot sooner. However, I finally refused to be a codependent glutton for punishment, and I paid a high price before I was delivered from the sin of relational gluttony. Because of my codependence, I had a way of drinking from toxic fountains. No man or woman should be held hostage to a relationship that refuses to fulfill God-given roles. A man should not be held captive to a conniving woman, and a woman should not be captive to a compromising man. Of course, the Bible teaches how the believing spouse is bound to the unbelieving spouse, but it does not say the believing spouse should be bound to the abusive spouse. Abuse is a Serpent issue. Wives have torn down husbands with their words, and husbands have torn down Wives with their works.

Healing rarely takes place in marriage and ministry between couples together or divorced because the dysfunction has not been adequately detected and dealt with. Usually, it is only discussed. If so, it is discussed in pseudo safe zones where one person does all the talking. One-way conversations are usually with people or professionals who will only condone the dysfunction instead of confront it. Fortunately, Adam and Eve had the best marriage counseling session that ever took place in history after they had fallen. God was their Wonderful Counselor who understood the violations of both the man and woman. He began dealing with each person and each issue in way that made them aware of their own individual iniquities, but He still gave them hope that life goes on, even if they had to die to live. For the Christian man and woman, if God brings consequences to failed relationships that last for a lifetime, they can yet have hope to know there will be neither Male nor Female in the Afterlife. Thank God that there are no marriages made in Heaven.

The question is, who is at home? Some believe the Wife's place is not in the home. The Bible begs to differ. The Wife's place is in the home, and so is the husband's. Home is marriage's main ministry base that should operate on terms mutually exclusive from those required of the local church. Mary Wade recalled to me how J. C. Wade, Sr. would come home from church and relieve her of duties at home. She told me countless occasions of how he would romance her with love songs. I loved to see her eyes widen and her face blush as she stated how romantic he was to her. On other occasions, he would do chores at home and get down on his knees and hand-clean the floors, even if he had to use a toothbrush.

The pastor's object of affection should be his Wife, just as Jesus is affectionate with His Wife, the Church. God's people are the apple of His eye (Zechariah 2:8). Adultery is committed on levels far beyond the bedroom. Adultery also comes in a form of a twisted sense of spirituality that is unfaithful to how God defined us to be males and females totally devoted to Him. A pastor has the awesome command to not fall out of love with his Wife and develop an adulterous relationship with Jesus' Bride, (the Church) of which his Wife has become the surrogate. Jesus assumes responsibility for loving *His* Bride (the Church), and the pastor should assume responsibility of loving *his* bride (his Wife).

Ephesians 5:22-32 emphasizes Jesus' pattern of how *He* loves the Church and how the Church is commanded to submit to Him. That means, we all as Christians must submit to how Christ wills to control every aspect of our lives, including our marriages and ministries. In our contemporary age, there is a tendency for many to love the local church more than they submit to Christ. Well, there are many people who are attracted to a person's body, but they can do away with the head that is on their shoulders. Unfortunately, many of us as Christians are the same way. We are attracted to the Body of Christ, but we have issues with Christ, who is the Great Head of the Church.

Instead of Christ doing the thinking, we (local churches) are doing too much thinking for ourselves. Thus, too many local churches have their own interpretation of the Bible, and too many of our marriages past and present operate on conniving and compromising norms. I can personally testify that we pay a high price when we do that. While marriage is usually emphasized the most in this passage. Paul is explicitly stating that his ultimate purpose for giving the pattern for marriage is to let the hearers know that he is speaking concerning Christ and the Church.

Regarding Christ and the Church, there must be authority, submission, and order in a sexual way. In other words, he spoke of Christ in the masculine gender and the Church in the feminine gender. So, sexuality and order do matter. Jesus in no way depicts the Church as equal with Him in role or responsibility. As members of the Church, we constitute the rib of Christ's body. Notice how Paul says in the above-mentioned verse that we (the Church) are like Eve was to Adam, members *of His body, of His flesh, and of His bones*. Adam also says to Eve, "*This is now bone of my bones and flesh of my flesh*" (Genesis 2:23).

The Church consists of vital organs of Jesus' Body of which He is the Head (Ephesians 5:30). We are to aid the perpetuation of the Kingdom paradigm by serving the purposes of our Head (Christ) for whom we were created. We were created to the praise of Christ's glory and not vice-versa. In like manner, the Wife was created to the praise of the husband's glory (I Corinthians 11:7). A woman's deception and a man's disobedience must be discussed simultaneously if there is to ever be any health in the anatomy of a marriage or a divorce. If a woman comes to me in counseling and says her husband was disobedient, I will also examine if she has been deceived and deceptive. If a man comes to me in a counseling session and says his Wife has been conniving, I will also examine if he has been compromising.

How have we come to know so much, yet know so little? Our information is coming from the wrong source. Prophetic revelation is still the satanic norm used to deceive marriages and ministry in the 21st-century church. Eve was under prophetic revelation when she was communing with Satan and when she gained knowledge of good and evil. Unfortunately, receiving prophetic revelation can be just as much a satanic exercise as a godly one (I Kings 22:22). Revelation is not the major problem. The problem is in discerning which spirit certain revelations come from. Thus, some Wives heard something God did not say, but make no mistake about it, they *are* hearing something. As a matter of fact, they are hearing a whole lot. Furthermore, too many of us as husbands did something with our Wives God did not tell us to do.

The Serpent has grown legs again. The legs belong to demons who are saying to men that a woman can do a man's job. There are also legs that belong to demons who suggest to women that a man cannot do his job. Truthfully, most women do better jobs than men in most things. That reality can be perceived from two angles. Either it says a lot about the woman, or it does not say much about the man. Either way, the man is still a silent vowel in the sentence. Many are hearing confirmation from the spiritual realm that there is more to attain than the confines of a marriage that places women in submission to a man and ministry that holds their freedom of expression bound to biblical absolutes. This is strange fruit that is dangling in our day from tricky trees with twisted truths.

So many women in ministry are working tirelessly to get the job done. It takes so much out of them to get the simplest things done because they must cross so many gender barriers to get there. They are giving everything they have with the taunting voice in the back of their minds saying to them that it still is not enough. Many women in ministry are measured by a ruler they can never see. They never truly know if they measure up. They always feel like more could be said and done. Some are under a heavy yoke, and that yoke does not fit them well. Many women in misguided ministries are hurting beyond measure in ways that even their ministries are not healing because their marriage history is hurting. As a matter of fact, their ministries are hurting. You can see the pain in their eyes. You can often see the blame and bitterness. More importantly, if certain Wives' eyes were open to the real consequences of husbands who refuse to lead, they would commit their husbands to God, influence them to take their places as the head, and dedicate the rest of their lives to the power of submission to the Lord and their God-ordained lover.

There *are* real pastors' Wives who tapped into the power of real womanhood by letting the man lead. They are a rare species in today's marriages and local church ministries, but they are real. If he fails to do so, they do not feel it is their obligation to come to his rescue. They let him stand, and they let him fall because they realize God will either pick their husbands up if they fall or leave them lying on the ground if they fail to learn from their mistakes. They also recognize the fact that if they assume the role of becoming his savior, there will come a day that will come back to haunt them. They understand to become his savior means they will one day be crucified. If they get to that point, the husband's sins will cost them everything they have. So, they must leave that man alone, not try to play God, and allow God to work in his life to correct and chastise him in ways they never could.

Looking again at I Timothy 2:11-15, Adam allowed Eve to usurp his authority. The Greek word for "usurp" is *authenteō*. It means *to dominate or have mastery over*. Eve gained mastery over Adam. However, the context of I Timothy teaches us that she did not do it on her own. Adam allowed Eve to dominate him. A man must never have a weakness for bondage. Adam's Wife gained mastery over Adam after Satan gained mastery over her. Thus, domination of this sort is a satanic act. Bondage should never be a man's fetish. Men who are attracted to bondage are usually men of great power and privilege. Adam had great power, but he took his privileges for granted. Maintaining power is a sleepless responsibility and a lonely life for a man (Genesis 2:18). Many men in great power get lonely. They do not always want to do their job. Instead, they sometimes want a woman to do a job on them.

Adam sought to protect his loneliness at the expense of his leadership. Like Adam, a man may not want to be left behind with no woman by his side. Therefore, the temptation to relax obedience is present. The fear of losing a Wife can do many things to the psyche of a man, especially a pastor. Some of us react to fear of losing our Wives in a way that we do not want to be stigmatized as restricting or controlling husbands. Thus, many seek appreciation from their Wives by supporting them at all costs, even if it means allowing them to have unrestricted access to toxic opportunities.

What is seldom realized is the fact that Eve had more of a God issue than a husband issue. It is interesting how Satan was enticing Eve to believe she could succeed apart from her husband while Adam feared living without her. Eve was prone to an evil exit from their relationship, but Adam was compromising to keep their marriage together. If a man must keep a marriage on compromising terms that usurp his authority, he might as well let that relationship go and let the chips fall where they may. Eve was bold enough to believe she could be complete without him, and Adam was timid enough to believe he would be incomplete without her.

Marriage can demand something you never signed up for. The harsh reality is in the fact that when men are silent, a woman's respect for him decreases, and some will even be tempted to expect him to give more and say less. She may complement him because he is quiet but inwardly resent him because he never says enough because he is not a man of conversation. Whenever godly restrictions are removed, there will always be an insatiable lust for more. Some husbands remove godly boundaries because they realize how some Wives attract to freedom more than accountability. Unfortunately, freedom without accountability will never breed satisfaction or appreciation in any normal individual. The truth is in the fact that you never get enough of what you want, Male or Female. This type of behavior is in the realm of lust. Lust never satisfies, and it leaves us wanting more. Eve was no exception. She may have been a woman, but she was still human.

Adam was trying to keep up with his Wife when he should have been focusing on standing down with God. The moment she became deceived, she was too fast for him. She had Satan, seduction, and selfishness on her side. God is the only leverage a man has when it comes to a woman of this sort. She is too smart for him if he does not stay under God's ordained radar. He must be obedient to God to maintain that leverage. The only way Adam could have survived was to stay in his lane.

When a man removes himself from accountability to God, it leaves his Wife exposed to all kinds of evils. Of course, she must give an account for her actions, but the man must do the same. Adam left the gate open. Our loneliness as men must incite us to suffer consequences of standing tall on God's word, even if we come short in marriage by coming to the Garden alone.

Men are required to develop a work ethic that refuses to use or allow women to do all or most of the churchwork and homework. Submission will produce more results than the burden leading could ever accomplish. The Church is most powerful as she submits to Christ. The moment she seeks to usurp authority from Christ, she gets in trouble with Christ. Unlike Adam, Christ will never allow his Bride (the Church) to take His place and have her own way. In addition, Christ will not bite into her suggestions of what will make her more appealing. Our sufficiency is in Christ and not within forbidden Antichrist-like options of marriage and ministry.

When we understand the dynamics of how the local church is to operate, we will discover that a pastor's Wife can do more for her husband as a member of his body than a member of his local church. Why? Because she is bone of his bone and flesh of his flesh. She is his rib. A pastor's Wife is a greater influence in the pews than the pulpit if she sits correctly. This is not to downplay Wives who have tremendous spiritual gifts in the local church. They should somehow operate within the context of ministry within the local church. It is only to give the *up-side* of Wives who are uniquely gifted to stand by their men behind closed church doors.

With a little play on words, Mary Wade knew how to sit, and she knew where to sit. As a member of Salem Baptist Church of Omaha, Nebraska, Mary Wade sat in one spot. She never moved from that one spot. She did not parade all over the church. If I remember correctly, it was somewhere along the second or third row at the old Salem Baptist Church on Lake Street, in the middle isle, on the far end of the pew. She did everything from that seat. She watched her husband's enemies from that seat. She gave the church a sweet aroma of a virtuous woman from that seat. She encouraged her husband from that seat. She prayed for her church from that seat. She was faithful to that seat. She almost saw everything from that seat. For that, Salem Baptist Church and their succeeding pastor, excellent exegete, and my dear brother (Pastor Maurice Watson) honored her to the day of her death. I was there the day he instituted a financial promise at J. C. Wade, Sr.'s funeral that she would never suffer lack. God bless my dear brother for keeping his promise.

Wives on Mary Wade's level refuse to lust for manpower. They have a power of their own. Mary Wade was too wise to lust for manpower. She knew where her edge came from. Her edge came from having self-respect and being a descendent of virtuous, secure, and strong-willed women. She enjoyed being a woman and Wife because it was her decision. She did not trick J. C. Wade, Sr. into marrying her. She took pride in being single and demanded that men respect her as such. When J. C. Wade, Sr. first set eyes on her, he saw a Wife, but to her, J. C. Wade, Sr. was "That Ol Esau." Because she had pride and security in who she was before she met "Daddy Wade", she protected that pride in her marriage in a way that he could do nothing but respect her for it. Mary Wade had such a relationship with God that she was too wise to partake of the Tree. She ate from her own gardens and planted in her own backyard. She did not believe in what she called "crossing over". She came from a deep family background that believed in trusting God. Her mother who went by the nickname of "Mama Frazier" was a woman who had still waters that ran deep. "Mama Frazier" was no joke. She had such a relationship with God that she picked her dying ground. Her prayer was that when it was her time to die, she would die in her sleep. That is exactly how she died. Like her mother, Mary Wade's heart simply stopped beating a few years from one hundred years old. Both simply transitioned into their rest. If a Wife who does not have a faith like that who is at least my age (fifty-two), compared to the life span of Mary Wade, maybe she has at least forty-seven more years to get it right.

God has a way of taking care of a woman who takes care of her husband, even if he does not deserve it. God allowed Mary Wade to outlive her husband to complete his story. She put the finishing touches on "Daddy Wade's" life. She was the predicate. She rarely threw anything away that pertained to her husband. She kept old newspapers of articles written about his accomplishments that became the evidence needed to prove his works when his history was in question. She did not try to remove chapters from the pages of his life. Instead, she cherished chapters of the pages of his life. Such collections of his data became necessary for the city of Omaha, Nebraska to honor him in countless ways, including the naming of the J. C. Wade, Sr. Post Office of Omaha, Nebraska. When James C. Wade, Sr. died, the closest thing to remind me of J. C. Wade, Sr. was his Wife. When I was around *"Big Annie"*, I got that *J. C. Wade feeling*.

Although many pastor's Wives do not stem from deep godly roots, God's grace will be with them if they have a mind that refuses to be too smart for their own good. A woman who knows too much may have a difficult time keeping what she knows to herself. While she thinks what she says makes her wise, it only makes her look foolish. There is a sinister impulse that will tempt her to chew too much information instead of spit it out. Then, she offers what she knows to others and tempts them to also eat. When we know too much, we are no good for God because He cannot trust us with secrets. What God told Eve was not to be shared with Satan (Genesis 3:1-2). Because Satan can only be in one place at a time, who are deceived women sharing their secrets with? What Satan deceived her to do, she was not to share with Adam. If she damaged her own life, she should have left his alone. Yet, the woman deep on the inside of Eve never meant Adam harm. She could not help him if she could not help herself. Eve was a good woman gone bad.

When we condone women to be released into levels of a lack of accountability, we are sporting them, stripping them of their virtuous garments, leaving them naked and exposed to the spirits of deception and seduction. A pastor must protect his Wife in this hard-hitting, snake-biting, contact sport of ministry and marriage. Being a Wife is hard enough, but being a pastor is even harder. If we do not believe it, just ask the real pastor's Wives. They see their husbands come home from church battered and bruised. They have a thick book of blank pages because they are wise enough to know they cannot tell it all. So, they do not even try. They just walk with a power-strut that epitomizes a real woman who refuses to fall for Satan's tricks.

Satan wants to deceive us into biting into the lie that freedom is an anti-venom to the Serpent's bite of male-chauvinism. Instead, pastors have the mandate to come out of the thickets of the Garden, stand by their Wives, and protect them from the snakes in their gardens that deceptively lead them to turn what God gave them into a venomous marriage and ministry. After husbands have stood by their Wives and have given them godly accountability, if their Wives still choose the voice of the Serpent, God will no longer search for the man in the Garden because the man will have no reason to hide. We do not have to hide from God when we have done nothing wrong, and we cannot hide from God when we have done something wrong. We have no reason to hide, naked and ashamed in the 21st century when we refuse to compromise regulations required *for men only.*

On the horizon, ministry will reveal Wives in ministry who validate the paradox of a new-found freedom by preaching sermons and developing ministries that mask themes of the sin of silent men. On the other hand, it is critical to understand the *Universal Church* Jesus promised to build is in good shape and will be simply fine (Matthew 16:18). It is the local church who has a massive degree of uncertainty. Jesus's marriage to the Bride will be intact. All of us can rest assure that Jesus is not engaged to even one of our local churches. Jesus' Church is much larger, stronger, more submissive, more beautiful, and more attractive than any of our local churches are or will ever be. Only a remnant within our local churches are the Bridesmaids who will be raptured and welcomed to the wedding. While we (pastors) sometimes have a compulsion to count our members, who among those members can God really count on? Those are most likely the ones who are true members of Jesus' Church.

When Wives exercise their side-by-side capabilities or rib-responsibilities, the influence they have on their husbands can have a powerful and positive outcome. When influence is misused, the husband may find himself in situations in which his Wife's magnetism is malicious. Notice how long it took Eve to buy into Satan's trick but how quickly Adam bought-in to Eve's treat. She gave to her husband, and he ate it. A combination of power and pity produces a man who will almost bite into anything a seductive Wife suggests. A woman's seductive influence is powerful, and a man's stubborn disobedience is pitiful. When these two forces of power and pity combine, God will come for the man with a searching question, i.e., "*Man*, where are you?" Next, he will come for the Wife with a sobering question, "*Woman*, what is this *you* have done?" Notice the ramifications of the question to both Male and Female. To ask Adam where he was reveals how he was still in serpent-like stealth-mode, silent, and hiding. To ask Eve what she had done reveals how she was still in demonic denial.

Marriages are so intimate that people rarely know the real deception and disobedience that took place in such relationships unless they were there to see the sin of both parties. Only God was there all the time, and only God really knows the heart of both the husband and Wife. God sees more than the couples themselves because it is only God who knows the deceitfulness of our hearts (Jeremiah 17:9). As couples in failed marriages mature, they begin to see their own individual sins that ruptured the relationship. Couples who are blessed to stay together must maintain accountability toward God instead of measuring their togetherness on how well they can satisfy each other's agendas. That only leads to pride and codependence.

Submissive Wives who have strong, loving, protective, nurturing, providing, and masculine husbands find relief through their husband's headship and not their own. I do not believe a

Wife can respect or appreciate a man who is too *boyish* or too *bending*. A boyish man throws tantrums if things do not go his way, and a bending man does not care at all if things ever go his way because he has no way at all. He has no sense of direction. A boyish man must grow up, and a bending man must straighten up. Lack of male leadership for Wives would mean experiencing the naked consequences of coming out of the comforts of a covering. Therefore, rare but wise women experience submission as a covering and not a curse. Through the power of submission, these wise Wives are no longer responsible for the daunting task of being accountable for the outcome of their marriage or their husband's ministry. They are free. If the marriage goes sour, the woman will never have to confess to God that she also had something to do with it. Therefore, she will never feel the compulsive need to explain herself or shade her side of the story.

Adam and Eve were missing these dynamics. Adam did not have a consecrated Wife, and Eve did not have a committed husband. They were only committed and consecrated unto a certain point. Eve went from consecration to conniving, and Adam went from devotion to desecration. In some way, they sought relief from what God truly ordained and deceptively and disobediently believed they could keep God in the equation.

Adam and Eve sought something outside of what their humanity could handle as he gave Eve female temptations and Adam male ones. Eve's temptation was in gaining *more*, and Adam's temptation was to settle for *less*. Eve wanted to be more like God. Adam wanted to be less than a man. He just wanted a Wife. A man can easily make that grave mistake. He can have the whole world in his hands and trade it for his Wife's world and eventually lose everything he had. Some women make their share of mistakes in their man-selection as well. Ambition and boredom plague husbands and Wives who have difficulty standing still and standing down in a relationship. So, they feel they are not productive if they do not keep it moving. Sometimes, it is not that complicated how some of our marriages and ministries got out of control. Every now and then, the root problem is that anxiety causes one to refuse to accept what God sanctioned or refused to sanction. Satan masters in giving couples more or less than what they signed up for.

Marriage is not a commitment to, *as long as*. Marriage is a commitment to, *in spite of*. God dealt with both accordingly when they failed to realize that. Nobody wins in a conditional relationship. Everyone loses in an *as long as* marriage or ministry. No matter what a husband or Wife has done, it basically comes down to that. Everything else becomes a wicked outgrowth of thinking anything outside of God's ordained roles for marriage is a viable solution.

On March 8, many celebrate International Women's Day. On this day, many women refrain from working because they want the world to know what the world would be like if there were no women. They also refer to this day as, *"A Day Without a Woman."* On this day, many women champion their rights and fight for gender equality. While I personally believe in this needed national day, some abuse this day to detest the authority of men, an exact phenomenon that occurred in the Garden of Eden. The woman was seeking what she felt was an equality she was not privy to. Because Eve assumed authority she did not have, if Adam would have obeyed God, the consequences for him would have been *a day without a woman* (Genesis 3:4).

While I am a stark proponent of gender equality, I am not a proponent of an equality that sends negative signals about authority or submission. It may sound harsh, but it is probable that the best response to those who protest against male authority is to understand that when one woman attempts to usurp authority from a man, God will ensure that another woman can easily take her place.

If only Eve would have disobeyed, only Eve would have died. It still would not have been good for Adam to be alone. Consequently, God would have eventually given him another woman.

Wives who feel they must assert themselves may indicate the need to remove themselves from their husband's covering. Some women can have the ability to have their bodies in one place and their minds on the other side of town. They can have several windows open and look out of all of them at the same time. God created women with the unique ability to multi-task. So, some Wives accept doors men swing open for them, but they walk through them with one eye open and the other eye on the back and side doors. They will even go out the window if they must. If all doors are closed, they will even tear the roof off to get out of the house of a passive or pressuring husband. One eye sees an entrance, and the other is looking for an exit. In relation, they do as some often do when they have had enough. They hang in there until they develop an exit strategy for either a new man, new meaning, new ministry, or all the above.

Women trapped in these types of relationships who have no way out figure a way in. They may deem it necessary to rib the man and pierce his vulnerable organs to relax his authority. If he is passive, she squeezes authority out of him and usurps it for herself. In her mind, somebody must lead. If he does not, she will. Satan wants her to get under his skin and gain leverage. If he is overly authoritarian, it is she who cannot breathe. When some women cannot breathe, they will do what they must to breathe again. Some refuse to suffocate in this type of submission. In fact, suffocation is not submission. Suffocation is the testimony of a dying woman. The only problem is that God never sanctions the woman who dines with the Devil to gain resuscitation through false life support systems. She must get her second breath from God (Genesis 2:7).

Consequently, an evolution of leadership in the local church takes place in the psyche of some women in ministry marriages. Unless they return to God, they get more of a distorted view of men than they do ministry. After all, it was not the ministry that let them down. It was their man who let them down. Therefore, they leave their man and join another man or lead another ministry. One thing is for certain, they will never let another man lead them or their ministry ever again on that level.

Thus, the pulpit is populated with silent men who have lost their voice through disobedience and bitter women with loud voices who are damaged by their own deception. Here is where one of the saddest parts of ministry takes place in the local church. It is nearly impossible to convince a man or woman that pain is never to be the motif for ministry. Just because we have gone through indescribable pain, that does not give us the right to make a ministry out of it. After Adam and Eve were confronted by God, they corrected their errors and learned to live with their losses. The average woman is not going to tell off on herself in front of an audience of women. She is smarter than that. That is suicide because she knows how brutal some female audiences can be. So, they divert attention from themselves and play the role of a victim in front of an audience of victims. On the other hand, it is almost impossible to give an accurate testimony if there has not been an accurate confession unto God. We are confronted with the truth of God's word regarding role-reversals. God commands us to refuse to press the envelope and justify our jeopardies by creating marriages and ministries that cover our nakedness.

Every testimony is not to be told. All testimonies are not true anyway. Most people never could handle Truth. Truth is total. It is not told in parts. So, most of the truth told are half-truths. Most cannot even handle the truth about themselves. Truth has boundaries. It is not designed for all. It is only designed for those who want to be made free (John 8:32). When truth is told about another individual, that is not Truth. It is snitching, being a tattletale, or even being a false witness (Exodus 20:16).

People who want to stay bound in blame and develop a voice as victims want to be lied to in a way that makes them feel loved. When Eve told God about Satan, she did not realize how that only exposed her truth that she failed to be accountable for her own actions. Therefore, she received no sympathy from God. When Adam told God about Eve, he did not realize how that only exposed his truth that he failed to man-up. Unlike Adam and Eve, the Serpent at least had enough sense to realize he had no comeback God would condone. When God confronted the Serpent, he just went on his belly and took the heat deserved from God (Genesis 3:14). The fact that Moses described the evil as a serpent in the book of Genesis in no way disarms the argument that the serpent was Satan in the flesh. The following verse proves that fact (Genesis 3:15). We know it was Satan because God further states that He would put enmity between the serpent's seed and her seed.

We do not get in the ministry because we have come through a mess, and we are not called into the ministry because we have a message. In addition, we do not get into the ministry because we have a testimony to tell. We get into the ministry because we have been tested. God tests us to get us to the level in which He can trust us with *His* Truth and not our own (II Timothy 1:12). Thus, we must refuse to deify our deception or disobedience. Our testimonies of torment have no saving power. They will only persuade people to believe in a side of God that does not exist. God only embodies His saving grace in the testimony of Jesus Christ. Christ only embodies His sacrificial love in the Gospel.

As a result, we recognize the pulpit and teaching platform is not a platform to address our foolishness or the foolishness of another. The ministry is not about our miseries. It is about God's message. The pulpit and teaching podium are not platforms to start a revolution or movement predicated upon human misery. We are to testify of Jesus and not of ourselves (II Corinthians 4:5). Any ministry built on the foundation of pain is personal. We can never be effective in ministry if we take things to a personal level. We cannot afford to take ourselves that seriously. We do not get into the ministry because we had trials. We get into the ministry because we have been tried. We get in ministry because we have gone through God's fire and not our spouse's fire. We all must be purged before we can truly preach (Psalm 51:12-13; Luke 22:32; II Timothy 2:21; I Peter 5:10).

Mary Wade was a four-sided Wife. She always knew there were two other sides to the husband and Wife's story. Although she knew there was another side, she was wise enough to not want to hear the other side. There were some things she did not want to know. She knew there was God's side of the story. She also knew there was a satanic side of the story because she recognized how busy the Devil is. Therefore, Satan could not tempt her to bite into blame or something she could not chew. She even advised marriage couples to not get into the *"what ifs"*. She always said that although *"if"* has two letters, it is a big word. She advised men and women to not ask hypothetical questions because you never know what you would do with the real answer, what you would do under any given situation, and there are some things you don't want to know. She had a lot of hard sayings that would throw couples off if motives were not right. Satan got Eve into the demonic realm of *"if"*. He deceived Eve into thinking that *if* she ate, she would be better off.

Instead of Eve being submissive God, she was submissive to Satan. In addition, instead of Adam being submissive to God, he was submissive to Eve's whims. No passive man can stay on that level without having a secret outlet somewhere. That is really what happens in a lot of failed marriages many do not know. Strong men do not have to prove they are not intimidated by powerful women. It will reveal itself in time. Strong men have no more to prove in the ministerial gardens of today than God does. God did not feel as though He was not *God enough* for Eve. God did not feel as though He had something to prove to her. God was secure in the fact that He had done *His* job.

When God lets couples sign their own death warrants through conniving and compromising, He cannot promise them life (Genesis 2:17). He previously told them not to partake of the forbidden fruit or they would surely die. Eating of the forbidden fruit was Adam and Eve's personal problem they had with God. What women are failing to be should not be the man's problem. Likewise, what men are failing to be is not the woman's problem. This is where relationships get in trouble. When a man takes the woman's problem as his own, he is assuming too much responsibility. He must leave the woman to experience the consequences of her own decisions, even if it kills her (Genesis 3:4). On the other hand, Eve needed to know that giving Adam a bite of the same fruit was not going to make him or her any better. If she really wanted to help him, she did not have to enable him. If Adam were so hungry for knowledge of good and evil, he would have eaten from that tree a long time ago on his own terms.

When a Wife takes on too much responsibility for what the husband fails to do, she will be permanently impaired by his decisions and never learn how to move on with her life. Even if she is gone, she will never go away. The fact of the matter is that *we* are our number one problem. When Adam and Eve ate of the forbidden fruit, God held each of them accountable to put their personal problems in proper perspective. When a couple disobeys God, neither wins. God does not only bring chastisement on the couple. He also chastises devilish third parties who helped bring division in the marriage (Genesis 3:14). If God did not even want parents involved in their children's marriages, He sure did not want so-called friends to be involved (Genesis 2:24).

For there to be true revival in ministries and restoration in marriages, it is not necessary to break down gender barriers by putting men and women in the same positions or putting them down. We need to raise gender barriers. If we are to be restored to Cross-shaped marriages and ministries, gender barriers must be raised. A real women's ministry will encourage women to keep their skirts down, and a real men's ministry will encourage men to keep their pants up.

We know the blame game continues if men raise standards for women and lower standards for themselves. It also continues if certain women raise standards for men but ignore their own issues. Mary Wade had high standards for herself, and her husband, J. C. Wade, Sr., had high standards for himself. When a marriage couple has built-in insecurities and higher standards for each other than they place upon themselves, a sense of betrayal arouses when one or the other fails to satisfy those standards. As a matter of fact, the standards we place upon one another in marriage will always be unrealistic and unreachable. Then, the victim in the marriage can easily become the victimizer.

In Adam and Eve's marriage, there was too much pressure that neither of them could handle or identify. Eve could not handle the pressure Satan placed upon her to eat of the forbidden fruit, and Adam could not handle the pressure Eve placed upon him to eat of the forbidden fruit.

In venomous marriages and ministries, when we open our mouths, our tongues are longer than we think, and we will choke on our own words. Sometimes, it is the Serpent's tongue that is doing all the talking. Whenever we bear the yoke of God's chastisement, we keep silent until God restores us to where we belong. After that, it is only God who gets the glory and not we ourselves. Then, we shout praises to God instead of hiss bitterness and blame towards the spouse. When we take full responsibility for our own actions, God may allow us to surface in a salvific and supernatural way after we have sinned, been scandalized, scorned, or seduced.

The truth of the matter is in the fact that Jesus may not return within the next decade or century because looming on the horizon is His Church populated with marriages of displaced heads and bodies. It takes time to secure the head back on the body. Jesus is coming back for a Bride without spot or blemish. For that to happen, Jesus may have to perform a sex-change on the Church because the roles are reversed. His Bride (the Church) has become too masculine. In other words, she has assumed too much authority. Jesus is looking for softer and more submissive servants.

When a man and woman co-exist in their God-ordained roles, they are a powerful unit that is unstoppable. We have examples of pastors and their Wives who exemplify this trait throughout the Body of Christ. They are the real power-couples. This reversal back to God's original design may take generations before it happens on larger scales. However, there can be a *slowdown* of the speed of role-reversals for the benefit of the next decade. Then, perhaps another generation can begin a U-turn in the right direction.

Regardless, there is a remnant in each generation who resembles God's original design who have no problem with traditional family values. Also, they are pastors, Wives, and members of our churches filled with women who know how to sit down and men who know how to stand up. Mary Wade's generation knew nothing of role-reversals in the Church or home. If there was divorce, it was rare, and the parents co-parented in raising their children. The children never heard any negative word from their parents toward one another, even if they were divorced. Her generation of pastors and Wives were on a much simpler but significant scale. Those who constitute the remnant are voices within the new Church wilderness who are keeping ministry and marriage simple. They are teaching their kids about traditional values and reminding them of vices that baptized most of our children in a culture of confusion and compromise. In addition, their children are listening. They are not popular in the Christian marketplace, but they are powerful. They have not bowed to the gods of convenience, ecclesiastical idolatry, deception, or ambition. They have more pictures of themselves together as Husband and Wife at home than they do on their church website. They are simply, "*Just Married.*"

My heart is for all regardless of whether I agree with their practices or not. The purpose and premise of this book is still the same. If I have enemies or critics, it is for their healing as well. It is for *anyone* who is sincere about marriage and ministry to be delivered from some internal perspective or external pressure that has defined them. It is for those who have been judged by people, but they have been justified by God. It is healing for those who may have everything on the outside, but on the inside, they are still left with that naked and fake feeling. It is for women who feel they must be hard to survive a marriage, and it is for men who feel they must be soft to survive a marriage. In the words of pastor Derek L. Winkley, "When a woman moves from under the submission of a man, she ceases to be soft." Before Eve sinned, her name was "Woman". The word for "Woman" is אִשָּׁה (ishshah, also transliterated ishah) which means, *womb of man* or a softer version of a man. When Eve sinned, she became hard. Adam then named her "Eve", the mother of all living because she was soon to die, and so was he along with all humanity.

I believe at the core of all our dysfunctions, most of us are or were doing our best with what we know or once knew. No one sets sail with the purpose of sinking in the storm. I do not wish to believe any are attempting to do so with ill motives. Some Wives may just be deceived, and some husbands allowed themselves to be dominated. Most in ministry and marriage are putting their hearts and souls into it. One thing they cannot be guilty of is laziness. Their work ethic is impeccable. At the end of the day, let God be glorified.

All I am saying is that it should help if we can see that God is our only source to restore us to true standing with Him. We live in a church-life culture that will convince you that you are a failure if you do not fit the norm. Ministry has been so normalized that success is only credited to us if we reach certain platforms. I just want all readers to know that many of those platforms are not worth standing on. Everything that glitters is not gold. My goal is to encourage readers to be who God called and created them to be while being held to biblical absolutes instead of cultural norms.

For the wonderful and wise Wives who dare defeat the odds by tapping into a power much greater than assuming manly roles and battling for an already ordained equality, there are countless women in the Bible and our local churches who gained favor with God, men, and themselves through feminine power on a godly level. These women of God are extraordinary, to say the least. One would have no problem believing Deborah was a major military leader (Judges 4:6-7). In addition, one would not find it hard to believe Esther was chosen *"for such a time as this"* (Esther 4:14). One would not find it hard to believe women courageously stood by Jesus at the foot of the Cross until the end. One would not find it hard to believe women were the first heralds of Jesus' resurrection, nor would one find it hard to believe Anna (the prophetess) was a major recipient of the good news of Christ's birth (Luke 2:36-38). One would not find it hard to believe Paul was surrounded, sustained, and supported by a core group of women who he labeled co-laborers with him in the Gospel. It would not be hard to believe much of Timothy's discipleship was from his mother (Eunice) and his grandmother (Lois). One would not find it hard to believe the Chosen Lady of II John was a woman, who was most likely a major influential leader in the church (II John 1:13). These women operated within the context of God's regulations of submission and authority and not outside or despite them. In addition, it is not hard to believe virtuous women are rare in the 21st century (Proverbs 31). I do not find it hard to believe the most influential person in my walk with God was my dear Aunt Eloise Temple, who is a virtuous woman. Maybe I am still alive today because of *Big Annie's* prayers. Every time I saw her, she would say, "I pray for you every day."

If Mary Wade and J. C. Wade, Sr. could do it, so can we. We must remember they were cut from a different cloth along with countless pastors and Wives of their generation. They came from a hard-working generation who knew how to make it on a little. They were the generation that came before some Baby Boomers who blurred the lines and the succeeding generations who blamed the lines. Like James Commodore Wade, Sr. and Mary Wade, Husband and Wife look a lot like this:

We do not see them much anymore. Although they are almost extinct, they do exist. They are pastors who learned to love and lead, and they are Wives who learned to love the liberating flow of submission. They are no longer championed by our society, but their hearts ache at the sight of anemic husbands and anxious Wives. They are a ministry team, but their central base of operation is the home front. In this type of marriage, the husband is also capitalized. The Husband is no less at home than the Wife, and the Wife is no more at home than the Husband. They are dear to their church because they have demonstrated marriage can pass through the fire and still come out unsinged. They love and care for one another just as they care for themselves. They bear each other's burdens and are not repulsed by each other's infirmities because they have committed their lives to each other in sickness and health. They predict each other's movements before the other moves. They complete each other's sentences before the other speaks. They feel each other's pain before it strikes. They sit side by side and have conversations for a lifetime without ever saying a word because they know each other well. She does not talk too much, and he is not too quiet. When one succeeds, it is not at the other's expense, but it is at the other's loving sacrifice. One's sadness is revived by the other's joy. They are together in every sense of the word. They are reserved for each other, and no serpent can talk them into falling out of love with one another. One's values are more precious than the values of the other, but they do not mind. There is no competition because they are on the same team, and their only opponent is the Devil. They have enough scruples not to major in minors. They truly love the Lord. The important thing is that they stay together. They are one flesh. They are simply:

Just Married

Chapter 9

THE PASTOR AND HIS ARMS

Authority Meets Attitude
(An Excerpt from the Life of Paul:
A preacher who survive credibility assassins)

<u>Tribute</u>: To Jack Hayford (Pastor-Emeritus, The Church on the Way of Van Nuys, CA from 1969-1999)

Pulling down strongholds, casting down imaginations, intercessory prayer, spiritual warfare, invading the impossible, and being a pastor of pastors are just a few signatures of Jack Hayford. Literal shepherds in Bible days were strong. To pastor effectively, a man must have strong spiritual arms. The weapons of their warfare must not be carnal but mighty for the pulling down of strongholds (II Corinthians 10:4). I had the privilege of meeting him personally while attending one of his pastoral consultations for an entire week many years ago as well as joining a group of pastors to visit his home and meet his dear wife, Anna. How do I know Pastor Jack has a strong spiritual arm? He laid his hands on me, stretched out his arm, and prayed for me.

The loss of credibility is a silent killer of leadership of any form. It is a sophisticated way of saying a man's authenticity is in question. Many acids erode credibility. Every now and then, plain old taking the pastor for granted will chew at the pastor's credibility. Unfortunately, when the pastor feels it slipping away, he may do more introspection on himself than his constituents do among themselves. The pastor relentlessly searches for areas in his life that may be inhibiting his authority from flowing in its fullest strength. The pastor's arm is made of complex spiritual muscle. The results tested regarding the accuracy of his spiritual authority may not come back immediately. It takes time. Yet, when Satan enters the scene, a pastor's credibility can collapse, and his arms can drop in a matter of seconds. Satan is a strategist at playing on the minds of God's people. Sometimes, it is due to the carnality of his critics. Satan takes advantage of the minds of Christian constituents and places them in strongholds of defamation.

As stated in the first chapter of this book, the Corinthians doubted Paul's apostolic authority. Although Paul announced he was chief of sinners, it was of no sin of Paul's that the church developed prideful and ascending attitudes toward his leadership that needed to be *cast down*. Paul's loss of credibility was one of Satan's assaults upon his leadership because their carnality allowed Satan to erect a demonic playground within their imaginations.

When a pastor's credibility is in question, he discovers progressive restrictions placed on him by the people who were supposed to be in his circle. After a while, the pastor is no longer free to do the simplest things without experiencing criticism, judgmentalism, skepticism, sarcasm, or indifference. Paul the Apostle became his own defense attorney by protecting his rights to forbid to marry, expect compensation for full-time service to ministry, claim the benefits of a true apostle as well as describe his apostolic authority to go to war spiritually do defend his credibility:

The Pastor And His Arms

"Am I not an apostle? Am I not free? Have I not seen Jesus Christ our Lord? Are ye not my work in the Lord? If I be not an apostle unto others, yet doubtless I am to you: for the seal of mine apostleship are ye in the Lord."

(I Corinthians 9:1-2; KJV)

"For though we walk in the flesh, we do not war after the flesh: (For the weapons of our warfare are not carnal, but mighty through God for the pulling down of strong holds;) Casting down imaginations, and every high thing that exalteth itself against the knowledge of God, and bringing into captivity every thought to the obedience of Christ; And having in a readiness to revenge all disobedience when your obedience is fulfilled."

(II Corinthians 10:3-6; KJV)

Weapon in this text is *hopla*, which means, *arms* or military might. The Corinthian church arrogantly proclaimed Paul was only bold in his letters, but he would be timid when face-to-face. Paul responds by stating the fact that if he were to visit them personally, he would not only be bold, but he would also be *battle minded*. To diffuse premature insinuations that he would cause physical harm, Paul assured he did not war after the flesh (II Corinthians 10:3). However, he would come with weapons. He would use spiritual arms to pull down attitudinal strong holds that possessed the judgmental thought processes of the Corinthian Believers.

Because their attitudes were becoming aggressive in their accusations, Paul had to use apostolic authority to *disarm* their criticisms. Listen to the text again, considering the context of the Corinthians' questioning of Paul's apostolic credentials.

> *"For though we (apostles) walk in the flesh, we (apostles) do not war after the flesh: For the weapons of our (apostles) warfare are not carnal, but mighty through God for the pulling down of strong holds."*

(II Corinthians 10:3-4; KJV)

Many interpreters make assumptions that this text refers to the spiritual authority of every Believer. However, the context only describes the arms of the *apostles* in spiritual warfare. The central idea in question among the Corinthian church was Paul's apostolic credibility. When Paul referred to the terms, *we* and *our*, he was referring to the apostles and no one else. The weapons of the *Believer's* warfare are mentioned in the sixth chapter of Ephesians. Remembering the role of apostles was to lay the foundation (Jesus) for the Church, we find in II Corinthians 10:3-6 that Paul was saying apostles were authorized to use spiritual arms to pull down vain imaginations as an act of spiritual warfare and church discipline, of which the apostles had hierarchy (Matthew 18:18). Thus, Paul was using the principle of binding and loosing as an act of Church discipline against the Corinthians for attacking Paul's credibility. This act of church discipline occurred because Satan captured the minds of carnal Believers through arrogant judgmental attitudes that sponsored flagrant disobedience and insurrection against the foundation on which the Church is built, who is Jesus Christ (I Corinthians 3:11, Ephesians 2:20).

Just as Believers are restricted from laying claims to the authority given to apostles, pastors are to do the same. Yet, pastors can learn principles of how to deal with people who devote themselves to defamation demons:

> *"For the weapons of our warfare are not carnal, but mighty through God to the pulling down of **strong holds**; Casting down **imaginations**, and **every high thing** that exalteth itself against the knowledge of God and bringing into captivity every thought to the obedience of Christ."*
>
> (II Corinthians 10:4-5; KJV)

The word for *strongholds* is ὀχύρωμα [*ochuroma/* okh·oo·ro·mah/]. It can have several connotations. Strongholds can refer to *fortifying by holding safely*. It also had a literal translation that referred to a *castle or fortress*. However, this cannot be the literal meaning because the context does not imply apostolic weapons are mighty for the pulling down of castles or fortresses. Yet, there is an additional meaning of the word, *strongholds*. It can also refer to the *arguments by which one who is a disputant can engage in to fortify his opinion and defend it against his opponent*.[1] Greek sages were known to identify battle against false ideologies as a war. Paul appears to borrow this battle language. Paul is defending his apostolic right to go to war with false ideas, "arguments" (NIV, NRSV, TEV) or "speculations" (NASB).[2] The Corinthian church developed false arguments against Paul's credibility that were

---

[1] Strong, J. (1995). *Enhanced Strong's Lexicon.* Woodside Bible Fellowship.

[2] Keener, C. S. (1993). *The IVP Bible background commentary: New Testament* (2 Co 10:3–5). Downers Grove, IL: InterVarsity Press.

imprisoned within their minds. Their arguments were so fortified that they were defensive and attacked Paul's credibility because they thought he was their opponent in practical matters regarding the Church.

Paul's apostolic authority was also mighty for the casting down of imaginations. The word for *imaginations* is λογισμους (*logismous*). It refers to reasoning. Furthermore, λογισμους (logismous) is taken from the old word λογιζομαι (*logizomai*), which means *to reckon*, used only here and Romans 6:11. In this sense, their imaginations were equated to forts or citadels that needed to be conquered.[3] These imaginations were reasonings in the minds of the Corinthian church that were hostile to the Christian faith that needed to be conquered. Their opinions became oppressive. Such reasonings were arguments against Paul's credibility that they did not realize was an attack upon Jesus Christ and His Church. To discredit Paul was to discredit Christ. They no longer thought Paul was worthy of serving in the Church as a leader. Therefore, they disqualified him in their minds. The Corinthian church had a temporary case of satanic amnesia. They quickly had forgotten that it was Paul who founded the church of Corinth. Therefore, in their minds, he was only credible when he confirmed them.

The word for *high things* is ὕψωμα (*hypsōma*), which can mean *arrogance* or *pretension*.[4] It also refers to an elevated barrier or bulwark within a castle or fortress. Paul is using fortress terminology to describe the fortified and arrogant reasoning of the Corinthian congregation. To break through the fortress of their arrogance, he needed spiritual weapons. Every arrogant argument

---

[3] Robertson, A. T. (1933). *Word Pictures in the New Testament* (2 Co 10:5). Nashville, TN: Broadman Press.

[4] Swanson, J. (1997). *Dictionary of Biblical Languages with Semantic Domains: Greek (New Testament)* (electronic ed.). Oak Harbor: Logos Research Systems, Inc.

that exalts itself revolves around the pride of Satan before his fall when he attempted to exalt himself above God. The synthesis of this text gives an understanding that the context of spiritual warfare is within the mind. Therefore, the Corinthians were in a battle for their minds. In a practical sense, we can say that whenever someone attacks the credibility of a leader on this level, they are *losing their minds*.

The sixth chapter of Ephesians states that we wrestle against spiritual beings in high places. From Ephesians 6, we recognize the locality of *demonic beings*, i.e., in high places. However, in II Corinthians 10:4-5, we recognize the locality of *demonic battlefields*, i.e., within the mind. Therefore, the nature of the Corinthian's skepticism was evil, and the playground for Satan to spurn prideful and idolatrous attitudes was within their minds. Paul discerned that he must go deeper than reason and teaching to combat the mindset of the Corinthians. Paul would use spiritual arms to war with spirits that capitalized on the Corinthian's consciences. Paul could guarantee that their minds would change, and their disobedience would be brought into captivity to the obedience of Christ because he was battling prideful spirits deeper than mere skepticism. Their skepticism was satanic.

Whenever a pastor goes to war on judgmental spirits, victory is guaranteed if spiritual weapons are used with a strong arm. Paul would have been powerless to change their minds because that would have been mind-control. God does not endow pastors with the powers of mind-control, but He does endow pastors with the spiritual powers of *malignant-control*.

On the other hand, carnality within the local church is a work of the flesh that demands pastoral attention on aggressive levels. When all a pastor can do is pray and preach within local churches who refuse to be transformed, the power of praying and preaching must never be underestimated. Carnality will not evolve into spirituality on its own. Christians do not automatically mature over time, especially carnal Christians.

Shepherds in ancient days were not timid, but they were warriors who needed strong arms. With strong arms, they were required to protect sheep from predators and lay down their lives for the sheep. Their arms were strong to pull down, tear down, and take down predators who threatened livestock. In the spiritual sense, Satan was the predator seeking to take down the sheep (Believers) of Corinth. Paul was coming to assist them although they were attacking him.

Human nature is a very strange and fickle force. Therefore, the lines get satanically blurred within the local church. Initiating organizational change, spiritual transformation, and structural re-alignment can be very frustrating tasks for a pastor, depending upon who holds the reigns in local churches. In these types of local church settings, the only thing the pastor can do is wait until the unchanging generation of that church dies. For many pastors, it takes many years before real change takes place. God must remove strongholds before the pastor can truly take the church to the next level.

The New Testament concept of shepherding transliterated into spiritual shepherds who were to guard the flock of God (Acts 20:29-32). John descriptively portrays Satan as *the Wolf* (John 10:12). Contrary to popular opinion, Satan is not *the thief* who comes to steal, kill, and destroy in John 10:10. As we study the text, the context suggests the *thieves and robbers* to whom Jesus was referring were Pharisees who were attempting to raid innocent sheep (Israel) through false doctrine (John 10:1-10). According to verse 8, all who preceded Jesus were thieves and robbers (Pharisees and Sadducees). The *hirelings* were also Pharisees who made false claims of spiritual authority over God's people, but they did not guard the sheep. The Pharisees (hirelings) only fleeced the sheep for capital gain and made God's temple a den of *thieves* (Matthew 21:13). In other words, Jesus' house (the Temple) became a den of Pharisees and Sadducees.

The Pharisees had dual roles. They were *thieves and robbers* who were falsely claiming to be shepherds. Instead, they were also *hirelings* (John 10:12-13). The Pharisees were doing Temple business for what they could financially gain from the temple enterprise. Jesus contrasts His shepherding skills to those of the Pharisees, who were nothing but hirelings who flee when the Wolf (Satan) comes (John 10:12). Thus, Satan is the Wolf, and the thieves who come to steal, kill, and destroy were the thieves and robbers who desecrated the Temple through money changing.

In contemporary language, the thieves and robbers are false apostles, false shepherds, false teachers, false prophets, and false prophetesses. They have no conviction, calling, courage, or consciousness to defend the sheep when Satan or demons attack the flock because their arms are too weak to war on behalf of the sheep. You would even find occasional mentioning of demon-possessed people in the synagogue who the Pharisees ignored or shunned (Luke 4:33). Just as The Good Shepherd (Jesus) lays down His life for the sheep, the *under-shepherd* or *pastor* is endowed with strong spiritual arms to give his life in combat against the attacks of the doctrine, deception, and damage of demons upon the local church body.

Demons do not travel aimlessly in the air like floating butterflies. Instead, they target people to occupy. Their gateway of entrance into human bodies is within people's minds. If demons can control people's minds, they can control their bodies. Many Christians today have strange things going on in their thought lives. Many Christians also have *strong things* (strongholds) on their minds. Many are thinking more stubbornly and strangely than ever, and they are also thinking *strongly*. Many Believers are strong in their opinions. Their minds are like fortresses that hold good thoughts captive. Because they are so strong in being wrong, they refuse to be persuaded. Instead, they are influenced by satanic revelations that distort the true essence of the critical truths of Christianity. These lying spirits undermine the foundation on which the Church is laid. Therefore, they attack the credibility of certain leaders of the Church. Under such circumstances, accusations of that sort are satanic. Satan is the Accuser of the Brethren (Revelations 12:10). Many need to be saved from the strongholds that have captivated the minds of so many within our ranks who are not simply wrong, but they are also *strongly and strangely wrong*. In short, Christians have become strangely aggressive in their accusations of leaders.

Conservative understandings of the Bible assumed to be known are curious and unusual facts to the average Christian today. We are not referring to the world, but we are referring to the *mental health* of many within the local church. Demon possession has been deceptively diagnosed as bi-polar disorders. While there are legitimate mental cases of bi-polar illnesses or schizophrenia, many of these cases are a misdiagnosis. Many Christians have strange revelations they think are of God, but they are diabolically opposed to accountability to their spiritual leaders, the local church, and Christ. In other words, they have allowed their personal issues with leaders in the Church to become a satanic issue in their minds that seeks to destroy the credibility of a God-called man.

The vulnerability of many Christians to vindictiveness is evident because they have not taken seriously the discipline of guarding their minds (Romans 12:3). Thus, their minds are often an open battlefield for demons to play on by inducing strange perceptions and principles about leaders. Pastors are confronted with the surprisingly satanic ways people think about them. The entire culture of Christianity is in a stronghold. This is some of the context Christ-called pastors often scratch their heads about. They have been compressed by the delusion of contemporary Christian practices that defy foundational truths that never warrant other Christians the right to attack a pastor's credibility.

Paul stated he would exercise spiritual arms in the presence of the Corinthian congregation. Contact and communication are integral to combating demonic attitudes of skepticism. One of the traits of skeptical critics is that they form their opinions, but never come to the source to verify if their opinions are valid. Out of all my critics, I never hear from any of them personally. I only heard it through the grapevine or some indirect informant. Pastors who are experiencing credibility critics rarely get a phone call or one-on-one conversation with his critics. They get ugly letters from their critics, but most of them never put their names on the letters or give their identity. A real preacher can never accept criticism from a coward.

I remember when my pastor, M. V. Wade, Sr. on a Wednesday night solicited dialogue from his congregation regarding how they could grow in their attendance at Wednesday night Bible studies. He gave them the option to even write letters. As his Assistant, I thought I had a grand idea to get more of an honest response from the members. I suggested in my youthful vigor to have them write anonymously. In his wisdom and experience, he simply responded, "No son, that is not a good idea. I don't want to breed cowards."

It is even a lethal mistake to attempt to do battle with aggressive skepticism while away from our churches. By the time we come back to our churches, an organized stronghold will have developed that will be virtually impenetrable. Old school pastors would call this, "*Staying close to home*". The pastor must stay close enough to effectively neutralize carnal critics. He must be close enough to have visual accuracy of where wolves try to lie down with lambs.

Because the pastor's arms are spiritual, *pulling down* has little to do with *reaching up*. The strongholds are on people's minds. Therefore, pulling down strongholds has more to do with supernaturally correcting people's patterns of thinking than yanking demons out of the sky. Instead, pastors must utilize the spiritual forces of abstract aggression. In other words, we battle not against flesh and blood, but we do battle against all forms of spiritual wickedness in demonic realms.

Like Paul, the best way to sometimes check people is for the pastor to defend himself. When we are referring to the pastor's arms, we are referring to his ability to gather sheep unto himself in a correcting and nurturing fashion. When a shepherd would gather lost sheep that wandered from the fold, he would often break the leg of the sheep and carry it back to the fold in his arms or on his shoulders. The reason for breaking the leg of the sheep was to prevent the sheep from wandering again. While the sheep's leg was healing, he would spend time with the sheep, training it to stay within hearing distance of the shepherd. In like manner, when people's attitudes wander from biblical absolutes, the qualified pastor may employ painful corrective measures that break people from allowing Satan to gain an opportunity to play with their minds.

As a wise master builder and apostle, Paul's fingerprints were all over the foundation of the Corinthian church. Therefore, his fingers were connected to a corrective hand. Each Believer was to be warned of how he or she was to build upon that foundation (I Corinthians 3:10). Satan uses critics to try to erase the leader's imprint on the lives of those he leads or those who he once led. Like many churches that forget their founder, the Corinthian church's pride attempted to smear every fingerprint of Paul's in helping establish the Corinthian church.

Paul could have easily personally taken the assaults on his credibility and left the church in major disarray. This battle really was not Paul versus his church. Instead, the battle was Paul versus Satan who deceived his church. Be mindful, Paul did express deep feelings of love for the Corinthians as he suffered a godly sorrow for their condition. However, he did not allow the personal assaults that they hurled to deter him from being lovingly devoted to them. If Jesus commanded us to love our enemies, the pastor must also love his executioners, especially if they are members of his own constituency. Unlike his critics, the pastor can never grow bitter. When I think about my critics, I feel sorry for them. I really do. They do not know what they are doing, and they do not know what they are talking about. They are very unhappy people because out of what little time God allows us to have in this brief life, they can find time to focus on me. Anyone who focuses too much attention on me will be a miserable person.

Pastoring is a vocation that requires unconditional love for who we serve regardless of how we are personally assaulted by their actions and vice versa. People can treat the pastor no better than they treat God, themselves, or one another. It was not a sole coagulated effort against Paul that was the issue with the church of Corinth. Corinth also had internal schisms among themselves (II Corinthians 12:20).

It can be extremely easy to take affronts of people on our lives personally. However, God told Samuel that the people were not rejecting him, but they were rejecting God (I Samuel 8:7). Pastoring is not easy, but it is a privilege and should be entered without complaint or grumbling (Philippians 2:14). Despite the subjective damage Paul faced, he allowed himself to stay in protective distance of the people of Corinth. His protective distance was not only in protecting himself from hellish harassment but also in protecting them from the demonic disease of immaturity and self-centeredness. Taking battles personally amputates our arms.

It is always interesting to look at the reasons for Moses' disqualification from the Promised Land. It was not necessarily the case that Moses was disqualified because he got angry and struck the rock twice. If he would have been cool-headed and struck it once or not even struck at all, he still would have been disqualified. The Bible shows a completely different twist to Moses' disqualification from entering the Land of Promise:

> *"And the Lord spake unto Moses and Aaron,* ***Because ye believed me not, to sanctify me in the eyes of the children of Israel****, therefore ye shall not bring this congregation into the land which I have given them."*
>
> (Numbers 20:12; KJV)

God judged Moses and Aaron because *they did not believe God, and they refused to treat God as holy among the people.* God previously commanded Moses to *speak* to the rock, and water would be supplied. Out of resentment, Moses added his own twist:

> *"And Moses took the rod from before the Lord, as He commanded him. And Moses and Aaron gathered the congregation together before the rock, and he said unto them,* ***hear now, ye rebels; must we fetch you water out of this rock?*** *And Moses lifted up his hand, and with his rod he smote the rock twice: and the water came out abundantly, and the congregation drank and their beasts also."*
>
> (Numbers 20:10-11; KJV)

Moses and Aaron began to practice the ministry in the wilderness meanly as he brought water out of the rock with a double-strike and a double-tongue. No matter how bitter people become towards a pastor, the pastor must still honor God and not fight with an arm of flesh. When God tells a leader to do something, he does not have to become threatening or use sarcastic sentences as insults toward them. As matter of fact, we are not to strike at all. All it takes is God's word, and the job will get done. A godly word personifies our obedience to God. We are to communicate to God's people on God's terms and in God's tone. God's tone was one of love, and Moses' tone was lashing. God's tone was redemptive, and Moses' tone was resentful. Moses shamed the people instead of being obedient to serve the people. Despite Israel's complaining, God designed water to come out of the rock blessedly and not bitterly. Disqualification occurs when we strike and slash instead of serve God's people. When we administrate and preach out of frustration or bitterness, we are striking twice.

Moses *stopped believing God*. It is futile to pastor a congregation if we lost our faith in God's methods for coming to our defense and their deliverance. For the five years I served as Assistant to M. V. Wade, Sr., although he went through bitter challenges, I never heard him preach from a bitter spirit. The seasoned preachers had a way of sanctifying God when people were crucifying them. In my youthfulness, I could not wait until it was my turn to preach so I could let some of them have it. For a while, I could not understand how he could speak so graciously as if nothing ever happened. He preached as if his sufferings were irrelevant. God does not sanction us when we are on the persecuting end of pastoring, soft-skinned, and ready to fight when opposed. This type of attitude must be harshly corrected because the pulpit is not the platform to cut God's people down no matter how many times they try to cut the preacher down. God will bury us for that behavior, especially if we have a past ourselves. Moses had a past criminal record himself (Exodus 2:12). Paul also had a past of being a mass murderer of Christians. When we know that we have a past, it is even more vital to minister out of perfect obedience although we are far from perfect.

For Moses, it was as if the people were complaining about water, and Moses went to the faucet, poured barrels of water, and splashed it in their faces saying, "You want water, here's water, you rebels!" God is not like that. He does not barrel water in our faces when we are thirsty. Either He will feed us graciously, or He will not feed us at all. God does not throw food on the floor when we are hungry and treat us like disobedient dogs. God feeds us like a Shepherd and provides for us like a Father. God disciplines out of love and not hatred, bitterness, or frustration. He upbraids not, even when we are undeserving (James 1:17). If Moses and Aaron were to continue in that kind of arrogance, God was sure to take them out personally, and He eventually did just that.

On the contrary, many pastors are criticized by many people because of their shortcomings, but God uses them mightily and preserves their pastorate because they are professional in the pulpit, and they are not personal. They know how to separate their sufferings and get down to the business of preaching. Among many reasons, God uses these types of men mightily because they know how to handle critics in a Christ-like way, and they have a level of integrity amid their iniquities. In other words, although some of God's people may not trust certain leaders, God can trust certain leaders with His people. God cannot trust a preacher's critics with the Gospel because it is a Gospel of reconciliation and not a gospel of retaliation. It is the Gospel of victory and not a gospel of vindication.

Jesus could trust Paul (II Corinthians 5:18). Despite God-called pastors' shortcomings, they make sure people know the difference between them and God. This is what it means to sanctify God among the people. These great men of God let the people know that even though they are pastors, they are not God. These types of pastors are not proud of their weaknesses, and they have not forgotten their faults. They are simply testimonies of the power of God working in them. For these reasons and more, they know how to preach, and their critics do not. When they stand behind the sacred desk, mature Christians know these types of pastors are standing behind God, and they respect that at all costs.

Mature people will put up with a lot of things from their leader, but they will not put up with arrogance. Even if a pastor has flaws but leads with an integrity only God can give, most people will trust their lives in his hands. They know he will handle them in a godly and unconditional manner of love. When Moses spoke out of turn to the Israelites, he lost his credibility with God and the people. People can easily see when we stoop to their level. When we do, we just lost them. Israel only drank because they were thirsty, but they would never forget the bitter way Moses turned on the faucet.

God could have easily embarrassed Moses, but God still let the waters flow. When God's waters flow, they always flow abundantly. However, God would make sure the people would not credit Moses for being the miracle worker. God was more concerned with quenching their thirst instead of protecting Moses from their threats, even if they were an ungrateful group. He would deal with Moses later. We must not be disillusioned when the waters flow if we strike out of frustration or angry motives. If God allows the waters to still flow, it is only because He is concerned about satisfying the thirsty souls of those we lead. If we fail to remember God, we can believe we have an authority beyond accountability. God will hold us accountable for ministering out of madness. Our extras will never give people their exodus. Make no mistake about that.

I recall when Mary Wade told me a story of a member who viscously opposed Pastor J. C. Wade, Sr. when he was the pastor. Each time the man would do something to assault her husband, the assailant's leg would swell and break out in sores. Pastor and Mrs. Wade would visit, pray for him, and Mrs. Wade would put a home-made ointment on his leg. Then, his leg would heal. After a brief period, he would do well, start the cycle again and oppose Pastor J. C. Wade, Sr., and his leg would swell up and break out into sores. They would go and pray for him, and his leg would heal. This cycle repeated several times. He would seek to harm. They would seek to heal. Technically, they were pulling down strongholds. That is what real pastoring is about when our credibility is in question. Pastor Wade's philosophy of ministry was to love God's people, and trust God that He would take care of him if he did so. No wonder he earned such credibility with the entire city of Omaha, Nebraska. He was more powerful than the Mayor and any political or city official of Omaha because He refused to rule with a retaliatory rod. He won the city and his church through love and not popular opinion, force, or coercion. If he was not loved, he was at least respected because he had proven himself in loving service to his church and state. He knew mayors, city councilmen, chiefs of police, judges, and many more just as intimately as he knew his own congregation. Yes, there was a core group of members who aligned with the gates of Hell to oppose him, but no man took his life or ministry. He laid it down.

Jack Hayford called the people he led, "Loved Ones". It was not just a fuzzy phrase he used to coerce them to cuddle under his covering. The first time I heard him make that statement, I could not wait until I became a pastor so that I could have the privilege of loving the ones I was with. Although I have seen many members come and go, I do not believe there is even one of them who can accuse me of not loving them. Some may not admit that I love them, but they sure cannot say that I hate them. Learning to love people is the basic motive for ministry. I believe one of the simple fallacies developed in the quest to get into our pastoral promised lands is forgetting that among all our ambitions of leadership, we are called to love the people we lead, even our enemies.

Moses stopped loving Israel. Initially, he loved them so much that he slew an Egyptian for killing an Israelite and even interceded for God not to kill His people when they made idols out of gold at the foot of Mt. Sinai. Later, Moses got so engulfed in the cycle of the rebellion of God's people that he became rebellious also. The pastor must never become who or what he is fighting against.

Pastoring the people of God is a high calling and high privilege although we are often on the brunt end of their issues with themselves and God. People did not call us to preach or pastor. Therefore, their confirmation or criticisms do not determine our wealth or worth in God's heavenly account. God called us. We can also be on the brunt end of our issues and stand in our way. When people attack the pastor's credibility, they are not at themselves because they are also under attack. They allowed themselves to become the victims of evil and have allowed some unresolved issue in their own lives to surface at a pastor's expense. At times, pastors may realize this truth all too intimately by allowing their compassion to override combat or their own guilt to override their grit. We can be tempted to take a sympathetic approach to the assaults hurled against our people and succumb to the demons of passivity. Yet, there is a difference between a pastor being persecuted versus one who is a glutton for punishment. Inherent within people under satanic attack is a paradoxical cry for the pastor to lead them, even if it means skillful confrontation with the evil powers that bind them.

Paul was aware of approaching the people in a way that would give them greater avenues to oppose themselves. To avoid this, he admonished us to let our speech be seasoned with salt, and to confront people with the truth in a spirit of love (Ephesians 4:15). Because love disciplines, a strategic balance of a shepherd's arm and a shepherd's heart are integral to an effective *exercise* of pastoral authority and *exorcise* of demon critics.

I will often refer to the pastor who trained me for pastoring. Pastor Melvin Wade would train younger preachers not to lead out of frustration because it breeds sarcasm. The pulpit then becomes our platform to spit Truth at people in a way that insults rather than inspires them. We lose a sense of credibility when we confront congregations carelessly. It is a strange experience when we allow ourselves to become the victims of our congregation's vices. We cannot afford to allow people's issues to pull us into their world. As we minister according to God's dictates, we pull them into God's world. Each instance when we give up on people or resort to our own human tactics, we release them from an accountability to God we did not even know existed. God has a reign on people's hearts and minds despite how they behave. If we minister apart from God's standards, we tighten the reigns and choke their ability to come to their senses (II Timothy 2:25).

If a pastor is not careful, he can allow critical Christians to drive him crazy. Every pastor must have a release valve that is victorious instead of a vice. Unfortunately, these are some of the unspoken reasons why some of us as pastors resorted to medicating ourselves through some type of immorality. Although pastoring is painful, it is a privilege. Thus, we must master our miseries and not become self-sabotaging servants (I Corinthians 9:27).

Leadership demands the pastor to be disciplined when it comes to the battle of the mind. Just as a disobedient child tends to gravitate to the parent who exercises controlled discipline, local churches are more prone to recognize whose arms they truly belong when the pastor is exercising control over criticism. At the end of Paul's letter to the Corinthians, there is a gradual shift from correction to compassion. Being a pastor is an art that poses threats in new dimensions regularly, especially those in which our effectiveness in leadership becomes the axis on which opposition swings.

Any real pastor can tell you that the local church is a strange beast. "Daddy Wade" would always say, "Boy, don't try to figure out church people. I have been in the ministry well over sixty years, and I still can't figure them out." He never said anything skeptical about the disciples of Christ, just some church people. Extraordinarily little of how to deal with the psychology of local churches is detailed in the Bible. It takes a lot of prayer, preaching, observation, experience, wisdom, and common sense to lead people.

Unfortunately, I did not have much of either when I first became a pastor. I had skills, but I was not seasoned. I had talent, but I had not been tested and tried. It took several deaths other than the death of my mother for me to understand what all that meant. It took the death of relationships, jobs, dreams, hopes, assignments, the death of churches, and the dying of myself to the Lord's will. I would make decisions in relationships and ministry that were attempts to make others happy, but those decisions would sabotage my health at the same time. If somebody asked me, "What do *you* want?" I would not know how to answer that question. I tended to give it all away in codependent relationships until I had nothing left for myself. I was a more faithful number-two man than a number-one man. Then, I finally broke and fell to self-medicating myself. I would always want to do what would meet the expectations of those who I admired or loved. I codependently surrounded myself with dysfunctional people on many levels who loved to talk about themselves so much that they could not find time to listen to me. That pattern finally backed up on me and became the reason why I fell into self-destructive behavior that nearly cost me my life. Over the last half of my ministry and life, I put away childish things and childish people. My time is my new money. Therefore, I do not have time to entertain toxic relationships on any level. I no longer surround myself with people who always want something but never have anything to give.

Moses usually did just that, but Paul always did that. If the people complained or criticized him, Moses would not argue or contend with them. He would just go to God, and God would tell him what to do. Yet, Moses allowed that pattern of good behavior to fool him into thinking he could vent for once in his lifetime. Like Pastor Broderick Huggins would say, "You can do so well for so long and tolerate so much that you can be deceived into thinking you owe yourself a little sin every now and then."

There are many pastors (including myself) who have been faced with strongholds that would not release their grip despite how hard they prayerfully pulled. Retrospection teaches many reasons why demons refused to relinquish their claws off those congregations. Some of them were stubborn demons that demanded succeeding shepherds if they were to lose their power. In other cases, what we thought were churches were synagogues of Satan that even Jesus refused to shepherd. If a pastor has been accused of making a mistake and losing his tenure at a church, if that church never gets back on its feet, I do not believe it was the pastor who was the problem. Our efforts were futile because we were unknowingly attempting to make disciples out of demons and were pastoring synagogues of Satan.

Pastoring is like watering an unpredictable plant. Every church has its own personality and progress rate. Although there are things about each church that are standard, there are other things about each church that are unique and unexplainable. Even the most seasoned pastors scratch their heads, trying every sanctified method they can to increase the quality of the life of the church of which they are overseers. So, how can one judge the crisis of another pastor who scratches his head also? There is no experiential paradigm that works for every church; only a biblical one. In the local church business, no one is an expert. Pastoring is a lot like golf. Once you master one hole, the next hole can totally embarrass you. Every now and then, the operations of God are so deep within the soils of some people's hearts that we must maintain the stance of a faithful farmer and sow and plow faithfully, realizing the results of our planting are at the mercy of heavenly laws. One thing is for certain: We are to never lose sight of who we are regardless of the outcome of our efforts. If our constituency has become bewitched, we must always remain shepherds (Galatians 3:1). Under every circumstance, no work consecrated to God is in vain (I Corinthians 15:58).

To show you how the local church is a fickle entity, each local church in the New Testament is no longer in existence. God will never bless a church or people who persecuted their pastor. Regardless of whoever the next pastor will be or whatever new church they join, there will still be stunted growth until they resolve their issues with the previous leader who loved them. It was not just persecution that scattered local churches in the New Testament. The disintegration of those churches was also due to how they persecuted their founder, Paul (Philippians 4:15)

When we realize that our *pastor-ship* is not permanent, we will never be baffled by shattered sanctuaries and skeptical Saints. Nevertheless, we *have* received a Kingdom that cannot be shaken, and we are participants in a spiritual building program for Jesus' true Church that the gates of Hell cannot destroy (Matthew 16:18). Our Lord authorized us to exercise the keys of the Kingdom (church discipline) to restrict the operations of evil within our settings if they are to be in alignment with Jesus' true

Church. We may not have the keys to some of our local churches, but we do have the keys of the Kingdom. Regardless of the outcome of our local churches, we are adding spiritual bricks to the Universal Church in the spiritual realm. We are not only pastoring local entities, but we are also participating in an invisible one. Our arms stretch beyond our present local churches into the realm of the eternal virtues of Christ's true Church. No pastor will ever have a sense of true fulfillment unless he prioritizes the Kingdom of God above his local church. If Jesus were to come back for local churches, none would stand. Only a remnant of true Believers in those churches will be raptured. It is only the Invisible Church that Christ will return for and bring into everlasting glory (Ephesians 5:27).

As we re-examine our arms, we realize we have been entrusted with power to defend ourselves and possibly create an anointed anti-venom for poisoned minds. We have Jesus as our model for meekness as He exemplified strength under control. Therefore, we cannot afford to operate under any forms of madness. Taking the insults and opinions of people personally by publications or into the pulpit will always result in some form of pastoral insanity.

Sometimes, our authority will demand that we take the road of humility. Our weapons are to be used when the sheep are in danger of wolves (false teachers and the spirit of the Antichrist), but we are to never use our weapons upon the sheep. *Shepherds are never to fight sheep.* We are instructed to warn, discipline, rebuke, and even convict, but we are never to fight them. We are not to sue them, but we are to serve them. We may be subpoenaed to their courts, but they are never to be subpoenaed to ours (Luke 12:11). In addition, we are not to use our weapons to defend ourselves. We are to use our *armor* to defend ourselves but never our *arms*. Our arms are our offensive weaponry. The purpose of our weapons is to extract evil spirits that brainwash the progression of God's purposes from our parishioners' perspectives.

Whenever Paul was attacked by the Sanhedrin or wolves of his day, he never pulled out a human sword. Because God was his defense, he knew he would not die by their swords until his work was done. When persecuted, we are to bless God and endure hardship as good soldiers because suffering is redemptive (II Timothy 2:3-4; Romans 8:35-36).

If the office of an apostle is still valid today, claiming the office of an apostle in today's church is not a position of supremacy. It is a position of suffering. It is not an office of prosperity. It is an office of persecution. We must know when to hang up our guns. When people come to the sanctuary, we must prepare them to worship and not get caught up in the center of warfare. Therefore, there should never be such a thing as a *church fight*. It takes at least two to fight. Church fights are the consequences of inheriting churches that are set up on a western civilization system that structures churches as organizations governed by boards and big wheels. In a church business meeting of a church established on such a corporate world structure, it takes forever to even get people to agree on what color the church walls are to be painted, but in a church prayer meeting, things can get done with supernatural speed. Battles in business meetings are political battles. If a pastor does not learn to be a shrewd politician, he will never survive a full tenure at that kind of church.

It is interesting how Jesus dealt with His own house when they corrupted it by polluting it with politics. He lost battles, but He won the war by letting them have it. Honestly, some churches are not worth having. Their candlestick has already been removed (Revelation 2:5). There may be many who attend, but there will never be an anointing. It is best to learn to walk away from churches like that. Jesus turned the keys of the Temple over to the Pharisees and Sadducees and cut a new set of keys that gained members entrance into the Kingdom of God and become buildings not made by hands (Matthew 16:19; Matthew 23:28).

An epidemic broke out in a local Walmart in 2014. One person grew angry and impatient when the line seemed to be moving slowly. Next, another person saw the other's anger and grew angry also. The anger spread from one person to another until a large number of people in the store began to grow angry. Then, a riot broke out, and people were fighting one another without even knowing why. Little did they know that they fell prey to a sociological phenomenon that happens with people in a crowd. Dealing with people individually is vastly different from dealing with crowds. My heart goes out to every pastor who pastors a relatively large crowd. Large crowds are more susceptible to contagion. The sociological phenomenon to be cognizant of has to do with realizing that emotions are contagious. Thus, wise pastors of large congregations are experts in mob psychology.

Another frightening reality in the local church of the 21st century is that people appear to be gravitating to more wolf-like leaders. Christians need to understand the difference between a wolf-leader and a leader with a weakness, especially carnal Christians. They usually confuse the two. Wolf-leaders are the types of leaders who are dominating and portray more threatening styles of leadership. They prey on people instead of pray for people. Their doctrine is diluted and delusional. They feed Christians cotton candy instead of the meat of the word of God. They tell people what they want to hear instead of what they need to know. They use that as bait to keep people devoted and addicted to them. The psychological dynamics of people who devote themselves to wolf-leaders consist of people who suffered major abuses in their lives, sometimes at regular intervals. People who have been held in subjection for a significant time fear empowerment. Because they are so damaged, they are dysfunctional, and they are highly codependent. There is a desire within these types of people to be micro-managed rather than to be ministered to. Although they have been set free in Christ, they do not mind being in servitude to male or female leaders who have control issues.

Some of today's sermons sound like preschool teachers who tell children Bible tales or short stories. Masses appear to gravitate to more controlled leadership and more controlled environments where people are left with only a few options as the pre-school preacher points to the pictures and flips the pages. Carnal churches do not like to read, let alone, study. Instead, they want all the attention devoted to pacifying their infancy. No real words, just illustrations, props, and creative uses of the imagination; no real Word, just allusions to the Word; not much preaching but a whole lot of personality.

On the other hand, leaders with weaknesses are the men and women who God uses, and it will not be long before members of the churches they lead discover their weaknesses. God uses leaders with weaknesses so the glory of God can be seen in their lives. Every God-called leader has a weakness whether he acknowledges it or not. It is always wise for a pastor to work with his weakness. Paul had a serious weakness he identified as pride and arrogance. Yet, in his weakness, he was strong because his infirmity kept him depending upon Jesus. These are leaders who carnal and immature Christians criticize and cannot comprehend because it would demand a strength from them that they do not have.

The mark of true ministry is the extended arm of the pastor to crippled people, challenging them to take up their beds and walk. The pastor is authorized to challenge people to be edified in ways that places requirements upon them to land and live on their own two feet rather than keep them crippled by promising them a prosperity that will keep them paralyzed (Acts 3:6).

When we concluded our consultation with Jack Hayford, he went around the room and laid hands on each of us. Although that was an honor, what he said to us touched me more than his hand. His closing words were something like this, "My fellow-pastors, Satan has targeted you in your city. He will attempt to do everything he can to destroy your credibility. Be on guard against that." Then, he prayed for us that God would cover us in our cities. Keeping your credibility is more important than keeping your church. Never pastor in a fashion that you keep your church but lose your credibility. Keeping our credibility has nothing to do with covering our sins. Paul let the churches know he was a wretched man (Romans 7:24).

Any real preacher does not mind telling his truth if people can handle the truth. At least I do not. Whether Paul was a wretched man in the past or present tense is not the issue. It has everything to do with the fact that sins critics expose for the world to see are sins God has already covered a long time ago, somewhere around AD 30-33 (over 2,000 years ago). Never become a coward to keep a church. It will not be worth it. When you pastor with credibility, at least you are consistent. They may not like you, but at least they will respect you. The best way to keep credibility is to glorify God at the expense of our reputation.

When Paul threatened to come, he was not coming to condemn. He was coming to correct, but the process would have meant going to war with the *images* that were gaining demonic clarity within the *imaginations* of the Corinthians. Sometimes, it is necessary to visit your critics by any spiritual means necessary. Paul desired to delay his coming to allow them to repent and be restored. Internally, he ached for communion with the Corinthians as they continually attempted to shun his love and leadership. However, Corinth eventually became known as what Dr. Paige Patterson called, "*The Troubled Triumphant Church*" because of

Paul's dedication to heal them from the multifaceted damages of demonic delusion. Believe it or not, when people come against a preacher on that level, it is not personal. It is only because they have lost their minds. Yet, our God is not only a heart-fixer, but He is also a mind-regulator. Listen to Paul's love for the ones who lashed out at him. If a pastor's love can save at least one of them, it is better than losing them all:

> "...*To the weak became I as weak, that I might gain the weak: I am made all things to all men, that I might by all means save some. And this I do for the gospel's sake, that I might be partaker thereof with you.*"
>
> (I Corinthians 9:22; KJV)

Chapter 10
THE PASTOR AND HIS LOINS

∞

From Perversion to Power
(An Excerpt from the Life of Samson:
A leader who looked for love in all the wrong places)

Tribute: To my cousin, whom I affectionately call, "Uncle James"; James Commodore Wade, Jr. (Pastor Emeritus, Zion Missionary Baptist Church of East Chicago, IN)

When he prays, he prays with the intensity of Elijah. When he speaks, he speaks with the authority of Moses. When he walks into the room, his presence is felt, like Samuel. When he preaches, there is a shaking in the valley, like Ezekiel. When he pastored, he was a gritty shepherd who did not mind getting his hands dirty, like David. If I were to think of one word to describe Uncle James, the word would be…STRENGTH. During the beginning of my ministry in Dallas while driving J. C. Wade, Jr. to DFW airport, I asked him what the greatest advice was he could give me as a young minister. He reminded me of the story of Samson as he attempted to shake himself loose after he confessed to Delilah. However, Samson did not know the Lord left him. Uncle James gave me solemn words that I cannot forget: "Don't ever do anything that would cause the Lord to fire you!"

If there are skeptics who are sincere about understanding dynamics that cause pastors to fall into sexual sin, it is wise to read the saga of Samson. A vice that can grip the strongest of men is an undisciplined sex-life. God never ignores sexual sin among His servants or lust among his leaders. Samson's relationship with Delilah was preceded by dynamics that are not foreign to many men. "*The Pastor and His Loins*" refers to the pastor's sexual drive. The rising seductions of our time warrant aggressive embraces of Scripture that portray the drama of sexual impurity in many of God's most powerful men. Examining every sexual episode of the failure of God's men in the Bible provides a framework to evaluate sexual failure. Because the Bible has more truth to discover regarding the sexual sins of a man of God than any other source, God always has the last and most accurate word regarding sexual lust among leaders. At the end of the day, God nobly buried Samson and commended him for making a comeback. As a result, Samson is noted in the Hallmark of Faith (Hebrews 11:32). However, Samson had to face a death sentence before he truly lived, and he had to lose his eyes before he could truly see.

Rarely do God's men fall into sexual sins simply because of the heat of the moment. Samson began with humble beginnings and supernatural prophecies upon his life. God promised his barren mother that she would bring forth a Nazarite son who would begin to deliver Israel from the hand of the Philistines. That man was Samson (Judges 13:5). Samson's parents followed the Lord's directions in how they were to raise him (Judges 13:8). Samson began his ministry with great parenting, power, and privilege. However, Samson failed to maintain a perpetual anointing:

*"The Spirit of the Lord began to move him **at times** (when) in the camp of Dan ..."*

(Judges 13:25; KJV)

Samson's anointing occurred on certain occasions when he would go into some form of battle against the Philistines. Samson allowed the Spirit of the Lord to move him *at times and seasons*, but he did not allow the Spirit of the Lord to move him at all times. During the intervals of his battle with lust, there was no anointing Samson would summons. Samson refused to summon the Spirit of the Lord to give him strength to move away from the wrong women.

Samson's failure also occurred because *he began to treat his anointing as if it were a toy* he could pick up at his leisure. The strongest man on Earth tended to play with his power. Early in his life, he developed a keen eye for toxic women. Because leaders often operate in a different dimension, so do the women who can sap our strength. The Devil has damsels destructive to a pastor's destiny. God warned Samson not to play games with Philistine women. More importantly, he was not to play games with his gift. Ironically, God wanted to use Samson's relationship with a Philistine woman of Timnath to be a vehicle of infiltration into the Philistine camp, but for God, this was no game. On the contrary, it was a war strategy. Samson noticed this woman and asked permission to marry her. Samson's agenda was physical and psychological instead of spiritual:

> *"Then his father and his mother said unto him, Is there never a woman among the daughters of thy brethren, or among all my people, that thou goest to take a wife of the uncircumcised Philistines? And Samson said unto his father, Get her for me;* ***for she pleaseth me well*** *(she looks good to me)."*
>
> (Judges 14:3; KJV)

At this point, we see dynamics developing within Samson regarding patterns of lust. His parents recognized the potential threat to the Nazarite vow and immediately tried to convince Samson to choose a daughter of Israel, but neither the parents nor Samson recognized the purposes of God in ordaining Samson to marry this woman (Judges 14:4). Here is a strange truth portrayed in the wisdom of God: ***Certain marriages are condoned by God if they bring glory to God and serve God's purposes rather than our passions.*** I remember Eloise Temple (my aunt) telling me that marriage is about purpose. Marriage is not based upon a physical attraction or a psychological placement of complimentary values. We fall prey to all types of failure if we do not marry the woman who God told us to marry or when we marry the woman who God told us to marry for the wrong reasons. It really gets that simple. Then, it gets simply complicated. When we fail to do so, an unsanctioned marriage becomes seriously complicated. Samson had a problem with passion, poise, and purpose. He often missed the point. He was a man of God gone wild.

Any man who has his eye for a woman wants to impress that woman in some fashion. Samson was hoping to impress his wife of Timnath with the muscle that came along with his ministry. He was flexing his ministerial muscle everywhere. We may better understand this by realizing how the Bible in no way depicts Samson as a muscular man. Yet, we do know Samson's strength was supernatural, and his ministry was muscular. The truth is even more amplified if Samson was an ordinary-sized man. If so, we can more greatly see how he had a hard time being humble in harnessing his supernatural strength.

On Samson's way to see his future wife, a young lion attacked him. The Spirit of the Lord comes mightily upon Samson and enables him to rip the lion to pieces with his bare hands. Samson does not tell his parents of the episode and continues his journey

The Pastor And His Loins

to have her to marry. God gave Samson supernatural strength to defeat a lion because it was not time for Samson to die. His ministry had not even begun. On Samson's way home, he brings honey produced from bees that harnessed in the carcass of the lion he slew. Samson takes the honey out of the carcass and begins eating. He gives some to his parents when he arrives but does not tell them where it came from. The Nazarite vow also consisted of not tampering with corpses. Samson violated that vow. This is most likely the reason why he did not tell his parents where the honey came from. During Samson's wedding feast, he tells thirty of his companions a riddle regarding the bees and honey. He promises the companions to give rewards to whoever figured the riddle. He had no intention of telling them the meaning of the riddle because he knew they would in no way figure it out. He is protecting his violation of a vow to not touch corpses by toying with the truth that he did tamper with corpses. Thus, Samson playfully protects his secret sin. He is using the sin of deflection. The fact that he even tells a riddle reveals the fact that he had no conviction about his careless compulsion to flaunt his anointing.

Our secret sins are no joke. The fact that a lion attacked him was serious, but the fact that he toyed with the triumph by eating honey from the corpse of a lion was a joke to Sampson. When or if we get caught up in secret sins, we must not have clever ways of diverting attention from our guilt as if it is a joke:

> "Out of the eater came forth meat, and out of the strong came forth sweetness"

(Judges 14:14; KJV)

The Bible states none could figure the riddle for three days. When we play games with our gift and trivialize our triumphs, our enemies play for keeps. Satan was not pleased with the fact that there was a young leader on the horizon groomed for Philistine destruction. Out of the riddle came an evil plot. Thirty companions threaten Samson's wife and tell her to seduce him to reveal the riddle. They also sought to demonstrate their seriousness over the matter by threatening to burn she and her father's house with fire if she did not comply. As a result, she seduces Samson with tears to tell her the meaning of the riddle. At first, Samson refuses to confess, but because Samson has a weakness for women, he gives in after she continually presses upon him with the crying game.

You hear a lot about the sexual sins leaders fall into, but you never know who or what is pressing them (Judges 14:17). Remember, this was not some woman on the side Samson had. This was his wife who God ordained for him to marry. Yet, her fear that led to turning Samson in was her fault. Samson tells her, and she immediately runs and tells her countrymen. The men tell Samson that they figured the meaning of the riddle. Samson is infuriated because he can put two-and-two together, realizing his wife had something to do with it. In Samson's anger, the Spirit of the Lord comes upon him, and he slays thirty Philistines while fulfilling his word to reward those who figured the riddle. Notice, the Spirit of the Lord came upon Samson although he violated the Nazarite vow to not tamper with corpses. The Spirit of the Lord always moved upon Samson within a Philistine context. Once again, God is still getting the glory through Samson's life, but Samson begins the process of embezzling God's glory.

Samson goes to her father's house and discovers his wife was given to Samson's companion by her father (Judges 15:1-2). Her father used Samson's lack of anger management as an opportunity to break up Samson's marriage. Samson's father-in-law tells him that he gave her to a companion because he figured Samson would be so outraged with her betrayal that he would not want her anymore. We know Samson's lust blinded him in a way that he overlooked her betrayal because of what happened next. After he discovers how she betrayed him, all he wanted to do was have sex with her (Judges 15:1). Samson was so devoted to his passions that he resorted to a type of sex that is called, *escape sex*. Escape sex involves not dealing with the issues by trying to resolve hidden hurts through sex. Samson failed to realize that marital issues cannot always be buried in the bedroom. Samson foolishly wielded his power for selfish motives. He put his power on a platform to play with people rather than please God. However, God's anointing cannot be outwitted. God still used Samson although Samson wanted to be used by the Lord for personal gratification.

Power has been argued to be the ultimate aphrodisiac. The affections of a self-preserving woman can shift when the chips are down. At the end of the day, Samson's wife turns against him when *her* security was at stake. In her eyes, she did not sign up for all of that when she married Samson. Yet, Samson's wife was not the root of his rebellion. Samson's weakness was. Currently, Samson is not appreciating who he really is. Samson was the strangest Nazarite who one ever had seen. He was different, but he was dangerously different at this time. Instead, he should have been divinely different. If he would not have played games with his anointing by telling riddles, she never would have been placed in that predicament in which she had to make a choice. Samson did not take his ministry or marriage seriously. Although his wife had a choice, it is understandable how she felt she had no choice. It is never wise to put a woman you love in a predicament in which she feels forced to choose between her love and her life.

Toying with our power is not just an issue with women. **Most of God's men who commit sexual sin do so on enemy territory when some type of war is raging**. In other words, they are in some type of battle for more noble causes. Sometimes, the issue has more to do with winning than women. Samson hated to lose. If he was going to be a winner, hating to lose was a necessity. Yet, when you hate to lose, it is important to have someone on your team. At least we think it is important. Like the men who surrounded Sampson, men who should be on the front lines with us can become dangerously competitive of our calling. We know they hate us or envy our spiritual *swag*. In a feeling of betrayal, men with an unusual anointing can mock them because of their lack of loyalty and fool them because of their lack of fidelity to the fraternity. Because we cannot justifiably retaliate against jealousy, arrogant ways of toying with our enemies can be developed in a way that jokingly jabs at their jealousy. We can frustrate them by giving puzzles we know they cannot piece together. God will use the *Samson* within us, but in the end, we will pay the piper if we refuse to remove riddling routines from our anatomy and learn to play by God's rules.

Well, what does a woman have to do with it? It is all about loyalty. Loyalty is a priceless and rare commodity in leadership. For a God-called leader, a good man really is hard to find, but so is a good woman. In leadership, most of the time, if you want something done right, you must do it yourself. However, Satan's men never break rank. Since a good man was hard to find, Samson not only looked for love, but he also looked for loyalty in the wrong places, usually with women. Nevertheless, Samson failed to realize that was one main reason why God gave *him* the strength to get the job done singlehandedly. Samson had the strength of three hundred men, one man per jackal (Judges 15:4).

When we don't allow our sexual anatomy to flow in alignment with our anointing, a tendency to develop a vindictive attitude toward repercussions surface, not realizing the fact that some of us wouldn't have to deal with consequences if we would have maintained a perpetual anointing and have been wise in our woman-selection. After his father-in-law gives his daughter to another man,

Samson goes into a rage and ties the tails of three hundred jackals and sets them on fire on Philistine crops. Unusually, this was a feat done with no mention of the Spirit of the Lord coming upon Samson. However, it is most probable he performed this task with supernatural strength. We can conjecture many truths from that fact, but one thing is certain: God did not approve of his outraged response. During this episode, Samson is fighting consequences and digging a deeper hole for himself because he has not learned key lessons about harnessed strength. We can be most dangerous when we war in the flesh. Although wronged, Samson sees arrows pointed at everyone but himself. Samson has muscle, but he has no maturity. Our talents mean nothing if they do not align with our gift, and our gift means nothing if it does not align with the God who gave us our gift.

Sexual sin always produces a downward denial spiral, even if we never get caught. Things get worse, and the Philistines retaliate by burning his wife and her father with fire. Samson is furious and paying the price, but he is still destroying Philistines. God will get the glory one way or another. A spiritual leader can get much accomplished amid serious dysfunctions, even if they are sensual. Yet, God never dismisses our dysfunctions. Instead, he disciplines by teaching us how not to allow our dysfunctions to derail our destiny. Samson teaches us why God keeps some of us in ministry despite our madness. Often, it has nothing at all to do with us, but it has everything to do with God's ultimate purpose. God keeps us for His name's sake and not ours or any other's (Psalm 23:3). However, sooner or later, God will draw the line, especially when His name is at stake. If we do anything that will cause God's glory to fade, our Lord will strip us of all our successes and strengths.

Samson gained such foolish momentum that he could hardly stop. At this point, Sampson is not a sex addict. *He is an anointing addict.* He is abusing his anointing and using it with the wrong ambitions. In like manner, he is a power-addict. His assumption that God's power will always flow through his veins never happens at all costs. He will learn that eye-gouging lesson later. He slaughters Philistines with a great slaughter. While it may be tempting to assume God only anointed Samson when he was right, God often anointed Samson when he was wrong. God's anointing is for *His* purposes, whether we are right or wrong. However, if we digress to lustful levels and power perversions, the anointing can be removed, and our ministries and even our lives can be cut short.

Finally, Samson is brought to a pause regarding his foolish path of lust and anger as three thousand men of Judah talk sense into him. God has men who are not afraid to slow us down when we are fast and furious. Although Samson has supernatural strength, he was no match for the men of Judah. God had more invested in Judah than in Samson. Jesus would later come through the line of Judah. We can take to heart an important truth: **God has more invested in His Kingdom than He does in us.**

They tell Samson to turn himself in because his outrage has resulted in harsh dangers for the people of God. Samson knew that if he did not, there was a possibility they would kill him themselves. It is always wise to take responsibility instead of being forced to be accountable. When we take responsibility, we learn to live with the mess we made. When we are forced to face accountability, we may have to face godly authorities who can personally bring an end to our ministries. No matter how strong and powerful we are, we are never as strong as those who are on our side. The men of Judah were painful but necessary reminders to Samson that he was not a victim.

The pastor's anatomy is unique. At his greatest outbursts, there lies a tenderloin that can be touched. When we get news of the slightest possibility of greater damage we may have inflicted on who we lead and love, the lion in us lays down like a lamb.

Three thousand men of Judah convince Samson that his foolish acts would place a heavier yoke upon them by the Philistines. Sometimes, it is the ones you love who motivate you to turn yourself in. Touched by their plea, Samson allows the men of Judah to take him into custody into the Philistine camp (Judges 15:10-13). When we get too far out of control, it ties the hands of those who are on our side. Although their hands are tied, God's hands are not. When we surrender to the consequences of unbridled passions, God's Spirit can return.

Upon arrival into Lehi, the Philistines began to taunt Samson. Samson tended to be sensitive to slander. Although Samson has begun his ministry foolishly, God knows it is not Samson's time to die. Samson recognized how these taunts were against the purposes of God. The Spirit of the Lord came upon Samson as he slew one thousand Philistines with the jawbone of a donkey (Judges 15:14-16).

The most remarkable occurrences happen in our anatomy when we are willing to take responsibility for our actions. In our anatomy, stronger than normal drives exhaust us, and we do not know how depleted we are until we have paused from our perverted patterns. Samson now has a strange case of post-adrenaline syndrome. He is fatigued from two powerful currents moving within his anatomy, i.e., lust and the Spirit of God. As a mere man, he is exhausted and most prepared to call on God. After his single-handed defeat of one thousand Philistines, he is just a man, and he is thirsty.

Resources to replenish our souls can be scarce, especially if we have spent too many days playing the fool. Yet, Samson calls on God, gives God honor for bringing deliverance, and God miraculously provides water out of the jawbone of a donkey (Judges 15:18-19). The mercies of God can flow powerfully in the middle of our madness but even more powerfully when we have humbled ourselves to call on God for replenishment. Because of God's love,

He pardons and places Samson where he first believed although his accountability partners (the men of Judah) gave up on him and were too afraid to support him. If a pastor has gone too far, his peers have a right to give up on him, but God's faithfulness is greater than those who were once on our team. Thus, we still have a partner in God, even when we are no longer popular or precious in the sight of our peers.

Samson is now revived and restored, but he is not healed from the hurts of a betraying and self-preserving wife. So, he begins to play the fool again. Samson is on an addictive cycle of power and passion with hidden wounds under his supernatural cloak. Because God has unique methods for dealing with His servants, we can often deceive ourselves after mercy has been extended and feel as though we can return to our foolishness. The purpose of God in restoring Samson after exhausting fits of rage was to prove to Samson a more anointed way to act. However, Samson's deliverance was not complete because he failed to obligate himself to the price he had to pay for his power, which brings us to the next reason for Samson's downfall.

Whenever we do not allow restoration to set us on a committed path of dedication to the Lord, we degrade to a lower level of lust. Sexual sin is degrading. When Samson refuses to break his pattern of pride, he degrades into more perverted forms of sex. When Samson had his wife from Timnath, it appeared that he was monogamous. He appeared to be completely intoxicated with her. Now that his relationship with his wife is dead, Samson visits a prostitute. A dead marriage can do that to a minister if he allows, especially if he has not fully processed how both partners killed it. Samson still has his ministry, but his marriage is dead, thereby causing him to feed an already existing love deficiency that degraded to looking for love in all the wrong places. When a man has a dead marriage, he may pay almost any price for sex because he has an intimacy deficiency and a problem with his God-ordained purpose.

It was much more than sex with a prostitute that was the issue. He was trying to pay a woman to be everything he wanted in his wife, even if it was only for one night. A prostitute was not the only woman he paid. He later paid a high price for Delilah, and we will soon discover that. Distraught from his previous wife's betrayal, Samson develops the habit of paying women to cooperate with him. Sadly, many damaged wives ask their husbands, "What do you see in a woman like that?" If some husbands were honest, they would simply answer, "Cooperation." Little did Samson know that he could not pay a real woman to cooperate with a man gone wild. If a prostitute is defined as a woman who will trade sex for an agenda, Delilah fit that category as well, even if she was not standing on some street corner.

Samson goes to Gaza and has intercourse with a seemingly cooperative harlot. Samson's visit is known by the Gazites, and they lay in wait all night for Samson to come out. Then, they would ambush him. Interestingly, Samson decided to leave at midnight. Perhaps, Samson was beginning to realize that looking for love in all the wrong places never satisfies. The only woman he loved was Delilah. Perhaps that is why he chose her to be the next woman who he would know. Nevertheless, this move saved Samson's life. God still had a plan for Samson. Therefore, in God's sovereignty, it was not time for Samson to die. He rises from the bed of a prostitute at midnight and rips the city gates off hinges and escapes (Judges 16:1-3). Once again, Samson exemplifies unusual strength with no mention of the Spirit of the Lord moving upon him. It is hard for me to believe the Lord would give a man the anointing to escape a hotel with a prostitute. Yet, I do know God will give him an advantage. When his own goodness will not give him an exit, God's grace will. Common sense will also do it, even if conviction does not.

Most importantly, the Spirit of the Lord cannot be used to escape our iniquities without honest confession unto God. Our sexual anatomy has a power of its own if it is unbridled and has the power to rip gates off hinges that hold us. I do not mean this literally. There are times when we possess unusual power to save our own skin. Fear of getting caught can give a man skin-saving skill. Fear can cause a minister who is trapped in sexual lust to become abnormally strong and strategic in his quest for survival. He may be able to escape his enemies, but he can never escape his sins because sin is the greatest bondage for even the strongest of men. In those times, dangerous patterns of pride, arrogance, and a false sense of invincibility can be developed. A man of God is never in his greatest troubles when his enemies are trying to trap him in his sins. A man of God is in his greatest troubles when he is trapped in his own triumphs.

We see a subtle sense of numbness to the naughtiness of his nature as Samson rips gates off the hinges. He does not set the gates down and free himself of unnecessary weight. Instead of laying aside the weight and sin that so easily beset him, he carries the doors of the gate of the city and the two posts, bars and all to the top of the hill. Although this can be an act of haste as Samson is seeking to get out quickly, this can also be a portrait of the selfish pride and arrogance of a man who refused to break his sex-cycles. If he had power to rip gates off hinges, he also had power to set the gates down. The same power that we possess to pick up certain degrading practices is the same power at our disposal to put them down (Hebrews 12:1).

Although Samson escaped, his pride has not escaped. Pride never escapes on its own. You must lay it aside. If we do not, God will. If we fail to submit, God will lay us aside. Samson is degrading into a pit that will cost him his life. Herein lays the deception of an unbridled sexual anatomy. ***Samson's failure also came when he made the mistake of thinking his calling would outlast his consequences.*** We can never fail to be reminded that God will fire us if we do not get on the job. I cannot forget how Pastor George Banks, III would say, "God will take you up before He lets you tear things up!"

We have evidence of divine favor and fleshly strength in our files that successfully delivered us from traps in the past. Somehow, when our sexual anatomy is not tamed by a perpetual anointing, we can deceive ourselves into thinking more sin breeds more opportunities for displays of God's power. If God is allowing us to continue in the ministry despite unbridled lusts, He is only patient with us and protecting people from our foolishness. That is all. At some point in time, God's watch will stop, and playtime will be over. Samson is not only in a web of lust, but his sexual lust is evolving into a fixation on foolishness. Now, Samson will use any power at his disposal to gratify his quest for personal glory, even if it is by the power of his own sensual anatomy. If we operate outside of God's boundaries, we will eventually meet our match, and we will catch the deadliest sexually transmitted disease that exists. It is called, *The Delilah Syndrome*.

Before we get to this infected woman who went by the name of Delilah, it is critical to understand Samson's context. He was an extremely gifted man. God gave him an anointed advantage above and beyond his peers. He had more haters than lovers. Most people who were in his circle competed with him instead of supported him. Everywhere Samson went, he never quite fit in. As he was looking to them for loyalty, they were looking at some strength he had that they wanted. His parents even had a hard time processing God's purposes for his life. This and much more put him in a class all by himself, surrounded by envy, jealousy, and disloyal women.

There is fire, but I am just clearing a little smoke. Beyond popular opinion, Samson was not a womanizer. A womanizer is a man who preys on innocent and vulnerable women. Every woman we know who Samson was with pretty much had their minds made up regarding what they were going to do with him. They all were sexy, sneaky, sensual, stubborn, and strong-willed women. His wife of Timnath was self-preserving, the prostitute was a professional who had many customers before she ever met Samson, and Delilah was money-hungry and an opportunist. Samson did not have a problem finding women. Women would find him. He was a magnet for manipulative women. He did not always hunt for women. He was also hunted by women. Samson's blindness for love made him vulnerable to women who were man-eaters. Every woman he chose was a woman he was worse off with than he was without. Most women noted in the Bible who Samson had relations with turned him in. The prostitute he was with was most likely a trick than a treat. No event in his life was normal, but the people in his life were. They could not handle a man who was as different as he. He did not fit into their norm. He was cut from a different cloth. Women could not handle him, and men could not hold him. Because Samson could not handle such great power and privilege, he craved normalcy. He was an unusually strong man. If he picked up a glass, he had to be careful that he did not accidentally crush it. If he wanted to politely open a door, he had to make sure he did not rip the knob off. If he knew people were thinking of ways to trap him, he had to avoid the sin of playing with their minds. In other words, whatever he did seemed to matter more than anyone else if they made the same careless mistakes. His anointing required for him to have the skill of paying detailed attention to everything he did and said. Samson had to learn to see a principle that applies to every strong man: "To whom much is given, much shall be required" (Luke 12:48).

Whenever God has uniquely carved a man, his cravings to fit into regular molds are never satisfied. If he does not accept and appreciate the fact that he is in a class all by himself, his consequences will also be abnormal. Whenever a man uniquely carved for ministry depreciates his uniqueness, his enemies will eventually discover his patterns of weakness. They recognize that he does not really know what he has going for him. In this sense, a man's enemies know him more than his friends.

Although Samson has been unmatched so far, he is about to meet his match with a woman who has a sexual anatomy of her own. So far, Samson is undefeated although he is bruised and battered on the inside. He is strong outwardly, but he is losing strength every day on the inside. Keeping a strong shell on the outside, shelving trophy after trophy while yearning for someone who would be totally devoted to him was killing him softly.

However, Samson had to learn the hard way that victory may also come through defeat. Samson's immune system is not strong enough to defend himself against Delilah's syndrome. Delilah was also fast and furious. She was faster and more furious than Sampson. His strength came from God, but her strength came from her own goals. Thus, Delilah paid close attention to herself while Samson tended to ignore himself. She had to earn everything she had, but Samson received God's gift for free.

The advantage she had over Samson was in the fact that she was also focused. Before Delilah, there was no mentioning of anything or anyone Samson really loved. To the best of my knowledge, the text does not even say that Samson loved God. However, the Scriptures boldly emphasize Samson's love for Delilah (Judges 16:4).

Whenever a man gives his strength away to a woman of this sort, she becomes an untrusted container of his secrets. The same plot that was successful with his wife from Timnath is executed with Delilah. Samson's weakness for women is evident, and the Philistine lords bribe Delilah into finding the secret of Samson's strength. Delilah attempts several times to seduce Samson, but he plays the riddle game. At this point, Samson feels invincible, and he is once again, toying with his anointing and enemies. Do not forget, he is still grieving over his dead marriage, developing personal vendettas against his enemies (the Philistines), and poisoned by his visit with a prostitute. Although chosen by God, he is a wounded dog. Yet, a wounded dog is better than a dead lion (Ecclesiastes 9:4). However, he was not too wounded to lie to the woman he loved. Later, we will discover that he also was not wounded enough to avoid telling her the truth. Telling the truth and giving up divine information can be two totally different things. He should not have lied or given up his truth to Delilah because she was sure to use his lies and his truth against him. If he would have truly paid attention to the wounds incurred through his wildness, he would have devoted his life to the worship of God and not saying another word to Delilah for the rest of his life. Instead, he was so wounded that he worshiped Delilah. That is when he got in terminating trouble with God.

If a man plays games for so long, he will eventually begin to play games with himself and be in denial of the fact that he was sleeping with the enemy. The most dangerous bed Samson ever slept in was the bed of the only woman he loved. Samson kept convincing himself that Delilah was perfect for him. He was in the dangerous game of denial.

Three consecutive times, Samson gives false sources of his strength and sends Delilah and the Philistine lords on a wild goose chase. What is interesting about this episode is that Samson knew

Delilah was trying to trap him, but he refused to break off the relationship. When a man is in a toxic relationship, he sees the signs early, but the persuasive package she offers is more valuable to him than the price he must pay. Delilah even tells him she wants the source of his strength *so that he may be bound and afflicted* (Judges 16:6), and she does it continually. Although Samson is stubborn, he is far from stupid. Notice the sequence. First, Samson gives her a false source of his strength. Delilah tells the lords, and they bind Samson, assuming he is powerless. Samson breaks the fetters, and Delilah tries again. The cycle repeats three times. Each time, the Philistines bind Samson, and he breaks the fetters. Samson connected the dots in his first relationship when his previous wife of Timnath told the thirty countrymen the answer to the riddle. It is undoubtedly true that Samson knew the only way the Philistines were aware this time was through the agency of Delilah. How did they know to bind him with seven green withs (cords) that were never dried, new ropes that were never occupied or seven weaved locks upon his head unless Delilah told them? Samson was not only strong, but he was also smart. As a matter of fact, he was too smart for his own good. **When we are too smart for our good, we develop a weak intelligence and a strong stupidity**. We cannot see things that even a blind man could see. Therefore, blindness was the avenue God would have to allow Samson to experience before he could truly see.

Love and life are things that can never be played with. Both are extremely fragile. The Delilah Syndrome can destroy both love and life. Eventually, somebody is going to get hurt or even get their lives cut short. Whenever you play with love, you must be wise enough to realize that you are only playing the fool. While Samson is skillful at playing the riddle game, he has no skill in playing the game of love. Love is no game. Love has a blinding effect when it co-mingles with lust, pain, and loyalty. Although

Samson knew that Delilah meant harm, he did not want to believe she could stoop that low. Once a man is burned by a woman like that once, he is blind as a bat if he allows that to be done to him again. Although Samson had great power, he did not have the power to make a woman love him, and he sure could not make a woman be loyal to him. Although the Philistines had not previously laid a hand on Samson, he was still wounded. Samson was a hurt man long before Delilah hurt him. Delilah's persistent nagging dug into an open wound that Samson never closed.

To further describe patterns that led to Samson's downfall, we learn that **we can fall into tricky trust levels when we fail to close old wounds**. Samson still thought he could trust Delilah although he saw clearly how manipulative she was. Delilah openly nags him to tell her how he may be bound (Judges 16:13). Finally, Delilah manipulates Samson's love-level in a way that she pressured him to despair of her continual request. How can this be? The text shows Delilah implying repeatedly, "If you really love me, you will tell me the source of your strength." Since love was a greater weakness for Samson than lust, Delilah had him right where she wanted him. Because Samson had a love deficiency, he did not know what love called for. Love also calls for a man of God to defend himself by not giving all his love away to anyone but God.

One thing a man of God cannot handle is getting to the point of vexation. Real love does not vex the relationship. Vexation is when you are at a point when your mind, body, and soul are at complete odds with one another. It is as if you are being pulled in three different directions by forces that will not let you go. It is usually someone or something in your immediate surrounding who is pulling you in a direction you do not want to go. Something must give. If not, you will be ripped in at least three pieces. The only way to not give in is to not give up. When we refuse to give up, God will break the chains that tear at us and set us free from that torturing environment of being bound by the three-fold chord of a vindictive woman, a love deficiency, and an unbridled lust. If we give in to either of those chords, we will be so broken down that we will have no defense left to protect us from the two remaining chords. Then, we lose on all ends. When one breaks, the others break, usually at the same time. Psychologists call that a *breakdown*.

During this spiritual, physical, and psychological breakdown, Samson knows all along why Delilah really wants to know the source of his strength. Samson knows she wants to sell him out to the Philistines. Just that thought alone was breaking him down. Samson allowed himself to be a glutton for Delilah's punishment. When a man has erroneously fallen in love, he will go through any means for that love to be reciprocated, and he can think opening his most disclosed secrets will cause her to love him more. He has a compulsive need for that woman to let go of the rope that rips his heart apart and set him free from her control. He does not want her control, but he does want her compassion. It is not just that Samson loved Delilah, it was also that Samson wanted Delilah to love him back. Love is a vexing thing if the one you love does not love you back.

Finally, Samson gives in and tells Delilah the source of his strength. The source of his strength also entailed Samson telling Delilah his weakness. Although Samson was going to lose his eyes, he was blind long before he laid eyes on Delilah. Therefore, he could not see her for who she really was until it was too late. The familiar idiom that says *love is blind* was true of Samson.

Notice Samson from another angle. Samson finally finds love after years of playing the dozens. When he met Delilah, he was looking for a woman he could settle down with. There was no way he could settle down with a prostitute. Now, he is ready to settle down, but he falls in love with a woman who is out to set him down. The wrong woman is concerned about some form of payment that comes from betraying the man she is after (Judges 16:5). In other words, it usually has something to do with money. Many women realize the fact that there are some things money cannot buy, but others do not realize that until they have a house that is not a home. Unfortunately, Delilah was selling him out for personal gain. Delilah's motive was money. She was marketing Samson's weakness and profiting from Samson's pain. She could care less about his strengths.

You can never conquer love. No matter how strong you are, love will always conquer you. For these reasons, it is important to love on the level that God commands rather than the level our loins demand. In addition, it is important to love someone who is going to love you back. Delilah never reciprocates but continually seeks to dominate. That alone will break a man's heart. Every minute of Samson's relationship with Delilah was a control issue and a one-sided love affair.

Next, the process that weakened Samson's will to give away his secret was that **he was dying from a broken heart** (Judges 16:16). The text says that his soul was vexed unto death. Something psychological and dysfunctional was occurring the longer he stayed in his relationship with Delilah. In other words, his relationship with Delilah was killing him softly long before he died. He allowed Delilah to break his spirit. Delilah nagged him until he finally gave in, disappointed, and drained from the fact that nothing he did could get her to love him in a way that would support his strengths. She tricked him into trying to prove his love. A woman with an agenda is never impressed with the size or strength of our muscles, ministry, or manhood. She is impressed with the size and strength of our weakness. To her, you are nothing but a silly boy and a silly fool. It does not matter how much you have. She wants it all. All is never enough for anybody. A toxic woman is not in alignment with the soul of a man of God.

The Pastor And His Loins

The text has a strange implant in Judges 16:19. The latter part of verse 19 says Delilah began to *afflict* Samson as he lay upon her knees. In the Hebrew text, the word for afflict is עָנָה ('ā·nāh)), which means, *to oppress, humble, to be put down, mishandle, to humiliate.*[5] Interestingly, the word also means, *to silence, cease, stop, i.e., cause a state to cease to exist or be ineffective, as an extension of conquering or subduing an opponent.*[6] This all happened *after* she cut off Samson's hair and while he was sleep. The order is extremely important. Look at what happens first. When Samson was awake, the text says that she *vexed* him:

> "*And it came to pass, when* **she pressed him daily with her words**, *and urged him, so that* **his soul was vexed unto death**."
>
> (Judges 16:16; KJV)

This was not a magical spell. She was simply pressing him with the same hard truth he did not want to accept. She kept saying, "Give me the secret of your strength". Sampson heard what she did not say in words. He heard the voice of her heart. Sampson knew she was truly saying, "I don't love you like that!"

Secondly, we see what happens next. After he cooperated and confessed, she never let him live it down. She kept putting him down, humiliating him, criticizing him, demeaning him, and breaking him down to his knees. She had a skillful and satanic

---

[5] Strong, J. (1995). *Enhanced Strong's Lexicon.* Woodside Bible Fellowship.

[6] Swanson, J. (1997). *Dictionary of Biblical Languages with Semantic Domains: Hebrew (Old Testament)* (electronic ed.). Oak Harbor: Logos Research Systems, Inc.

way of destroying his confidence. After he jumped through all her hoops, she cut him down with her words.

Thirdly and finally, something satanic and witch-like begins to happen. She seduced him to sleep. When he was asleep, she *afflicted* him after she vexed him:

> "*And she made him sleep upon her knees; and she called for a man, and she caused him to shave off the seven locks of his head;* **and she began to afflict him,** *and his strength went from him.*"
>
> (Judges 16:19; KJV)

Do you see the order? Samson did exactly what she asked him to do. He was not a man who wanted illicit relationships. He was a man who only wanted one woman. He wanted a woman whose loyalty would last for a lifetime. However, a loyal woman had nothing to do with what God planned for his life. The only loyalty Samson needed to be appreciative of was the fact that God would be loyal to him and never turn him in. God is a jealous God. When Samson placed his passions to please the only woman he loved before his Lord, that upset God on the highest order. *That* was the problem. Just like Adam, Samson allowed the woman he loved to dominate him.

As he was asleep, Delilah worked her witchcraft. The Devil was in the details. Because she was against him, she was against his God. She was cursing his God and cutting him down at the same time. The other side of God is Satan. She is on Satan's side, dominating him by the powers of her darkness and the Philistine gods she grew up with since her childhood. She was using the skills she developed in her upbringing that was connected to the underworld. She learned her skills from the streets. The text says his strength went from him as she afflicted him. Simply put, Samson's disobedience gave way for Delilah's witchcraft to take its course. Had not Samson given the secret to the strength of his ministry *first*, her assaults and insults would have been useless to his downfall because they would have rolled off his sleeves. No ill-intentioned woman can do anything to a man unless he gives her leverage. We are to never trade leverage for love. Samson fell prey to the song that says, "If Loving You is Wrong, I don't Want to be Right."

Because Samson was ill of love, he made sick choices in relation to women. Because he had a lovesickness, he chose sick women. Because he was love-sick, he chose women who were sick of love. The woman who means a man of God harm resents everything that man is proud of. Samson's deficiency for love was so strong that he gambled, hoping that she would appreciate the fact that he gave her all he had. So, he did just that. He gave her all he had. Every muscle he had was wrapped around her. She had him wrapped around her finger. Any woman who places an ultimatum on a man is an enemy of that man's strength. Any woman who challenges a man's love for her on that level has no respect for his Lord. Her goal is to strip him of his strength. Because Samson did not appreciate the man who God called him to be, how could he expect a woman like Delilah to do it?

The final deathtrap with a woman is falling in love in a lustful context. Whenever a man lives a life of lust on consecutive occasions, another woman is never the answer. If he gets another woman, the cycle will start all over again. He will only jump from the skillet to the frying pan. The ultimate problem is not with the woman. The problem is with the man, and God is the answer. After days, months, or years of sexual immorality, the love of the game sets in, and deadly consequences are nearby. The truth regarding any game is that sooner or later, the game will be over. Before then,

God's mercy was extended because Samson's unbridled passion did not eclipse his passion to destroy Philistines.

It may sound raw, but there are some things God will put up with regarding us as leaders as long as our issues do not personally affect Him. When Samson foolishly wielded his power, God still used Him for His glory because it was still in a Philistine context. Whatever was said about Samson, they could never say he was not doing his job. He was like a drunken man who immediately sobered up the moment he clocked in for work. If he was drunk at 8:59 a.m., by 9:00 a.m., he was ready for work, sobered by the Spirit. Samson was killing Philistines left and right and clocking in on time.

What appears to have truly brought Samson's ministry to a halt was not his sexual weaknesses or women. What brought Samson's ministry to a halt was the fact that he made a decision that impacted God personally. God personally told Samson not to allow anyone to become privy to what only He and Samson knew, i.e., the secret of his strength. If he would have told anyone, God would have ripped his muscles, even if he never met Delilah. When he revealed divine confidential information, he breached his contract with God. Without the anointing, there was no way Philistines could be defeated. God hired him based on that contract. Because Samson broke it, he would be soon fired by God. Previously, Samson had a vengeance against the enemies of God that kept him employed. Now, Samson does not care about the Philistine's destruction or his job description. All he cares about is Delilah.

When a preacher falls in love with the wrong kind of woman, it robs him of his desire to preach and strips him of his confidence. When pastors fall out of the ministry based on a toxic relationship, it is often because some of us may have already fallen away from God much earlier. Somehow, we allowed our power to be drained because of overexertion in a relationship with a woman who could never be satisfied. My mother always taught me to never give all my strength away to a woman like that. Always make sure you have something left for yourself.

    Samson wanted to spend the rest of his life with Delilah. He put his livelihood right in Delilah's lap. She would never support his ministry because she never wanted it in the first place. All she wanted was her future secured. That is why she took the money for her life and left the man for dead. Samson no longer had a desire to destroy the works of God's enemies or do God's work. At that point, God had no organ of Samson's anatomy He could use. He was useless. Samson was good for nothing. It is understandable why one of the saddest sentences in the Bible is recorded when the Philistines came upon Samson with one blow. Listen to the saga of Samson as he is about to undergo a rude awakening:

> *"And he said, I will go out as at other times before, and shake myself. And **he wist not** (he knew not) **that the Lord was departed from Him.**"*
>
> (Judges 16:20; KJV)

    It is one thing to lose God's power, but it is quite another to lose God's presence. More than Samson's power being gone, his God was gone. God's presence is more important, even if a preacher no longer has God's power. Not only did Delilah leave him for dead, but God did also. When God is gone from a pastor's life, there is nothing he can do but ask God for one more chance. When a pastor experiences a sense of godlessness, he will not last very long. There is no worse feeling for a God-called man than to have a vacant God. None of the consequences of Delilah's satanic afflictions, the Philistine's counsels, or Samson's painful past could compare to the harsh realities he experienced when his God was gone. When his wife of Timnath was gone, he still lasted although he was wounded. When God was gone, his life ended quickly. When God is gone, we are at the mercy of the godless. When this happens, we should not retaliate against Delilah or our enemies first. The first thing we must do is go after our God. When God returns, we can surface, but not until God returns.

Suicide has been one of the most ignominious debates when the walls fell upon Samson. The Hebrew writer heralds Samson in the Hallmark of Faith because of his last noble act. If suicide were the case, the text would have commended Samson for committing suicide by faith, but suicide was not the scenario. He was dying, but his last noble act of faith extended his minutes. Samson's final plea was for the Lord to *let* Samson die with the Philistines (Judges 16:30). Suicide is when one *takes* his life and not when one *gives* his life. Samson did not have the power to take his life. His power was gone. God permitted Samson to die killing Philistines rather than permission to kill himself. God allowed Samson to live his last moments doing what God called him to do. Samson did not want to finish the rest of his life in Philistine hands. Instead, he wanted to die in God's hands. Samson did not commit suicide. He sacrificed his life for God. God sanctioned Samson's sacrifice of his life, but it had to be done God's way. Samson could have asked for an extension of life in years, and God could have easily granted it. However, Samson wanted to give God something he had never given before, i.e., his body as a living sacrifice.

How shall we resolve these last moments with Samson? Is this a happy ending, a sad ending, a victory, or defeat? Is this the story of a man with deep pornographic issues? Is this the testimony of a wild man? Is this a story about witch-like women? Not by a long shot. It is the story of a man whose life was transparent for all to see. Yet very few understand the meaning of it all. It is the story of a man so gifted that he attracted enemies who were in submission to the Lord of the Flies (Satan) wherever he went. His life was full of people who were walking parasites, thirsty for his blood, envious of his ability, and threatened by his uniqueness. Samson could not make one move without someone being acutely interested in what he was doing. He was hunted and turned in by the only woman he ever loved (Delilah), and he was betrayed by the woman who loved him (the woman of Timnath). We see the stench of his sins, but too many people fail to pay attention to the flies who preyed on his spirit. Samson was different, envied, and surrounded by haters. He had an accountability group (the men of Judah) who gave up on him and virtually left him for dead. When he moved in his anointing, he did not need them anyway. There was nothing the men of Judah could say that would give them credit for supporting Samson. It is the story of a man who had so much of an anointing that he could not believe in himself. Samson grew up and lived in a shady context of people who had agendas. His parents were codependently confused about God's call upon his life. Most of the people he was surrounded by were trying to save their own skin. No one seemed to understand what loyalty meant, but they dared to demand it from Samson. They all seemed to protect their assets.

When you have unusual strength, you cannot always handle the fact that you are not strong enough to make anyone love or be loyal to you, but you do have to be strong enough to remember that God is love, and God is loyal. If we do not, we will look for love in all the wrong places and begin a life of a self-medicating ministry that will be ended.

Somewhere within the pastor's anatomy is the capacity to demonstrate decency amid moral failure. People who are considered to be heroes usually detest being called heroes. They simply state the fact that they did what they believed anybody would do in that situation. Samson did what any man of God would do if God left him. He asked God to come back into his life and help him finish strong. Although Samson was not trying to be a hero, it was an act of heroism to ask God for permission to die among the Philistines.

Samson never lived a life of consecutive obedience to God or his anointing. God was with Samson most of the time, but Samson paid severely for every mistake he ever made. His anger was the cause of his wife and father-in-law getting killed. He risked greater hardship on his brethren because of his brashness. He suffered reproach by being seen in public as he was going to lay with a prostitute. He suffered his wife being in the arms of another man. He suffered a broken heart to the point of death from the only woman he ever loved (Delilah). The Lord left him. His eyes were gouged. He was tortured. He was psychologically tormented and belittled by the only woman he loved. He was placed under the spell of witchcraft from Delilah. He placed God in a place of contempt because of his foolishness. He suffered mockery, humiliation, and reproach. He died before his time. Did he not suffer enough? The greatest sin he committed was telling the woman he loved too much information.

For the first time, Samson's heart was right with God, but it took the process of moral failure to succeed. I like to describe Samson as a noble savage. When Samson discovered he was in a position that would afford him one last opportunity to gain victory for God, he took it. Although Samson failed God miserably, God's grace allowed him to be placed in a position of power. As he leaned on the pillars, he was not premeditating how he was going to get out of the hell he got himself into. Samson was premeditating how he could get into the Heaven he neglected. Samson realized that he did not need a cure to fulfill his calling. All he needed was his anointing restored. Samson was prepared to die, but he did not want to die by the consequences of his own sins. He wanted to die doing his job, killing Philistines, and not be killed by the Philistines. Samson's last ministry motto was, "If I go down, my enemies are going down with me."

Yet, the very enemies who gouged his eyes were the same ones who placed him in a position to see God. That is exactly what the enemy does. When enemies think that they have a man of God in a position of defeat, in all actuality, it is a position that elevates him. When Delilah betrayed Samson, it became obvious that there was a vast difference between she and Samson. If they would have stayed together, we never would have known who the culprit was. When two codependent people exist in a relationship, both share the blame. If they separate, the one who takes responsibility for his or her actions becomes evident. Delilah came out smelling like a rose. Yet, roses quickly fade. I heard a wise man say, "Cut flowers don't last long!" Samson was the one who came clean with God.

Thinking they destroyed him, the text reveals why they mocked and laughed at him. They got careless by putting him in a position they thought would trap him, but all it did was elevate him. They put him between two pillars (Judges 16:25). His enemies just did not know how to quit. If they would have just left him alone, he would have died from depression. Yet, they had to keep going, pressing the envelope, and publicizing his foolishness. Whatever position the enemy sets a man of God in after that man has repented is only a position of promotion. Within Samson's anatomy, he had enough scruples to know that although he failed God miserably, God allowed him to be in position to bring the house down. When we fail God, He has a way of allowing the enemy to place us in paradoxical predicaments that display God's power. That which does not kill us only comes to make us strong.

In Judges 16:28, Samson's call on the Lord epitomizes a sinner's cry that God will never forsake the cries of His servants.

Samson cries, "Lord, remember me!" I never read an instance when that prayer was prayed by anyone in the Bible, man or woman, and God turned them down.

Samson could have asked God for perpetual strength and length of days, but he asked for strength just one more time. After moral failure, arrogance asks for everything back, but nobility asks for only one thing back, i.e., "Lord, remember me!" We never want the Lord to forget us. If God remembers us, we will always finish strong. Samson was asking God to open the gates of Heaven after he brought down the gates of the Philistines. He begged God to prepare him for Glory. He asked God to graciously receive him into Heaven after he finished his assignment on Earth. Samson heard and sensed that he had an opportunity to leave a legacy behind, and he went for it. Blinded, bleeding, and buffeted. Samson used his better senses. His ear became keen to his surroundings, and he smelled the stench of Satan cheering and mocking he and his God. Samson grew hungry to do ministry and looked for every opportunity to go for it at all costs. All he needed was the green light from God, and he would break the enemy's back with a vengeance upon his assassins and a holy anger that would bring judgment upon the Philistines.

The tides began to turn. Although blind, he could hear the noise and taunts against God and quickly calculate that if he could have one more chance to slay the Philistines, he would do it. He also realized that he could do more in one moment of complete surrender to the Lord than a lifetime of partial submission. Although blind, he was beginning to see Heaven open and the sweet chariots of the Lord coming forth to carry him Home, but not until his work was done. Samson's sins are now blessings in disguise that transformed him into a sanctified savage. Now, the Philistines are in trouble.

Nobility is seen when he requests to die *with* the Philistines. He realizes that it would be ludicrous to think he could go any further. Samson realized why God deserved more than a blind judge. When we have suffered permanent impairments because of our foolishness, there are some ailments we should not ask God to heal. When a man has understood the full ramifications of the depth of this type of failure, he can transition gracefully into Glory, and the next man can take God's work to the next level. Although most of the judges had some type of handicap, blindness was not one of them. Eyes were an integral part of longevity in winning future battles. He realized his carelessness shortened his days. He was just as realistic as he was restored. Restoration must involve being realistic. That is a painful lesson learned after we have gone too far with God. Most of all, he recognized how his carelessness cost him his eyes. He was not just blind. His eyes were gone. To ask God for sight is one thing, but to ask God for a whole new set of eyes is pushing God to the limit. **When we violate the most precious things that God has given us, some things are irrevocable.** Although God could restore him as a judge, God would not restore his eyes. Some things God will not put back in our sockets when we let sexual lust and a lack of loyalty gouge certain things out of us.

So, he requested to die in dignity and honor God in a way he had never done before and leave room for another who would not lie down or die down in Delilah's lap. Instead, God needs men who stand down. The last judge was Samuel. There was no way Samuel would fall prey to women. Samuel had impeccable integrity. Samuel valued his eyes. A prophet must be a seer to prophesy. Samuel used his eyes to see into the spiritual and not the sexual realm. He valued his calling and standing with God. Samuel took nothing for granted.

Whether we are at a stage of unbridled passions or victorious disciplines, our chief aim is to glorify God. God called Samson to defeat Philistines and not fool around with tattling wives or tormenting women. Previously, Samson's calculated defeat added up to the slaying of a lion, thirty men at a bridal party, three hundred foxes, an unknown number slaughtered, one thousand Philistines at Lehi, and ripped gates from their hinges. None of these compared to what Samson was going to do in one final feat. When we give God partial obedience, many of our accomplishments are nothing but vanity compared to the trophies we collect on our ministry shelves that are the amazing graces God bestowed upon us that are greater than our sins (Romans 5:20).

The glory is seen in the fact that **God's grace still allows us to accomplish what He called us to do, even after we lost our most precious commodities.** With no eyes, Samson slew three thousand men in his final days. Interestingly, that is the same number of godly men who stopped believing in him (the men of Judah). We do not have to have a number of friends or gain popularity among our peers, but we must take down as many enemies of the Cross that we possibly can.

It is ironic that when Samson had his eyes, he could not see. Now that he has no eyes, he can see better than he ever has before. When a man can say, "I once was blind, but now I see", his enemies ought to run for the hills, and the angels can prepare to open Heavens gates because a *seer* is soon to come Home. The glory is seen in the fact that Samson realized God was allowing him to fulfill his destiny and attribute to God a major portion of the glory he once squandered. When we have lost our eyes, Samson teaches us that we can still see. We can see that God is faithful to His call upon our lives. We see our sins and how they separate us from our Savior. We also see the lives who were destroyed by our depravity. Nevertheless, our sins never separate us from the Savior's love or the possibility of the salvation of the Lord if we call on Him to give us another chance (Romans 8:35). When we turn to God once and for all, He will restore us to the frontlines of His purposes for us in the Earth.

When God wrote about Samson, the last chapter did not condemn him. God's last chapter of Samson's life honored him for who he always was. It just took Samson a long time to realize who he always was. He was born a man of God, and he died a man of God. That is how I was born, and that is how I will die. When our concern is to glorify God regardless of our state, whether sinful or sanctified, blind or seeing, sick or well, God will remember us, and our calling can be completed. God already has our ministries, but he also wants our manhood. He wants us to give up our pride, ego, arrogance, unbridled passions, fear of standing alone, and codependent compulsions. Yes, we are called amid a deadly context of snakes and scorpions. Yet, we can take up snakes and trample upon scorpions when we keep what God entrusted to us and not squander it with people who will only use our advantage against us. We are God's property, and He has ways of reminding us and anyone who seeks title deeds of our lives that we belong to Him.

Learn from Samson, myself, and others. Only God can save us from the long line of deficiencies we inherit or instigate. When you have lost strength and sight, if you are *strong enough* to call on the Lord and *seeing enough* to perceive how God is the strength of our lives, He will allow you to bring the house down. It is not about how long your life and ministry last. It is all about how strong your loyalty to God is. When we are loyal to God, we do not have to risk being fired by our greatest Friend (God). God will keep you employed. He may even give you a raise. Perhaps, He may give you some overtime.

Chapter 11

THE PASTOR AND HIS THIGH

Facing Failure
(An Excerpt from the Life of Jacob:
A man of God who left people feeling robbed)

Tribute: To my uncle, Donald Ray Temple; (former Pastor, New Hope Baptist Church of Greenville, TX; Marlin Baptist Church of Marlin, TX)

I preached the eulogy of a dearest relative on my mother's side of the family. Pam Boddie was her name. She was a Caucasian lady who married my cousin, who was an African American male. She was one of the kindest and most tenderhearted women who I ever knew. As the officiant, it was important to me that the atmosphere of her funeral reflected the non-prejudicial woman she was. Yet, at her funeral, Blacks sat on one side of the church, and Whites sat on the other side. God told me to have my uncle sing to bring about a desegregated atmosphere. I was privileged to have Uncle Donald Ray Temple sing. I liken Uncle Don to a male mockingbird when he sings. People may presume the female mockingbird does all the singing. However, it is the male mockingbird who sings, but it is the female mockingbird who chirps loudly, usually once. Then, she makes her long screech (no pun intended). Ironically, he sang "His Eye is on the Sparrow". The atmosphere of that funeral service was literally transformed. The way he sang unified the entire congregation under the presence of God. From that point on, there were no Black or White folks. We experienced temporary desegregation as one people under God. All God's men have a limp. God used Donald Ray Temple to make history that day. Donald Ray Temple is also a great preacher and teacher. He has a keen mind, and he is rich with deep theological insight. He is a man who has a mind that attends to detail. Many more gifts accompany Uncle Don. If he put his mind to it, he could be one of the greatest professors our seminaries have ever known.

Other than the Great White Throne Judgement, I believe the most dreadful appointment one faces is an appointment with *self*. One can spend his entire ministry avoiding an appointment with his dark side. This meeting with ourselves is a meeting we must attend sooner or later. Most attend the meeting late, when it's almost too late, at the last minute, somewhere around 11:59 in the p.m. of life, when we've reached rock bottom, when all Hell has broken loose, when we have nowhere to go but to this meeting, when we have no one to turn to but the Lord of the meeting, when we are all by ourselves and it is dangerous for anyone to be around us, when we are a menace to society, when we have to pay the piper, when we must lie down in the bed we've made, when we must reap what we've sown, when Esau is coming. When we undergo serious character deficiencies, there comes a day and time when every step we took in the past leaves footprints in front of us that are headed in our direction.

The consequences of one bad decision accumulate in one moment. Years of sweeping character flaws under the rug are contained within the capsule of seconds. In one small hourglass, we see our lives, all we have done, and all who we offended. We are running out of time. This is a frightening fact. Everything we deemed to be something no longer means a thing. We realize we are not really the champions we claim to be because we did not earn our trophies. We cheated to get them. What we gained, we gained dishonestly. We took someone else's credit away from them that they deserved. We pulled at the heel of our brother and beat him out of what was rightfully his. We could not stand to see our brother blessed. All that matters is that we change and hope for mercy extended to allow us to make up for lost time and lost lives.

No wonder this meeting is so dreaded. This appointment strips us to the bone and shows us what we are made of and who we are. It strips our titles and accomplishments to nothing. We have no one to impress, no one to preach to, and no one to pray for but ourselves. We have no reputation or pulpit to hide behind. Our opponent could care less about what we acquired and what success we attained. At this meeting, we are no longer impressed by our pastoral profile because we know what we really look like on the inside. We see ourselves in our bare skin as we look at ourselves in the mirror without our clerical garments, suits, or ties. We are no longer satisfied by the size or style of our congregations. We are no longer impressed by our sermons because we realize how much we have lived far beneath what we preach. Yet, all we want to do is win. That is all we ever wanted the moment we were called to preach. Winning was in our DNA before we were ever birthed in our mother's womb. Unfortunately, we pulled at somebody's heel to win. We want to be better and do better. We want to be changed, knowing that whatever games we play, we must learn to play by the rules.

Our opponent is not God, Satan, or those who are chasing us down. Our opponent is ourselves. The opponent is that other side of ourselves that needs to be pinned to the mat. If we are going to be our greatest friend, we must learn not to be our greatest enemy. We tried over and again to master our monster within, but the dark demon within keeps winning. He is strong and stubborn. We come to a point where we admit our need for help before we spiral out of control. We are professionals at masking our mistakes, but we do not care what we look like anymore to people because we want to be better men.

Jacobs' demons were born from seeds of several sowers, but God was not one of them. Personalities develop deep within the womb. Before Jacob was born, he pulled at his twin brother's heel while in the womb of his tricky mother, Rebekah (Genesis 25:26). The struggle of Jacob and Esau was a prophetic announcement concerning nations is often spiritualized to explain how Jacob and Esau's struggle is an illustration of the war in all of us between the flesh and the Spirit. However, neither of the brothers represent a good spirit. Esau was just as fleshly as Jacob on several levels. Squandering the birthright was one of them:

> *"And Esau said, Behold, I am at the point to die: and what profit shall this birthright do to me?"*

(Genesis 25:32; KJV)

Human personality is formed before the foundation of the world (Jeremiah 1:5). There are unforeseen elements that hinder us from our best behavior. Of course, our sin nature is no exception. Scripture teaches us that we were born in sin and *shapen* in iniquity (Psalm 51:5). Yet, we cannot blame it all on the Devil. The sin principle was at work in our DNA before we became pastors. However, the sin nature and character development must not get confused. Character deficiencies cannot be blamed solely upon our sin nature. We will have a sin nature until we die, but we must not die with a sinful character.

Understanding forces that develop our dark sides is valuable to winning battles with ourselves. Not only before and during birth but also during childhood were traits evident that nurtured our dark sides. This principle is deeper than some psychological cop-out as an excuse for failure. *Jacob's parents nurtured his selfishness.* If parents do not think they have favorites with their children, they should ask the siblings. Jacob was the product of dysfunctional parents who competed for God's approval at the expense of their children. When parents compete, it adds to the already ingrained sinful tendencies children inherit within their sin nature. Isaac favored Esau, and Rebekah favored Jacob. Deeper than favoritism, it was twisted love they had for each of their sons:

> *"And Isaac loved Esau, because he did eat of his venison; but Rebekah loved Jacob."*
>
> (Genesis 25:28; KJV)

This type of discriminating parenting did not cause Jacob to be the deceiver he was, but it nourished the dark child within. Jacob was being nursed from breasts that had spoiled milk. Therefore, Jacob was spoiled. We recognize the outgrowth of Rebekah's manipulation and how it included Jacob as part of the scheme to trick Isaac into giving *The Blessing* to Jacob. Jacob was not only wrestling with his dark side, but he was also wrestling with generational dark sides that had not been resolved in his family line. The apple really does not fall far from the tree. The godly line of Jacob was preceded by generations of lying, manipulation, and partiality. His grandparents (Abraham and Sarah) were not exceptions to the rule. What made matters worse is that it was all over not fully apprehending the promises of God by faith. Jacob and Esau watched their parents compete for God's promises. If Jacob was going to win the battle against his internal iniquities, his parents made his personal battles even more difficult.

God's call on our lives is not only a mandate to live up to but a deliverance to be thankful for. This explains why we have deficiencies we often discover *after* our calling. We discover how we have not only developed new flaws, but we have also come to realize the power of our generational ones. When we look at our family trees, some of us will be surprised to discover we were not the blackest sheep of the family.

In our deepest failures, the pastor's anatomy is wired to have strong feelings of guilt, condemnation, disqualification, hypocrisy, resignation, or even a polished passivity regarding his perversities. We can easily misread the signs. Yet, they are sensors designed to remind us to keep our appointment with our adversarial ambitions. When we run from, dismiss, or excuse the battle with ourselves, we are denying ourselves the victory of a lifetime. All other victories are traditional bouts regardless of our degrees, awards, or promoted positions in ministry. The battle against ourselves is most significant because the stakes are much higher. The reward for winning this self-battle is the regaining of our royalty.

Jacob already had recognition and respect because of his steeling status. However, behind the mask of a successful patriarch was a man who had not been healed from spiritual theft. Jacob was too old to be re-parented. He needed to be transformed. Whenever we reach points of status in ministry without ordering our private world, we are robbing ourselves of the joy of looking in the mirror and not being deceived by who we see.

Although he was a grown man, Jacob was still a fetus pulling from the womb of life every opportunity he could to get ahead of the next guy. Competitiveness, envy, insecurity, and jealousy are all vices that come from a man who has not gone to the mat with God. Sometimes, when a preacher is buried in despair, it is a *matless* minister who will shovel the last mound of dirt on top of him. It also involves protecting what was mischievously acquired at the expense of realizing much of what we have belonged to someone else. Even in a religious context, a man who is success-driven with an underdeveloped ego will steal anything. He will steal sermons, ideas, members, money, churches, someone else's wife, positions, and many other things from another to get ahead.

When a healthy relationship with God is established, we acquire a more grounded relationship with ourselves and others. We are then, free from establishing an unhappy identity based upon what we have or do not have. We no longer need to be notorious by possessing certain ministerial niceties when we have conquered our demons within. When we become tainted by our tangibles, it is a sign that we fear the fight of a lifetime. One who runs into the ministry but flees transformation has not gone to the mat with God. When we get in the ring with God, we have only two options, i.e., to live or to die. The man who flees self-confrontation refuses to get his knuckles bloody in the ring of change. If we have not been trained to be transformed, we may be well-polished with our ministries manicured, but our temperaments have not been tamed. A man who has not gone to the mat may do the most polished things to get ahead to avoid exposure. Yet, everyone who intimately interacts with him leaves feeling robbed (Genesis 25:31).

We must win against our darkest sides because they intercept our communion with God, focus on our families, and realization of what is rightfully ours and what rightfully belongs to another. Herein was Jacob's problem. He spent a critical portion of his life manipulating for status while jeopardizing his chance to be championed as a changed man. Our ability to hold on to God for change determines if we want the blessing or the *Blesser*.

Meetings with ourselves do not always come when we are at our lowest points. They sometimes come when we are at the height of experiencing *the good life*. When we are recipients of lofty inheritances, whether they are material or spiritual, we are often at our poorest points in character development. Big bills can be spent faster than small change. Sometimes, we waste more when we have more. At the top, we are less tempted to be transformed because we deceived ourselves into believing we have arrived. Jacob's wrestling match was approaching when he could have been considered in his prime. Our achievements can be the detectors of our downfall. Jacob had great wealth before this dreaded appointment took place. Rock bottom is not always the place to make a turnaround. One of the most dangerous places to be is at the pinnacle of the temple. If we made it to the top of the religious order, that does not mean we are accomplished. The top could be where we experience the deepest dives. From high religious positions, we can be tempted to sin in a religious way. From the pinnacle, we can miss knowing the fact that how we stay grounded is a matter of coming to terms with the danger of jumping to our own conclusions. (Matthew 4:6).

Although Jacob was successful, he became successful in a sneaky way. The most important truth when we reach higher ground is how we got there. If we climbed the mountain with our own two feet and bare hands with the help of the Lord, we got there honestly. If we stepped on the back of someone else without their permission or robbed them of their climbing gear, our ministry has never truly begun.

If we run from transformation, just when we feel as though we are in our golden years, the haunting of some dumb decision we made years ago springs with new life. The issue is not resolved by settling with demons of our past by paying them off to keep quiet so that our reputations are not ruined. The first step is not to make peace with our pursuers. The issue of silencing old demons resides in making peace with God.

Now, Jacob has two wives and many livestock. His past catches up with him when he has attained great wealth and possession through the consequences of being haunted by his brother, Esau.

The Pastor And His Thigh

Because Jacob had not settled his issues with God, Esau had issues with him. Notice how Jacob had to liquidate his assets for fear of his life:

> *"And he rose up that night, and took his two wives, and his two women servants, and his eleven sons and passed over the ford Jabbok. And he took them, and sent them over the brook and sent over* (all) *that he had."*
>
> (Genesis 32:22-23; KJV)

When we settle our issues with God, we do not have to change lanes when we see consequences coming. Although Jacob had great wealth, he had no land and no landing. God desires our appointments with the grave to be a safe landing into our eternal rest and not some casualty because we were too stubborn to submit. He was a fugitive. Until we are delivered from our darkest dispositions, our entire lives will be spent running from our reality. We must have somewhere *to land* when we come down from perverted progress. The world is getting smaller. Just when we think we landed in a safe place, there is something in our past that reminds us that we still must face the Hell we caused someone else. Jacob had nowhere he could run to claim protection from his past. There was nowhere he could settle. He had success, but he had no sanctuary. He had fortune, but he was a fugitive. He was rich, but he was restless. Whenever we acquire any form of wealth the wrong way, there will come a day when we can no longer get a good night's sleep. Our eyes may be closed, but our guilt remains wide open.

Those who have gone to the mat with God know this is not the point when life ends. On the contrary, it is the point when our lives have only just begun. When we send over all of what we gained dishonestly, we can embark upon the process of a purged personality, and we will become purposeful preachers. Sometimes, we do not know how much we are in God's hands until we release everything we have out of our hands. Instead of stealing status, we must sell all we have. We must sellout to be sold out to God. If we do not do it willingly, God must wrestle everything we hustled and hankered out of our hands so we can hold to His unchanging hand. If we are holding on to the wrong goods, we will never get a good grip on God.

This wrestling match with God has one central theme although it has been variously interpreted: We can only go so far, last so long, and do so much in life and ministry without that divine appointment when we finally realize a change must come. God is faithful to bring about change in our lives, but opportunities for change will not always be with us. To take advantage of the possibilities for personal power, Jacob teaches us how opportunities for change will not always pass us by. Often, opportunities for change can catch up with us and take us down. In God's eyes, Esau was going to be either Jacob's opportunity or opposition, depending upon how tightly Jacob could get a grip on God.

When we make certain errors in life, the need for change can pursue us. Sometimes, it comes in the disguise of our friends who we made into enemies because we did not relate to them justly. We must seize the time of change and not let go until God approves our fighting efforts to be the men He predestined us to be.

Jacob arose "that night" (Genesis 33:22). Even the day will be dark because we must settle being alone in the night of life. To say goodbye to our past, we must say hello to sleepless nights. No man with good in him can keep sleeping on what he has stolen. Sooner or later, his consequences will not let him rest until he returns his stolen items to where they belong.

We do not always return those items to those we stole them from. Until our victims have been changed, they will only be vicious and use our stealing status against us. Whatever we owe them, they will keep us indebted no matter how much we pay them. They will only charge an interest rate we cannot afford. We return them to the Lord because our birthright and blessing comes from Him. This type of theft is an unusual crime. It is one in which we never held anyone at gunpoint although we were guilty. We were unarmed but, in some capacity, they also were partners in the crime. Yet, they were still robbed because we got the better end of the deal in a cheating fashion. Once we have been transformed, God can distribute to both parties what is rightfully theirs if both parties are willing to make amends. It is never about getting back what you lost or have stolen. It is about appreciating what God still allowed you to have.

The heart of a champion gives opportunities for the challenger to have a shot at the title. God is the Champion, and He grants the opportunity for us to challenge Him to a shot at the title of transformation. When we challenge God to change us, we will always win if we hold on to Him regardless of how hard God hits us. Real change never comes without pain. Jacob later came to realize the truth that if God did not wound him, there would be no way he could win.

It was so dark that night that at one point, Jacob did not know he was wrestling with God. The fight with God is a dark fight, but it is a good fight. It is a fight night. Exegetically, in round one, Jacob had no idea it was God with whom he was wrestling. To Jacob, he was wrestling with some hard-hitting human, but the day had not begun to break. If God would have wrestled with Jacob until daybreak, Jacob would have lost focus and quit too soon. God did not want Jacob to see who he was wrestling with at that time. God wanted Jacob to see himself. It is possible that for at least a fleeting moment, he could have easily assumed he was wrestling with Esau. However, he knew too much about his brother to believe the *man* he was wrestling with was Esau. After all, they were twins. Esau was a good fighter, but Jacob realized the *man* he was fighting with was much more skilled and stronger than Esau. When our enemies are against us, we know their fighting styles, and we can easily tell when we are up against a natural or supernatural opponent because He (God) is much stronger than they. We will eventually realize it is God who is trying to tell us something.

God can take us through trials in which our fleeing efforts are developed into fighting efforts. God leaves us with powerful punches we cannot deflect to cause us to reflect. We must hand over our hustle and accept the fact that *we* are our number one problem. He puts us in rings of repercussions in which we have no defense. In round one, consequences are allowed by God, and we must not attempt to control them. In addition, we should not run from them. We must stay in the ring and figure out how to fight right. Remember, Jacob was guilty of causing Esau to have a spirit of bitterness although Esau brought it upon himself. It is careless to curse consequences, and it is not rational to run from repercussions that lead to redemption, restoration, and reconciliation. If Jacob would have ran from the ring of change, God would have tagged the Angel of Death to step over the ropes and finish Jacob off. God picked this fight, not Esau.

> "...*Jacob was left alone...there wrestled **a man** with him until the breaking of the day.*"
>
> (Genesis 32:24; KJV)

This *man* was the only man who Jacob could not manipulate. He defeated his dad when he lied and tricked him into bestowing upon him *The Blessing*. He defeated Esau when he tricked him into selling his birthright. He defeated Laban by working faithfully to earn the right to marry his daughter, Rachel. Notice how everyone in Jacob's circle had serious shadiness as well. They were not angels. They had a track record that showed how they did not always play by the rules. They all were gamblers. Isaac could not be trusted because he leaned more towards one son. Such was also the case with his mother, Rebekah. Esau could not be trusted because he traded *The Birthright* for his interests. Laban could not be trusted because he used his daughter (Rachel) as leverage to get more labor from Jacob and deceived him to do so. None walked the road to Glory on a truthful track. They were all tricky and twisted. They tended to put their twist on life and throw curveballs to strike someone else out. Jacob was raised within a context of connivers and a home of hustlers.

However, neither of them could hustle God. God does not gamble. God gives or gets what He wants on His terms. God wanted to get some good out of Jacob and his entire family of frauds. God was giving Jacob constant wake-up calls, but he kept hitting the snooze button:

> *"Jacob awaked out of his sleep, and he said, Surely the LORD is in this place; and I knew it not."*
>
> (Genesis 28:16; KJV)

Regarding all these soon to be converted criminals, it helps to recognize the difference between *The Birthright* and *The Blessing*. *The Birthright* was a natural inheritance, but *The Blessing* was a spiritual one. Esau could care less about his birthright, but he was offended greatly when *The Blessing* was stolen from him. Notice Esau's unappreciative attitude of his birthright:

> *"And Jacob sod pottage: and Esau came from the field, and he was faint: And Esau said to Jacob, Feed me, I pray thee, with that same red pottage; for I am faint: therefore was his name called Edom. And Jacob said, Sell me this day thy birthright. And Esau said, Behold, I am at the point to die: and **what profit shall this birthright do to me**? And Jacob said, Swear to me this day; and he sware unto him: **and he sold his birthright unto Jacob**. Then Jacob gave Esau bread and pottage of lentiles; and he did eat and drink, and rose up, and went his way: thus **Esau despised his birthright**."*

(Genesis 25:29-34; KJV)

However, notice Esau's attitude about *The Blessing* Jacob had stolen from him:

> *"**Esau hated Jacob because of the blessing** wherewith his father blessed him: and Esau said in his heart, The days of mourning for my father are at hand; then will I slay my brother Jacob."*

(Genesis 27:41; KJV)

This is where Jacob got in trouble with Esau. Esau in some since could tolerate the offense that occurred when Jacob had taken his birthright because he should have at least realized that he had something to do with it as well. However, when Jacob stole his blessing from under his arms, Esau added the past offense of *The Birthright* to the equation as well:

> *"And he said, Is not he rightly named Jacob? for he hath supplanted (deceived) me these two times: he took away my birthright; and, behold, now he hath taken away my blessing. And he said, Hast thou not reserved a blessing for me?"*

(Genesis 27:36; KJV)

A double portion of the inheritance was passed down to the son who received *The Birthright* (Deuteronomy 21:17). In the time of the patriarchs, *The Blessing* was like a last will that was greatly valued because it was a means of revealing God's will. In a strong sense, in Esau's eyes, his battle with Jacob was spiritual. In some sense, Esau cared more about spiritual things than material things. Yet, he seemed to care when it was too late. So, Esau was bound to a life of regret of what he could have had and what he should have done. Whenever a person lives in regret of what they should have done, they can go after you with a deadly vengeance.

From this historical occurrence, we learn that Esau later realized that possessions can easily be replaced, but royalty is hard to recover. People who feel robbed of their true purpose in life hold killing grudges. To them, it's not about money or material things lost that greatly offends them. It is more about the status that they lost because of the deception of someone else. They believe that their lives are never the same and will never be what they could have been because of what someone has done to them. Thus, they feel as though their *lives* have been stolen from them. In a strong sense, another person's character flaws can cause others that kind of damage. What we do matters in the lives of people, and they can easily have a case for being embittered for what some of us may have deceptively done to them. If Jacob was ever going to be a true patriarch of people, he would have to do some serious soul-searching because he would have caused damage to more lives in the future.

For what Jacob had done to Esau, God had to go to work on Jacob. Because God desires change, He will induce the need for change in striking measures. God struck Jacob's thigh because Jacob needed to know how much he had more of a desire to change than he realized. If Jacob could hold on despite a divine blow, he was qualified to accept the change that blow would inflict. If a man is willing to hold to God, he will let go of everything else.

When we have not faced our failures for so many years, we must never resign to believe that they are much too old and strong to overcome. Jacob was fighting an opponent older than his opposition with Esau. Jacob was fighting with an issue that was as old as he. Jacob was fighting with himself. Jacob was his own problem long before Esau became a problem for him. Jacob was born pulling at the heel.

We can become settled at being set in our ways. As an undefeated opponent, God made sure Jacob could not get settled. So, God struck him in the thigh and stifled his stance. We can discover our will to live and lead is stronger than we thought when death comes knocking and pain strikes. When God strikes, it is an issue of life and death. Jacob's match with God was a deathmatch. His life depended on the first few rounds. God was not going to kill him, but the consequences of his sins were. Esau was coming. Esau was trying to destroy Jacob because he felt his life was destroyed by Jacob. After God hit him hard, Jacob discovered a drive within he did not know existed as he responded to God's chastising hand with a resilient and rewarded reflex:

"I will not let thee go, except thou bless me."

(Genesis 32:26; KJV)

    The similarity of Jacob's experience with God to his experience in the womb of his mother cannot be underestimated. A terrifying temperament was developing in the womb of Rebekah. Rebekah was giving birth to a manipulative monster. Remember, it was Jacob's sin to grab the heel of his brother when he was in his mother's womb, and he would not let go. Jacob had a habit of *holding on*, even if he was holding on to the wrong things or wrong people for the wrong reasons. Everyone he held on to, he hustled. When he thought he had nothing to lose, he had a grip on who he felt could help him. Jacob was born holding on. His little fetus had strong fingers. He also held Rachel because he loved her too much. He held on to his mother (Rebekah) although she was poisoning him against his father and nurturing him to be a momma's boy. In his mother's womb, he was maliciously holding on to Esau's heel. Jacob was holding on to his old ways. However, in the womb of Jabbok he was wrestling with himself. If he were to win, he would have to let go of his old ways and find someone worth holding on to. Jacob could not manipulate God. The only one worth holding on to for dear life was God. As God was moving away from Jacob, he was holding on to the heel of God for a new inheritance. Jacob was seeking another blessing that far exceeded the one he had stolen.

    Now, Jacob is in the womb of Jabbok, grabbing for something better than what he has. He is in the womb of change, realizing he must be born again. If not, he would be aborted. A preacher can die in the womb of change if he is not careful. We have a long line of preachers we know who died before their time. In Jacob's mind, whoever this was inflicting pain in his life was also inspiring him. Although Jacob was losing breath from the battle, God was breathing enough life into him to keep him from quitting. If he would have refused transformation, by the time Esau caught up with him, Jacob would have already been a dead man. If Jacob would have let that moment slip away, he would have died the same person he was when he was born. He also began to realize it was not Esau who he was wrestling with because Esau would have killed him in round one. God was sparring with Jacob, training him to be a strong contender of the Faith. It was God's tough love. The precision and impact of the strike upon Jacob's thigh taught him to know this blow was intentional and inspirational. Jacob knew the being he was wrestling with could have given him a blow to the heart, lungs, throat, or head in a way that could have killed him if God wanted to. When God struck Jacob in the thigh, it was a leg issue. Jacob knew he was in no condition to run from Esau. This dark, dangerous, and difficult deliverance was all he had.

God spared Jacob from wrestling with anyone other than himself. Jacob had reason to wrestle with his mother (Rebekah), brother (Esau), dad (Isaac), father-in-law (Laban), and even his wife, Rachel. Yet, if he were to spend time wrestling with either of them, he would have been wrestling for the rest of his life because none of them had the power to change him or the will to change. Jacob did not have the power to change them. If we waste our lives wrestling with those who are part of our dysfunction, our fight will be forfeited. Their desire for change can easily be challenged. Usually, they never change. They just strategically learn to play the victim. There is no victory in being the victim. At the end of the day, people with a victimized mentality can never be satisfied, and they will always slip up somewhere. No matter what anyone has done to inflict damage in our lives, the wisest prayer to pray is, "Lord, change me."

There is no need to throw in the towel if we feel personal change can never take place. If we do not resign from the ministry, never resign from the mat. We must never resign from the ministry unless we have not gone to the mat with God and refused to hold on until He beats blessed behavior into our being. This type of resignation has never proven to be necessary even though it appears to be noble. If we have been changed, we can stay in the ministry until God says otherwise. In fact, purposeful pain is the beginning of real preaching. No preacher is useful to God until he has been hurt by God badly.

Adversely, forced resignation bears the tone of pastoral euthanasia as one chooses to allow his ministry to die in an apparent dignified fashion. The testimony of this type of pastoral suicide never breeds nobility but it does breed mourners. Nothing but sorrow is the result of quitting too soon. While we or others may suggest we throw in the towel, God is sparring with us, developing us to go the distance necessary to develop our true definition. If we resign from the ministry and never go to the mat with God, we will have a failing shadow that will hover over our heads for the rest of our lives, even if we stepped down and moved off the radar.

Traditional, political, and religious treatment of moral failure seeks resignation over and against the transforming virtues of resilience, rewarded reflexes, and restoration. Sadly, counsels, denominational parent bodies, church governing boards, and other pastors force failing pastors to resign for political, personal, or partial reasons. Simply put, they do not want the failing pastor's shadow to fall on them. So, the pastor who failed in some fashion becomes the scapegoat. I only mention this because those who do not know the politics behind the pulpit never truly mature from the political ejection of some of God's best men. They just look one day and discover their pastor is gone. In some capacity, he has been politically removed by some hypocritical party.

Some of God's greatest leaders are the ones who got caught just as Jacob finally got caught. Getting caught does not mean one cannot be a conqueror. In addition, it does it mean he was ever hiding. There is conquest after getting caught if that same man's character has been cured. People prematurely disqualify a staggering man because they never truly know the dynamics of what makes a preacher walk uprightly. Staggering men of God are men who transcended the hypocrisy of religious, bitter, and political enemies by holding on until God blessed them. After transformation, everybody wants to know your name, even many of the ones who previously tried to erase it. We are to fight for transformation and let the divine chips fall. We must be more concerned with our reward for being redeemed more than our own reputation. God determines the extent to which He uses us for His glory despite our gloom.

I cannot forget a statement my cousin, Pastor W. Terrell Snead II made during the fading of one of his ministries. Before I was honored to have him become the Executive Pastor at our church, he witnessed the closing of one of the churches he pastored. He told me about his prayer that confirmed it was time for him to move on. As his membership was declining, he asked the Lord to give him a sign. He asked the Lord to remove the remaining members from his ministry if it was time for him to move on. That following Sunday, he came to his church, and the only members present were virtually he and his family. While some picture that as failure, the rest of us know that was faith. When a pastor learns to let go of his church and hold on to change, he is a man who is a champion.

I borrowed that prayer from my cousin because one day, I knew it would be my turn. Years later, I prayed, "Lord if you want me to fold it up here as the pastor of this church, you fold it and I will put it on the shelf." I failed so miserably that I was ready to ride off into the sunset and hang up my guns like some drunken cowboy, who was previously a sharpshooter. Instead of God folding my ministry, He ironed it out. Although I am still pastoring, only God knows how much I gave that church up in my heart. Under no circumstances does God hold anyone responsible to put their lives or ministry in their own hands. Also, we are not to allow some uncertified ecclesiastical physician (critic) to pull the plug on our preaching or our pastoring.

I believe that although Satan and people who are offended by the failures of pastors have a strategic and systematic way of coming for pastors, it is not those who have such evils in their hearts that cause pastors to bite the dust. I believe something within a man of God breaks long before his consequences chase him down. Once that man's spirit breaks, he quit long before he was caught or condemned. For such reasons as these, God is a pastor's only hope for healing. If or when we truly go to the mat with God and are willing to take whatever chastisement God inflicts upon us, we can survive the assaults of anyone who is trying to kill our calling.

Most of all, it is important to understand encounters with God on this level are not death sentences. They are life sentences. When we truly get in the ring with God, He is asking us if we want to live and lead. He is asking us if we want to win. As we stand in the ring of God with no real chance of winning against such an apparent opponent as He, we must realize God is not our opponent. We are our own worst nightmare. If we want change, God is our changer, teaching us how to defeat our defects within. Once we do that, our external circumstances shift in reconciling dimensions because the people who are coming for us will have to go through God first. The man who they are coming for is no longer there because he is a changed man. If or when they catch up with him, he would have already changed so much that they can hardly recognize him. When God can get us to see that in its clearest dimensions, He takes the reigns on the hearts of our harassers. After Jacob became a changed man, Esau could either live by allowing God to reconcile their differences and learn how to appreciate what he still possessed, or he could die a slow death from the cancer of bitterness and boxing with a man who survived twelve rounds with God.

Honestly, it is selfish to quit, especially when we never really started. That would be the cowardly thing to do. The most courageous thing to do is face our failures and go the distance with God in the twelve rounds of repentance. Once we have been transformed, the most courageous thing to do is allow God to maim us back into ministry with nothing and no one else but God as our crutch.

The old idiom, *"You can't help others until you've helped yourself"* is not always true of pastoral ministry. Thus, many content preachers need to be crippled by God. Contentment can be delusional. Ironically, a preacher *can* help a lot of people, even if he has a flawed character. I was such a one. Paul reveals a frightening reality. We *can* possess the power to help others while risking personal disqualification (I Corinthians 9:27).

The power that operates within to help others is often difficult to wield against our own personal dark sides. Picture a doctor who is a successful surgeon, performing skillful operations on his patients. However, the doctor becomes sick and must operate on himself. He must figure out how to anesthetize himself and stay conscious to perform his own procedure. He must also figure out how to utilize his tools and place his body in a position that frees his hands to work. He must use his scalpel in a way his vital organs are in view while operating on himself upon his back. After surgery, he must stitch himself up and not lose consciousness. The procedure is a virtual impossibility. However, it has been done.

The Pastor And His Thigh

Leonid Ivanovich Rogozov, a Soviet general practitioner performed an appendectomy on himself on May 1, 1961. Some assistants were holding a mirror for Rogozov to observe areas not directly visible. Ivanovich was positioned half-way on his side in a semi-reclined position. The operation was not without complications as he accidentally injured his cecum and had to suture it. He also had strong bouts of weakness and nausea that developed thirty to forty minutes into his operation. As a result, he would repeatedly have short pauses of rest. Nevertheless, his operation was successful. If the pastor uses the same tools on himself that he uses on others, it can be a nauseating operation. However, if he has a mirror, it is possible. God was the mirror through which Jacob could look to see his sickness. We must do as my cousin, Melvin V. Wade, Jr. would say, "We must do what we know to do until God gives us greater light."

Yet, when God operates on us, it is less risky, but it will require more resilience. God wants us to be awake every step of the way to behold each incision necessary to bring us into wholeness and forever remember that the ring of change is not to be entered into lightly. If we want to win, we must put in the work. Yet, we need a hand to hold. We are to consciously hold to God's hand when God appears as though He is shutting down the operation before we are completely cured. We hold His hand and cry out to Him, "I will not let your hand go. I will not let you stitch me up until this operation is over!" While we are in a state of consciousness, we do not have the privilege of an anesthetic that deadens our pain, and we do not have the privilege of controlling the incisions God induces in our character. We need to feel the pain of the operation because we must discover when there is no pain, there is no gain. Change is painful, and pain is often, change; make no mistake about it. When God sees we are still holding on to His hand while He is also cutting us with corrective cures, His grace transforms our wounded anatomies into vessels of honor sanctified for His use. We possess within the will, drive, and desperation to fight for what God placed within our reach, and deep within, He knows we will do anything to never rob ourselves or anyone else again. It is after our transformation that we are left with graceful, yet obvious reminders of the robbers we used to be.

Understanding God's desire for Jacob's transformation and Jacob's desperation to be transformed, it is quite clear why God impaled Jacob's thigh (hip joint). Jacob's limp has nothing to do with God using us despite our faults although that principle is true. Our limps are not sins we must learn to live with. Instead, our limps keep us from running toward sins that can kill us. Our limps are the painful measures God induces in our lives that delivers us from ourselves. To properly understand Jacob's limp is to recognize Jacob would be heavenly handicapped for the rest of his life as God stunted Jacob's mobility so that he could never run from transformation again.

Jacob had been on the run from Esau long enough to realize he had nowhere else to run. Everything and everyone he cared about was slowing him down from the limp of a lifetime. His success was slowing him down. His marriages were slowing him down. He was not a single man anymore. His family was slowing him down. Now, he is married to two wives, and he has children. Jacob had too many titles that tainted his transformation. Thus, he had too many responsibilities that kept him too busy to focus on himself. He was a father, a husband, and an heir. All those titles can keep a man busy and distracted from dealing with his dysfunctions for the rest of his life. God had to give Jacob a temporary separation from his wives and pull his children out of the nest prematurely for Jacob to focus on the fact that he truly couldn't help others until he learned how to help himself.

Jacob also had a certain level of status with great material wealth (*The Birthright*), and great spiritual wealth (*The Blessing*). He had his family and possessions with him, and they could not keep running because of him. It was not their battle. If he were to sustain his inheritance, he could not continue with the corrupt character he condoned and covered. His family had done nothing wrong. He could not let his foolishness jeopardize everything and everyone he loved. When someone is bent towards destroying you, they will go after whatever and whoever you care about. They will even try to shrink your circle. Then, you may discover that not all who were in your circle were in your corner. You must strategically move those who you love out of the way of the stray bullets of the carelessness of those who you offended. People who we may have robbed are not straight shooters. They think they are, but they are not. They are too full of the sin of vengeance to think or see clearly because they have meanness on their minds and rage in their retinas. Everyone in Jacob's family was in danger of a man they were related to, i.e., Esau, Jacob's brother. Esau was either their uncle or brother-in-law. Esau was so bent on catching up with Jacob that even his family meant nothing to him.

Although we have no stated evidence that Esau would have harmed his own relatives, Jacob's fear of his family being in danger lets us know the potential threat Esau was to them as well. If Esau cared about Jacob's family, who were his relatives, he would have realized hurting Jacob would have hurt them. Vengeance runs wide. When one takes vengeance personally for offenses done, such a one will have issues with anyone in your circle who is loyal to you. Those who are offended lose all sensitivity to the bigger picture. Because Esau felt violated by his brother, Esau was a miserable man. When misery takes hold to a person on this level, such a person develops tunnel vision. The only person they see is the one who they are hunting.

Little did Esau understand that it was *he* who did not value what he had. Esau should have been hunting for his own history lesson. Of course, Esau knew he let his success slip away, but he could not connect the dots and just move on with the rest of his life and appreciate what God still allowed him to have. He had to try to take Jacob down because he saw no way up. Jacob valued *The Birthright*, even if it meant taking advantage of Esau to get it, but Esau threw it all away for the *meat* of the moment. Notice the text:

"...Lest there be any fornicator, or profane person as Esau, who for one morsel of meat sold his birthright."

(Hebrews 12:16; KJV)

While Esau could only see himself as a robbed victim, God described him as a profane person. Esau sold his birthright for one morsel of meat. One little hunger game can turn a person's life around for the worse. When Esau tried to get everything back that he let slip away, he discovered how he had gone too far. Now, Esau is permanently unhappy because he sees why he can never get back what he took for granted. Esau was dealing with that old saying, *"You don't miss your water til' your well runs dry."* Since Esau was not happy, he didn't want Jacob or anyone within his circle to be blessed by what Jacob had. Esau's bitterness blinded him to the fact that there was a God. The same God who reminded Esau that he let it all slip away was the same God who was going to make sure Jacob paid for everything he had stolen although Jacob couldn't return a dime of it to Esau.

One of the greatest prices a man can pay for his sins is to become purged. Change comes at a high price. The price Jacob was going to pay was a divine blow from God, and his limp was his receipt of payment. I love God, but when I am wrong, I do not want God to touch me because the hands of God are mighty heavy. When God touches us up, it can be terrifying. As a matter of fact, it is the most painful experience we will ever know. Heavenly pain keeps a man accountable for his actions on Earth. When God hurts a man on this level, he feels that pain for the rest of his life. Sanctification stings. Do not think for one moment that the pain Jacob experienced when God struck him on the thigh ever went away.

Spanking children is prohibited today, but I thank God it was not when I was growing up. If we spare the rod, we spoil the child (Proverbs 13:24). When my father spanked me, I would sometimes pull a stunt, fall to the floor, and play dead. I would do this as a trick to get him to have sympathy for me. Instead of getting affection, it made my father even angrier. He spanked me so hard that I thought he was trying to kill me. Well, it never worked. He would say, "Get up boy, you *ain't* dead. You should have thought about how bad this would hurt when you did what you did!" I understood that, but he would say something I just could not understand at the time. He would say, "Son, this hurts me more than it hurts you!" His spankings were controlled, but they were extremely painful. That was his point. If it did not hurt, it did not help. I remembered the pain, days, months, and even years later. I can almost feel it now. The pain went away a few days later, but the memory of the pain stings to this very day. It was the pain that reminded me to never do that again. Because I remember the pain, I remember my problem. My father spanked me in a way that made sure I never became guilty of repeated failures.

Most of all, when God disciplines us, it hurts Him more than it hurts us. Once we get that point, we sacrifice our gloom on behalf of his Glory. God disciplines in ways that prevent us from repeated failures. There was no way God was going to let Esau or Jacob get away with thinking they were hurt more than God was.

God taught Esau to never chase down a man who cheated him, and never let what God ordained slip away because of some hunger game. When Jacob was healed from within, his limp taught him the pointlessness of running from his past. With a limp, Esau would be sure to catch up with Jacob. It is easier to face your enemies when you learn to live with your limp. Then, it does not matter whether your past catches up with you or not. Although Jacob was running from Esau, he was running from himself a lot longer and a lot faster. With a healed character, it did not matter anymore to Jacob whether he was dead or alive. Jacob could let his past take its course. A limp would slow Jacob down enough to face his foes. With a broken spirit, God was sure to catch Jacob's attention as well. A pastor who has been changed can know that at the end of the day, it does not matter what Esau tries to do to him. Here is a powerful truth: ***Our past only has the power to overtake us when we continue to run from it.*** Doesn't this make sense? Since it is only God who can perform such an operation on our character, it is only God who can turn the hot pursuit of our past into a predestined purpose.

I am fifty-two years old. I am too old to be young, and I am too young to be old. I always loved basketball. Until the last seven years, I would play basketball quite frequently. However, I acquired a tender and sore spot in my left hip joint. Regardless, I attribute my pain to a lack of exercise. Those closest to me chuckle and tell me the best is yet to come. I am aging. My mind still tells me I can run several pick-up games just as I did years ago. However, as I get out of bed, I sometimes feel a pain in my left hip joint that reminds me to think twice before I try to run like I used to. Such is the case with Jacob's limp as well as our own. God leaves us with painful and aging reminders that we cannot *run game* like we used to. After we have been transformed by God's painful measures, God reminds us why we cannot *run away* like we used to; neither can we *run around* like we used to. When our minds want to tell us we can, our injuries God inflicted upon us remind us that we cannot. Now that I have aged, I still play basketball. However, I play smarter and not harder. When we have matured and learned to accept the fact that God slowed us down, we work in this life smarter and not harder.

Sometimes, it is hard to see the need for change since we were born with a flawed character. ***Until we have been changed, a subtle way of surviving and selfishly succeeding is all we know to do.*** It was our coping mechanism and our survival skill. It can also be challenging to remember where we came from after God does a work in our lives. It is easy for any of us to get beside ourselves now that we are more mature. However, a huge plug out of your hip will remind you that you were not born doing everything right, and we will not die doing everything right.

It was God who gruesomely gashed Jacob's hip. Jacob was not born with that deformity. Leaders are not born leaders, but they are made to be leaders. We were not born changed men. Once we say we have been changed, God will often put us on bumpy and long roads our legs cannot endure without His help. The road to Glory is a tedious journey. This reminds us that we need *Him*, and it also reminds us to never become self-sufficient and sole survivors ever again. We need a permanent plug taken out of our lives to remind us that we do not have it all together. Our natural inclination is to be self-sufficient. Once we have gotten to certain levels, we can tend to forget the simplest and most significant things and people in life. There is a self-sufficiency that will rise within us that God calls, *pride*. Pride can trip us up at any given moment. God gives us permanent impairments to keep us conscious of the fact that pride goes before destruction, and a haughty spirit goes before a fall (Proverbs 16:18).

It is not until we have been metamorphosized and maimed that we realize truths of triumph. God has a way of slowing us down so that we pay attention to future steps we take. Thus, it is much more gratifying to embrace our limps and be grateful for our gropes. Our limps are those personal but painful ways God has of reminding us not to allow our characters to be polluted by unseen forces, seeds of iniquity sown within the womb, dysfunctional families, unbridled ambitions, personal torments of insecurity, and indescribable demons. In addition, our limps are those painful ways God causes us to depend upon Him for every future move we make so our steps will be ordered by Him (Psalm 37:23). From that point on, God was going to be Jacob's crutch. It is a beautiful thing to be crippled by God when God is your crutch.

Regarding pastors, our healing is not always as complete as others. God leaves us with a crippling calling. When others are healed, one does not always see scars remaining. When pastors are healed, our scars may be seen. Our wounds are our witness. Our torn tissues are our testimonies. Jacob's limp would give others an obvious and perpetual glance at a change in Jacob's walk. It was also ugly enough for people to see how God hits hard. They see something messed up about us as ministers, but we know it was God who messed us up in a merciful way. God's men never get away scot-free. There is always a high price a preacher must pay for purposeful promotion. God sometimes puts the receipt in others' hands for them to understand how much it cost a preacher for God to turn his life around.

It was not Esau who motivated Jacob to change. Esau just motivated Jacob to stay out of harm's way. Jacob was motivated to change when God struck him with something he could feel. Anybody who vindictively puts a changed man's receipt of payment in the streets is giving him a free advertisement. It only puts him on a platform for the grace of God to be seen in his life. As Pastor

Sylvester Washington of the Pleasant Hill Baptist Church would say, *"If you live right, no matter what you have done, God will allow you to live down whatever others said about you."*

God removed Jacob's swagger and gave him a stagger. Every changed man of God is a staggering man. A stagger will get a preacher further with God than his swagger. Swagger impresses people, but a stagger impresses God. A staggering man has been painfully impaled by God in a way that reminds him where his true help comes from. When we have been changed, God has a way of making sure others know it. They see our change more than they see our chastisement. They see our new successes more than they see our sins. After God was finished with Jacob, Esau could not help but see a man who had been divinely disciplined and faithfully forgiven. In my opinion, Jacob stands out more as the man who wrestled with God than the man who was a deceiver. Although Jacob was healed, he lived with a stigma that would stay with him for the rest of his life. People still tend to see Jacob as the Deceiver. Rarely do people call him who God called him, i.e., "Israel" (Genesis 32:28). Jacob was no longer concerned about looking polished, but he was consecrated to living on purpose.

God did not allow others to see the intense fight He instigated with Jacob, but He did let others see the outcome. You can look at the face of a boxer after a match and tell if he was in a brutal battle, even if you did not see the fight. God could have easily induced an audience to view the fight of the century: God versus Jacob the Deceiver. God could have caused his family to make a U-turn and view Jacob's operation through the windows of the eyes of God. God could have picked a fight with Jacob in front of his family and given them front row seats. He could have also done it in front of Esau. However, what good would that have done? To Jacob's enemies, that would have only been entertainment. As far as his family was concerned, all they would have done was try to protect Jacob from the fight of a lifetime because God hit Jacob so hard, they wouldn't have been able to stand the sight. Thinking it was a man, they would have come to Jacob's defense and got severely hurt in the process. It is not wise to interfere when God is working on one of his men. It is also possible they would have been pleading with God to stop the fight. Family will unintentionally enable you, but God will intentionally disable you.

The things a pastor must fight are his fight. No one has the right, ability, or authority to get too involved, even if they have good intentions. If a pastor wronged anyone, he hurt God and himself more than anyone else. It is interesting how some people take a pastor's flaws personal. When we examine the inner struggles of men and women of God who battled for the change of their lives, they were never in the face of a live audience. Each major contender in the Holy Scriptures who had deep struggles of soul battled with God behind closed quarters. Moses wrestled on the back side of the desert, alone. Abraham wrestled on Mount Moriah, alone. Hannah wrestled in prayer, alone. The only signs Eli could see of Hannah's struggle, he mistook for drunkenness. David's struggles with his soul were alone. Saul was struck down on the Damascus Road, alone. All observers could see was a light, but they could not hear God's conversation with Saul. Hezekiah prayed for healing, alone. Jesus wrestled in Gethsemane, alone. The disciples could not even tarry for an hour. Jeremiah stood amid ashes, alone. Boiled alive in a cistern before being exiled, John was on the isle of Patmos receiving *The Revelation*, alone. God wrestled racism out of Peter when Peter received God's vision on the rooftop, alone. Samson stood between two pillars, asked God for a new burst of power, and defeated the Philistines, alone. Jonah was in the belly of the whale, alone. Habakkuk wrestled with the discipline of losing everything, alone. Job asked for an appeal for God to answer him during his days of testing, alone. The operations of God on His servants must be done in secret, alone.

God desires intimacy with who He loves. Transformation necessitates intimacy with God. Anyone present or involved other than the Transformer (God) would be bad company. They would be an interruption of that intimacy. God delights in one-on-one encounters with His men although many dread them. Oftentimes, when we seek transformation, we wish we were in the company of others who could hold our hand as we go under the knife of God.

People often want to know what made a man change. The most important thing is that he changed. They would not understand, even if we told them. We do not even fully understand what really happened on that dark night of deliverance for Jacob. It is not always consequences that change a man. It is an encounter with God that changes a man. If Esau would have caught up with Jacob before God did, all Jacob could offer Esau was an apology. Our apologies do not cleanse, comfort, or cure the ones we offended, but God is pleased by our confessions (I John 1:9). Sometimes, what God uses to induce change is secret and sacred. People may mistake the process, but they cannot deny the power. Of all the things people could say, they could never say Jacob walked the same. In addition, they could never say Jacob walked alone. They could easily see that God was with him. Sometimes, our walk will do the talking. Change has a language of its own, and real change induced by God will always be heard.

This striking of Jacob's thigh was no mere puncture. It was a deep abrasion of the tendon that caused a powerful defect in Jacob's joints. When God strikes His men, it hurts like Hell, but it heals like Heaven. After God afflicts us, what we say after that becomes the reflexive comment that turns our lives around. After God hit Jacob, his next response was not, *"That hurts"*, but his next response was, *"Lord, I need Thee, every hour."* More accurately, *"I won't let You go until You bless me."* Jacob did not walk with a subtle limp, but he walked with an ugly dragging of his leg that even the strongest skeptic could not deny. Herein is the measure of our transformation. Although our enemies seek to do us great harm, no man could have wounded Jacob like God did. When Esau saw Jacob, he knew something divine struck him.

When God profoundly changes our lives, it becomes uniquely obvious and sometimes, it gets downright ugly. Although our afflictions may be ugly to others, they are beautiful in God's eyes because they come from Him. Even if there may be some *unusual* who denies our drag, a divine drag in our steps is obvious to anyone who understands the deadly sport of wrestling with God. With a drag-walk, we never walk alone. His limp was so severe that no cane or companion would have been enough to support him. He needed God to prop him up on every leaning side and not just on the side of his limp. Now, Jacob has learned to take the Lord with him everywhere he went.

Pastor M. V. Wade, Sr. preached a sermon on this passage and entitled it, "Living with a Limp." During that time, I was quite self-sufficient. Somehow, I knew one day, I would learn to know what that really meant. Now, I know for myself. When we learn to live with a limp, God goes with us, assisting us along the way, just in case we stumble. With a limp, we should no longer worry about what is behind us. All we must do is keep our gaze on what God has set before us. God is not interested in the speed of our flight from our past. God is interested in us walking the road to Glory, one step at a time, one day at a time and in God's own time. He is concerned about ordering our steps. He does not want us to get in a hurry to move forward. Furthermore, God does not want us to rush our way into royalty. We will receive our crowns *after* we bear our crosses. The walk of faith is a slow, drag-like walk that keeps us depending upon Him every step of the way. The pastor who has been transformed has godly impediments and not worldly ones. The world is behind us, and the Cross is before us. We must never forget that. God keeps our feet from falling and guides us along life's highway.

With an ugly incision in our lives, God gives us an ugly grace. More emphatically, a *gracious ugliness* is applied to our lives that is most precious to us as changed men. A *divine deformity* is the by-product of God's gracious methods of making us princes according to His good pleasure (Genesis 32:28). A *merciful malady* is induced in our anatomy to not only keep us in remembrance of the real forces that induce change but also to keep us changed. With a *weakened walk* and a *ruined run*, we will never trot from transformation. A *stumbling stability* is the most precious commodity that divinely assures we will never be quick to turn out of the way of salvation ever again.

Maimed ministers are not a mistake although they made mistakes. They are the broken men who God uses. That is what this book is about. Staggering preachers are the ugly men who have an unction. God blesses men with broken bones, broken lives, broken hearts, broken families, and broken spirits. Such men limp toward the pulpit and walk by faith while those who deny transformation make futile leaps in life, only to fall flat on their faces. God's men have a stumbling way of striding. If they cannot run, they walk. If they cannot walk, they crawl. Either way, they will get there. They will be just fine. People in question are not the crippled men of God who have been struck by the Master's hand. People in question are those who are too proud to beg to be beaten by God into a tenderized servant of God. People in question are the ones who feel they cannot afford to live on one leg as they despise God's discipline and curse His correction (Provers 3:11).

Jacob admitted who he was not for God to make him into who he truly was. While others glory in our success, we glory in our shame. While men praise us for our strengths, we boast in our infirmities, that the power of God may rest upon us. Because we have gone to the mat with God, we know it is only when we are weak that we are made strong. How we remember the day when we gave up on ourselves, but God never gave up on us. We can run to the ring when we are right and when we are wrong. We graciously preach that privilege to others, and we shout that *God saves* from the mountaintops. God will ensure we are recipients of that same grace. When we preach how Jesus saves on behalf of some, they receive it in a salvific fashion. When we preach how Jesus saves on behalf of ourselves, others receive it in a scandalous fashion. Nevertheless, salvation belongs to whom God wills, even if it is for the preacher who once was lost, but now is found.

Not everyone wants us to be a recipient of that same grace. That is only because they have not been changed. You see, when we all have been changed, we look the same because we become more like Jesus. God will not forget us, and He will remember our humble cries and give us the graces to grope our way to Glory. When we get there, God will remove the marks of that sanctifying stroke and give us a blessed body and fresh pair of legs. When we get to Heaven, we will drop that drag and take flight like birds in the morning. We will be Home, and we will not have to cry for change anymore because we will be changed (I Corinthians 15:51). We will not have to limp in the Afterlife. We will walk that road to Glory, our Lord and ourselves. We will leap through Heaven's gates with lively limbs and glorified bodies, thanking God for how He brought us over.

There was a day when we cried because we felt we were deprived of that which would give us significance. Then, we cried due to the consequences of taking what was not ours to take. Now, we cry because we are broken behind the buffeting grace extended to us on that nocturnal day as we accepted God's challenge to become champions. We needed that night, and He gave us a shot at the title of transformation and a new beginning. We praise God that we serve a God who does not mind losing. The battles God loves to lose are the ones He wants us to win. God does not mind losing the battle for change. God does not need to change, but we do. As a matter of fact, God never changes. True champions in this life are the ones who win the battle for change. Now, we weep because we are grateful for a deliverance we did not deserve.

Our guilt and shame have been removed. Our only disappointment is in the fact that there will yet be others who refuse to partake of God's saving grace. That grace is free, but it is not cheap. It will cost. It will cost a bracing of the body that stands resilient enough to endure a pain induced by God that could kill you if you cannot stand to be corrected. We live with deadly deficiencies that only God's sustaining grace can prevent from taking us to the grave prematurely. We can never judge cheaters, thieves, robbers, and liars who were ambushed by ambition. If we were ever granted that mammoth ministry to minister to the manipulative, our only desire is to serve the scandalous the same comfort wherewith we were comforted.

These are the *ugly unctions* that makes men meaningful ministers. They understand that God must sometimes hurt us to heal us. We have seen God face-to-face, and by His grace, our lives were spared, and we have prevailed (Genesis 32:30). Yes, there is an ugliness about most of us. Make no mistake about it. We are not the most attractive men in the eyes of most, but God sees us as princes who won the war for our souls. We may not be everything we should be, but thank God, we are not who we used to be.

Chapter 12

THE PASTOR AND HIS KNEES

Prayer, the Most Unpopular Practice in the Church
(An Excerpt from the Life of James:
A preacher whose actions were louder than his words)

Tribute: To James A. Temple, (Pastor of Pilgrim's Rest Missionary Baptist Church of Omaha, NE)

James A. Temple is my uncle who baptized me at an early age. He spoiled me rotten, but he also challenged me to be a man. He has a graceful way with his words, a powerful thinker, and a preacher who can teach flatfooted on a Sunday morning. Yet, he does most of his thinking on his knees. He is a praying man who gets his thoughts from God. Among preachers, I can easily guess our peak levels of interest in preaching. However, it is quite difficult to assess what our true peak levels are in praying. Most of us do not do it as often as we should, and we struggle at it if we are honest. Not so with Uncle James, when he prays, he comes alive. It is almost as if you are looking at a completely different man. There are a lot of preachers who we love to hear preach, but how many do we love to hear Pray? We love to preach, but do we love to pray?

The Epistle of James was written around AD 45. For this reason, the book is considered the earliest of New Testament writings. Traditionally, most scholars agree it was written by James, the brother of Jesus. The book of James was addressed to the twelve tribes of the Dispersion during great persecution. The linguistic style of the book is written in precise Greek language while maintaining strong Hebraic imagery. James was exhorting Believers to stand fast, knowing their trials would produce perseverance. The book is noted for its extensive discourse on faith and works, declaring we are justified by works of faith. James' basic premise is that genuine faith has works that follow. To be justified by works is to be justified by a works that is the result of faith.

James was a straightforward writer who strikes at the root of practical local church issues. When I was earning my B. A. Degree in Biblical Studies at the Criswell College many years ago, Dr. David Allen was one of my professors. During that time, he believed James to also be the author of Hebrews; a view that was very unpopular, especially during that time. I would not doubt if James also wrote the book of Hebrews.

Nevertheless, James' discourses on prayer address methods to pray in a way that powerful results follow. He is one of the most unpopular men in Christendom because he addresses issues head-on with truthfulness and frankness. The brevity of the book of James in no way hinders its effectiveness. It is dynamic in nature and pointedly calls for radical Christian responses in at least three of the most important dimensions of a Christian's life, i.e., Christian persecution, Christian practice, and Christian prayer.

As we are caught unexpectedly by trials of all sorts, we are on a continual character-building, leadership-challenging, faith-developing wheel. How we position ourselves in prayer is a vital element for maintaining a healthy pastoral personality. Because we are pastors, we have a vast amount of spiritual disciplines at our disposal when it comes to adversity. When it comes to our own personal crisis, one of the problems is trying to figure out which way is up. We need wisdom that supersedes knowledge. Wisdom narrows our option and is obtained through prayer (James 1:5).

The Greek word for wisdom is *sophia* (σοφία), which refers to understanding how to apply what we know. Much of our pastoral perplexity is in knowing that we are involved in a delicate profession that demands accurate application. We have been prone to have suffered heart attacks, strokes, stressful diseases, ulcers, high blood pressure, and even moral failure because some of us made the wrong moves under pressure. It takes skill to apply God's commands to our crisis. When in the fire, the Bible promises that God will give us the skill to know exactly what to do if we ask in faith. Scripture is definitive about what conditions the prayer of faith should be exercised:

> *"But let him ask in faith, nothing **wavering**. For he that **wavereth** is like a wave of the sea driven with the wind and tossed. For let not that man think that he shall receive anything of the Lord."*
>
> (James 1:6-7; KJV)

The word for wavering is *diakrino* (διακρίνω). It refers to a kind of doubt that comes from one's instability. This instability causes the person to be easily swayed by opposing forces. There is a dangerous doubt that can kill an answer to prayer. An unstable man will not receive answers to prayer. Instability comes when we allow circumstances to sway our beliefs. This type of doubt will cause one to sink in the storm. It is not the power of the storm that sinks him, but it is the power of his duplicity (doublemindedness) that sinks him in the storm. Doubt is not always in God's ability but in our own stability to trust God in the trial. The consequences of such doubt are frightening. If we doubt, we will not receive *anything* of the Lord; not even the wisdom that we need.

God is almost merciless when it comes to our lack of faith (Matthew 17:17). Without faith, it truly is impossible to please God. Jesus has been known to be angered at unbelief regardless of the power of the tests and the persons who are tested. The *prayer of faith* is prayer that is not talking to God about the pressure as much as believing God will mature us into realizations of His purpose and power in the pressure. We do not wait on God to move the problem, but we wait on God to release the solution. The prayer of faith will fortify us in the fire, but it will *back-fire* if we attempt to utilize it for personal agendas. James addresses a selfish and entitled sense of praying. James 4:1-3 reflects how the lustful nature within can become a major hindrance to the prayer of faith. Prayer is not always a noble exercise because there are different types of prayer. There are prayers of doubt, selfish prayers, and hypocritical prayers with vain repetitions. Prayer is not an end in and of itself, but it is a means to an end. Prayer is not to be deified as if it has an inherent power of its own.

God does not answer certain types of prayers. When God goes silent under the sound of our supplications, James reminds us to monitor our motives and recognize every good and perfect gift comes from the Father of lights (James 1:17). One *yes* from God may lead to another request from us. Lust for more luxuries keeps us from learning when enough is enough. We may ask for a building, and God grants it. Next, we may see an opportunity to own the adjacent building, and God grants it. Next, we may want the entire block. One campus leads to another campus. Growth is one thing, but greed is another. Sooner or later, we can come to know when to be content with what God has allotted and respect the borders that God granted to another.

Seasoned generations of pastors in the past appeared to respect the fences that separated one pastor's ministry from another's. Pastors were not interested in duplicating or competing with a specialized ministry another pastor possessed. They were wise enough not to reinvent another pastor's wheel. Furthermore, pastors were not interested in overlapping another pastor's allotment. James Temple respects other pastor's borders. He is not jealous. He just seemed to resent the fact that others appeared to appreciate their borders while depreciating his. He is a supportive cast to other preachers and pastors.

What we acquired by personal ambition becomes our liability during trials and tests. A large percentage of the tangibles we acquire in and for ministry can be to our own demise. The time we spent acquiring unnecessary wealth makes us weak. The energy we extend in acquiring externals leaves us empty of joy during suffering. Material things mean nothing when we are in the fire. As a matter of fact, our material things add more fuel to the fire. When we have nothing left but our faith, the fire will eventually die because fire cannot burn faith. It only purifies it as pure gold (Job 23:10).

As we streamline our requests to the nature of the objectives God called for us to obtain, the answers to our prayers flow into our hands more gracefully. Then, we have something to believe in, and God has something to give. As we bear a conscience that remains discerning to the slightest touches of vainglory and personal ambition, God can trust us with *enough* because we will take our blessings seriously and use them soberly.

Fortunately, when we are under pressure, ambitious, envious, and covetous desires no longer matter. *More* does not matter when we are in the fire. The only thing that matters when we are in the fire is *enough*. As long as God's grace is sufficient, we have *enough* to endure. Sufficiency is one of the most critical commodities of Christianity. What matters is that we have enough faith, enough perseverance, enough patience, enough wisdom, enough strength, enough grace, and enough Christlikeness to get through the day.

The knees are the most humiliating organs of our anatomy because we are forced to abandon erect postures that portray dispositions of self-sufficiency. Most of us as pastors like to walk tall because we are proud of our profession. Our most powerful posture is on our knees. The knees balance us by soberly reminding us who God is and who we are not. James reminds us that we bow before a God who resists the proud but gives grace to the humble (James 4:6). Our anatomy is incomplete unless we learn to bring every organ to the knee. At the knee, we consecrate every function of our anatomy to operate in faith. It is on our knees that battles are won, and our most sinister motives are revealed. We need not suffer the examination of men because we are allotted private time with God to place our dirty linen in His throne room. We have the advantage of settling our selfish pursuits with God alone and arise off our knees with a cleansing that critics presume never existed.

One of the humbling measurements of the quality of our churches is to examine if we have a praying church. A praying church constitutes a healthy church above and beyond a core group of Believers who are the church's prayer warriors. Furthermore, we are not referring to a sophisticated or specialized intercessory ministry that is reserved for a few. Prayer is not just a core group ministry. It is a corporate mandate. In a strong sense, our churches are no larger or stronger than the power of our prayer gatherings.

James teaches us how to make faith *work*, how to make persecution *work*, how to make prayer *work*, and how to make healing *work*. The last mention of prayer is in the last chapter of the book of James. Out of the blue, James appears to crescendo to another melody. He reveals the power of prayer and how prayer brings results in the corporate dimensions of Believers. James' emphasis is more on a healthy church than a huge one. The type of health that he is concerned about is deeper than superficial healing of the body or some healing and deliverance service. The problem with the church of whom James was addressing was that they were not healthy regardless of how many members they had. The sicknesses in that church had much to do with sin, demonic afflictions, divisions, strife, envy, and fighting. James related healing to the condition of our souls:

> *"Is any among you afflicted? Let him <u>pray</u>. Is any merry? Let him sing psalms. Is any sick among you? Let him call for the elders of the church; and let them <u>pray</u> over him, anointing him with oil in the name of the Lord: And <u>the prayer of faith</u> shall save the sick, and the Lord shall raise him up;* **and if he hath committed sins, they shall be forgiven him. Confess your faults one to another**, *and <u>pray</u> one for another, that ye may be healed. The effectual fervent <u>prayer</u> of a righteous man availeth much."*

(James 5:13-16; KJV)

In four verses, prayer is mentioned five times. Precision is James' style. He is sharp and to the point. The issue is once again, the power of prayer, especially the prayer of faith. James is pointing to a particular type of prayer. The prayer of faith operates like a formula. When administered under the right conditions, *it works* every time. There are certain conditions that must occur that warrants the usage of the prayer of faith.

First, one must suffer the satanic. The word for *afflicted* is *kakopatheo* (κακοπαθέω), which means, *to suffer ills due to evil*. When one suffers evils, the antidote is prayer. Prayer counters evil when we pray with that objective. James is giving the remedy for demonic oppression in the formula of the prayer of faith.

Secondly, one must be sick. James 5:13-16 almost seems too good to be true. It is interesting how widely James' teachings on counting it joy are accepted, but his teachings on healing are often rejected, diluted, or taken out of context. James is showing us how faith works. Just as faith works under fire, faith also works when we are feeble. While it is true that God does not heal all sicknesses, God will answer the prayer of faith when applied in its proper context. God does not answer every prayer that is *offered in faith*, but God does answer every *prayer of faith*. The essence of James' argument is within teaching the church to enlist in a form of prayer that works. When certain sicknesses arise, prayer is also to be employed. In this type of scenario, the formula of the prayer of faith is to be exercised, and the Lord will raise the individual off the sickbed. In James 5:14, the word for sickness is *astheneo* (ἀσθενέω), which refers to the feebleness of body.

Sick and feeble bodies were to be anointed with oil. Although James commands the elders to anoint with oil, the formula for healing has very little to do with oil or elders. The Greek word for *anoint* in this passage refers to anointing with oil for medicinal purposes. If interpreters put more emphasis on the oil, they would have to be consistent by recognizing they would also have to put the same emphasis on medicine. However, James does not say that medicine will raise the individual nor does he say that it is prayer accompanied with medicine that will raise the individual. Furthermore, elders do not constitute the reason for the healing of the sick, but it is the *prayer of faith* that will raise the individual that constitutes healing regardless of whether medicine oil and elders are present or not.

It is also important to remember that New Testament elders were equivalent to pastors. Yet, the presence of anointing ointments and elders must not be dismissed. If these pastors or elders are to exist today, they are to have a healthy understanding of

Hamartiology, Pneumatology, Christology, and Theology for healing to truly take place. A healthy church also consists of a plurality of pastors (James 5:14). Yet, these were no ordinary pastors. They were elders who had just as much prayer power as preaching power. Notice the fact that there is no emphasis on faith-healers. Thus, elders (pastors) must have a sound theology of healing that realizes why and when God *does* want to heal the sick.

Thirdly, one must be a sinner. Part of the premise for healing is based upon the fact that God wills a healthy Church. James teaches us that much of church health has to do with confessing our sins. Some sicknesses are the result of sin. Sin and faults make the Body (Church) sick (James 5:16). It is not Jesus' will to have a sick Bride. Thus, James refers to a type of healing that addresses sins at the core. As a result, healing involved deliverance from sin as much as it involved deliverance from sickness. There are some diseases that will remain because the sin remains. Herein lies an important principle in the theology of healing. The healing of the disease is *not* Jesus' number one priority, but the forgiveness of the sin is (Mark 2:9). The arrangement of the grammar in relation to the raising of the sick off the sick bed is about a sickness that is unto death. James is referring to those who have been afflicted with illnesses and are dying before their appointed time due to some unconfessed and continually practiced sin.

Some illnesses are self-inflicted. Therefore, further discourse on sickness is given. Because of the confession of sins and faults, we may continue to be healed (James 5:15). There is a strong level of integrity that must accompany healing. In other words, God does not desire to heal a person who continues in a sinful lifestyle, and neither does He desire to keep a person in bondage to sickness who has confessed and forsaken his or her sinful lifestyle. James is exemplifying in leadership what should be imitated in his followers. Kingdom laws establish the fundamental truth that

God has not chosen to do certain acts apart from the prayers of His people. He has facilitated our victory by giving us formulas of prayer that will activate miraculous results when we pray and pray mightily.

James beautifully places a capstone on how the sinner is converted from his ways that led to his sickness. James even states that a brother who errs from the truth and is converted by another Believer is saved from death. The context suggests the death that James is referring to is one that would have been the result of a sick-inflicting sin. When we understand this context, James 5:19-20 takes on a totally different twist regarding prayer that saves a person from deadly diseases.

Fourthly, one must have supplicating stamina. What distinguishes this type of prayer is the type of person who prays and the type of praying that is prayed. The person who prays with the prayer of faith must also have the stamina, character, and strength of Elijah (James 5:17-18). James even makes Old Testament reference to Elijah, which bridges dispensational gaps and teaches us about a type of prayer that is accurate for our age. The same power that Elijah tapped into is available today. The difference is not *that* he prayed, but *how* he prayed. There is no distinction in who is praying. James tells us that Elijah was a man who was subject to the same passions as ourselves. Yet, Elijah prayed effectually, fervently, and earnestly.

The word for *effectual* is *energeo* (ἐνεργέω), which means *energetic, strong, alive,* and *power-induced* praying. We get our English word, *energy* from this Greek word. To think of *energeo* in terms of modern-day energy would dilute the transliteration of the Greek word. James' praying was not electrifying or explosive. It was forceful. Studying how energy worked for Elijah, one cannot remove the Spirit by which Elijah flowed. His ministerial flow was in the Spirit and with power. When we think of the energetic praying of Elijah, it was strong, Spirit and power-induced praying. It was forcefully supernatural.

There were additions to Elijah's praying. James 5:16 states how the *effectual fervent prayer of a righteousness man has much force*. The prayer referred to in this text is *deēsis* (δέησις), which has to do with continual supplication. This type of supplication involves bearing a matter to God continually until there are results. It is the same type of praying that Elijah did when he was praying for rain. He continually prayed until rain broke forth. Notice Elijah's prayer in verse 17 was a *prayer prayed earnestly*. Notice how distinctively James utilizes the Greek language in verses 16-18:

> *"The effectual fervent **prayer** (deesis) of a righteous man availeth much (verse 16). Elias was a man subject to like passions as we are, and he **prayed** (proseuche) **earnestly** (proseuche) that it might not rain: and it rained not on the Earth by the space of three years and six months (verse 17). And he **prayed** (proseucheomai) again, and the heaven gave rain, and the earth brought forth her fruit" (verse 18).*

"*Prayed*" in verses 17 and 18 is not the same as verse 16. The word for prayed in verse 18 is *proseuchomai*, which means to *offer prayers* (plural). The word for *prayed earnestly* in verse 17 is proseuche, which means, *to pray*. In verse 16, the word for pray is *deesis*, which means, *supplication*. Interpreting the text, it would read like this:

> *"The strong, Spirit-empowered, continual bearing up of a matter before God of a righteous man has much force . . . and he prayed, praying that it might not rain....and he prayed prayers again..."*

The kind of praying James is referring to is comparable to a man who is pushing an object until it is in its proper position. The old folks in my family called it, "praying until you get a prayer through". It is prayer that pushes back the darkness (James 5:13) and the disease (James 5:16). James' concept of prayer that brings results is a type of praying that is strong, Spirit-induced *pushing-praying* that is persistent until the promised results are in perspective. We are not pushing God to do anything. We are pushing back the darkness or disease through energetic, spirit-filled, and believing prayer to God. Therefore, it is God who is really doing the pushing and not ourselves or our prayers. Since God is doing the pushing, miracles begin to happen. There is no power in prayer. There is only power in praying to a God who answers prayer.

When Elijah was praying for rain, he did not offer one prayer. Instead, he prayed prayers until there was rain. Before Elijah prayed, there were no signs of rain. All he had was the promise of God that it would rain. When he prayed, he still saw no signs of rain. On the seventh time, his servant looked toward the skies and saw the sign of a cloud about the size of a man's hand (I Kings 18:44). Of course, the cloud was not that small, but it typifies the distance of the rain cloud that only looked the size of a man's hand because it was so far away. Sometimes, our answers are far away. As a matter of fact, they are as far as the Earth is from Heaven. Somehow, we must pray our way into Heaven or pray until Heaven makes its entrance into us. Sometimes, that is a long way. Yet, as we pray, God gives us signs of deliverances that are in development.

What was seen in the distance could have been a cumulonimbus cloud. Cumulonimbus clouds produce severe thunderstorms and large amounts of rain. What is powerful about this experience is that Elijah had already been promised rain by God. Elijah received the promise of rain before he saw signs of rain. Then, he prayed for the promise to come into fulfillment. It would be easy to conclude that the promise of rain and the perception of the cloud would have been enough for Elijah to just wait until the cloud developed and produced the promised rain. Yet, Elijah recognized something spectacular about God. Although God's promises will come to pass, there are occasions in which the method by which those promises are actualized is through a partnership with God in persistent prayer. If Elijah stopped praying, the rain cloud would have dissolved in the distance. At certain times, if we do not pray, nothing will develop. There are many things that will never come into fruition if we don't forcefully and faithfully ask (James 4:3).

This process of looking for a sign of rain took place at least seven times. On the seventh look, the servant saw a cloud that was the size of a man's hand. Here is where numbers do matter. When it comes to prayer, numbers matter. It does matter how many times we pray. The number seven is the number of perfection. When it comes to prayer, we must be persistent to the point of perfection. Nothing short of perfection in persistence should be the product of our prayer lives, especially when it comes to demonic oppression and confession that provides healthy lifestyles.

Elijah was praying for rain to stop and start again for the space of three years and six months. He prayed many prayers for this supernatural phenomenon to occur. When it comes to healing and the prayer of faith, it is not a one-time formula that is applied on all occasions but a continual persistence in prayer until sickly elements have been completely removed by the healing hands of God. In other words, it takes a whole lot of praying, even years of praying! It is praying on top of praying. This type of praying is praying at its best, requiring concentrated, continual effort, inducing forceful results. This type of praying partners with the power of God in each situation that God promised us that He would intervene in. It is more intense than merely bringing someone down the aisle and standing in a prayer line until someone comes and lays their hands upon them. It is even deeper than the traditional altar call. The type of praying that Elijah had in mind consisted of a concentrated team of pastors (elders) who were totally devoted to the Lord, performing a perpetual practice of Spirit-induced prayers, giving their lives in total prayer (even if it took days, months or years), and believing on behalf of individuals who were honest in confession about the source of their sickness.

The church was also commanded to continue in believing prayer on behalf of such individuals until healing resulted. Until that point, the prayer life of the church was in complete disarray as people were only making personal prayer requests, praying only for personal gain by asking God for blessings that they coveted from others. They were also a church who was naïve to enduring hardship as a testing of their faith. So far, their faith was not working. Nothing was working with this church because there was no spiritual accountability in place. Accountability is deeper than having restrictions to prevent us from doing what we should not do. The goal of accountability is to place us in positions in which we are required to do what we should do.

There are *prayers of adjustment* to the sovereign will of God when we pray, *"Thy will be done"* (Matthew 6:10). There are also *prayers of alignment* when we pray according to God's will (1 John 5:14). The Bible describes all types of praying. However, in James' context, there are *prayers of attainment* that invoke the power of God to intervene and heal certain manners of sickness under confessing and sanctifying contexts.

While many of us are aware of many exaggerated emphases of healing and theological fallacies, there is no argument on Earth that can accurately refute the power of this passage regarding the prayer of faith. The challenge is not to seek ways to dilute healing. On the contrary, the challenge is to seek ways to deliver healing.

During the Christmas season of 2015, my granddaughter (Aniyah) asked me repeatedly about toys that she wanted for Christmas. In a sense, she was supplicating. She kept asking until her request got through to me. It was already in my will to shower her with toys. However, when I was going to do it and what I was going to give her was along a completely different line. She would have to tell me exactly what she wanted. It was not until she showed up at my house a few days before Christmas that the process began to take effect. On that day, she asked me where her gifts were. I hadn't purchased them yet because I wasn't quite sure when I was going to give them to her, when she was coming over, what I was going to give her, and where I was going to go to get the gifts for her. When she asked me, I decided that very day was the best day for me to go. *I decided to get the gifts when she asked.* Yet, I still did not know what exactly she wanted. I decided to go to Toys R Us and let her pick whatever she wanted. I carted her through each aisle, and *she picked out exactly what she had in mind.* Finally, she said to me, "Well Poppy, I believe that's enough toys for today."

Prayer is a lot like that in relation to our Heavenly Father. Although God has it in His mind to heal, had we not asked, He would not have healed. We also must have in mind what we specifically want Him to do for us. In addition, we must be believing and persistent enough to pick out what is already in Heaven's supply and on Heaven's display. Never did my granddaughter doubt that I was going to do it for her. Because of her faith in me and continual persistence, I was determined to not let her down. After all, it was already in my will to do it for her because I wanted to bless her. It was a win-win situation. Especially in the prayer of faith, God wants us to trust Him, and never doubt. After all, it is already in His will to do it for us. At the core of God's care for us is an eternal compassion to bless us in every way beyond measure.

By the way, my granddaughter did not want a lot. She just wanted enough. When we keep God's sufficiency as our priority, we too can say, "Lord, that's enough for today."

We should not be discouraged if we see no results after a one-time, sincere, concentrated effort to ask. We are to continue in prayers until we capture Heavens attention; better yet, until Heaven captures our attention. Pastors' anatomies are afflicted and attacked on a regular basis. Overall, God desires for us to be in good health and prosper, even as our souls prosper (III John 1:2). That scripture means exactly what it says. It does not say anything at all about being rich, but it says everything about being prosperous. Our bodies are the temple of the living God, and they are the vehicles that God wants to occupy to demonstrate His wonder-working power.

Many years ago, my younger son (Alonzo) had a stomach virus. I bought him some antacid pills, but he was somewhat disturbed why they were not working right away. I explained to him that they must be taken consecutively and patiently, and each pill contains elements that will dissolve the virus, but they must be taken on regular intervals. Each pill empowers the other, but they are not designed to be taken alone. Much is the case with prayer. Prayers must often be offered consecutively to attack and kill viruses that infect members of the Body of Christ. One prayer empowers the other, but they should not be offered in single or irregular doses. Deadly viruses occur because of sin's killing power. We are not to faint in prayer because each prayer empowers the next when offered with Spirit-filled force and faith. When these enemies of the soul of the Church seek to assault the life of the Church, a local church that rises in effectual, fervent prayers will be revived for the glory of God and the Great Head of the Church, Jesus Christ.

This concept of partnership in prayer continually amazes me. To know that there are many instances when God will do nothing apart from our prayers is mind-boggling. I just must believe it because the Bible says so, and because I experienced that phenomenon a thousand times. At the heart of God, He created us for Him. He wants as intimate of an involvement with us as possible. He did not create us as a civilization that He could wind up like toy soldiers and watch us work according to His plan. God created us to exist and move through fellowship with Him. It is in Him that we live and move and have our being (Acts 17:28). The process of partnership in prayer involves us making the loving decision to stay connected to Him by upholding our end of the relationship to commune with Him through prayer. It is a harmony of relationship that takes place when we pray. God is on one end, and we are on the other end working in perfect harmony. When we fail at performing our end in prayer, the harmony is broken, and the music stops. The difficulty in getting results is not in a God who is refusing to give. Instead, it is in our inability to allow God to prepare us to receive. The analogy is almost as simple as a father's relationship to his children. There are times in the children's lifetime when they will receive of their father *only because they asked*. When God honors the prayer of faith, He answers only because we asked (Matthew 7:11).

The benevolence of God must not be argued away with healing. These passages on the prayer of faith are packed with promise because God is good. God is benevolent, and He desires to raise us up when we are bowed down. God desires to restore us when we have fallen prey to sin's infecting power. God is not calling us to sharpen our theology on *why* He doesn't heal, but He is calling us to sharpen our theology on *when* God does heal. When we understand more clearly when God does heal, we can more greatly accept why He does not.

I recall a time when my older son, Derrick Jr. was suffering from a chronic condition at birth. After his birth, I learned an important lesson about the will of God and healing. I led his mother to a small room at Cedar Sinai Medical Center of Los Angeles, California. I led in prayer and committed him to the Lord. I did not ask the Lord to heal him. I prayed for the Lord's will to be done. I remembered a statement from Jack Hayford years before that occurred. He said these exact words, "There is a great deal of wisdom in praying for the Lord's will to be done." When we pray God's will to be done, we are not building up stamina to accept a divine "No" from God. To pray God's will does not imply that we must prepare for the dark side of the inevitable. To pray God's will to be done is to recognize how much God's way is healthier than our most wholesome imaginations. God's will brings Heaven to Earth, and takes us from Earth all the way into Heaven. God's will connects us to His divine purposes in a way that brings a peace in our hearts that passes all understanding because we opened our hearts to God's ultimate good for our lives.

Derrick soon recovered because *the Lord* wanted him to recover. God had His way. Had we not prayed God's will to be done, something far worse could have happened. To pray God's will to be done is not a prayer that will enable us to accept the worst, but it is a prayer that will align us with God's best. What God wills, He wants. What God wants, we must allow. God wants to heal more than He wants us afflicted by sin, Satan, or selfishness. All we must do is believe God for the impossible to happen. The prayer of faith truly does invade the impossible.

Most of the times when God does not heal, they come from the fact that we are not willing to pay the price of perfect persistence in prayer. It is not always a theology of sickness and healing that is our problem. It is often a problem of pride and lack of persistence. Some of us may not wish to be embarrassed by spending elongated amounts of time and energy asking for something that God may not supply. What pastor wants to stand before a congregation and ask God to heal, only to discover that the person dies after he prays? During other times, we can become too proud to beg. Secondly, we may not be willing to commit to the process of living a life of wholeness. God doesn't want us to be repeat offenders. If our sicknesses are results of our sins, God wants us to stay healed by staying away from deadly sins. Regardless, our responsibility is not to second-guess God. Our responsibility is to pray and leave the results to God. If we do, we just might be surprised. God may do above and beyond what we could have ever imagined or thought.

I remember when my Aunt Doretha Wade-Wilkerson was diagnosed with cancer. She was not given long to live. To show you how deep this story is in my heart, she knew my secret faults, and we had long conversations about them. Our offices were adjacent at Mt. Moriah Baptist Church of Los Angeles, California. So, we had a lot of quality time together. In my mind, I still feel as though she died before her time. Although I have a praying family, I also believe that the prayers of "Big Annie" (Mary Wade, who was her mother) kept her living if she did. At the time, my father gave me a tremendous amount of wisdom. He said that there are times when God doesn't heal, but He will give us the grace to bear the illness. There was nothing heavy or deep about his statement. What made his statement so profound was his discernment to know that it was not God's will to heal her. Instead, it was God's will to make her whole. God's grace makes us whole. Sometimes, God's sufficiency is all the healing we need (II Corinthians 12:9). As a matter of fact, God's sufficiency *is* healing. If we have God's help, we can live without God's healing. God may not always heal us, but He will always help us.

To James, healing was equated with confession and forgiveness. In no way would I be condescending or compromising the text if I say that when one confesses and is forgiven, he or she is healed regardless of their physical condition. To James, one's spiritual condition took priority over one's physical condition. It takes a great deal of wisdom to recognize the difference (James 1:5-6). Sooner or later, we all will fall prey to some type of disease if we keep on living. Our theology of God will be crucial to our Christianity during that season of sickness. When that diseased day strikes, God will make it crystal clear which way we He would have for us to go down the road of prayer. Just be assured that God is good all the time.

Prayer does not move God as much as it positions us to receive what God already promised. Heaven made its decrees, but sin has so warped our ability to believe and receive direct interventions of God's mighty power that prayer must serve as a positioning discipline to ready our souls for what God has prepared for the good of them who love Him. As we pray, we are reminded of the fact that the greatest work is not happening above. Instead, it is happening below. As we pray, we are not moving Heaven. Heaven is moving us. We are not preparing God, but God is preparing us for the impossible. We are not empowering God, but God is empowering us. We are not reaching out to God as much as God is reaching down to us. As we pray and pray mightily, God is doing a work on the inside of us that begins to transform us into beings who can welcome the entrance of His Kingdom power upon us and our selfish, sinful, satanic or sickly elements.

We see the transforming glory of God when Moses was on Mount Sinai with God. When he finally came down, his countenance changed. We see the transforming glory of God when Jesus prayed on the Mount of Transfiguration, and His countenance was changed. In no lesser way does Spirit-induced prayer transfigure us. Prayer does not transfigure Heaven, but prayer transfigures Earth. God's will is already settled in Heaven (Psalm 119:89). As we pray, we come into realizations of the God-intended health of our anatomies. We are fearfully and wonderfully made, and we come into realization that when we pray for healing, we are restored to our original design. The goal of Satan and sin is to disfigure us, but prayer's objective is to transfigure us. When we cease to pray, we cease to be transfigured.

One of the greatest works that will ever take place in our pastoral lives is not what we accomplish externally, but what we allow prayer to accomplish through us internally. When Elijah prayed earnestly, a lot was happening on the inside of him. What he prayed for manifested outside of himself. While this may sound strange, the point in the prayer of faith is in realizing that God is seeking to get us to attain what Heaven has assigned to us. Nothing on Earth can resemble Heaven's best until God comes down. Sometimes, God only comes down when we invite Him through prayer. God wants us, but He wants us to want Him. No sickness is too far from God's will to heal. No attack is too demonic for God. No crisis is so confusing that God will not give us the wisdom to conduct ourselves in a persevering manner. Nothing is too hard for God.

At the root of all impossibilities is a God who comes down, especially when He is invited. When God is welcomed in the most diseased and demonic moments, the sick and tormented will never be the same. The point is that Satan is real, and he is assaulting God's children on a masterful level. Sin is real, and some of us can sometimes make choices that cut our lives short. If these be true, how much truer is it that God wants to bring us back into *attainment* with what He offers? For our bodies to come into alignment with God's original design, sickness must sometimes go. After all, the children who Satan is oppressing are God's children. The sins that James is referring to that induce sickness are the sins of God's children (Exodus 15:26). Therefore, God has a will for His children, God has a word for His children, and God has a way for

His children to recover. James is telling us to line up with God and P.U.S.H. (*Pray Until Something Happens*) our way back into wholeness through consistent dependence upon God in prayer.

God takes sin seriously. Sometimes, the greatest miracle is not that we were healed, but it is in the fact that we confessed our sins. If that is not the case, the greatest miracle is in the fact that we prayed believing that God will miraculously intervene. It takes a lot of humility for us as God's people to bow down on our knees and call upon God while He may be found. It takes humility for God's people to seek His face and turn from their wicked ways. The sight and thought of God's people bowing down before God's throne in total dependence upon Him is a beautiful sight and a virtuous thought. Prayer is humbling. Our status, abilities, degrees, and achievements can never compare to what prayer can do.

Like Elijah, we all have like passions, and we all have knees that are made of the same type of bone as Elijah's. To see Heaven's best, all a pastor needs is a good set of knees. There is sweet relief in knowing God's greatest men were made of no different material than that from which we are made. If there were ever any differences, they would be in the character and faith-level that they allowed God to develop in their lives. None of God's men or women were born believing. God shaped men and women of faith through a process of years of disappointments, failures, attacks, battling beasts, high waters, dry deserts, strong storms, and fiery trials (Hebrews 11:1-40). Yet, they endured the trying of their faith. Therefore, their faith endured. As we fall on our knees, we should no longer be intimidated by those who were noted for prayer or faith. We are not to bow down on *their* knees. We are to bow down on our own.

Whether it be manifold misery that catches us at the most unexpected moments, seasons of hidden lust that lurk within, evil afflictions that tease our bodies with irritating moments, or sickness that festers in our bloodstream because of some unsettled sin, God is summoning us to His throne of grace to find mercy in our times of need. While He calls us, He is inviting us to a transformation of character within and cures without because He is eager to invade our physical vices with His metaphysical virtues. It is not Jesus' will for His Church to be sick-and-shut-in. *He wants His Body* (the Church) *healed.* God is anxious to intercept all that obstructs our fullest created capabilities, and He wants us to enjoy a reasonable portion of Earth before we experience the unimaginable portions of Heaven (I Corinthians 2:9). All need not be dreary on this side of life. Jesus came to give us a life abundantly that begins where we are and crescendos from glory to glory until we meet Him face-to-face. Our ultimate destiny is to be somewhere around the Throne, and the earthiest way to get there is down on our knees. The prayer of faith allows us to have a taste of Heaven until our ambitions are transformed into appetites that hunger and thirst after His righteousness instead of coveting worldly success. As we fall on our knees, great and mighty things await us that we know not of but are ours for the asking if we would only ask in this God-type faith until Heaven has our undivided attention.

When we think of the prayer of faith, we see our lives from Heaven's point of view. Heaven is announcing that God wants to invade our impossibilities. God wants us to have more of Him in all His glory. Because we cannot endure His full glory in our mortal bodies, we can experience glimpses of His glory as He ejects evil from our midst, touches our bodies with healing-life, and restores our trust in Him to know that we serve a mighty God and a mighty good God.

I will never forget when I was a little boy who observed a prayer phenomenon that would take place. In the Black Baptist Church, we had what was called, "Devotion". Devotion was the period before the worship service began when the deacons would line up before the church and lead in songs and prayers. It was our way of getting consecrated for the rest of the worship service. It was like a warm-up before worship. My childhood days were at Bethlehem Baptist Church of Dallas, Texas. As a member of Bethlehem Baptist Church, Deacon Sanders' prayers were criticized because he prayed so long. I must be honest, he prayed for a long time. Whether his prayers were legitimately received or not was not my interest. What impressed me was not how *he* prayed but what he said when *others* prayed. Although many failed to encourage him in his prayers, he always encouraged others when they prayed. When it was another's opportunity to pray publicly, he would say, "Pray mightily, pray mightily". Before we criticize, theologize or analyze what is true, false, possible or impossible in the context of God's powerful manifestations in our midst, God and James (the brother of our Lord) pleads for us to "pray mightily" and see what the end will be. We can be guaranteed that when we pray, and pray mightily, the end will not be the end. When we pray and pray mightily, it is not over. When we pray and pray mightily, we have only just begun. So, let the healing begin…

Chapter 13

THE PASTOR AND HIS FEET

∞

(A Collection of insights on Expository Preaching: Preachers who avoid laziness in the library)

Tribute: To Dr. Joel Gregory, former Pastor of the Travis Avenue Baptist Church of Fort Worth, TX and First Baptist Church of Dallas, TX

*W*hile studying to obtain my B.A. Degree in Biblical Studies at the Criswell College of Dallas, Texas, I never will forget a preaching seminar that was held that week. It was known as, "The School of the Prophets". I looked on the platform at the guest lecturer of Homiletics. By the looks of him, he did not appear as though he would have much to deliver. Without any insult, he just had an innocent, docile-like disposition, and the simplicity of his facial features suggested a mild-mannered man would exude from his presentation. Anyone acquainted with Dr. Joel Gregory knows that is far from the truth. That man stood up with a voice that sounded like thunder, and so did the rest of that week. It was a storm all week long. It was an expository storm, and the truths that came from Dr. Gregory were raining down on me. Expository truths thundered from the lips of a man who I never heard of before, but I will never forget. Those who are serious *about expository preaching should know his name and read his notes. I can safely say that Dr. Joel Gregory has Gospel feet.*

Within this last organ of the pastor's anatomy, inserts on preaching have been given that I pray will be helpful for those who are serious about the dynamics of true preaching. Those familiar with the disciplines of expository preaching will know these observations are not reinventions of the wheel but restatements of the spokes of the expository wheel that has been developed by the great expositors in ages past.

Special thanks and recognition must go to my preaching mentor, Pastor Donald Parsons (Pastor of the Logos Baptist Assembly of Chicago, Illinois). Donald Parsons introduced me to a book entitled, *Preaching*, by Fred Craddock when he allowed me to pick his brain when I was a younger preacher. He had just concluded a revival at the Eastgate Baptist Church in Dallas, Texas. I want to also thank Professor Chuck Ward, who was my professor of Homiletics at the Criswell Center for Biblical Studies (The Criswell College). Dr. Ward stressed the importance of developing the *Central Idea of the Text*. I also want to thank Dr. Danny Akin, my former New Testament professor at the Criswell Center for Biblical Studies and now, President of Southeastern Baptist Theological Seminary. I thank Dr. Akin for his example of discipline in the word of God. I have never seen a man who put so much disciplined effort in study and preparation of sermons and lectures as Dr. Akin except for my pastor, M. V. Wade, Sr. Then, there are observations I gleaned from John Stott's book entitled, *Between Two Worlds*. I also want to thank my pastor and uncle, Melvin Von Wade, Sr. who taught me how to preach in a church setting. He would always tell me, "Son, our people here at Mount Moriah may not have gone to seminary, but they read their Bibles. So, preach the Bible, son." I also thank Uncle Melvin and E. K. Bailey for leading me to Criswell College when Bishop College closed. They taught me the importance of going to a college that would teach me how to use all the tools necessary to know and study the Bible.

Dr. E. K. Bailey became the reformer of expository preaching in the African American preaching context. Dr. Bailey accepted my appointment with him in my first few years of ministry. I also want to acknowledge his widowed wife, Sheila Bailey, who (in my opinion) is the epitome of a woman regarding the teaching of God's word. Mrs. Bailey was always a model to me of what a woman can do gracefully in the context of teaching God's word and women's ministry.

I want to acknowledge a young giant of expository preaching and my brother in the ministry as we share the same spiritual father (Melvin Von Wade, Sr.) by the name of H. B. Charles, Jr. who is continuing the expository journey and paving the way for the next generation. He is one of the greatest textual generals of the 21st century. Lastly, I would like to thank my father in the ministry, Derek L. Winkley who taught me how to study with just a Bible in my hand and take simple texts and discover their meaning. Although Pastor Winkley never attended seminary, I never will forget his discipline when I visited his home every Sunday after church. I would hear him preach on any given Sunday in a way that I had never seen. He taught me not only how to study but how to hear from God. I would go home with him after church and see the process of how it all happened. On his dining room table was around ten to fifteen books that were opened and highlighted. He would get his thoughts from God and then consult commentaries and expository helps. He only highlighted the thoughts that were in alignment with what God spoke to him. When I pick up a highlighter, I more than often think about Pastor Winkley. He has a unique revelatory approach to the text that I truly admire and respect.

I attempted to digest the expository pills that have been given to me from men who have invested in my ministry over the years. As I digested them, I have made these truths my own and scripted them as they flow from the depths of my soul in my own words:

Developing a Life of Study

- *Developing a life of study must be distinguished from studying only for a sermon.*
- *When a life of study is developed, the sermons become an overflow of what has been processed within the anatomy of the preacher.* I recall John MacArthur state that he rarely studies to preach a sermon. He just studies. Therefore, when he stands, he never runs out of material because his sermons are an overflow of his studies.
- When study is confined to sermons only, the sermon will be undernourished.
- A life of study prepares the minister for many occasions, most of which are without notice because *no other profession has such a busy intersection as the profession of the preacher* (Fred Craddock, *Preaching*).
- *Today's Christians are more formally educated than ever.* Our congregations are loaded with professionals of all sorts. In like manner, the preacher must be a professional in his field of the Bible.
- A life of study allows the pastor to master the subject in a way that creates a wider range of communicative methods.
- Do not feel inspired to resist the need to study.
- Pastors need to study because of the nature and need of the word of God:

"All Scripture is given by inspiration of God
(Nature), *and is profitable for doctrine, for reproof,*

> *for correction for instruction in righteousness: That the man of God may be perfect, thoroughly furnished unto all good works* (Need)."
>
> (II Timothy 3:16-17; KJV)

- We are to also study because it is a command (II Timothy 2:15).

Hindrances to the Life of Study

- When preparing for study, *eliminate time wasters* (Joel Gregory).
- *Local church parish ideas of ministry and study* that do not allot their pastor time to study. It takes at least twenty hours for the pastor to get a reasonable handle on the text. Yet, these are minimal hours for those who are deeply rooted in expository preaching. At the beginning of one's ministry, large or small, teach those to whom you minister to respect your time in study. Your time spent in study is time also spent with them.
- *Our western culture rarely affords educators and institutions acute environments for study.* Therefore, study and reading are not a cultural priority in America.
- For some pastors, *early school traumas hinder a life of study.* Childhood memories of certain teachers, taunts, or even parents with unrealistic educational expectations on their children may be silent demons that breed insecurities in the pastor when he becomes an adult. The most silent demons of many pastors are those who plague pastors with reading deficiencies. When a man cannot read as well as others, it hinders his self-esteem on deep levels.

- *Strong study habits are not the norm of our western civilization regarding our childhood education.* Children of other countries learn up to three languages throughout their education. America's math, science, and language disciplines are poorly lacking. English is one of the most inconsistent and difficult languages to learn. Yet, children in other countries learn our language while we have little or no knowledge of theirs.
- *Poor transition from college or seminary into the local church setting.* Many seminaries have professors who have little or no experience in a local church setting and are not able to provide relevant facts that balance doctrine and practice. Thus, their concepts of local church ministry are reasonably theoretical. Graduates become highly disillusioned with the practical dynamics of the local church and suffer severe burn-out.
- *Pastors who have not been privileged to attend theological institutions may have poor selection skills when it comes to reading quality material.* On today's Christian bookshelves, we must be aware of the evolution and propaganda of books. One author may be known for a best-seller and decide to write a sequel. In the theatrical or entertainment arena, the sequel is rarely as good as the original. Such is the case with Christian books. Many Christian books are mere propaganda (Pastor Ralph West).
- *Study is hard work.* As a matter of fact, real study is painful. Real study requires the discipline of the mind, body, and soul to resist every temptation to answer any distraction that may impede study. Along those lines, there are myths to study that need to be addressed. It is not always true that experience is the best teacher, but it is true that the exposition of God's word is the best teacher.

- *We live in a world that is filled with people who are attracted to ecstatic experiences.* Sound expositors are more theologically inclined, and they concentrate on reverence and awe of God versus ecstasy and superficial thrills. Ecstasy affords individuals the ability to abandon moral absolutes. Reverence and awe require individuals to be accountable to the very absolutes they abandon. In many of today's churches, if some people do not feel or see something happening, they erroneously conclude the worship experience is lacking. It is vital the pastor does not feel the same way. One of the acid tests of a church is if it can endure the simplicity of worship and the Word.

Suggestions for a Life of Study

- *Be realistic regarding your study life.* The most important concept in relation to the quality and quantity of study is quality. It is important to work smarter as well as work harder. Quality study enhances the interpretive process because human faculties are operating at higher levels of interest and investment. One of the best practices in preparation and preaching a sermon is getting proper amounts of rest (Pastor James A. Temple).
- *Determining when to quit studying for a sermon.* I remember Dr. Gregory stating that one of his greatest struggles was not knowing when to pull away from his desk of study. I can identify with that. He recalled times when he would literally have to be pulled from his office on Sunday mornings because he still saw more in the text to deliver. I remember J. C. Wade, Sr. having a saying to me, "You can't preach it all."
- *The use of imagination is integral in communication.* I asked M. V. Wade, Sr. what was one of the differences he saw

in today's preaching versus the preaching of old. He said today's brand of preaching has lost its sense of creative imagination.

- *Broadening your horizons in literature broadens intelligence* (Pastor Donald Parsons).
- *Resist the temptation to cease studying once an idea emerges.* Allow the idea to become God's through full investigation of the text and getting to the intended meaning of the author. If not, we have received more flash than light (Joel Gregory).
- Because we live in a high-tech society in which information can be accessed in a matter of seconds online, it would be wise to *take advantage of the information highway* (Bishop James Edward Henry).
- *Setting up an efficient library* is a key factor to developing and enhancing study skills. Leave new books on your desk until they are read and try to read one book per week (Pastor Donald Parsons).
- *Read and re-read material until you digest it and it becomes a part of you.* Then, restate it in your own words (Reverend Earnest Estelle, Jr.).

Principles of Exposition (Professor Chuck Ward)
- One of the fundamental steps of exposition is to *locate the Central Idea of the Text*. Why should we isolate the dominating theme or C.I.T. (Central Idea of the Text)?
    - Because every text has a main theme. God is saying something.
    - People will not remember all the details anyway.
    - All the succeeding points of the sermon should support the C.I.T.

The Investigation of the Text

- Investigate the historical and literary settings of the text.
- Investigate the *syntactical and verbal specifics of the text*. How sentences and words are arranged is crucial to interpretation.
- Investigate the *doctrinal and theological significance* of the text.
- Read the text and not merely look at the text and read into the text what we want to preach. Re-reading the text gives the pastor a sense of the flow of the text. John Stott advised to read the text at least fifty times before studying the text (John Stott, *Between Two Worlds*). Reading and re-reading the text shortens the pastor's distance between the two worlds of the Bible and our age. It also gives the pastor a greater handle on the text due to increased familiarity with the text.
- *Be aware of the specifics of the translations we are using.* Without a proper understanding of hermeneutics (the science and art of biblical interpretation), one may assume the most understandable Bible is the one that has the most accurate translation. However, there is a difference between transliteration and translation. Transliteration is the conversion of one script to another, thereby preserving the actual words transferred. Translation has more to do with taking the actual Hebrew/Greek words and giving the best words of one's known language that has the same or closest meaning to the Hebrew/Greek texts. Unfortunately, translations are often contemporary misinterpretations of what Hebrew and Greek sentences mean. For example, most Bible readers know Easter is a pagan holiday, but some have found the passage referring to Easter in the KJV Bible, and they conclude that Easter is biblical. Easter

is a KJV translation, but it is an erroneous transliteration of the actual Greek word. Instead of *Easter*, as it is translated in the KJV, the transliteration is *pascha* in the original Greek (Acts 12:4). Therefore, a proper translation would be, *Passover*.

Procedures and Tools

- Tools help to get a job done better and faster. The problem is not in using tools but knowing which tools to use. Tools should relate to the true grammatical, historical, contextual, and cultural relevance of the passage studied.
- *Original language texts are important.* It is vital to know the majority texts of Greek and Hebrew manuscripts. The pastor should not read majority texts with a minor attitude. The majority Greek and Hebrew texts have stood the test of time and are the most accurate transliterations of the grammar of the original Hebrew and Greek. There is always some parishioner who has encountered some ancient script that undermines the credibility of the Bible. However, very few have ever seen majority texts written in the actual Hebrew and Greek languages.
- Interlinear Bibles, word study books, expository dictionaries, Bible Atlases, Bible dictionaries, and Bible encyclopedias are helpful tools that have an intimate relationship with the biblical world and words.

Developing a Proper View of the Text

- <u>Observation</u>: Observation involves getting an overall view of the text. Within the process of observation are disciplines of *deduction* and *induction*. Deduction is the act or process of reasoning from the general to the particular, from the universal to the individual, and from given premises to their necessary conclusions. *Inductive Bible Study* involves examining the immediate data of the text to find verification in the context. Induction is the act or process of reasoning from a part to a whole.

- Observation is critical to the scientific method. Whatever the area of study, it is critical to let the data speak for itself. Expository preaching is valuable because it *exposes* the real data and definition of the text. This is another reason why expository preaching is not a style. It is a science by which we communicate a passage. To read into the text something that is not there is the fallacy of not paying attention to the textual data. To do so is poor observation of a passage. Hermeneutics is the science and art of biblical interpretation. No scientist is wise who overlooks the data or makes conclusions on limited data. In addition, a scientist is unwise if he makes general conclusions based on only one piece of data. There is much data to consider before reaching a proper interpretation of the text.
- There is the *complex* world of the biblical text. There is a danger of glancing too easily at the surface of a passage and making a quick evaluation.
- Then, there is the *context* world of the biblical text.
  - For example, when we observe Psalm 30:8, people in pain often race to this text as an emergency scripture to draw from: "*Weeping may endure for a night but joy cometh in the morning.*"
  - However, within the context of this scripture, Psalm 30 deals with David's morning over *sin* as he suffered God's chastising hand. David found himself weeping from the pain of being chastised by God in the night of life. Joy comes in the *morning* to those who are in mourning over their sins. From the context, we can

see that it does not apply to those who suffer hardships due to righteous living. God's anger endures for only a moment to those who weep and mourn over their unrighteous living. God favors life for those who confess they have sinned greatly. Therefore, God graciously gives them a joyous morning if they are repentant of their sins. The point David is trying to get across is that we do not have to be sorry for our sins forever. We can have new joy as God gives us brighter days. However, those brighter days only come to those who have experienced God's chastising hand that causes dark nights. When we acknowledge our transgressions, as sure as there is a night (God's discipline), there is also a morning (God's deliverance).

The Importance of Exegetical Analysis

- Preaching is often pleasurable, but it can also be a drudgery (Dr. Gardner C. Taylor). One major importance of exegetical analysis is that you can get to work whether you are inspired or not (Dr. Joel Gregory).
- Exegetical analysis is important because measuring Truth on emotional levels is a misguided measurement. Study is as much of a mental process as it is a spiritual one. The emotive processes become the motivator when inspiration or passion is the drive that moves the pastor *into* the study. The emotive processes can also be sustainers *during* the venture of study, depending upon the nature of the material covered and strength of the pastor's drive. Lastly, the emotive processes are the recipients of Truth discovered through a long line of disciplines exercised in coming to the true meaning of the text. It is not what we *feel* the

passage is saying or how we feel about the passage. On the contrary, it is what we *know* the passage is saying.

- In exegetical analysis, the preacher is gaining a hands-on relationship with the primary documents, i.e., the Scriptures. Exegetical analysis is a process that requires the pastor to dig, dig, and dig some more. Each process requires the pastor to handle the text with a hands-on, mind-on approach. Scripture and intense linguistic texts are the primary documents used to arrive at the meaning of the text. The usage of primary documents is a basic principle of effective research on any level. The same is true of exposition. The usage and skillful handling of primary documents strengthens the preacher's convictions and systems of analysis because he becomes less dependent on the interpretations of others or his own private interpretations. Although no scripture is given for private interpretation, there are many who interpret the Scriptures privately. If the preacher is a slave to secondary documents (ex. commentaries), he has no real system of accountability to establish with various interpretations. There are countless times when some refer to documents such as the works of Josephus as if those works are undisputed truths. However, such works are secondary documents and are not always inspired by God. However, all Scripture is inspired by God. The works of Josephus are only historical documents that may or may not have hermeneutical relevance to a given passage.
- Exegetical analysis protects the pastor from major subjective interpretations and exaggerated emphasis. Using exegetical analysis, we suspend our own conclusions and allow the textual data to speak for itself. One textual data of exegetical analysis is in relationship to the other. As the pastor

is gaining acute intimacy with the textual data through such analysis, the enthusiasm resulting from individual discoveries is heightened. The pastor has a deep sense of ownership of the analytical and interpretive process. Then, he becomes a biblical scientist. He is an exegete. He is partnering with God in the process of deductive revelation and reasoning. With a strong sense of ownership, the creative processes are ignited because a strong interpretive foundation has been established by staying true to the text. From that vantage point, the preacher will have authority when he preaches because he is preaching the Word.

- Creativity and imagination have safe foundations upon which to build as well as textual foundations when the preacher is true to exegetical procedures. The pastors of old in the African American context called this, *"using your sanctified imagination"*. The mind can pursue different forms of communicating Truth justifiably discovered. The world of metaphors, analogies, and symbolic forms of expression are permitted because they are used in the communicative process rather than the fundamental interpretive process. The imagination is risky when primarily exercised in the interpretive process because there is a strain to bridge a relationship between images and reality. Once the reality is established, the images are more easily detectable and detailed through the imagination. Then, *communication* becomes an art and science, which is the fullest definition of homiletics. The knowledge of the *content* becomes an art and a science, which is the fullest definition of hermeneutics. Never should reality be established based upon the imagination. However, imagination should be based upon the realities (data) of the text encountered through safe interpretive guidelines.

- Expository preaching is the foundation for all kinds of preaching because it is true to the literal meaning of the text. Whether the method of preaching is topical, dramatic, or storytelling, the essence of the passage is communicated because the chosen style of communication is based upon what has been the literal meaning exposed through accurate hermeneutical disciplines. Topical, dramatic, or story-telling preaching is not a curse if it is based upon the Truth of the text. Probably, one of the best storytellers and users of the imagination in the African American context is Pastor-Emeritus Johnny Ray Youngblood of the St. Paul Community Baptist Church of Brooklyn, New York. This type of preaching is no more a fallacy than the usage of illustrations in the expository preaching setting. If the illustrations are supportive of the Central Idea of the Text, they can enhance the communicative process. In like manner, topical, dramatic, or story-telling styles of preaching are justified if they are founded on the literal meaning of the text. Once the expositor has gained a handle on the central theme, the basis for various styles of communication becomes available. Although a thesis and three supporting points is an awesome way to communicate, they do not work in all settings. We must always remember Jesus never preached a three-point sermon. He preached one-point sermons. Jesus had one Truth He was stating. Technically, Jesus was a topical preacher who used a series of illustrations to communicate a central truth. Although we tend to glean several truths from parables, Jesus used parables to communicate one truth. The type of exegetical preaching we often see today is known for having an attention-getting introduction, three supporting points, and an inspiring conclusion. This method is simply an essay method derived from an English grammatical communicative model that had nothing to do with preaching. This type of communication is structured in such a way because of the low levels of brain functionality and detention the western mind has due to poor cerebral exercises of the mind. The introduction is to get people's attention. The supporting points are to nail the point home and support the theme because people tend to not retain the main idea of any conversation, let alone a sermon or Truth. The conclusion is to inspire people to action because people are more motivated by feelings than facts (Joel Gregory).

Planning Exegetical Bible Study

- Remembering that observation involves examining every aspect of the text to come to an understanding of the writer's intended meaning (better known as, the Central Idea of the Text or theme), it is important to plan an approach to observation through specific points of view.
- To gain a general view of the text, the *setting* or background is important.
- Getting an overall feel and understanding the *historical setting* is critical because it opens many other frames of reference that allows the pastor to get a more intimate understanding of the biblical world of that passage.
- The *cultural setting* is also important because it gives the pastor an idea of why specific terminology was chosen. The culture also provided ways of communication, along with ways people thought, felt, and behaved during the times in which that passage was written.
- *Chapter setting* provides the internal context of which a scripture was written and provides relative information on the proposed text of analysis. It often sheds light on

the immediate setting in the observation process. It is also important to remember English translations of the Bible do not accurately categorize chapters of thought in the original Hebrew or Greek. Therefore, a changing of chapters in our English translations is not always indicative of a change of thought in the original Hebrew or Greek.

- The *geographical setting* allows an overall view of the land and physical environment of which the text pertains. The geographical setting has often been undermined or overlooked in the process of exegetical analysis, but it is just as important as any other discipline in the deductive process. Remember, expository preaching involves the art of exposing the meaning of the text. Every item analyzed warrants exposure and has meaning relevant to the literal intent of the passage discovered. Therefore, the geographical setting must also be exegeted.
  - As the Assistant to the Pastor at the Mount Moriah Baptist Church of Los Angeles, California, I can recall a perfect example. While preaching, I studied the geographical setting of a passage I was attempting to preach. After the sermon, I was lovingly humbled by my pastor (M. V. Wade, Sr.) as he smiled and said, "You know that land that you were describing? I have been there." I was preaching about a land I studied. If he were to preach of that same setting, he would have preached about a land on which he stood. When we are studying a passage's geographical setting, unless we stood where they stood, we are preaching from an educated reality instead of an experiential one. In this sense, experience is the best teacher. If we are not afforded the experience of standing on holy

grounds, the least we could do is to be better educated about them.
- *Textual setting* is a critical factor. Developing a detailed view of the text involves dealing with the details of the text. This is the process of text-handling where we are applying skilled hands and tools to divide the text into its individual parts to understand the individual meaning of words and their relationships within the passage. This would involve the process of rightly dividing the Word of Truth.
  - I remember a documentary detailing how many members of a church died because their pastor engaged them in snake handling based upon Mark 16:18. Biblical hermeneutics reveals the pastor and parishioners took the text out of context. The dangerous practice of snake handling was the ultimate fault of their pastor who suffered a major deficiency in interpretation. Jesus promised in the sixteenth chapter of Mark that *"signs would follow them that believe"*, but He did not promise *these signs were to be tested by those who believe*. The point of the matter is that it is a dangerous practice to not only handle snakes, but it is also dangerous to remove a text out of context. Furthermore, it is dangerous to test a text. In other words, it is dangerous to push the literal meaning of a text to the limit. Taking a text out of context is also the reason for doctrinal heresy within the Body of Christ that has taken place on universal dimensions. As a matter of fact, taking a text out of context was also the reason for Jesus' crucifixion. The Jews had taken the Old Testament out of context, and their false interpretations bred a generation of vipers and an

unbelieving nation that eventually shouted, "Crucify Him" (Mark 15:13).
- The pastor must also be *grammatically* accurate. Notice Matthew 5:18:
  - *"For verily I say unto you, Till Heaven and Earth pass, one jot or one tittle shall in no wise pass from the law, till all be fulfilled."*
  - True biblical grammarians know the jot and tittle were Hebraic and Greek grammar marks that had detailed significance. Jesus is stating the fact that God's word is accurate, right down to the punctuation marks. I recall Dr. Troy Welch, founder of the Channel Islands Bible College and Seminary, making a major observation on God's faithful preservation of His word as it passed through human hands. Mind you, Dr. Welch can take a Hebrew or Greek text and read, parse, and interpret it fluently without any aids. He stated that it is more than remarkable that out of all of the ages of transferring biblical texts from one hand to another, as scribes re-copied the oldest manuscripts, less than 0.1% of the transliteration of these documents is known to have an error. Astute textual critics may believe the percentage to be larger, but if so, the percentage is no larger than 1%.
- Because of the accuracy of the Scribes, we must have *morphological* accuracy. When we speak of morphology, we are referring to the study of forms and structures of words. Word studies can also be mishandled. One definition of a Hebrew or Greek word does not always guarantee the proper meaning of a text. If a man had only one to two years of Greek and/or Hebrew, he knows just enough to be dangerous. Biblical words have forms that dictate the

actual meaning of the word that must also be understood. Knowing how and why a word is formed impacts the interpretive process.
- Therefore, the pastor must also have *syntactical* accuracy. Syntax refers to the forms and structures of sentences.
- *Semantic* accuracy is a necessity because semantics involves the study of words and their etymology. Certain words have the same root but different meanings, and some words have different roots but the same meaning.
- The pastor must be *doctrinally* accurate. Understanding the text breeds sound theology because the text will reveal something about the nature and character of God as He is revealed in the context of Scripture. Therefore, the question must always be asked, "What is the theological message of the text?" Dr. Gary Galeotti, former professor of the Old Testament at the Criswell Bible College and Southeastern Theological Seminary, had a saying regarding the preaching of a passage. He summed it up in three simple questions: (1) What does the passage say about God? (2) What does the passage say about man? (3) How do the two relate?

The Subject of the Text

- Revisiting the Central Idea of the Text or theme is a necessary art in knowing the meaning of the text. The theme must be crystallized. When we refer to crystallizing the theme, the sequence cannot be developed until the subject becomes clear. The Central Idea of the Text involves being able to say what a scripture or cluster of scriptures are saying in one sentence. Understanding the C.I.T. forces the exegete to narrow a body of material down to one concise statement. This is where the true power of expository preaching resides.

The Structure of the Text

- The structure of the text should come out of the exegetical analysis of the text. The main points should come out of the C.I.T. (Central Idea of the Text).
- What is the dominating *theme*? What are the integrating thoughts? Each point must be *biblical*. Each point must be *logical*. There must be a logical flow of each of the stated points of the sermon outline. If there is more than one point in the sermon, *Point One* should transition into *Point Two*, and *Point Two* should transition into *Point Three*, depending upon how many points there are in the sermon.
- Each point must be *practical*. When it comes to exposition and preaching, we should never leave doctrine to duty. We must preach the points in a manner by which they can be applied, but we must not leave the application to the hearers only. The listeners must know how to apply what they hear. The preacher must leave them with no excuse for not knowing how to do it. To assume that just because we are doctrinally sound, the people will know how to make an accurate decision is a deep fallacy. They can know what we are saying to be true and know how it relates to their experience but leave with a sermon that cannot be translated into their reality. One helpful hint is to develop in our study of the passage the objective, *"Once they hear this message, the people will be able to…"* This is preaching with purpose. It is also known as, *the motivating thrust* (Chuck Ward, former Professor of Homiletics). Being doctrinally sound without relevant application to the ills of the people is not enough. To do so is like a doctor telling a patient, "You see this medicine on the shelf? This is penicillin." After that, he dismisses the patient and says he is free to leave. The patient is told what the medicine is, but

he has not been given a chance to experience what the medicine can do for his illness. Why? Because the doctor did not take it off the shelf. He did not give him a prescription that he could use to apply the power of the penicillin. The expositor who just explains the passage is no better than the doctor if he says, *"You see this passage? This is what it means. God bless you all, that concludes my message. Lord I pray that this message will be a blessing to all those who hear it. Amen."* Nothing happened other than the expositor explaining what the medicine is and what it can do. He has not taken the truth of the passage off the shelf. In this instance, the expositor failed to give the people a prescription. This is one of the challenges of great expositors who preach in a theological environment. Preaching to preachers can be quite intimidating. There is a temptation to meet the expectations of peers with our expository skills. There can be a tendency to put our exposition on display. Then, our preaching lacks dynamism and movement. Old preachers would say that type of preaching isn't portable. It sounds good, but listeners are not left with anything to apply to their lives.

- What is the *motivating thrust*? In other words, what will the sermon achieve? Regardless of our desires for people to be at a level of discipline in which they are not moved by their emotions, most people are. The sermon must have some form of motivation that awakens their emotive processes to act upon what they heard. Some pastors are inherently gifted in their preaching anatomy to motivate people with little effort while others must work to achieve motivation. In the African American preaching context, this is known as having a strong close or *closing-out* the sermon.

- Each point must be *critical*. Each point must have a purpose intended, and it should communicate to the people a crisis of decision. We must communicate in a way they know the Truth revealed must be acted upon.
- When we speak of homiletics, we are only referring to the way in which we package our sermons to make the sermon more memorable and understandable. Sermons with all points beginning with the letter "A" (for example) were designed to make the points easy to remember for the people. However, a sermon with three "A's" does not always constitute an expository message. In addition, it does not mean the sermon is homiletically accurate.
- Whether there are three "A's" or six "P's" in our outline, they all must be related to one another because the points should flow out of the Central Idea of the Text. These points are also known as the *integrating thoughts*. Pretending what follows is a sermon, I have used fruit as an example to describe homiletical accuracy as well as inaccuracy. The first two examples are examples of homiletical inaccuracy because they are not related to the Central Idea of the Text. Pretending the central theme is *"pears"*, the points should be related to one another and support the theme. Remember, sermons one and two are homiletically *inaccurate*.
  - Sermon 1: Pears (point 1), Porcupines (point 2), Peanuts (point 3)
  - Sermon 2: Pears (point 1), Lemons (point 2), Grapes (point 3)
  - Sermon 3: Pear seeds (point 1), Pear cores (point 2), Pear stems (point 3)
  - Sermon 3 has homiletical accuracy. Pear seeds, pear cores and pear stems relate to the central theme of

the text (pears). If the central idea of the passage were *fruit*, sermon 2 would also have homiletical accuracy although it does not have three *P's*. Of course, sermon 3 would also be homiletically accurate because pear seeds, pear cores, and pear stems pertain to fruit. If a sermon has three points that are not related to the subject or Central Idea of the Text, the sermon has three mini sermons compacted into one sermon. There is a trend in preaching today in which most sermons have homiletical inaccuracy and hermeneutical unrelatedness. Such sermons would be indicative of sermon 1. Yes, there are three *P's*, but the points are unrelated. It is hard to tell what the theme is in sermon 1 because the points are vastly unrelated.

The Substance of the Text

- When we communicate in expositional preaching, if we use the essay method (an introduction, at least three supporting points, and a conclusion), the *introduction* should be carefully thought out. It should be a brief attention-getter. Overpowering as well as boring introductions must be shunned. The average attention span of Believers in a preaching setting is less than one minute. If their attention is not gained in the first few minutes, they will potentially be lost for the entire sermon. If the congregation is highly literate in expositional preaching, the preacher can get straight to the text without an attention-getting introduction because he already has their attention through their conditioning to expositional preaching.
- If the introduction is powerful, a weak body and conclusion must be avoided. Dr. Joel Gregory and Dr. Caesar

A.W. Clark would call this, "building the foundation for a skyscraper and putting a chicken coop on top of it."
- In the act of exposition, during the communicating event, introduction, explanation, illustration, application, and inspiration (motivation) are the five major ingredients of a homiletical sermon.
- Most Christians cannot understand abstract reality. Truth is abstract and immaterial. Therefore, *illustrations* are vital in making the abstract concrete. Illustrations are not a form of enabling. Jesus was aware of the importance of illustrations to communicate a message, comparing the Kingdom of Heaven to a mustard seed or even a treasure (Matthew 13:31 and 13:44, respectively). As a matter of fact, Jesus used illustrations to communicate the deepest truths. I am not sure if it is a consistent practice today regarding John MacArthur's usage of biblical illustrations, but during my student years at Master's Seminary, Pastor MacArthur didn't put much emphasis on extra-biblical illustrations. However, he emphasized the latitude an expositor may have in using biblical illustrations. Yet, one can never lose by using Scripture to illustrate other points of Scripture.
- As the introduction serves as an attention-getter, the *conclusion* is to serve as an action-getter. The conclusion is designed to motivate people to action. We mentioned previously how motivation is important to the application of Truth. Having a good sermon full of doctrinal content and profound Truth is good, but a weak, emotionless conclusion is like watching a good movie, and the conclusion just leaves you dangling. What is your evaluation of the entire movie if you sat through the movie for an hour and a half with suspense, excitement, and intense interest, but the

conclusion is totally off base or ends abruptly? We usually conclude that the movie was awful.

- However, there are times when it may be effective to leave the people hanging, in a sense. Such was the case in the book of Jonah. The story just stops with no real conclusion. It is indicative of Jonah's response to his calling. He never fully swallowed the idea of Nineveh repenting, but he had enough sense not to fight it. So, God ended the book with a question mark (Jonah 4:11). Sometimes, it may be helpful to leave the sermon with one final word or question. It depends on the content of the message and the condition of the hearts of the congregation. If they are wrestling with submitting to God's truth, it may be best to leave them with one last sentence and cut it short to inspire them to think. It leaves people with the understanding that God will not always strive with them. It also relieves the pastor of co-dependent tendencies to overly press a point. Sometimes, we can overdo it, at least I can. A one-liner helps me shut it down. There are some passages of Scripture that are too clear to overstate.
- All of what has been referred to so far is in the context of preaching. Yet, there can be a difference between preaching and teaching. All preaching is not teaching. Yet, expository preaching is also a form of teaching. In addition, all teaching is not preaching. It is impossible to teach a sermon. A sermon must be preached. It is also difficult to preach a lesson from Scripture. A lesson must be taught.
- Thus, the final factor that distinguishes preaching from teaching is the *dynamism* of the event. If the preacher communicates the word of God effectively, it will have a dynamism that accompanies it. If it is in the demonstration of

the Spirit and in power, it is most likely, preaching. Listen to Paul's definition of preaching:

- *"And I was with you in weakness, and in fear, and in much trembling. And my speech and **my preaching** was not with enticing words of man's wisdom, but in **demonstration of the Spirit and of power**. That your faith should not stand in the wisdom of men, **but in the power of God**"* (I Corinthians 2:5; KJV).
- Notice how Paul approached the people. He approached them in weakness, fear, and much trembling. Notice how Paul approached his preaching. He approached preaching in a way that was a demonstration of the Spirit and power. He approached them in weakness, fear, and trembling because he was going to be the vehicle through which the power of God was going to flow in the preaching event. He was claiming the preaching event and not a teaching event. Many pastors do not have this ability. I will use myself as an example. Although several preachers and people call me a great preacher, I believe I am a more effective teacher than preacher. I guess I could say that I am more of an *expository teacher*, teaching-preacher, or Pastor-Teacher. Yet, I love to preach, and I love to hear preachers preach. I used to do a lot of preaching, but God slowed me down and grounded me to my better niche and our congregation's greater need. Our church needed more teaching than preaching. Yet, there are church settings conditioned more to preaching than teaching. If I teach in those settings, I run the risk of losing their attention. The adverse is also true.
- Pastor Maurice Watson (one of the greatest expository preachers of our age) taught me early in my

ministry that it can also be anti-climactic to preach a certain way in certain church settings. When I communicate God's word through teaching, I am trying to impress upon people God's *principles*. Yet, I believe the goal of preaching is to impress upon people God's *power*. Every pastor should be a teacher according to Ephesians 4:11. However, real preaching needs to be recovered. Most of the attention has been devoted to preaching because it is becoming a lost art in today's 21st-century brand of preaching. I look up to the *real preachers*. I am amazed at how they do it. These are the pulpit masters who use various styles and methods to communicate the Truth of God. They are not bound to styles or structures. They use the tools that God has given them to get the job done. I love to see the demonstration of the Spirit and power of God flowing through them. I am tickled pink whenever God allows me to preach. Yet, I am comfortable in my own skin, and I get back to what He specialized me to do. God has called me to stand flat-footed and teach the word of God with simplicity, and even preach the word of God with profundity.

Anyone familiar with expository preaching has heard of what I mentioned previously or something of the like regarding the principles of expository preaching. There may have been a different linguistic twist, but the common denominators of expository preaching are virtually the same. In short, *expository preaching is simply, preaching what the biblical passage is saying in a dynamic way.*

The laws of hermeneutics are the standard by which expository preaching flows. Some expositors are better at exposition than others. The key is in developing the discipline to respect the laws of hermeneutics and applying them in an expository context. Pastors and preachers who are sincere at getting to the root of a passage to determine its literal meaning embrace any expository suggestion that would legally enable them to do so. Reading into a passage a meaning that is not there is hermeneutically illegal. Those who avoid doing so are wise and true to hermeneutical laws. The best expository preachers are the ones who pay the closest attention to hermeneutical laws and the biblical data. Some preachers are more committed to this process because they have the stamina to endure the hermeneutical distance required to be the best at the craft of expository preaching. All the above-mentioned disciplines detail why expository preaching takes time and diligent effort.

However, none of these disciplines encompass the entire dynamic of the preaching event. It would be arrogant to suggest such an idea because preaching is a supernatural event. These disciplines are meant to serve as safety devices to help protect the pastor from interpretational and communicational error. God's word has been entrusted unto us, and we are required to be faithful stewards of His word. The diligence required of any science demands tremendous and enormous amounts of reverence, time, and effort. Plainly put, one who is crafty must respect the craft. Preaching is no exception. Because preaching is ultimately a dynamic event sponsored by the Holy Spirit, we never fully master these methods. However, we are attempting to prove to God that we respect and honor His word, and we are not taking the privilege of rightly dividing His word lightly. We are acknowledging the treasure of the Gospel has been entrusted to clay vessels, and we are admitting our frailty when we study with all our might. We are saying to God that we recognize we are only human, and we are aware that there are enough fragile elements of our anatomy that can warp the studying and preaching event. Therefore, we approach the people in weakness, fear, and trembling. If we lose our sense of a shaking in our souls, something has gone wrong. We are attesting to the fact that a simple dependence upon God's power is not enough because we can even err in our dependence. Not only must we be dependent upon God, but we must also be disciplined for God. Discipline requires that we abide by the law. We must follow the biblical laws of interpretation. When we preach expository messages, we are attempting to make every effort to make our calling and election sure. We are worshipping God in the Word when we study because we are presenting our bodies, minds, and souls as living sacrifices, allowing them to be slain on the altar of study.

When we speak of expository preaching, we are speaking from the symposium of a plethora of God's greatest preachers who passed their discoveries to succeeding generations. Our responsibility in the dynasty of expository preaching is to protect and perfect the discipline of true hermeneutics and homiletics. Our pulpit fathers wanted us to be better than they, but it appears we still have a long way to go. We are simply building on a foundation that is already laid by the ancient pulpit masters long before the Puritans. We are advancing what has already been activated and are perpetuating a science that originated with Jesus. Jesus was indeed the *Exegesis* of God, and He was diligent in how He communicated who God is. We are seeking to emulate Jesus' style with the contemporary graces God has bestowed upon us.

Our literary tools and techniques are with sincere accountability to the system of biblical accuracy. When we exegete the Scriptures, we are declaring our love for the original language of the Hebrew and Greek language God chose to use in the process of inspiration. If we consider ourselves to be expositors, we are committed to make every effort to avoid our interpretations becoming misaligned with God's revelation. We admit, there are seasons when the pipeline of God's revelation flows directly through our anatomy and out of our lips, causing us to communicate semi-prophetically. However, most of our preaching is the result of human exercises that discipline our minds and souls to be still and search the Scriptures daily.

We fear to deter from the literal meaning of any passage because it is Truth that makes us free (John 8:32). To deter from the literal meaning of a passage is to deter from our freedom. We are committed to represent God's terms as He outlined them in Scripture by restraining our proclivities to lean on our preferred theological walls. The system of interpretation we developed and perpetuated is designed to restrain us from operating on our own tangents. While we recognize the power of the Holy Spirit in the revelatory event, we dare not set up habits of heresy. We couple studying with our dependence upon the power of the Holy Spirit. When we preach expositional and study exegetically, we are challenging all other methods of communication and communicators to fall in line with the true soldiers of study. We are unashamed of the Gospel of Jesus Christ and have discovered the power of knowing God's word *literally*. Internally, we burn with a passion to continue to dig into God's word until we have discovered its intended meaning.

While we seek to be patient with our misinformed contemporaries who hold to revelation and experience only, we cannot resist the temptation to be constructively critical of any forms of shallow preaching. Expository disciplines afford us the graces to be able to immediately differentiate the men who received their thoughts from God from those who received their thoughts from another spirit (I Kings 22:22; I John 4:1). When we see the wrong spirits preaching from the platforms of Christ's Church, we feel a need to protect God's sheep from powerless, pragmatic, personal, and perverted preaching. While we are committed to having a lifestyle pleasing to God, we recognize our preaching must be loftier than our lifestyles. In our best days and in our worst days, we are still earthen vessels, and God has trusted us with the Gospel. Although we have sinned and come short of the glory of God, we never fail to preach. When we witness those who preach for ulterior motives, our sole concern is that the Gospel is preached, even if it protrudes out of pretentious vessels. Expository preaching sets a standard we must abide by in our walk with God. If not, we risk disqualification (I Corinthians 9:27).

Expository preaching is not a style or an alternative form of preaching, but it is an obligation and absolute way to preach. At the heart of expository preaching is the central theme of Paul's charge to Timothy to preach *the Word*. Make no mistake in failing to know our chief agent in interpretation and communication is the Holy Spirit. However, we depend not upon the Holy Spirit to fill a mind that has not been consecrated in deep study and prayer. Our reliance upon the Holy Spirit is not only in the event of preaching, but it is also in the painful exercise of study. The Spirit drives us into the study, detains us in the study, and only delivers us to the pulpit after we have studied. We depend upon the Comforter to guide us to the right passages, clarify our understanding of the grammar, help us understand the flow of the Hebrew and Greek language as well as bring revelation to obscure passages. We depend upon the Holy Spirit to help us understand clearer passages to help interpret passages not so clear. We depend upon the Holy Spirit to grant the stamina necessary for our mortal bodies to endure the process of staying in our seats of study until God releases us from our sacred desks.

Expository preaching demands an exegetical discipline that can gain true meaning where the grammar, etymology of words, and the morphology of words are difficult to interpret. It is the Holy Spirit who teaches us when to stop digging and keep the main idea of the text priority. The Holy Spirit is flowing throughout every fiber of our being when we study. We are not only depending upon

Him to touch our lips when we preach, but we are also depending upon Him to touch our lives when we ponder biblical passages. We depend upon Him to touch our minds and remove any negative thought processes formed before we accepted our call. We depend upon Him to reprogram our minds for revelation and discovery. We depend upon Him to teach us the power of analytical thinking and critical exercises of the mind. We depend upon the Holy Spirit to align our minds with our hearts, so that we will have the learning and the burning. We depend upon Him because He gives us a passion for what we discovered in a way that Truth will forever be with us and not just on Sunday morning in front of an audience. We do not seek to impress people. We are seeking to make an impression upon them. We also depend upon Him to give us a sense of approval before we mount the pulpit to be accepted of Him. When we get divine approval that we were good and faithful servants in the study, it no longer matters to us that we are not applauded for our wisdom or oratory accomplishments. As a matter of fact, for us, that would be a total failure on our part if they did. We already received our badge as we buffeted our bodies into subjection and brought every thought into obedience to our Lord and Savior, Jesus Christ. We mount the pulpit with authority and confidence that God has placed us behind the pulpit as men on a mission who have been trusted with a message.

The expository preachers of today are the sons of preaching. Those who have gone before us are our fathers. Our expository fathers ache at contemporary preaching sons who have chosen more convenient and cute methods of communication. We recognize to preach any other way than expository is an exercise that breaches fellowship with the Spirit of the living God. Unless that preacher knows no other way to preach, the grace of God is frustrated. The question is not whether expository preaching is the only way to preach or not. The question is whether there is any other way to preach other than expository. Expository preaching is not a style. It is substance. It is preaching the Word. If we do not preach the Word, we are not preaching.

Those who have been enlightened to the need to be true to the text and have refused to do so must come up with new inventions every Sunday. It is one thing for a preacher to do the best he can with what he has versus one who has been warned to preach expository and has refused to heed sound preaching advice because it demands too much from him. Many of our fathers did the best with what they had and have established an expository legacy worth loving. Those who seek to abandon our true preaching history are left with the consequences of refusing to communicate in a consecrated way. When we preach in an expository manner, it is not always necessary to preach from the top down. We do not have to depend upon God to reveal something new every week. All we must do is faithfully declare what He already declared within the context of the sixty-six books of the Bible from the bottom up. We can now capitalize on the preaching enterprise by preaching from the Scriptures *up*. We preach *up* because we are preaching in a way that seeks God's approval. Therefore, expository preachers are *Word-up* preachers.

We live in a church era that is experiencing a decline of biblical preaching. Many have deviated from the whole Bible and dedicated themselves to the Bible in part. They have taken specific truths of the Bible and amplified them in a way that overshadows other scriptures that challenge their ideologies and styles of doing ministry. In addition, they have not placed demands upon themselves to get the education and schooling that many slaves of seminary sacrificed their lives for us to have.

While studying at the Criswell College, an African American pastor by the name of J. Lee Foster was awarded an honorary doctorate degree from Criswell College. He was one of the fathers of African American preaching. J. Lee Foster also had a teaching unction. He is a prime example of a man who did not attend seminary, but he earned a degree. He was one of the old-school pastors and preachers whose shoulders many of us stand upon. I remember visiting Dr. Foster as my colleague (Gregg Foster) shared his father with me. When J. Lee Foster pastored First Baptist Church of Hamilton Park, Texas, there I stood in his office with his son, Gregg. There, I asked "Daddy Foster" what books he was reading. He told me he did not read many books anymore except for the Bible. It is important to understand the core of what he was truly saying. He was saying the word of God became the only source he could truly depend upon. Expository preachers recognize that after all the tools, grammar, and disciplines have been exercised, the last law of hermeneutics states that the best interpreter of Scripture is Scripture.

Regardless of our education or lack thereof, God sanctions the pastor who teaches his people the Bible verse-by-verse. When we do so, antichristian forms of ministry will be shunned from our ministries and our people. In addition, we will witness the blessed phenomenon of slow growth in our churches. Sound teaching simplifies ministry to what is most important. When we do so, we will sadly begin to discover the Bible is not the ultimate priority of many members in local churches.

Expository preaching is a weapon. The expository preacher is in spiritual warfare every day because he is acutely interested in the Word. Our parishioners are experiencing the brunt end of the war between angels and demons. The war is over the souls of God's people. Only one type of preaching can heal them from the wounds of the fiery darts that scorch the souls of Saints. Only one type of preaching can help them overcome the battle of being a Believer. Only one type of preaching can nurture and develop them into the image of Christ. That type of preaching is expository preaching. ***If we arrogantly hold to any form of preaching that is not wholly consistent with the simplicity of the Word, we are crippling our congregations.*** Expository preaching is an element of warfare, and it is part of the pastor's armor. Listen to the apostle once again:

> *"Stand therefore, having your loins girt about with truth, and having on the breastplate of righteousness, and your feet shod with the preparation of the gospel of peace…"*

(Ephesians 6:14-15; KJV)

Our responsibility is to be able to stand on our feet. We (pastors) must take care of our feet. We stand on Gospel feet. Expository preaching allows us to stand strong, plant deep and not retreat. Expository preaching is flat-footed preaching. It is the kind of preaching the late E. K. Bailey (a dear friend of Joel Gregory) gave his life and heart to. He discovered a dynamic in expository preaching many needed to recover. He was willing to remove himself from popular preaching to purposeful preaching. He was passionate about it. He exemplified it. He breathed it. He meant it. Pastor Bailey recognized that if we were to win the war, we needed to return to God's word. Dr. Bailey understood the need to abandon philosophical ideologies, Liberal Theology, and return to the foolishness of preaching (I Corinthians 1:21). If he were alive today, he would be classified among the Baby Boomer generation. Yet, he was no Baby Boomer. He did not defy tradition. He was true to the expository preaching tradition. Contemporary, cute, and comfortable was not his style. He encouraged us younger preachers to preach *The Book*. You really do not know what type of man he was unless you met him. I could feel his passion for the Word. He did not care about what style a young preacher had.

As a matter of fact, he was cautious about style and committed to substance. If a young preacher had something to say in his sermon, he would listen. A preacher's gifts did not impress him, no matter how well he whooped and hollered, but a preacher's guts did. The only way to impress him was to preach from the gut and allow sincerity and study to overflow in our preaching. He adopted Dr. Joel Gregory into the African American preaching fraternity, and Dr. Gregory became our brother from another mother. Black preachers embraced Dr. Gregory like a brother because Dr. Gregory is true to real preaching. Dr. Gregory embraced Black preachers because he was true to real preaching. Real preaching puts us all in the same fraternity as co-laborers of the Gospel, even if we are brothers from different mothers.

There are many positions a seminary can take regarding the Bible. As Dr. Paige Patterson once said when he was my professor of Evangelism at Criswell College. We can have a position *alongside* the Bible, having all sorts of alternative ideologies we feel are just as important as the Bible. Other seminaries can stand *above* the Bible, producing practices in the realm of new revelations or modern ideologies void of biblical accountability. Then, there are the blessed seminaries that stand *beneath* the Bible by having a humble approach to God's word, teaching the students that God's word is the absolute authority by which we govern life and ministry.

Our people are exposed to so many voices and ideologies on a weekly basis that can weaken their consciousness of what God says. Our preaching must be packaged with theological content and sound doctrine because it strengthens their consciousness of God and restores them back on their feet. Some of the strongest, most prepared, and ready churches are those who appreciate the fact that their pastors are expository. Such congregations may not know the exegetical linguistics, but they have an attitude that demands

The Book. Because the pastor systematically preaches through the Bible and teaches ways people can apply Truth to their lives, they are conditioned for the Word and become the pastor's delight and the Devil's worst nightmare. Our pastoral role is to feed the flock of God and not entertain, enable, or arouse them. Their true nourishment will not come through any other means.

There is a thin line between educating people and feeding people. In education, there may be all forms of information that may enlighten them on relevant issues, but it does little for their spiritual growth if they are not the word of God. In the process of feeding God's people, the Word has nurturing and developing power if it is given in regular and proper dosages for them to digest it. Hermeneutics is the pastor's pedicure. Anyone who loves beautiful feet will love the pastor who preaches the Gospel. We must preach. If we refuse to preach, we will perish.

Early in my ministry, I remember our home church, under the leadership of Pastor Derek L. Winkley as we visited Pastor Lee Arthur Kessee when he pastored in Port Arthur, Texas. When I came into Pastor Kessee's office, he was reclining in his chair with his feet propped on his desk with hands folded in the peaceful posture he often exudes. Although I have always been impressed by his preaching prowess, the most impressionable stamp left on my life from Pastor Kessee was his posture. I admired what he stood for and how he stood. One of the most remarkable contributions Pastor Kessee gave my ministry was a paperweight. Yes, a paperweight. He had a paperweight on his desk that read, "Preach or Perish!" He did not give it to me, but I took it. I did not take it literally. I took it to heart. I read it. I watched him do it. I remembered it. I will never forget it. If we refuse to preach the Word, we perish. I remember Pastor Kessee saying to me, "When you stand on the Word, no matter how young you are, you don't have to back up for anybody." Whatever we acquired in our pastoral repertoire will not save us if we refuse to preach.

We must never forget that we have Gospel Feet. Gospel feet require Gospel shoes. Our feet must be shod with Gospel shoes. We are not to lace our preaching feet with shoes the Gospel cannot comfortably wear. If what we wear in ministry cannot contain the Gospel, we should put those shoes back on the shelves we got them from. Too many preachers today are standing in the pulpit bare-footed. They have taken off their Gospel shoes and put on secular slippers. Unfortunately, one of the most missed practices in many churches today is the preaching of the Word in its rawest form. Ideas, methodologies, philosophies, liberalism, conservativism, politics, economic empowerment, equality, ethics, cultural norms, and trends are being preached instead of God's word. Many are preaching about the Word, around the Word, or above the Word. Much of preaching today is nothing but spiritual discourses on topics and issues. If that is not the case, much of preaching today is nothing but testimonials of personal lives. Testimonies have their place, and issues need to be addressed, but nothing is healthier to a church than a balanced diet of the word of God. Style has taken the place of substance, and trends have taken the place of Truth. There is a dire need for the return to the simplicity of the Gospel.

Therefore, I pay homage to men who are soldiers of simplicity. Most of all, we cannot forget those men who never made the preaching charts, but they are faithfully and rightly dividing the Word every Sunday. Real preaching will get us into trouble, but the same preaching will get us out of trouble. One of the most dangerous sins the pastor can commit is the sin of refusing to preach. We must preach in season and out of season, when it is popular and when it is unpopular, when we feel like it and when we do not.

Expositional preaching is burdensome to the lazy preacher. Expositional preaching is hard work. Nevertheless, diligent pastors must not apologize for their messages being masterfully crafted by the tools of expositional preaching. We must not apologize for being intimidating to our peers and realize people who have a heart for God will welcome expositional preaching although many of our preaching peers detest it. As we continue the journey of expositional preaching, we must remember how we are called to preach to people and not to preachers. Therefore, people eat the Word while preachers who refuse to study vomit it up. We must do as the old preachers did and make sure that we *do our homework* in the study, and we will be guaranteed that God will do His Heaven-work in the sanctuary. To skeptics of real preachers, let the text decide the beauty of those who have Gospel feet:

> *"How then shall they call on Him in whom they have not believed? And how shall they believe in Him of whom they have not heard? And how shall they hear without a preacher? And how shall they preach except they are sent? As it is written: How beautiful are the feet of those who preach the Gospel of peace and bring glad tidings of good things."*

(Romans 10:14-15; KJV)

CONCLUSION

(The Pastor and His Conscience)
<u>In Loving Memory of</u>:
My cousin, Pastor James Commodore Wade III

(Sunrise: January 24, 1964; Sunset: September 25, 2015)

On a Saturday afternoon, I received a text message from my cousin (CaSaundra Snead) to give her a call. Upon returning her call, she gave me the shocking news that James died. We all know the death of a loved one can redefine one's entire context of life. Now, a new perspective of life and ministry has overshadowed me as I even more, see through a glass darkly. I am not focused on the causes of his death as much as why God allowed him to be taken so soon. Several weeks after James' funeral, I remember watching Ralph West (Pastor of The Church Without Walls of Houston, Texas) on television as he preached a very profound sermon. He stated to the congregation and to those listening throughout the airwaves something I knew was just for me. Pastor West said, "Stop trying to have all the answers. There are some things we just can't understand, even if God explained it to us!" Well, God did not give me any answers to why He allowed my road dawg to be taken so soon. I heard about the cause, but I know that was not God's reason. All I can recall is tears flowing down my face while at my desk of employment. I informed a co-worker that I would be going to East Chicago to attend James' funeral. Without knowing any details or James personally, my co-worker simply said, "Whatever he was fighting, he won't have to fight anymore", and that was enough for me. If I could reduce this entire book to one or two lines, what I want remembered *most is the fact that I was trying to communicate one basic truth: Every pastor is fighting something. People confuse our faults with our fights. Regardless of what others say or think, we know our inward battles oh too well, but we must keep on fighting. Nevertheless, we can be assured that one day, we will not have to fight anymore.*

When we see Elijah, he was fighting against **fatigue**. Paul was fighting against **pride**. Jeremiah was fighting against **the conditions of his calling**. Ezekiel was fighting against **the idolatrous forces that killed his congregation**. John the Baptist was fighting against **abandonment**. Habakkuk was fighting against **the silence of God**. David was fighting against a **heart attack**. Adam and Eve were fighting for **supremacy**. Again, Paul was fighting against losing **his credibility**. Samson was fighting for **another chance**. Jacob was fighting for **change**. James was fighting for **a faith that gives results**.

The men of the Bible are men who had serious issues. Many of the men who I pay tribute to are men who others wished I erased out of the pages of this book. If that were the case, I would have to erase my name as well as every man who God ever used in the history of the Bible. God's grace sustained them every step of the way. These are the kind of men who are leading our most powerful churches today. Once we conquer one issue, another is standing in the ring challenging us to a confrontation. Once we win one bout, some of our foes within and without will demand a rematch, and we must battle all over again. If not, we face new challengers who want to take the championship title of change away from us. We yearn for that perfect day when our fight will be over. Yet, we must never forget we are God's prized fighters. All of God's men are struggling men who count themselves not to have apprehended. Our struggles may be unknown to all, but our struggles are there. With what others do know of us, the half has not been told because it is not their business. It is God's. We are not content with knowing we struggle. God deals with us severely when we cross Heavenly lines, but it is God who is ultimately responsible for how He deals with us. We are struck with awe and wonder at the grace of God that is utterly amazing that saves wretches like us. When we teach people of the grace of God, we know what we are talking about. Our teachings should never be underestimated because they flow from a plethora of rich but painful experiences.

God holds His men in the palm of His Hands while Satan tries every vile effort to pluck them out. God's men agonize and are not afraid of Hell's darts thrown against them, but they are sometimes afraid of themselves. They have owned the fact that they are their worst enemy (Romans 7:18). These are the kind of men who put their trust in God. Because they are so intricately structured, they fear being out of the controlling influences of God's grace. They will not be satisfied until God disrobes them of their failing flesh and grants them immortal bodies. They long for the day when they will study war no more. Until then, they press on and preach on with a compassion for anyone who is fighting for their lives. They understand struggle, and the chief lesson they long to teach those who are at odds with themselves is that the Lord will make a way somehow.

When I think of the life of my late cousin, James Commodore Wade III, he was a witness unto me. I can never remember a time when the grace of God was not upon his life. God's hand was on him always, even amid his weaknesses. He was a wonder to watch despite his personal bouts. To me, he was a better man on his worst days than I on my best days. Like Pastor Broderick Huggins would say, "When we keep our trust in God, we can accomplish more on accident than others accomplish on purpose." James Wade III was anointed, and anything he put his hands to do was blessed. My cousin taught me the meaning of grace. I mean, he *literally* taught me the meaning of grace. I started my ministry with a works and legalistic mentality. James Wade III sat me down, spent time with me, and explained the grace of God to me. James' life was a testimony of the grace of God. He was graced, and he was gracious. Other than his grandfather, James Commodore Wade, Sr., James III was the humblest and most gifted young preacher I ever knew. Everything he touched had a grace that accompanied it. When he touched the drums, they came to life. When he touched the bass guitar, it came to life. He even played with the piano a little, and it came to life. When he touched a song with his *Stevie Wonder-like voice*, the song came to life. As a matter of fact, when he touched people, they came to life. James could get along with anybody. When we attended Bishop College together, he was kind to all his preaching brothers. He had something positive to say about everyone he introduced me to. He was considerate. He esteemed others higher than himself. He made everyone he was with feel special, just like his grandfather, J. C. Wade, Sr. Yet, he was also human. When I attended his funeral, I wondered how his life would have been impacted if he knew how many people were touched by just the little things he said and did. When a pastor fights so many battles, he may wonder if anyone really cares about the good he has done. My father always told me that God blinds us (pastors) to how many people who are truly touched by our lives to keep us humble. James III teaches us that we *do* make a difference when we use our gifts gracefully and humbly. We may not get our flowers while we live, but God knows. E. V. Hill used to say that we are quickly forgotten by people.

I was more than discouraged about mistakes I made earlier in my ministry as I sat with a pastor who considered me to be his covenant brother. His name is Xavier Thompson. After cataloging my sentiments and pouring out my concerns, he said some simple words that settled in my soul like never. There are some areas I prayed for God to give me another chance in. He simply said, "God knows your heart." That is what I want to share with every pastor who did not always get it right. Be encouraged to know, God knows your heart. Maybe you feel as though God is against your ministry. Welcome to Habakkuk's world. Maybe you do not have what others would consider to be the best church in the world. Welcome to Ezekiel's world. Maybe your wife went satanically sour. Welcome to Adam's world. Maybe you have challenges with women. Welcome to Samson's world. Maybe you made one mistake you can never erase. Welcome to David's world. Maybe you have a resilient rival gunning for your head. Welcome to Elijah's world. Maybe you feel so many other's ministries are beginning on a good note and yours is ending on a sour one. Welcome to John's world. Maybe you are not the most attractive to look at because you have some ugly stigma about you. Welcome to Jacob's world. Maybe you just want to quit and leave it all behind. Welcome to Jeremiah's world. Maybe you do not have much credibility with certain people although you are the cause of many of their successes. Welcome to Paul's world. Whatever the case. God knows your heart.

One of the characteristics of romance is that it involves a plot and conflict. The beauty of romance is how a happy ending comes out of a dark conflict. The story of a pastor in relationship to his God is a romance that involves conflict before a happy ending. Every now and then, the pastor's friends, neighbors, churches, or even family see the conflict that has arisen and abandon the rest of his story because they are dramatically impacted by the conflict, fearing an unhappy ending. They do not want to be a part of the darkness of his drama. Therefore, many abandon him when the chips are down. The average person does not want to watch their hero in trouble and trapped by the villain. Some only want to relate when we are robed in our capes as if we are superheroes. However, when the capes come off and they see how human we are, many close their spiritual comic books in despair and run off looking for another hero. Some people could care less about Clark Kent. They only want Superman. However, people do not need another hero. They just need to remember the ordinary men they abandoned who were once their pastors. They should never forget the times when they were in trouble, and their pastor came to their side. When we think of pastors in conflict, most people only have a certain amount of tolerance for their troubles. These types of people have fantasized concepts of life and God. They become judges that defy the true essence of the romance of real ministry and real men. Such people want the conflict to be taken out of the romance because their perceptions of pastors can only stand so much dark realism.

Living in California, I got a chance to see movie stars and entertainers from a close-up view. I was amazed how some of them were shorter than they looked on television. Others had scars, and their skin was not as smooth as it looked on the screen. I saw how human they really were. There is something about a close-up view that shatters one's sense of idealism. When we see all the men and women of the Bible, God allows us to see them close-up. Ironically, the average Christian does not really look at them from a close-up point of view, even if the Bible is right in front of their faces. They look at them from a theatrical point of view. To them, the Bible is like a movie. To them, everyone in the Bible is a spiritual superstar. To those who keep it real, they realize people in the Bible were ordinary people. The pastor is no exception. If most of today's pastors had a background the men of the Bible had, most churches would not think to choose them as their pastor, and many women would dare not marry them. As a matter of fact, too many of today's churches would never have voted Jesus to be their pastor because He demanded more than what people were willing to give.

Conclusion

Whether people understand it or not, the problems pastors have are real. Their struggles are real. Their sins are real. Yet, their victories are real. It can demoralize the pastor and shatter his faith in God if he is living for the confirmation of the ones he loves and leads. If he is to experience the deliverance from conflict all pastors experience, he must keep in mind that he is the possession of God and God alone. His calling was from God before the foundation of the world, and his election is sure. He must learn to work out his own soul salvation with fear and trembling, reverencing the fact that much of his destiny will be realized when he makes some painful but necessary decisions to see himself from the eyes of God and no one else. The ultimate decision is not which way he will turn nor what will he do next as much as it is to accept the fact that he is in God's hands now.

We preach God's will and have studied the will of God to the extent that we realize the implications of where His will may lead us. I remember Bishop Kenneth Ulmer making a statement on a television show. It was simple but significant. He said, "*We, pastors must wake up every day realizing that we are on assignment.*" Our assignment will dictate the possibilities of us accomplishing other objectives. There are many noble desires we have that God will say "no" to because such desires are not within the realm of what He assigned us to do. Some of us are still living because God has an assignment for us. We realize oh so clearly that doing God's will can sometimes mean saying goodbye to the things or people we love most. We are not as intimidated by physical losses as we are by spiritual, emotional, and mental ones. We realize God's hands are powerful and purposeful. Being under God's control and in His care is a powerful event to experience and a sobering way to live. As a result, when we are in major conflict, we have a deep suspicion that we have only just begun regardless of how far we traveled.

The road the pastor travels is a road that gets narrower the closer he gets to Heaven. Yet, he presses his way through. At the close of our days, we are stripped to nothing but ourselves and God. Regardless of what we acquire, we realize we must say goodbye to it all the deeper we go in ministry. The calling of God is a constricting calling. When it gets down to it, all we have is God. The God-called pastors who have many tangibles know none of those things mean a thing at the end of the day. They are just grateful for what they have, but they do not hold those things tightly. We brought nothing into this world, and we can take nothing out of this world but our souls.

Conflict is our sober reminder that everything we believe about God is being placed in the furnace of His refining fire. We understand when others cringe and walk away from our crosses that God is up to something paradoxically powerful. Outwardly, we do not like it, but deep down inside our anatomy, we love it. Our anatomy senses more than the fact that we are in trouble, but it senses God lording over our troubles in a way that demands for us to know God will complete the good work He has begun in us. We are reminded that troubles do not last always. Somehow, the more pain we are in, the more powerfully we preach. We groan for redemption, but we sense the Holy Spirit praying for us in ways no tongue can express. While we know how we have come a long way, we know we have a longer way to go. We constantly undergo updates in our anatomy. Our anatomy is covered with the marks of the incisions of the Great Physician. We are constantly undergoing operations on our insides. Our mortal bodies will never be immune to Satan, sickness, or our sins. Yet, God's grace sufficiently sustains us.

Pastors are always fighting something. We experience bitter-sweet victories. Although they are victories, we live to see a casualty along the way that could have been avoided had we trusted in God a little bit more and embraced the better side of ourselves. Somehow, a quiet strength develops as we struggle in soul and spirit.

Although Moses was disqualified when he was outraged with his congregation, he was also confirmed when he could see the Promised Land. Although Samson's life was filled with unbridled passions, Samson had a sense of peace when he felt his strength returning for the final time. Although Jeremiah was disturbed by the conditions of his calling, his ministry was confirmed when he realized the perpetual presence of God's mercies. Habakkuk was calmed by God's power. Ezekiel was clear when he realized the victory in the valley. Saul was converted when he had seen the Lord. Although David had a divided house, the throne still belonged to him, and Heaven was his home.

Every God-called pastor gets to a point in which he refuses to please people or live up to his own unrealistic expectations. It is at this point when his preaching develops divine definition. He realizes that he cannot live up to their expectations. He cannot even live up to his own. When a pastor stops living for people, praise our prestige, his ministry grows from the inside out. His anatomy begins to work in alignment with his God ordained assignment. Then, he begins to touch more lives than a church building can hold. These men testify that purpose cannot be destroyed, and neither can they. There is a subtle disenfranchisement that exists within every God-called pastor. It is what Uncle Melvin (M. V. Wade, Sr.) calls, "A holy frustration." In other words, we are frustrated because we know there is more. The best way I can sum *The Pastor and His Anatomy* is from the pen of the apostle Paul. I pray the essence of this book will be understood by all who read it to be what Paul penned in four verses. Most of all, I pray every pastor and preacher will never forget:

"But we (preachers of the Gospel) have this treasure in earthen vessels, that the excellency of the power may be of God, and not of us. We are troubled on every side, yet not distressed; we are perplexed, but not in despair; Persecuted, but not forsaken; cast down, but not destroyed; Always bearing about in the body the dying of the Lord Jesus, that the life also of Jesus might be made manifest in our body."

(II Corinthians 4:7-10; KJV)

Amen.